FOUNDATIONS FOR FINANCIAL ECONOMICS

Chi-fu Huang

Sloan School of Management
Massachusetts Institute of Technology

Robert H. Litzenberger

The Wharton School
University of Pennsylvania

PRENTICE HALL, Englewood Cliffs, New Jersey 07632

Library of Congress Cataloging-in-Publication Data

Huang, Chi-fu.
    Foundations for financial economics / Chi-fu Huang, Robert H.
Litzenberger.
        p.   cm.
    Reprint. Originally published: New York : North-Holland, c1988.
    Includes index.
    ISBN 0-13-500653-8
    1. Investments--Mathematical models. 2. Finance--Mathematical
models.   I. Litzenberger, Robert H. II. Title.
HG4515.H83 1993
332--dc20   93-990
                                                          CIP

© 1988 by Prentice-Hall, Inc.
A Simon & Schuster Company
Englewood Cliffs, New Jersey 07632

Printed in the United States of America
10 9 8 7 6 5 4

ISBN 0-13-500653-8

Prentice-Hall International (UK) Limited, *London*
Prentice-Hall of Australia Pty. Limited, *Sydney*
Prentice-Hall Canada Inc., *Toronto*
Prentice-Hall Hispanoamericana, S. A., *Mexico*
Prentice-Hall of India Private Limited, *New Delhi*
Prentice-Hall of Japan, Inc., *Tokyo*
Simon & Schuster Asia Pte. Ltd., *Singapore*
Editora Prentice-Hall do Brasil, Ltda., *Rio de Janeiro*

To Our Families

TABLE OF CONTENTS

PREFACE

This book evolved from lecture notes we have used to teach introductory PhD courses in financial economics at the Massachusetts Institute of Technology, Stanford University, and the University of Pennsylvania. Its purpose is to provide the foundations for the study of modern financial economics. Rather than giving a superficial coverage of a wide range of topics, we have chosen to concentrate our discussion on individuals' consumption and portfolio decisions under uncertainty and their implications for the valuation of securities.

Chapters 1 through 6 discuss two–period models, where the consumption and portfolio decisions are made only once at the initial date of the economies. Chapter 1 analyzes an individual's behavior under uncertainty. This chapter also shows the comparative statics of an individual's optimal portfolio choice in an economy with one riskless and one risky asset when his initial wealth or attitude toward risk changes. Moreover, we provide sufficient conditions for these comparative statics to apply to economies with three or more assets. In Chapter 2, we discuss three concepts of *stochastic dominance*. The concepts of stochastic dominance identify conditions that allow risky assets to be ranked based on limited knowledge of individuals' preferences. Chapter 3 shows mathematical properties of a portfolio frontier – the collection of portfolios that have the minimum variance for different levels of expected rates of return. In Chapter 4, we give distributional conditions on the rates of return on assets so that individuals will optimally choose to hold portfolios on the portfolio frontier. As a consequence, expected rate of return on an asset is linearly related to its *beta*, which measures the contribution of the asset to the risk of a well–diversified portfolio. This is the *Capital Asset Pricing Model*. We also discuss in this chapter the *Arbitrage Pricing Theory*, which relates the expected rate of return of an asset to a number of *random factors*.

Chapter 5 begins our description of a state contingent security and its equilibrium valuation. A state contingent security pays one unit of consumption in one state of nature and nothing otherwise. Markets are said to be complete if there is a state contingent security for every state of nature. An allocation of consumption among individuals is said to be a Pareto optimal allocation if there is no other allocation that increases an individual's satisfaction without decreasing some other individual's satisfaction. We show how Pareto optimal allocations can be achieved in complete markets as well as in various other market structures. The allocational role of options, in particular, is demonstrated. This chapter also provides the necessary and sufficient conditions on individuals' utility functions for all Pareto optimal allocations to be achievable by holding the portfolio of all assets and borrowing or lending and discusses the relationship between these conditions and an aggregation result in securities markets. In Chapter 6, we present general pricing rules for securities that pay off in more than one state of nature and specialize these rules with additional preference restrictions. In particular, we derive a closed form solution for a call option written on a common stock when the random payoffs of the common stock and the aggregate consumption are jointly lognormally distributed and individuals' preferences are represented by power functions with the same exponent.

We discuss in Chapter 7 how multiperiod dynamic economies can be modeled. A multiperiod dynamic economy differs from a two-period static economy in that trading can take place at more than one date and individuals' expectations about future prices are therefore essential in an equilibrium specification. This leads to a notion of a rational expectations equilibrium. The general equilibrium valuation principles in a multiperiod dynamic economy are essentially the same as those in a two–period static economy. An important feature of a multiperiod economy demonstrated in detail is that a Pareto optimal allocation can be achieved by trading dynamically in a limited number of *long–lived securities*. Chapter 8 continues our discussion of a multiperiod economy with emphasis on valuation by arbitrage. We show the connection between an arbitrage–free price system and martingales. This connection allows us to compute prices of a derivative security in a simple way when the derivative security can be priced by arbitrage. As an example, we price a call option written on a stock when the stock price follows a binomial random walk.

A common feature of the economies in Chapters 1 through 8 is that individuals are endowed with the same information. In Chapter 9 we discuss economies in which individuals have differential information. We demonstrate that equilibrium properties can be very different from those in economies without differential information. Chapter 10 examines econometric issues of testing the Capital Asset Pricing Model. Some test statistics are given geometric interpretations in the context of Chapter 3.

Applications of information economics to financial markets have gained significant importance in recent years. Our coverage in Chapter 9 is limited in scope. Chapter 10 concentrates on econometric issues in testing the Capital Asset Pricing Model. Empirical aspects of many other theories developed in this book also deserve attention. Separate books can be written on the general topic areas of Chapters 9 and 10. Our selection of subjects covered in these two chapters is intended to be an introduction.

Besides providing material for introductory PhD courses in financial economics, this book can be used for a graduate/advanced undergraduate course in the economics of uncertainty. When supplemented with articles, this book can form the basis for a two semester course. Chapters 1 through 4 and Chapter 10 are recommended for the first semester, while Chapters 5 through 9 are recommended for the second semester. Although the level of presentation is rigorous in general, the necessary prerequisites are only intermediate level microeconomics, introductory econometrics, matrix algebra, and elementary calculus.

We owe a substantial debt to our academic colleagues who have contributed to the strong theoretical foundations of asset choice and valuation under uncertainty and to the empirical methodology for examining testable implications of the theory. This book presents and interprets materials in the existing literature and does not make original contributions of its own. In the end of each chapter, we try to give a brief attribution of the materials covered. But, undoubtedly, our attribution cannot be complete. Many of our colleagues provided either helpful comments on early drafts or encouragement throughout the years that this book was under preparation. Among them, special thanks go to Sudipto Bhattacharya and John Cox, from whom we have received continuous encouragement and invaluable suggestions on the selection of topics; and to Michael Gibbons and Craig MacKinlay, who have helped clarify some questions we had on the materials in Chapter 10. Many of our students have provided helpful comments and suggestions. Among them, special appreciations go to Ayman Hindy, who read through every chapter in detail and pointed out numerous mistakes in notation and derivations; to Caterina Nelsen, whose editorial help has proved indispensible; and to Ajay Dravid and Tomas Philipson, who gave helpful comments in terms of style and topic selection.

This book was completed when the first author was on a fellowship provided by Batterymarch Financial Management, whose generous support is greatly appreciated. The entire book is typeset by TEX designed by Professor Donald Knuth of Stanford University. Manjul Dravid helped us typeset some parts of this book. Our conversation with Hal Varian improved our understanding of some fine points of TEX, for which we are thankful. Last, but by no means least, we are grateful to our families for their encouragement and help.

Chi-fu Huang
Robert H. Litzenberger

FOUNDATIONS
FOR FINANCIAL
ECONOMICS

CHAPTER 1
PREFERENCES REPRESENTATION
AND RISK AVERSION

1.1. As we mentioned in the preface, the main focus of this book is on individuals' consumption and investment decisions under uncertainty and their implications for the valuation of securities. Individuals' consumption and investment decisions under uncertainty are undoubtedly influenced by many considerations. A commonly accepted theory of asset choice under uncertainty that provides the underpinnings for the analysis of asset demands uses the *expected utility hypothesis*. Under this hypothesis, each individual's consumption and investment decision is characterized as if he determines the probabilities of possible asset payoffs, assigns an index to each possible consumption outcome, and chooses the consumption and investment policy to maximize the expected value of the index. More formally, an individual's preferences have an *expected utility representation* if there exists a function u such that random consumption $\tilde{x}$ is preferred to random consumption $\tilde{y}$ if and only if

$$E[u(\tilde{x})] \geq E[u(\tilde{y})],$$

where $E[\cdot]$ is the expectation under the individual's probability belief.

In the first half of this chapter we give behavioral conditions that are necessary and sufficient for an individual's preferences to have an expected utility representation. We then go on to discuss the necessary and sufficient condition for an individual's preferences to exhibit risk aversion under the expected utility representation assumption. Different measures of risk aversion will be proposed and used to analyze the comparative statics of an individual's portfolio behavior when faced with one risky asset and one riskless asset. Finally, we will discuss sufficient conditions for the comparative statics for the one risky and one riskless asset case to generalize to the case of multiple risky assets and a riskless asset.

Before we proceed, we note that throughout this book we will use positive, negative, greater than, smaller than, increasing, decreasing, and etc. to mean weak relations. When a relation is strict, we will emphasize it by using a "strictly" to modify it, for example, by using "strictly positive."

1.2 Suppose for now that there are two dates, time 0 and time 1, and there is a single consumption good available for consumption only at time 1. Uncertainty in the economy is modeled by uncertain states of nature to be realized at time 1. A state of nature is a complete description of the uncertain environment from time 0 to time 1. We denote the collection of all the possible states of nature by Ω and denote an element of Ω by ω. At time 0, individuals know that the true state of nature is an element of Ω but do not know which state will occur at time 1. A *consumption plan* is then a specification of the number of units of the single consumption good in different states of nature. Let x be a consumption plan. We will use x_ω to denote the number of units of the consumption good in state ω specified by x. When there are five states of nature denoted by $\omega_1, \ldots, \omega_5$. Table 1.2.1 tabulates a consumption plan x, which has 2 units of consumption in state ω_1, 3 units of consumption in states ω_2, etc. As we defined above, a consumption plan is a vector specifying units of consumption in different states of nature. Since the time 1 realized consumption is uncertain, a consumption plan x can also be viewed as a random variable and we will use $\tilde{x}$ to denote it when we use the "random variable" aspect of a consumption plan.

x_ω	ω_1	ω_2	ω_3	ω_4	ω_5
	2	3	1	8	0

Table 1.2.1: A Consumption Plan

An individual is represented by his preference relation $\succeq$ defined on a collection of consumption plans. We will formally define a preference relation shortly. Roughly, a preference relation is a mechanism that allows an individual to compare different consumption plans. For example, given two consumption plans, x and x', a preference relation enables an individual to tell whether he prefers x to x' or x' to x. For concreteness, we would like an individual's preferences to be represented by a *utility function*, or H, in the sense that the individual prefers x to x' if and only if $H(x) \geq H(x')$. We will see later in this chapter that, under some regularity conditions, a preference relation can always be represented this way.

When the number of states is very large, a consumption plan x is a vector of large dimension and the function H will be complicated to analyze. It would be more convenient if there existed a function u that allowed comparison among consumption plans that are certain and a probability P that gave the relative likelihood of states of nature such that the preference relation can be represented as an *expected utility* in the sense that consumption plan x is preferred to consumption plan x' if and only if the expected utility of x is greater than the expected utility of x', that is,

$$\int_\Omega u(x_\omega)dP(\omega) \geq \int_\Omega u(x'_\omega)dP(\omega). \qquad (1.2.1)$$

Denoting the expectation operator under P by $E[\cdot]$, (1.2.1) can be equivalently written as

$$E[u(\tilde{x})] \geq E[u(\tilde{x}')], \qquad (1.2.2)$$

where we have used the random variable aspect of x and x'. Note that a consumption plan is *certain* if the number of units of consumption does not vary across different states of nature. Note also that in the above expected utility representation, if x and x' are both certain or *sure things*, that is

$$x_\omega = z \quad \text{and } x'_\omega = z' \quad \forall \omega \in \Omega,$$

for some constants z and z', then $E[u(\tilde{x})] = u(z)$ and $E[u(\tilde{x}')] = u(z')$. In this sense, u compares consumption plans that are certain.

Certainly not all preference relations have an expected utility representation. Indeed, we have to put a fair amount of structure on a preference relation to achieve this purpose. In general, there are two approaches for a preference relation to have an expected utility representation, depending on whether one treats the probabilities of the states of nature as objective or subjective. The former approach was introduced by von Neumann and Morgenstern (1953) and the resulting function u is thus called the *von Neumann-Morgenstern utility function*. The latter approach was taken by Savage (1972), who views probability assessments as an integral part of an investor's preferences and thus purely subjective. However, the distinction between subjective and objective probability assessments is inconsequential to our purpose in this book. Hence for the analysis to follow, we will not distinguish between them and always call the function u defined on sure things a von Neumann–Morgenstern utility function.

Before discussing the representation of a preference relation by an expected utility, in the next section, we give a definition of a preference relation and discuss conditions under which a preference relation can be represented by a utility function H.

1.3. Formally, let X be the collection of consumption plans under consideration. A *binary relation* $\succeq$ on X is a collection of pairs of consumption plans (x, y). If (x, y) is in the relation, we write $x \succeq y$ and say x is preferred to y. If (x, y) is not in the relation, then we write $x \not\succeq y$ and say x is not preferred to y.

A binary relation is *transitive* if $x \succeq y$ and $y \succeq v$ imply $x \succeq v$; that is, if x is preferred to y and y is preferred to v, then x is preferred to v. A binary relation is said to be *complete* if for any two consumption plans x and y, we either have $x \succeq y$ or $y \succeq x$; that is, any two consumption plans can always be compared.

A *preference relation* is a binary relation that is transitive and complete. We can also define an indifference relation and a strict preference relation. Formally, given a preference relation $\succeq$, two consumption plans x and y are said to be *indifferent* to each other if $x \succeq y$ and $y \succeq x$, denoted by $x \sim y$. The consumption plan x

is said to be *strictly preferred to y*, denoted by $x \succ y$, if $x \succeq y$ and $y \not\succeq x$. Note that a strict binary relation and an indifference relation can also be similarly defined for any given binary relation.

1.4. When X has a finite number of elements, a preference relation $\succeq$ can *always* be represented by a utility function. This assertion can be proved in a straightforward manner. The readers are asked to furnish a proof in Exercise 1.1. Here we shall give an example to demonstrate the essential idea.

Suppose that there are three consumption plans in X, denoted by x_1, x_2, and x_3. Pick any consumption plan, say x_3, and define

$$H(x_3) \equiv b,$$

where b is an arbitrary constant. Next take x_1. Since a preference relation is complete, x_1 and x_3 can be compared. We define

$$H(x_1) \equiv \begin{cases} b+1 & \text{if } x_1 \succ x_3; \\ b-1 & \text{if } x_3 \succ x_1; \\ b & \text{if } x_3 \sim x_1. \end{cases}$$

That is, compare x_1 and x_3. If x_1 is strictly preferred to x_3, we assign a value strictly larger than b to $H(x_1)$; and similarly for other cases. Without loss of generality, suppose that $x_1 \succ x_3$. Finally, we compare x_2 with x_1 and x_3, and define

$$H(x_2) \equiv \begin{cases} b-1 & \text{if } x_3 \succ x_2; \\ b & \text{if } x_2 \sim x_3; \\ b+\frac{1}{2} & \text{if } x_1 \succ x_2 \succ x_3; \\ b+1 & \text{if } x_2 \sim x_1; \\ b+2 & \text{if } x_2 \succ x_1. \end{cases}$$

Here we compare x_2 with x_1 and x_3 and assign values to $H(x_2)$ in a natural way. It should now be transparent that

$$H(x_n) \geq H(x_m) \quad \text{if and only if} \quad x_n \succeq x_m, \quad n, m = 1, 2, 3.$$

That is, H as defined above represents the preference relation $\succeq$.

When X has a countable number of elements, the above idea can be carried out in a similar way to conclude that a preference relation can always be represented by a utility function.

1.5. Matters are not as simple when an individual expresses his preferences on an uncountably infinite number of consumption plans. In such event, there exist well-known examples of preference relations that cannot be represented by utility functions. The so-called *Lexicographic preference relation* is one such example; we refer readers to Exercise 1.2 for a brief description. Thus, for general X, additional conditions on a preference relation will be needed for an expected utility representation to exist. It turns out that the additional condition needed is purely technical in nature and is stated in Exercise 1.2. Interested readers should consult Debreu (1954) and Fishburn (1970) for details.

1.6. Now we turn to the representation of a preference relation by an expected utility. Let P be a probability defined on the state space Ω, which can be either objective or subjective. (For the technically inclined readers, we are a bit informal here. When Ω has uncountably infinite elements, a probability is actually defined not on Ω but rather on a collection of subsets of Ω that satisfies a certain structure.) A consumption plan is a random variable, whose probabilistic characteristics are specified by P. We can define the distribution function for a consumption plan x as follows:

$$F_x(z) \equiv P\{\omega \in \Omega : x_\omega \leq z\}.$$

If a preference relation $\succeq$ has an expected utility representation with a utility function u on sure things, the expected utility derived from x is

$$E[u(\tilde{x})] = \int_{-\infty}^{+\infty} u(z) dF_x(z).$$

From the above relation, we see that if two consumption plans x and x' have the same distribution function, they will yield the same expected utility and are indifferent to each other. This demonstrates that the primitive objects on which an individual expresses his or her preferences are probability distributions of consumption. Note that two consumption plans having the same distribution function can have very different consumption patterns across states of nature.

1.7. To simplify matters, we shall assume that an individual only expresses his preferences on probability distributions defined on a finite set Z. In other words, the collection of consumption plans X on which an individual expresses his or her preferences must have the property that

$$x_\omega \in Z \quad \forall \omega \in \Omega, \forall x \in X.$$

For example, if $Z = \{1, 2, 3\}$, then the units of consumption in any state can only be 1, 2, or 3. This assumption can be justified, for example, when the consumption commodity is not perfectly divisible and the supply of the commodity is finite. In this case, we can represent a consumption plan x by a function $p(\cdot)$ defined on Z, where $p(z)$ is the probability that x is equal to z. Thus $p(z) \geq 0$ for all $z \in Z$ and $\sum_{z \in Z} p(z) = 1$. The distribution function for the consumption plan x discussed in Section 1.6 is then

$$F_x(z') = \sum_{z \leq z'} p(z),$$

and

$$E[u(\tilde{x})] = \sum_{z \in Z} u(z)p(z).$$

One can also think of a consumption plan as a *lottery* with prizes in Z. The probability of getting a prize z is $p(z)$.

We denote the space of probabilities on Z by $\mathbf{P}$ and its elements by p, q, and r. If $p \in \mathbf{P}$, the probability of z under p is $p(z)$.

1.8. The following three behavioral axioms are necessary and sufficient for a binary relation defined on $\mathbf{P}$ to have an expected utility representation.

Axiom 1. $\succeq$ is a preference relation on $\mathbf{P}$.

Axiom 2. For all $p, q, r \in \mathbf{P}$ and $a \in (0, 1]$, $p \succ q$ implies $ap + (1 - a)r \succ aq + (1 - a)r$.

This axiom is commonly called the *substitution axiom* or the *independence axiom*. Think of p, q, r as *lotteries* and $ap + (1 - a)r$ as a *compound lottery*: First an experiment with two outcomes (say head and tail) is carried out, where the probability of a head is a. If a head shows up, the lottery p is performed. If a tail shows up, the lottery r is performed. The motivation for this axiom is the following: The difference between $ap + (1-a)r$ and $aq + (1-a)r$ is what happens if a head shows up, so how an individual feels about $ap + (1 - a)r$ versus $aq + (1 - a)r$ should be determined by how he feels about p versus q. In other words, satisfaction of consumption in a given event does not depend on what the consumption would have been if another event had occurred.

Axiom 3. For all $p, q, r \in \mathbf{P}$, if $p \succ q \succ r$ then there exists $a, b \in (0, 1)$ such that $ap + (1 - a)r \succ q \succ bp + (1 - b)r$.

This is called the *Archimedean axiom*. It roughly says that there is no consumption plan p so good that for $q \succ r$ a small probability b of p and a large probability $(1 - b)$ of r is never worse than q. Similarly, there is no consumption plan r so bad that for $p \succ q$ a large probability a of p and a small probability $(1 - a)$ of r is never preferred to q. It is called an Archimedean axiom because of the resemblance to Archimedes' principle: No matter how small $z > 0$ is and how big z' is, there is an integer k such that $kz > z'$.

When p, q, and r are sure things, say when $p(z) = 1$, $q(z') = 1$, and $r(z'') = 1$, the Archimedean axiom says that there exists a lottery awarding z with a probability a and awarding z'' with a probability $(1-a)$ which is strictly preferred to the sure consumption level z'; and there exists a lottery awarding z with a probability b and awarding z'' with a probability $(1 - b)$ so that the sure consumption z' is strictly preferred to this lottery.

1.9. We will show in the following section that a binary relation $\succeq$ on $\mathbf{P}$ has an expected utility representation if and only if it satisfies the above three axioms. Before we do that, we will first record some very intuitive properties of a binary relation when the three axioms are satisfied. Their proofs are straightforward, and we leave them for the readers as Exercise 1.3 at the end of this chapter.

We will need the following notation. For $z \in Z$, let P_z be the probability distribution degenerate at z in that

$$P_z(z') = \begin{cases} 1 & \text{if } z' = z; \\ 0 & \text{if } z' \neq z. \end{cases}$$

That is, P_z represents the sure consumption plan that has z units of consumption in every state.

Suppose henceforth that $\succeq$ is a binary relation on $\mathbf{P}$ that satisfies the above three axioms. Then

1. $p \succ q$ and $0 \leq a < b \leq 1$ imply that $bp + (1-b)q \succ ap + (1-a)q$.
2. $p \succeq q \succeq r$ and $p \succ r$ imply that there exists a unique $a^* \in [0,1]$ such that $q \sim a^* p + (1-a^*)r$.
3. $p \succ q$ and $r \succ s$ and $a \in [0,1]$ imply that $ap + (1-a)r \succ aq + (1-a)s$.
4. $p \sim q$ and $a \in [0,1]$ imply that $p \sim ap + (1-a)q$.
5. $p \sim q$ and $a \in [0,1]$ imply that $ap + (1-a)r \sim aq + (1-a)r$, for all $r \in \mathbf{P}$.
6. There exist $z^o, z_o \in Z$ such that $P_{z^o} \succeq p \succeq P_{z_o}$ for all $p \in \mathbf{P}$.

The first property says that if p is strictly preferred to q, then any compound lottery on p and q with a strictly higher weight for p is strictly preferred to a compound lottery with a lower weight for p. The last property can be seen as follows. Suppose that $\succeq$ always prefers more to less. Since Z has only a finite number of elements, there exist a maximum z^0 and a minimum z_o. A sure consumption plan P_{z^o} is certainly preferred to any other consumption plan, and conversely for P_{z_o}. Other properties can be interpreted similarly.

1.10. Now we will prove that $\succeq$ has an expected utility representation. We take cases.

Case 1. $P_{z^o} \sim P_{z_o}$. Then $p \sim q$ for all $p, q \in \mathbf{P}$. Therefore any $u(z) = k$ for a constant k will be a utility function for sure things.

Case 2. $P_{z^o} \succ P_{z_o}$. For $p \in \mathbf{P}$, define $H(p) = a$, where a is a number in $[0,1]$ such that $aP_{z^o} + (1-a)P_{z_o} \sim p$. That is, we define $H(p)$ to be the weight a compound lottery on P_{z^o} and P_{z_o} assigns to P_{z^o} to make it indifferent to p. We know from property 2 of the previous section that a is unique. So $H(p)$ is well defined for all $p \in \mathbf{P}$. Note that by the definition of H and property 1 of the previous section, we have $H(p) \geq H(q)$ if and only if

$$H(p)P_{z^o} + (1 - H(p))P_{z_o} \succeq H(q)P_{z^o} + (1 - H(q))P_{z_o},$$

hence, if and only if $p \succeq q$. Therefore, H is a utility function that represents $\succeq$. This is not good enough, however. We want to show that there exists a function u defined on Z such that

$$H(p) = \sum_{z \in Z} u(z)p(z).$$

We will achieve this by construction.

First, repeated use of property 5 of the previous section implies that, for all $p, q \in \mathbf{P}$ and $a \in [0, 1]$,

$$
\begin{aligned}
ap + (1 - a)q \sim &a[H(p)P_{z^o} + (1 - H(p))P_{z_o}] \\
&+ (1 - a)[H(q)P_{z^o} + (1 - H(q))P_{z_o}] \\
\sim &(aH(p) + (1 - a)H(q))P_{z^o} \\
&+ (1 - aH(p) - (1 - a)H(q))P_{z_o}.
\end{aligned}
\tag{1.10.1}
$$

Note that by the definition of H we know that $H(p)$ and $H(q)$ are greater than 0 and less than 1. Hence, $aH(p) + (1-a)H(q)$ is between 0 and 1 and the right–hand side of the second indifference relation of (1.10.1) is a well–defined compound lottery. Since H represents $\succeq$, it follows that

$$
\begin{aligned}
&H(ap + (1 - a)q) \\
&= H((aH(p) + (1 - a)H(q))P_{z^o} + (1 - aH(p) - (1 - a)H(q))P_{z_o}) \\
&= aH(p) + (1 - a)H(q),
\end{aligned}
$$

where the second equality follows again from the definition of H. We thus conclude that H must be *linear* in that

$$H(ap + (1 - a)q) = aH(p) + (1 - a)H(q).$$

Next we define a function u on Z by

$$u(z) \equiv H(P_z) \quad \forall z \in Z. \tag{1.10.2}$$

We claim that this function is a von Neumann–Morgenstern utility function. Before we prove our claim, we remark that the above definition of u is a natural one. The von Neumann–Morgenstern utility function u is a function on sure things. Thus we define $u(z)$ to be the utility, according to H, for the sure consumption plan P_z. Here is the proof for our claim. Let $p \in \mathbf{P}$. It is easily seen that

$$p \sim \sum_{z \in Z} p(z) P_z.$$

Since H represents $\succeq$,

$$H(p) = H\Big(\sum_{z \in Z} p(z) P_z\Big)$$
$$= \sum_{z \in Z} p(z) H(P_z)$$
$$= \sum_{z \in Z} p(z) u(z),$$

where the second equality follows from the repeated use of the linearity of H, and the third equality follows from the definition of u. Thus any binary relation on $\mathbf{P}$ satisfying the three axioms has an expected utility representation. Finally, it can be shown that u is only determined up to a strictly positive linear transformation in that if $\hat{u}$ is also a von Neumann–Morgenstern utility function, then there exist two constants $c > 0$ and d such that $\hat{u} = cu + d$. You will be asked to provide a proof of this in Exercise 1.4.

Conversely, it is easily verified that if a binary relation $\succeq$ has an expected utility representation in that there exists u such that, for $p, q \in \mathbf{P}$,

$$p \succeq q \quad \text{if and only if} \quad \sum_{z \in Z} u(z) p(z) \geq \sum_{z \in Z} u(z) q(z),$$

then $\succeq$ satisfies the three axioms of Section 1.8. We leave the proof of this assertion to the readers in Exercise 1.4.

1.11. We proved the expected utility representation theorem for the case where Z is a finite set. When Z is an infinite set, for example when Z contains all the positive real numbers, the representation theorem is no longer true. We need a fourth axiom called the *sure thing principle*. In words, it basically says that if the consumption plan p is concentrated on a set $B \in Z$ such that every point in B is at least as good as q, then p must be at least as good as q. With this fourth axiom as well as some technical conditions, we have a representation theorem for general Z. We refer interested readers to Fishburn (1970) for details.

1.12. When consumption occurs at more than one date, say at times $t = 0, 1, \ldots, T$, our previous discussion can be generalized in a straightforward manner. Let Z be a collection of $T+1$–tuples $z = (z_0, \ldots, z_T)$, where z_t denotes the number of units of consumption at time t for sure. Suppose that Z is a finite set. A probability p on Z is a mapping with the following properties:

1. $p(z) \in [0,1] \ \forall z \in Z$; and
2. $\sum_{z \in Z} p(z) = 1$.

An individual expresses his preferences over the probabilities defined on Z, or, equivalently, an individual expresses his preferences on lotteries whose prizes are consumption at times $t = 0, 1, \ldots, T$. Denote the collection of probabilities on Z by $\mathbf{P}$. Now mimic the analysis of Sections 1.8 to 1.10 to conclude that the binary relation $\succeq$ is a preference relation satisfying the Substitution axiom and the Archimedean axiom if and only if there exists a von Neumann–Morgenstern utility function u on sure things such that for all $p, q \in \mathbf{P}$, $p \succeq q$ if and only if

$$\sum_{z \in Z} u(z_0, \ldots, z_T) p(z = z_0, \ldots, z_T) \geq \sum_{z \in Z} u(z_0, \ldots, z_T) q(z = z_0, \ldots, z_T),$$

where $p(z = z_0, \ldots, z_T)$ is the probability that consumption from time 0 to time T is $(z_0, \ldots, z_T)$.

For tractability, most analysis of the equilibrium valuation of risky assets in later chapters uses von Neumann-Morgenstern utility functions that are *time–additive*. That is, there exist functions $u_t(\cdot)$

such that

$$u(z_0, \ldots, z_T) = \sum_{t=0}^{T} u_t(z_t). \tag{1.12.1}$$

This is a rather strong assumption. It basically says that what an individual consumes at one time will not have any effect on his desire to consume at any other time. For example, it says that having a big lunch will not affect one's appetite for a seven course dinner. So, readers should be cautioned to note that results reported there are colored by this time–additivity assumption.

1.13. One implication of the expected utility theory is that a von Neumann–Morgenstern utility function is necessarily bounded when probability distributions of consumption involve unbounded consumption levels. This is a consequence of the Archimedean axiom. To see this, suppose that u is unbounded. Without loss of generality, let u be unbounded from above, and let Z contain all positive levels of consumption. Then there exists a sequence of consumption levels $\{z_n\}_{n=1}^{\infty}$ such that $z_n \to \infty$ and $u(z_n) \geq 2^n$. Now consider a consumption plan p such that $p(z_n) = \frac{1}{2^n}$, $n = 1, 2, \ldots$. This consumption plan has unbounded consumption levels. The expected utility of this consumption plan is

$$\sum_{n=1}^{\infty} u(z_n)p(z_n) \geq \sum_{n=1}^{\infty} 2^n \frac{1}{2^n} = \infty.$$

Now let $q, r \in \mathbf{P}$ be such that $p \succ q \succ r$. We know immediately that the expected utilities associated with q and r must be finite. It is then easily seen that the Archimedean axiom can not be satisfied.

The boundedness of a utility function is somewhat discomforting since many utility functions used in economic applications are unbounded. For example, the log utility function is unbounded from above and from below. Any power function, $u(z) = z^{1-b}$, is bounded from below and unbounded from above if $b < 1$ and bounded from above and unbounded from below if $b > 1$. There are, however, ways to get around this kind of difficulty. For example, if we only consider consumption plans that concentrate on a finite number of consumption levels, then the above problem certainly will not arise. This will be the case in many of our discussions in the subsequent chapters. There we usually take the state space Ω to have finite elements. Then a consumption plan naturally takes a finite number of consumption levels. The number of consumption levels is at most equal to the number of states of nature! In such an event, the consumption levels are certainly bounded.

Another possible resolution when Z contains all the positive consumption levels is to use a preference relation that exhibits *risk aversion* and consider consumption plans that have finite expectations. We will see in later sections of this chapter that risk aversion in this case implies that u is concave. Being a concave function, u is differentiable at some point, say $b > 0$. It then follows that

$$u(z) \leq u(b) + u'(b)(z - b) \quad \forall z, \qquad (1.13.1)$$

where $u'(b)$ denotes the derivative of u at b. Now let x be a consumption plan having a finite expectation. Then the expected utility of x is

$$E[u(x)] \leq u(b) + u'(b)(E[x] - b) < \infty,$$

where we have used (1.13.1). That is, if u is concave, expected utilities of consumption plans having finite expectations will be finite even when u is unbounded! Thus in applications, we can comfortably use unbounded utility functions as long as they are concave and random consumption plans considered all have finite expectations. When Z is composed of units of consumption at more than one date, the above analysis applies easily to the time–additive utility functions of (1.12.1) when u_t is concave and the random consumption at each time t has a finite expectation.

1.14.   Among the three axioms of Section 1.8, the one that is often violated in empirical experiments is the Substitution or Independence axiom. The best known example of this is the *Allais Paradox*. Consider the two pairs of lotteries in Figure 1.14.1. Lottery p_1 gives \$1 million for sure. Lottery p_2 pays \$5 million with 0.1 probability, \$1 million with 0.89 probability, and \$0 with 0.01 probability. Lotteries p_3 and p_4 of the second pair are interpreted similarly.

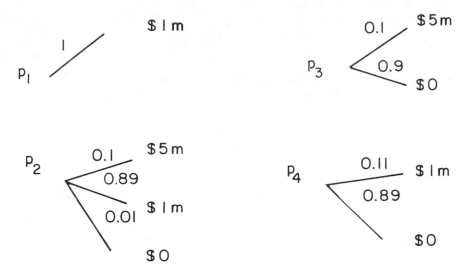

Figure 1.14.1: The Allais Paradox

Most individuals choose lottery p_1 over p_2 when faced with the first pair of lotteries. They prefer \$1 million for sure to a *high* probability of getting \$1 million coupled with *low* probabilities of getting \$5 million and \$0. On the other hand, most individuals choose p_3 over p_4 when faced with the second pair of the lotteries. This behavior, however, is a violation of the Substitution axiom. To see this, we first note that,

$$p_1 \sim 0.11(\$1m) + 0.89(\$1m) \qquad (1.14.1)$$

and

$$p_2 \sim 0.11\left(\frac{1}{11}(\$0m) + \frac{10}{11}(\$5m)\right) + 0.89(\$1m). \qquad (1.14.2)$$

Transitivity implies that

$$0.11(\$1m) + 0.89(\$1m) \succ 0.11\left(\frac{1}{11}(\$0m) + \frac{10}{11}(\$5m)\right) + 0.89(\$1m). \qquad (1.14.3)$$

We claim that

$$p_1 \succ \frac{1}{11}(\$0m) + \frac{10}{11}(\$5m). \qquad (1.14.4)$$

Suppose otherwise. That is,

$$\frac{1}{11}(\$0m) + \frac{10}{11}(\$5m) \succeq p_1. \qquad (1.14.5)$$

Then the Substitution axiom implies a contradiction to (1.14.3).
  By the Substitution axiom, (1.14.4) implies that

$$0.11(\$1m) + 0.89(\$0m) \succ 0.11\left(\frac{1}{11}(\$0m) + \frac{10}{11}(\$5m)\right) + 0.89(\$0m).$$

This is equivalent to

$$p_4 \succ p_3,$$

a contradiction to the experimental results. Thus the behavior of
choosing p_1 over p_2 and choosing p_3 over p_4 is inconsistent with the
Substitution axiom.

1.15. The experimental violation of the Substitution axiom
makes one cautious in using expected utility analysis for descriptive
purposes, as we will do in later chapters in drawing conclusions about
relations among equilibrium prices of risky assets by assuming that
individuals are expected utility maximizers. The ultimate test of the
"reasonableness" of the descriptive conclusions, however, is whether
the descriptive conclusions, to the extent that they are empirically
testable, conform with the observable data. This is a subject to be
discussed in Chapter 10.
  The expected utility analysis can also be defended at another
level by drawing on the work of Machina (1982). It is shown there
that the basic concepts, tools, and results of expected utility analysis
can be carried over to cases where the Substitution axiom is violated
provided that the following condition is satisfied: An individual's
preferences can be represented by a utility function H as discussed
in Sections 1.4 and 1.5 and H is differentiable in a certain sense.
Details of Machina's work, to which we refer interested readers, will
not be discussed here.

1.16. Throughout the rest of this chapter, we will assume that
individuals are expected utility maximizers. For brevity, whenever

we say a utility function, we mean a von Neumann–Morgenstern utility function unless otherwise specified.

As we are dealing with economies under uncertainty, it is important to characterize an individual's behavior when he is facing risk. The following section gives necessary and sufficient conditions for a utility function to exhibit behaviors that exhibit *risk aversion* behavior. Moreover, in order to discuss the comparative statics of an individual's behavior when his attitude towards risk changes, we need to have measures of risk aversion. These are the subjects to which we now turn.

1.17. An individual is said to be risk averse if he is unwilling to accept or is indifferent to any actuarially fair gamble. An individual is said to be strictly risk averse if he is unwilling to accept any actuarially fair gamble. Consider the gamble that has a positive return, h_1, with probability p and a negative return, h_2, with probability $(1 - p)$.

The gamble is actuarially fair when its expected payoff is zero, or

$$ph_1 + (1 - p)h_2 = 0. \tag{1.17.1}$$

Let $u(\cdot)$ be the utility function of an individual. From the definition of (strict) risk aversion, we have:

$$u(W_0)(>) \geq p\, u(W_0 + h_1) + (1 - p)\, u(W_0 + h_2), \tag{1.17.2}$$

where W_0 denotes the individual's initial wealth.

Using the definition of a fair gamble as in relation (1.17.1), relation (1.17.2) may be rewritten as

$$u(p(W_0+h_1)+(1-p)(W_0+h_2))(>) \geq p\, u(W_0+h_1)+(1-p)\, u(W_0+h_2).$$

The above relations demonstrate that risk aversion implies a concave utility function and that strict risk aversion implies a strictly concave utility function. A reversal of the above steps demonstrates that a concave utility function implies risk aversion and that a strictly concave utility function implies strict risk aversion.

Figure 1.17.1 illustrates the fact that the expected utility of gamble is strictly less than the utility of its expected payoff if and only if utility function is strictly concave.

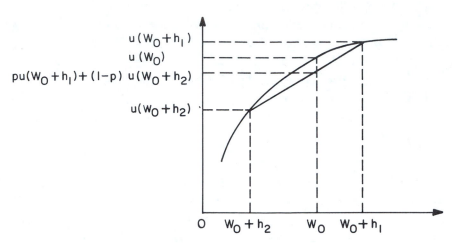

Figure 1.17.1: A Concave Utility Function

1.18. Consider a portfolio choice problem of a risk averse individual who strictly prefers more to less (has a strictly increasing utility function). If the individual invests a_j dollars in the j-th risky asset and $(W_0 - \sum_j a_j)$ dollars in the risk free asset, his uncertain end of period wealth, $\tilde{W}$, would be

$$\tilde{W} = (W_0 - \sum_j a_j)(1 + r_f) + \sum_j a_j(1 + \tilde{r}_j),$$

or equivalently

$$\tilde{W} = W_0(1 + r_f) + \sum_j a_j(\tilde{r}_j - r_f),$$

where

$W_0 =$ initial wealth,

$r_f =$ the riskless interest rate,

$\tilde{r}_j =$ the random rate of return on the j–th risky asset,

$a_j =$ the dollar investment in the j-th asset.

Thus the individual's choice problem is

$$\max_{\{a_j\}} \quad E[u(W_0(1+r_f) + \sum_j a_j(\tilde{r}_j - r_f))]. \qquad (1.18.1)$$

We assume that there exists a solution to (1.18.1). Since u is concave, the first order necessary conditions are also sufficient. They are

$$E[u'(\tilde{W})(\tilde{r}_j - r_f)] = 0 \quad \forall j. \qquad (1.18.2)$$

Note that, since u is strictly increasing, (1.18.2) implies that the probability that $\tilde{r}_j - r_f > 0$ must lie in $(0,1)$.

1.19. An individual who is risk averse and who strictly prefers more to less will undertake risky investments if and only if the rate of return on at least one risky asset exceeds the risk-free interest rate. To see this, we note the following. For the individual to invest nothing in or even short sell the risky assets as an optimal choice, it is necessary that the first order conditions evaluated at no risky investments be nonpositive:

$$E[u'(W_0(1+r_f))(\tilde{r}_j - r_f)] \le 0 \quad \forall\ j.$$

Equivalently,

$$u'(W_0(1+r_f))E[\tilde{r}_j - r_f] \le 0 \quad \forall\ j.$$

By assumption the individual strictly prefers more to less, therefore, $u'(\cdot) > 0$, and the above condition is equivalent to

$$a_j \le 0\ \forall\ j \quad \text{only if } E[\tilde{r}_j - r_f] \le 0 \quad \forall\ j.$$

Thus an individual with a strictly increasing and concave utility function will avoid any positive risky investment only if none of the risky assets has a strictly positive risk premium. When one or more risky assets have strictly positive risk premiums, the individual will take part in some risky investments. That is

$$\exists\ j, \text{ such that } a_j > 0 \quad \text{if } \exists\ j' \text{ such that } E[\tilde{r}_{j'} - r_f] > 0.$$
$$(1.19.1)$$

Note that j' may not equal j, because when there is more than one risky asset, $E[\tilde{r}_j - r_f] > 0$ does not necessarily imply $a_j > 0$. However, when there is only one risky asset, condition (1.19.1) indicates that a positive risk premium implies positive investment in that asset.

1.20. Henceforth until specified otherwise, consider a strictly risk averse individual who prefers more to less in an economy where there is only one risky asset and one riskless asset and where the risk premium of the risky asset is strictly positive. (Here we note that this individual will strictly prefer more to less.) Note that Section 1.19 demonstrates that a strictly positive risk premium would induce a strictly positive risky investment. This section examines the minimum risk premium that is required to induce the individual to invest *all* of his wealth in the risky asset. Let $\tilde{r}$ and a denote the rate of return of the single risky asset and the amount invested in it, respectively. For an individual to invest all his wealth in the risky asset it must be that

$$E[u'(W_0(1 + \tilde{r}))(\tilde{r} - r_f)] \geq 0.$$

Taking a first order Taylor series expansion of $u'[W_0(1 + \tilde{r})]$ around $u'[W_0(1 + r_f)]$, multiplying both sides by the risk premium, and taking expectations gives

$$\begin{aligned} E[u'(W_0(1 + \tilde{r}))(\tilde{r} - r_f)] = {} & u'(W_0(1 + r_f))E[\tilde{r} - r_f] \\ & + u''(W_0(1 + r_f))E[(\tilde{r} - r_f)^2]W_0 \\ & + o(E[(\tilde{r} - r_f)^2]), \end{aligned}$$

where $o(E[(\tilde{r}-r_f)^2])$ denotes terms of smaller magnitude than $E[(\tilde{r}-r_f)^2]$.

Risk is said to be small when $E[(\tilde{r} - r_f)^2]$ is small and terms involving $E[(\tilde{r} - r_f)^3]$ and higher orders can be ignored. Ignoring the remainder term, the minimum risk premium required to induce full investment in the risky asset may be determined by setting the right–hand side of the above relation to 0 and getting

$$E[\tilde{r} - r_f] \geq R_A\left(W_0(1 + r_f)\right)W_0 E[(\tilde{r} - r_f)^2], \qquad (1.20.1)$$

where $R_A(\cdot) = -u''(\cdot)/u'(\cdot)$ is the measure of absolute risk aversion defined by Arrow (1970) and Pratt (1964). Note that for small risks, absolute risk aversion is a measure of the intensity of an individual's aversion to risk. From (1.20.1), the higher an individual's absolute risk aversion, the higher the minimum risk premium required to induce full investment in the risky asset. Intuitively, the curvature of an individual's utility function would be related to the minimum risk premium required to induce full investment in the risky asset. The absolute risk aversion is a measure of the curvature of an individual's utility function. Note that von Neumann-Morgenstern utility functions are only unique up to a strictly positive affine transformation (addition of a constant and multiplication by a strictly positive scalar). Therefore, the second derivative alone cannot be used to characterize the intensity of risk averse behavior. The Arrow-Pratt measure of absolute risk aversion is invariant to a strictly positive affine transformation of the individual's utility function.

1.21. The characteristics of an individual's absolute risk aversion allow us to determine whether he treats a risky asset as a normal good when choosing between a single risky asset and a riskless asset.

An individual's utility function displays *decreasing absolute risk aversion* when $R_A(\cdot)$ is a strictly decreasing function. Similarly, $dR_A(z)/dz = 0 \; \forall z$ implies *increasing absolute risk aversion*, and a constant $dR_A(z)/dz \; \forall z$ implies *constant absolute risk aversion*.

Obviously, a single utility function may display more than one of the above characteristics over different parts of its domain. Several interesting behavioral properties of utility functions that display the same sign of $dR_A(z)/dz$ over the entire domain of $R_A(\cdot)$ were derived by Arrow (1970). Arrow showed that decreasing absolute risk aversion over the entire domain of $R_A(\cdot)$ implies that the risky asset is a normal good; i.e., the (dollar) demand for the risky asset increases as the individual's wealth increases. Increasing absolute risk aversion implies that the risky asset is an inferior good, and constant absolute risk aversion implies that the individual's demand for the risky asset is invariant with respect to his initial wealth. That is

$$\frac{dR_A(z)}{dz} < 0 \; \forall \; z \implies \frac{da}{dW_0} > 0 \quad \forall \; W_0;$$

$$\frac{dR_A(z)}{dz} > 0 \ \forall \ z \implies \frac{da}{dW_0} < 0 \quad \forall \ W_0;$$

$$\frac{dR_A(z)}{dz} = 0 \ \forall \ z \implies \frac{da}{dW_0} = 0 \quad \forall \ W_0.$$

The proof for only the decreasing absolute risk aversion case is presented as the proofs for the other two cases follow the same structure.

At an optimum, we have:

$$E[u'(W_0(1 + r_f) + a(\tilde{r} - r_f))(\tilde{r} - r_f)] = 0.$$

The change in the individual's optimal risky asset investment with respect to a change in initial wealth can be determined by:

1. Differentiating the first order condition for an optimum (that is determined for a given initial wealth level) with respect to his or her initial wealth;

2. Setting the first derivative equal to zero to move along the individual's optimal portfolio path; and

3. Solving for the implicit relationship between the change in risky asset investment and the change in initial wealth that would move the individual's risky asset investment along an optimal path as his initial wealth changes.

This process is referred to as implicit differentiation of a with respect to W_0 and gives

$$\frac{da}{dW_0} = \frac{E[u''(\tilde{W})(\tilde{r} - r_f)](1 + r_f)}{-E[u''(\tilde{W})(\tilde{r} - r_f)^2]}, \qquad (1.21.1)$$

where as usual $\tilde{W} = W_0(1 + r_f) + a(\tilde{r} - r_f)$ denotes the individual's end of period (random) wealth. The denominator is positive because strict risk aversion implies $u''(\tilde{W}) < 0$; therefore,

$$\text{sign } (da/dW_0) = \text{sign } \{E[u''(\tilde{W})(\tilde{r} - r_f)]\}.$$

Under decreasing absolute risk aversion, in the event that $\tilde{r} \geq r_f$, we have $\tilde{W} \geq W_0(1 + r_f)$ since the amount invested in the risky asset is strictly positive. Thus

$$R_A(\tilde{W}) \leq R_A(W_0(1 + r_f)). \qquad (1.21.2a)$$

Similarly, in the event that $\tilde{r} < r_f$, we have $\tilde{W} < W_0(1+r_f)$ and thus

$$R_A(\tilde{W}) > R_A(W_0(1+r_f)). \qquad (1.21.2b)$$

Multiplying both sides of (1.21.2a) and (1.21.2b) by $-u'(\tilde{W})(\tilde{r} - r_f)$ gives

$$u''(\tilde{W})(\tilde{r} - r_f) \geq -R_A(W_0(1+r_f))u'(\tilde{W})(\tilde{r} - r_f) \qquad (1.21.3a)$$

in the event that $\tilde{r} \geq r_f$, and

$$u''(\tilde{W})(\tilde{r} - r_f) > -R_A(W_0(1+r_f))u'(\tilde{W})(\tilde{r} - r_f) \qquad (1.21.3b)$$

in the event that $\tilde{r} < r_f$. Relations (1.21.3a) and (1.21.3b) imply

$$E[u''(\tilde{W})(\tilde{r} - r_f)] > -R_A(W_0(1+r_f))E[u'(\tilde{W})(\tilde{r} - r_f)], \qquad (1.21.4)$$

where we recall from Section 1.18 that the probability that $\tilde{r} > r_f$ must lie in $(0,1)$ for an optimal solution to exist. Substituting the first order condition $E[u'(\tilde{W})(\tilde{r} - r_f)] = 0$ into (1.21.4) gives the desired result.

Note that the property of non-increasing absolute risk aversion implies that the third derivative of the individual's utility function is strictly positive:

$$\frac{dR_A(z)}{dz} = \frac{-u'''(z)u'(z) + [u''(z)]^2}{[u'(z)]^2} \leq 0 \Longrightarrow u''' > 0, \qquad (1.21.5)$$

where we have used u''' to denote the third derivative of u. This follows because $u'(z) > 0$ and $[u''(z)]^2 > 0$. Thus $dR_A(z)/dz \leq 0$ implies $u'''(z) > 0$.

1.22. The property of decreasing absolute risk aversion is related to the dollar demand for the risky asset. Thus, an individual having a utility function displaying decreasing absolute risk aversion may actually increase, hold constant, or decrease the *proportion* of his wealth invested in the risky asset as his wealth increases. The Arrow-Pratt measure of *relative risk aversion* is $R_R(z) \equiv R_A(z)z$. Under increasing relative risk aversion, that is, when $dR_R(z)/dz > 0$

$\forall z$, the wealth elasticity of the individual's demand for the risky asset is strictly less than unity. That is, the proportion of the individual's initial wealth invested in the risky asset will decline as his wealth increases. Under constant relative risk aversion, $dR_R(z)/dz = 0 \; \forall z$, the wealth elasticity of demand for the risky asset would be unity, and under decreasing relative risk aversion, $dR_R(z)/dz < 0 \; \forall z$, the wealth elasticity of the demand for the risky asset would be strictly greater than unity.

The wealth elasticity of the demand for the risky asset, η, may be expressed as

$$\eta = \frac{da}{dW_0}\frac{W_0}{a} = 1 + \frac{(da/dW_0)W_0 - a}{a}. \tag{1.22.1}$$

Substituting the right–hand side of (1.21.1) for (da/dW_0) into the right–hand side of relation (1.22.1) and rearranging terms gives

$$\eta = 1 + \frac{W_0(1 + r_f)E[u''(\tilde{W})(\tilde{r} - r_f)] + aE[u''(\tilde{W})(\tilde{r} - r_f)^2]}{-aE[u''(\tilde{W})(\tilde{r} - r_f)^2]}.$$

Note that the numerator of the second term on the right–hand side of the above relation may be expressed as

$$E[u''(\tilde{W})(W_0(1 + r_f) + a(\tilde{r} - r_f))(\tilde{r} - r_f)] = E[u''(\tilde{W})\tilde{W}(\tilde{r} - r_f)].$$

Thus, the elasticity coefficient may be expressed as

$$\eta = 1 + \frac{E[u''(\tilde{W})\tilde{W}(\tilde{r} - r_f)]}{-aE[u''(\tilde{W})(\tilde{r} - r_f)^2]}. \tag{1.22.2}$$

The denominator of the second term on the right–hand side of (1.22.2) is positive because $u''(z) < 0$. Whether the demand elasticity for the risky asset is elastic, $\eta > 1$, unitary elastic, $\eta = 1$, or inelastic, $\eta < 1$, depends on the sign of the numerator. That is

$$\text{sign } (\eta - 1) = \text{sign } \{E[u''(\tilde{W})\tilde{W}(\tilde{r} - r_f)]\}.$$

Under increasing relative risk aversion,

$$R_R(W_0(1+r_f)+a(\tilde{r}-r_f)) \begin{cases} \geq R_R(W_0(1 + r_f)) & \text{in the event } \tilde{r} \geq r_f, \\ < R_R[W_0(1 + r_f)] & \text{in the event } \tilde{r} < r_f. \end{cases}$$

Multiplying both sides of the above relations by $-u'(\tilde{W})(\tilde{r} - r_f)$ reduces the relations to

$$u''(W)\, W\, (\tilde{r} - r_f) \leq -R_R(W_0(1 + r_f))u'(W)(\tilde{r} - r_f) \qquad (1.22.3a)$$

in the event that $\tilde{r} \geq r_f$, and

$$u''(W)\, W\, (\tilde{r} - r_f) < -R_R(W_0(1 + r_f))u'(W)(\tilde{r} - r_f) \qquad (1.22.3b)$$

in the event that $\tilde{r} < r_f$. Relations (1.22.3a), (1.22.3b), and the fact that at a portfolio optimum $E[u'(\tilde{W})(\tilde{r} - r_f)] = 0$ give

$$E[u''(\tilde{W})\tilde{W}(\tilde{r} - r_f)] < 0. \qquad (1.22.4)$$

Thus, under increasing relative risk aversion the wealth elasticity of demand for the risky asset is less than unity. If an individual were to have a utility function displaying increasing relative risk aversion, the fraction of his initial wealth that he invests in the risky asset would decline as his initial wealth increased. Using a similar derivation, the properties of decreasing and constant relative risk aversion may be shown to imply wealth elastic and wealth unitary demands respectively, as you are asked to do in Exercise 1.6.

1.23. The following utility functions are commonly used in finance to illustrate the properties of risk aversion that were discussed previously.

First, consider a concave quadratic utility function (which is sufficient for the demand for risky assets to be only a function of the mean and variance of portfolio returns):

$$u(z) = z - \frac{b}{2}z^2, \qquad b > 0;$$
$$u'(z) = 1 - bz;$$
$$u''(z) = -b.$$

For the marginal utility to be non-negative, z has to be less than $1/b$. The quadratic utility function is graphed in Figure 1.23.1. The quadratic utility function displays increasing absolute risk aversion:

$$R_A(z) = \frac{b}{1 - bz}, \qquad \frac{dR_A(z)}{dz} = \frac{b^2}{(1 - bz)^2} > 0.$$

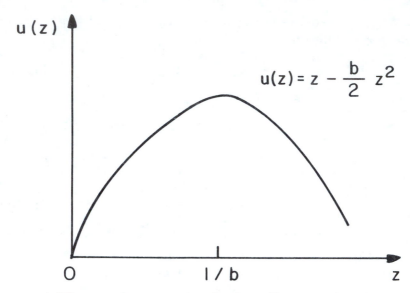

Figure 1.23.1: A Quadratic Utility Function

Thus, a quadratic utility function implies that the risky asset is an inferior good.

Consider next the negative exponential utility function:

$$u(z) = - e^{-bz}, \quad b \geq 0;$$
$$u'(z) = be^{-bz} > 0;$$
$$u''(z) = - b^2 e^{-bz} < 0.$$

The negative exponential utility function is graphed in Figure 1.23.2 and is bounded from above, which implies a finite utility level for infinite wealth:

$$\lim_{z \to \infty} u(z) = 0.$$

This utility function displays constant absolute risk aversion:

$$R_A(z) = b, \quad \frac{dR_A(z)}{dz} = 0.$$

Thus, the negative exponential utility function implies that the demand for risky assets is unaffected by changes in initial wealth, with riskless borrowing and lending absorbing all changes in initial wealth.

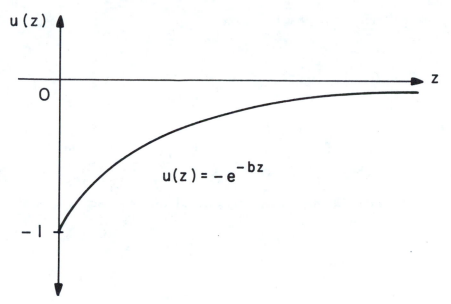

Figure 1.23.2: A Negative Exponential Utility Function

Next, consider a *narrow power utility function*:

$$u(z) = \frac{B}{B-1} z^{1-\frac{1}{B}}, \; z > 0, B > 0,$$

$$u'(z) = z^{-\frac{1}{B}}, \qquad u''(z) = -\frac{1}{B} z^{-\frac{1}{B}-1}.$$

Note the following:

$$R_A(z) = \frac{1}{B} z^{-1}, \quad R_R(z) = \frac{1}{B}$$

and

$$\frac{dR_A(z)}{dz} = -\frac{1}{B} z^{-2} < 0, \quad \frac{dR_R(z)}{dz} = 0.$$

Thus, for an individual having a narrow power utility function the *proportion* of wealth invested in the risky asset is invariant with respect to changes in his initial wealth level.

Finally, consider an *extended power utility function*:

$$u(z) = \frac{1}{B-1}(A + Bz)^{1-\frac{1}{B}}, \; B > 0, A \neq 0, z > \max[-\frac{A}{B}, 0],$$

$$u'(z) = (A + Bz)^{-\frac{1}{B}},$$

$$u''(z) = -(A + Bz)^{-\frac{1}{B}-1}.$$

Direct computation yields

$$R_A(z) = \frac{1}{A + Bz},$$

$$\frac{dR_A(z)}{dz} = \frac{-B}{(A + Bz)^2} < 0,$$

$$R_R(z) = \frac{z}{A + Bz},$$

$$\frac{dR_R(z)}{dz} = \frac{A}{(A + Bz)^2} \begin{cases} > 0 & \text{if and only if } A > 0; \\ = 0 & \text{if and only if } A = 0; \\ < 0 & \text{if and only if } A < 0. \end{cases}$$

Extended power utility functions exhibit decreasing or increasing relative risk aversion depending upon whether A is negative or positive. Note that when $A = 0$ an extended power reduces to a narrow power utility function.

Finally, we remark that the exponent of a (extended) power function is equal to the coefficient of z in the above examples. This is just for convenience in writing the derivatives. They do not have to be equal.

1.24. The analysis in Section 1.20 is essentially a local analysis. When risk is *small*, the higher the individual's absolute risk aversion at $W_0(1 + r_f)$, the higher the risk premium which is required for him to invest *all* his wealth in the risky asset. Thus, in a sense, $R_A(\cdot)$ is a local measure of risk aversion. Pratt (1964) showed that $R_A(\cdot)$ is also a measure of risk aversion in a global sense. That is, if there are two individuals i and k with $R_A^i(z) \geq R_A^k(z) \ \forall \ z$, then individual i will pay a larger insurance premium than k to insure against a (not necessarily small) random loss. Individual i is then said to be *more risk averse* than individual k. In the framework of Section 1.20, it will be demonstrated below that if individual i is more risk averse than individual k and they are endowed with the same initial wealth, then the risk premium required for individual i to invest all his wealth in the risky asset is larger than that required by individual k. The above statement is valid in a global sense where risk does not have to be small.

Suppose that

$$E[u_k'(W_0(1 + \tilde{r}))(\tilde{r} - r_f)] = 0, \tag{1.24.1}$$

where $u_k(\cdot)$ denotes individual k's utility function. Relation (1.24.1) is a necessary and sufficient condition for $E[\tilde{r} - r_f]$ to be the minimum risk premium that induces individual k to put all his wealth into the risky asset. If we can show that

$$E[u_i'(W_0(1 + \tilde{r}))(\tilde{r} - r_f)] \leq 0, \qquad (1.24.2)$$

where $u_i(\cdot)$ is individual i's utility function, then we are done. Relation (1.24.2) implies that individual i's optimal investment in the risky asset is less than or equal to W_0. This in turn implies that the required risk premium for i to invest all his wealth into the risky asset is greater than that required by k.

1.25. We will first prove a useful relation between u_i and u_k. We claim that there exists a strictly increasing and concave function G such that

$$u_i = G(u_k) \qquad (1.25.1)$$

if and only if $R_A^i(z) \geq R_A^k(z)$, $\forall z$. We will prove the necessity part first. Since u_k is strictly increasing, we define $G(y) \equiv u_i(u_k^{-1}(y))$, where u_k^{-1} denotes the inverse of u_k. Substituting $y = u_k(z)$ into the definition, we immediately have (1.25.1). We still have to show that $G(\cdot)$ is strictly increasing and concave. Differentiating (1.25.1) once gives

$$u_i'(z) = G'(u_k(z))u_k'(z). \qquad (1.25.2)$$

By the fact that $u_i'(z) > 0$ and $u_k'(z) > 0$, G must be strictly increasing in the domain of its definition.

Now differentiating (1.25.2) with respect to z gives

$$u_i''(z) = G''(u_k(z))(u_k'(z))^2 + G'(u_k(z))u_k''(z). \qquad (1.25.3)$$

Dividing (1.25.2) into (1.25.3) gives

$$R_A^i(z) = -\frac{G''(u_k(z))}{G'(u_k(z))}u_k'(z) + R_A^k(z). \qquad (1.25.4)$$

By the hypothesis that $R_A^i(z) \geq R_A^k(z)$ $\forall z$, (1.25.4) implies that G is concave. This completes the proof for the necessity part.

Next suppose that there exists a strictly increasing and concave function G such that (1.25.1) holds. By differentiation we have (1.25.2) and (1.25.3). Dividing (1.25.2) into (1.25.3) gives (1.25.4). Since G is strictly increasing and concave, we immediately conclude that $R_A^i(z) \geq R_A^k(z)$, $\forall z$, which concludes the proof for the sufficiency part.

1.26. Now we are ready to show that if $u_i = G(u_k)$, the minimum risk premium required for i to invest all his wealth in the risky asset is higher than that for k. We will first fix some notation. Let $\tilde{X}$ and $\tilde{Y}$ be two random variables. We use $E[\tilde{X}|\tilde{Y} \geq 0]$ to denote the conditional expectation of $\tilde{X}$ given that $\tilde{Y} \geq 0$; similarly for $E[\tilde{X}|\tilde{Y} < 0]$. Then we have by definition,

$$E[\tilde{X}] = E[\tilde{X}|\tilde{Y} \geq 0]P(\tilde{Y} \geq 0) + E[\tilde{X}|\tilde{Y} < 0]P(\tilde{Y} < 0),$$

where $P(\tilde{Y} \geq 0)$ denotes the probability that $\tilde{Y} \geq 0$ and similarly for $P(\tilde{Y} < 0)$. Using the above relation we can write

$$E[u_i'(W_0(1+\tilde{r}))(\tilde{r}-r_f)] = E[G'(u_k(W_0(1+\tilde{r})))u_k'(W_0(1+\tilde{r}))(\tilde{r}-r_f)]$$
$$= E[G'(u_k(W_0(1+\tilde{r})))\ u_k'(W_0(1+\tilde{r}))(\tilde{r}-r_f)|\tilde{r}-r_f \geq 0]P(\tilde{r}-r_f \geq 0)$$
$$+ E[G'(u_k(W_0(1+\tilde{r})))\ u_k'(W_0(1+\tilde{r}))(\tilde{r}-r_f)|\tilde{r}-r_f < 0]P(\tilde{r}-r_f < 0).$$

When $\tilde{r} - r_f \geq 0$, we have $W_0(1 + \tilde{r}) \geq W_0(1 + r_f)$. By the monotonicity of u_i and the concavity of G, we get

$$E(G'(u_k(W_0(1 + \tilde{r})))\ u_k'(W_0(1 + \tilde{r}))(\tilde{r} - r_f)|\tilde{r} - r_f \geq 0]$$
$$\leq G'(u_k(W_0(1 + r_f)))\ E[u_k'(W_0(1 + \tilde{r}))(\tilde{r} - r_f)|\tilde{r} - r_f \geq 0].$$

When $\tilde{r} - r_f < 0$, along the same line of argument, we get

$$E[G'(u_k(W_0(1 + \tilde{r})))\ u_k'(W_0(1 + \tilde{r}))(\tilde{r} - r_f)|\tilde{r} - r_f < 0]$$
$$\leq G'(u_k(W_0(1 + r_f)))\ E[u_k'(W_0(1 + \tilde{r}))(\tilde{r} - r_f)|\tilde{r} - r_f < 0]$$

Using the fact that $u_i = G(u_k)$ and summing the above two relations, we get

$$E[u_i'(W_0(1+\tilde{r}))(\tilde{r} - r_f)]$$
$$\leq G'(u_k(W_0(1 + r_f)))\ E[u_k'(W_0(1 + \tilde{r}))(\tilde{r} - r_f)]$$
$$= 0,$$

where the equality follows from (1.24.1). Therefore, the more risk averse an individual is, the larger the risk premium required for him to invest all his wealth in the risky asset.

1.27. The comparative statics we demonstrated in the previous few sections depend upon the fact that there are only two assets, one risky and one riskless. When there is more than one risky asset, in general we cannot say, for example, that the wealth elasticities of the demands for risky assets are greater than unity when an individual exhibits decreasing relative risk aversion. When an investor's initial wealth increases, he may want to change his portfolio composition of the risky assets such that the investment in one risky asset increases while the investment in another decreases.

Obviously, if an individual always chooses to hold the same portfolio of risky assets and only change the mix between that portfolio and the riskless asset for differing levels of initial wealth, then the comparative statics for the two asset case will be valid in a multi-asset world. In such event, the individual's optimal portfolios for differing levels of initial wealth are always linear combinations of the riskless asset and a risky asset mutual fund. This phenomenon is termed *two fund monetary separation*.

Cass and Stiglitz (1970) have demonstrated that a necessary and sufficient condition on utility functions for two fund monetary separation is that marginal utility satisfy

$$u'(z) = (A + Bz)^C \qquad (1.27.1)$$

or

$$u'(z) = A \exp\{Bz\}, \qquad (1.27.2)$$

where $B > 0, C < 0$, and $z \geq \max[0, -(A/B)]$, or $A > 0, B < 0, C > 0$ and $0 \leq z < -(A/B)$ for (1.27.1) and where $A > 0, B < 0$ and $z \geq 0$ for (1.27.2). The conditions on A, B and C are to insure that the utility functions are strictly concave and increasing.

The proof for necessity of (1.27.1) or (1.27.2) is tedious and we refer interested readers to Cass and Stiglitz's treatment. In what follows, we shall demonstrate the sufficiency of (1.27.1) or (1.27.2).

1.28. Let α denote the proportion of initial wealth, W_0, invested in the riskless asset, and let b_j denote the proportion of the remainder $W_0(1-\alpha)$ invested in the j-th risky asset. A risk averse individual solves the following programming problem:

$$\max_{\{\alpha,b_j,\lambda\}} \mathcal{L} = E[u(\tilde{W})] + \lambda(1 - \sum_j b_j),$$

where $\mathcal{L}$ denotes the Lagrangian, and

$$\tilde{W} = W_0(1 + \alpha r_f + (1-\alpha)\sum_j b_j\,\tilde{r}_j).$$

The necessary and sufficient conditions for an interior optimum are:

$$E[u'(\tilde{W})W_0(r_f - \sum_j b_j\,\tilde{r}_j)] = 0, \tag{1.28.1}$$

$$E[u'(\tilde{W})W_0(1-\alpha)\tilde{r}_j] = \lambda \qquad \forall\,j, \tag{1.28.2}$$

and

$$\sum_j b_j = 1. \tag{1.28.3}$$

Substituting (1.28.1) into (1.28.2) and using (1.28.3) gives, $\forall j$,

$$E[u'(W_0(1 + r_f + (1-\alpha)\sum_l b_l(\tilde{r}_l - r_f)))(\tilde{r}_j - r_f)] = 0. \tag{1.28.4}$$

Now suppose that (1.27.1) is true. Then (1.28.4) implies, $\forall j$,

$$E[(A + BW_0(1 + r_f + (1-\alpha)\sum_j b_j(\tilde{r}_j - r_f)))^C(\tilde{r}_j - r_f)] = 0. \tag{1.28.5}$$

Consider the same individual with a different initial wealth W_0'. Let α', b_j' be the individual's optimal portfolio decisions with respect to W_0'. Note that, by the strict concavity of the utility function, α' and b' are uniquely determined.

We must have, $\forall j$,

$$E[(A + BW_0'(1 + r_f + (1-\alpha')\sum_j b_j'(\tilde{r}_j - r_f)))^C(\tilde{r}_j - r_f)] = 0. \tag{1.28.6}$$

We claim that α, b_j and α', b_j' are related by

$$W_0'(1 - \alpha')b_j' = \frac{A + BW_0'(1 + r_f)}{A + BW_0(1 + r_f)} W_0(1 - \alpha)b_j \qquad \forall j. \qquad (1.28.7)$$

To see this, we substitute (1.28.7) into either (1.28.5) or (1.28.6) and check that the equality is satisfied.

Summing (1.28.7) over all j and using (1.28.3) we get

$$W_0'(1 - \alpha') = \frac{A + BW_0'(1 + r_f)}{A + BW_0(1 + r_f)} W_0(1 - \alpha). \qquad (1.28.8)$$

Now substituting (1.28.8) into (1.28.7), we have

$$b_j' = b_j \qquad \forall j,$$

which was to be shown.

Along the same line of argument, it is easily checked that (1.27.2) also implies two fund monetary separation.

1.29. The solutions of (1.27.1) include extended power utility functions:

$$u(z) = \frac{1}{(C + 1)B}(A + Bz)^{C+1}, \qquad C \neq -1$$

and log utility functions:

$$u(z) = \ln(A + Bz).$$

The solutions of (1.27.2) are exponential utility functions:

$$u(z) = \frac{A}{B} \exp\{Bz\}.$$

Narrow power utility functions ($A = 0$) and log utility functions exhibit constant relative risk aversion. Thus, the proportions invested in the riskless asset α and in the risky asset mutual fund $(1 - \alpha)$ are invariant to different levels of initial wealth.

The exponential utility functions exhibit increasing relative risk aversion. Thus as initial wealth increases, the proportion invested in the risky asset mutual fund will decrease.

Other comparative statics can be derived. Their analysis is a direct corollary of the comparative statics in the two asset case, therefore we leave them for interested readers.

Exercises

1.1. Suppose that X has a countable number of elements. Show that a binary relation on X is a preference relation if and only if it can be represented as a real-valued function.

1.2. Suppose that $\succeq$ is a binary relation. A subset Y of X is said to be a $\succeq$-*order dense* subset of X if for all $x, x' \in X$ such that $x \succ x'$, there exists $y \in Y$ such that $x \succeq y \succeq x'$. In words, given any two consumption plans that are in the binary relation $\succeq$ and can be strictly compared, there always exists an element of Y that lies between the two. The set Y is a *countable* $\succeq$-*order dense* subset of X if it is a $\succeq$-order dense subset of X and has a countable number of elements. A representation theorem for arbitrary X is as follows: The binary relation $\succeq$ can be represented by a utility function H if and only if $\succeq$ is a preference relation and there is a countable $\succeq$-order dense subset Y of X.

Now let $X = [0, 1] \times [0, 1]$ and define $(x_1, x_2) \succeq (y_1, y_2)$ if $x_1 > y_1$ or if $x_1 = y_1$ and $x_2 > y_2$.

1.2.1. Verify that $\succeq$ is a preference relation. (This is the so-called *Lexicographic* preference relation.)

1.2.2. Show that if $(x_1, x_2) \succeq (y_1, y_2)$ and $(y_1, y_2) \succeq (x_1, x_2)$ then $x_1 = y_1$ and $x_2 = y_2$.

1.2.3. Demonstrate that $\succeq$ cannot be represented by a real-valued function. (Hint: Show that there does not exist a counter $\succeq$-order dense set and use the representation theorem above for arbitrary X.)

1.3. Prove the properties of Section 1.9.

1.4. Show that a von Neumann–Morgenstern utility function is determined up to a strictly positive linear transformation. Show also that if a binary relation $\succeq$ has an expected utility representation in that there exists u such that, for $p, q \in \mathbf{P}$,

$$p \succeq q \quad \text{if and only if} \quad \sum_{z \in Z} u(z)p(z) \geq \sum_{z \in Z} u(z)q(z),$$

then $\succeq$ satisfies the three axioms of Section 1.8.

1.5. Prove that $dR_A(z)/dz > 0$ implies that $da/dW_0 < 0 \ \forall W_0$ and $dR_A(z)/dz = 0$ implies that $da/dW_0 = 0 \ \forall W_0$ in the context of Section 1.21.

1.6. Show that $dR_R(z)/dz < 0 \ \forall z \in \Re$ implies $\eta > 1$ and that $dR_R(z)/dz = 0 \ \forall z \in \Re$ implies $\eta = 1$, where η is the wealth elasticity of demand for the risky asset defined in (1.22.1).

1.7. Define *absolute risk tolerance* to be the inverse of the Arrow-Pratt measure of absolute risk aversion. Show that solutions to (1.27.1) and (1.27.2) all exhibit linear absolute risk tolerance.

1.8. Fix an individual with an increasing and strictly concave utility function u and consider the gamble of (1.17.1). Define the insurance premium z to be the maximum amount of money the individual is willing to pay to avoid the gamble. That is, z is the solution to the following

$$u(W_0 - z) = pu(W_0 + h_1) + (1 - p)u(W_0 + h_2).$$

Obviously, z depends upon the initial wealth, W_0, and we will denote this dependence by $z(W_0)$. Show that, when the risk is small,

$$\frac{dR_A(z)}{dz} < 0 \quad \forall z \quad \text{if} \quad \frac{dz(W_0)}{dW_0} < 0 \ \forall W_0;$$

$$\frac{dR_A(z)}{dz} = 0 \quad \forall z \quad \text{if} \quad \frac{dz(W_0)}{dW_0} = 0 \ \forall W_0;$$

$$\frac{dR_A(z)}{dz} > 0 \quad \forall z \quad \text{if} \quad \frac{dz(W_0)}{dW_0} > 0 \ \forall W_0.$$

1.9. Show that utility functions of (1.27.2) imply two fund monetary separation.

Remarks. Discussions in Sections 1.3 to 1.15 are adapted from Kreps (1981). For discussions of a continuous preference relation and its representation by a continuous real-valued function, see Debreu (1964). For representation of a preference relation by a continuous von Neumann–Morgenstern utility function, see Granmont (1972). The example of the unbounded expected utility of Section 1.13 is a generalization of the so–called *St. Petersburg Paradox*. Arrow (1970) is an excellent source for a discussion of this and other related issues. Nielsen (1985, 1986) develops a set of axioms under which a preference relation can be represented by a possibly unbounded expected utility function.

Discussions of Sections 1.17 through 1.22 are freely borrowed from Arrow (1970). Some of the results of Sections 1.24 and 1.25 are contained in Pratt (1964). The sufficiency proof of Section 1.28 is adapted from Rubinstein (1974).

We will discuss a stronger measure of risk aversion in Chapter 2 that gives some intuitively appealing comparative statics in a portfolio problem with two risky assets. Readers interested in different measures of risk aversion should see Pratt and Zeckhauser (1987). Machina (1982) discusses measures of risk aversion when an individual's preferences can be represented by expected utility only *locally*. For some negative results on the comparative statics for portfolio choice problems when there are many assets see Hart (1975).

References

Allais, M. 1953. Le comportement de l'homme rationnel devant le risque, critique des postulates et axioms de l'ecole Americaine. *Econometrica* **21**:503–546.

Arrow, K. 1970. Essays in the Theory of Risk–Bearing. Amsterdam: North–Holland.

Bernoulli, D. 1954. Exposition of a new theory on the measurement of risk (translation from the 1730 version). *Econometrica* **22**:23–36.

Cass, D., and J. Stiglitz. 1970, The structure of investor preferences and asset returns, and separability in portfolio allocation: A contribution to the pure theory of mutual funds. *Journal of Economic Theory* 2:122-160.

Debreu, G. 1954. Representation of a preference ordering by a numerical function. In *Decision Processes*. Edited by R. Thrall, C. Coombs, and R. Davis. John Wiley & Sons, New York.

Debreu, G. 1964. Continuity properties of paretian utility. *International Economic Review* 5:285-293.

Fishburn, P. 1970. *Utility Theory for Decision Making*. John Wiley & Sons. New York.

Granmont, J. 1972. Continuity properties of a von Neumann Morgenstern utility. *Journal of Economic Theory* 4:45-57.

Hart, O. 1975. Some negative results on the existence of comparative statics results in portfolio theory. *Review of Economic Studies* 42:615-621.

Kreps, D. 1981. *Single Person Decision Theory*. Lecture Notes. Graduate School of Business, Stanford University. Stanford, California.

Machina, M. 1982. Expected utility analysis without the independence axiom. *Econometrica* 50:277-323.

Nielsen, L. 1985. Unbounded expected utility and continuity. *Mathematical Social Sciences* 8:201-216.

Nielsen, L. 1986. Corrigendum. Mimeo. Economics Department, University of Texas at Austin.

Pratt, J. 1964. Risk aversion in the small and in the large. *Econometrica* 32:122-136.

Pratt, J., and R. Zeckhauser. 1987. Proper risk aversion. *Econometrica* 55:143-154.

Rubinstein, M. 1974. An aggregation theorem for securities markets. *Journal of Financial Economics* 1:225-244.

Savage, L. 1972. *Foundations of Statistics*. Dover. New York.

Von Neumann, J., and O. Morgenstern. 1953. *Theory of Games and Economic Behavior*, Princeton University Press. Princeton, New Jersey.

CHAPTER 2
STOCHASTIC DOMINANCE

2.1. In Chapter 1, we discussed the relationship between the risk premium and Arrow–Pratt measures of risk aversion in a context where there are only two securities, one riskless and one risky. The first part of this chapter addresses the following question: Suppose that there are two risky securities. Under what conditions can we unambiguously say that an individual will prefer one risky asset to another when the only information we have about this individual is either that he is nonsatiable or that he is risk averse? To answer this question, we will introduce two concepts of *stochastic dominance*. One concept turns out to be useful in comparing the *riskiness* of risky assets. This concept, however, does not allow us to compare any two risky assets, and in the terminology of Section 1.3, it does not define a *complete order* among risky assets. We will analyze the comparative statics of an individual's problem with a portfolio of one risky and one riskless asset when the riskiness of the risky asset increases. These comparative statics depends upon Arrow–Pratt measures of risk aversion in a complicated way. We will also demonstrate through an example that the Arrow–Pratt measures of risk aversion are too weak to study the comparative statics of

an individual's portfolio problem when faced with two risky assets.
A stronger measure of risk aversion that gives intuitively appealing
comparative statics is then discussed.

2.2.   We will say that risky asset A dominates risky asset B in
the sense of *First Degree Stochastic Dominance*, denoted by $A \underset{FSD}{\geq} B$,
if all individuals having utility functions in wealth that are increasing
and continuous either prefer A to B or are indifferent between A and
B. Intuition suggests that if the probability of asset A's rate of return
exceeding *any* given level is not smaller than that of asset B's rate of
return exceeding the same level, then *any* nonsatiable individual will
prefer A to B. It turns out that this condition is not only sufficient
but also necessary. Here we note that an individual is nonsatiable if
and only if his utility function is strictly increasing.

For ease of exposition, we shall assume that the rates of return
on A and B lie in the interval $[0, 1]$ throughout this chapter. However,
the results to be shown are valid in more general contexts when some
regularity conditions are satisfied.

Let $F_A(\cdot)$ and $F_B(\cdot)$ denote cumulative distribution functions of
the rates of return on A and B respectively. Suppose that:

$$F_A(z) \leq F_B(z) \qquad \forall \, z \in [0, 1]. \tag{2.2.1}$$

Since $F_A(\cdot)$ and $F_B(\cdot)$ are cumulative distribution functions, they are
continuous from the right and $F_A(1) = F_B(1) = 1$. However, $F_A(0)$
may not be equal to $F_B(0)$ since $F_A(\cdot)$ and $F_B(\cdot)$ can have different
masses at zero.

Relation (2.2.1) is graphed in Figure 2.2.1. For any z, the probability that the rate of return on asset A is less than z is less than
that for asset B. Putting it differently, the probability that the rate
of return on asset A is greater than z is greater than that for asset
B. Note that (2.2.1) does not mean that asset A has a *realized* rate
of return that is always greater than that of asset B. The following example illustrates this point. Suppose that rates of return on
assets A and B can only take on three possible values: 0, 1/2, and
1 with cumulative probabilities described in Table 2.2.1. It is easily
seen that condition (2.2.1) is satisfied. Ex post, when asset A has a

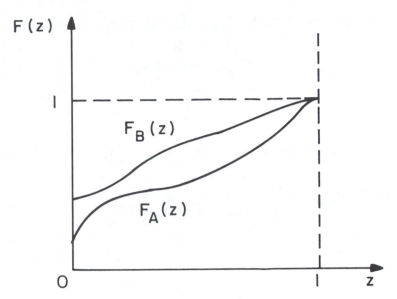

Figure 2.2.1: First Degree Stochastic Dominance

z	0	1/2	1
$F_A(z)$	1/4	3/4	1
$F_B(z)$	1/2	4/5	1

Table 2.2.1: An Example of First Degree Stochastic Dominance

realized rate of return 0, asset B can have a realized rate of return 1. If the rates of return on A and B were independent, then the probability that the rate of return on A is 0 and the rate of return on B is 1 would be 0.05.

2.3. Let $u(\cdot)$ be any continuous and increasing utility function representing a nonsatiable individual's preferences and assume without loss of generality that this individual has unit initial wealth. If the individual invests in asset A, his expected utility is $E[u(1 + \tilde{r}_A)]$ and similarly for asset B, where we use $\tilde{r}_A$ and $\tilde{r}_B$ to denote the rates of return on asset A and asset B, respectively. We want to show that

(2.2.1) implies that $E[u(1 + \tilde{r}_A)] \geq E[u(1 + \tilde{r}_B)]$, or equivalently,

$$\int_{[0,1]} u(1 + z) \, dF_A(z) \geq \int_{[0,1]} u(1 + z) \, dF_B(z),$$

where

$$\int_{[0,1]} u(1 + z) \, dF_A(z) \equiv u(1)F_A(0) + \int_0^1 u(1 + z)dF_A(z),$$

and similarly for the integral on the right side.

Integration by parts gives:

$$\int_{[0,1]} u(1 + z) \, d[F_A(z) - F_B(z)] = u(1) \, (F_A(0) - F_B(0))$$

$$+ \int_0^1 u(1 + z) \, d[F_A(z) - F_B(z)]$$

$$= u(1) \, (F_A(0) - F_B(0)) + u(1 + z) \, (F_A(z) - F_B(z)) \mid_0^1$$

$$- \int_0^1 [F_A(z) - F_B(z)] \, du(1 + z).$$

Since $F_A(1) = F_B(1) = 1$, we get

$$\int_{[0,1]} u(1 + z) \, d[F_A(z) - F_B(z)]$$

$$= - \int_0^1 [F_A(z) - F_B(z)] \, du(1 + z). \tag{2.3.1}$$

Now by the hypothesis that $F_A(z) - F_B(z) \leq 0$ and the fact that $u(\cdot)$ is increasing, the sign of (2.3.1) is nonnegative. Therefore (2.2.1) is sufficient for $A \overset{\geq}{_{FSD}} B$.

Next we establish that (2.2.1) is also a necessary condition for $A \overset{\geq}{_{FSD}} B$. Suppose that $A \overset{\geq}{_{FSD}} B$, and $F_A(x) > F_B(x)$ for some $x \in [0, 1)$. Note that $x \neq 1$, as $F_A(1) = F_B(1) = 1$. Since cumulative distribution functions are increasing and right continuous, there must exist an interval $[x, c] \in [0, 1]$ such that:

$$F_A(z) > F_B(z) \qquad \forall \, z \in [x, c]. \tag{2.3.2}$$

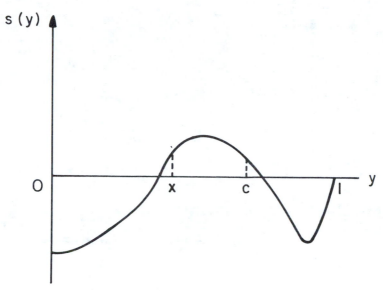

Figure 2.3.1: Relation (2.3.2)

If we put $s(y) = F_A(y) - F_B(y)$, then (2.3.2) can be depicted in Figure 2.3.1.

Note that $s(y)$ is the integrand of the right-hand side of (2.3.1). By (2.3.2), we know that $s(y)$ is strictly positive on $[x, c]$. If we can construct a continuous and increasing utility function that strictly increases only on $[1 + x, 1 + c]$, then (2.3.1) would have a negative sign, which contradicts the hypothesis that $A \overset{\geq}{FSD} B$. This can be accomplished by defining

$$u(1 + z) = \int_0^z 1_{[1+x, 1+c]}(1 + t) \, dt \qquad \forall \, z \in [0, 1], \qquad (2.3.3)$$

where $1_{[x,c]}(t)$ equals 1 if $t \in [x, c]$ and 0 elsewhere. It is quickly checked that $u(\cdot)$ is increasing and continuous. Moreover,

$$u'(1 + z) = 1_{[1+x, 1+c]}(1 + z) = \begin{cases} 1 & \text{if } 1 + z \in [1 + x, 1 + c], \\ 0 & \text{otherwise}, \end{cases} \qquad (2.3.4)$$

that is, the marginal utility is equal to 1 on $[1 + x, 1 + c]$ and 0 elsewhere, as graphed in Figure 2.3.2.

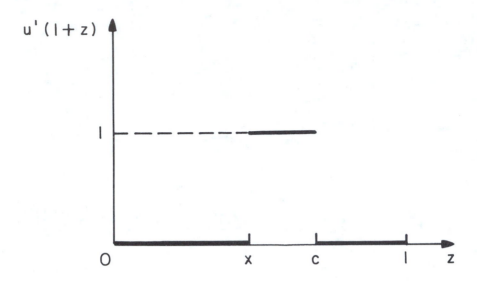

Figure 2.3.2: Relation (2.3.4)

Now using (2.3.1) and (2.3.2), we get

$$\int_{[0,1]} u(1+z) \, d[F_A(z) - F_B(z)] = - \int_0^1 [F_A(z) - F_B(z)] \, du(1+z)$$

$$= - \int_x^c [F_A(z) - F_B(z)] \, dz \ < 0,$$

which contradicts $A \ \overset{\geq}{{}_{FSD}} \ B$. Thus we must have

$$F_A(z) \leq F_B(z) \qquad \forall \, z \in [0,1].$$

A necessary and sufficient condition for $A \ \overset{\geq}{{}_{FSD}} \ B$ is thus established to be

$$F_A(z) \leq F_B(z) \qquad \forall \, z \in [0,1].$$

2.4. Another characterization of $\overset{\geq}{{}_{FSD}}$ is available. It can easily be seen that if asset A 's rate of return is equal in distribution to asset B's rate of return plus a positive random variable, say $\tilde{\alpha}$, then all individuals with increasing utility functions will prefer A to B, because:

$$E[u(1 + \tilde{r}_A)] = E[u(1 + \tilde{r}_B + \tilde{\alpha})]$$
$$\geq E[u(1 + \tilde{r}_B)],$$

for all increasing $u(\cdot)$. The inequality of the last expression follows from the positivity of $\tilde{\alpha}$ and the monotonicity of $u(\cdot)$. One can also prove that the converse of the above characterization is also valid. That is, if $A \underset{FSD}{\geq} B$, then there exists a positive random variable $\tilde{\alpha}$ such that $\tilde{r}_A \overset{d}{=} \tilde{r}_B + \tilde{\alpha}$. Since this characterization is quite intuitive; and its proof is technical, we omit its proof.

Combining the results of this section and Section 2.3, we thus have the equivalence of the following three statements:

1. $A \underset{FSD}{\geq} B$;

2. $F_A(z) \leq F_B(z) \ \forall z \in [0, 1]$;

3. $\tilde{r}_A \overset{d}{=} \tilde{r}_B + \tilde{\alpha}, \ \tilde{\alpha} \geq 0$.

From 3 above, if $A \underset{FSD}{\geq} B$, then asset A must have at least as high an expected rate of return as asset B. The converse is not true, however.

2.5. Suppose now that the only information we have about an individual is that he is risk averse. Under what conditions can we unambiguously say that he prefers risky asset A to risky asset B? This subject is examined in this section. Note that risk averse individuals may have utility functions that are not monotonically increasing.

We will say that risky asset A dominates risky asset B in the sense of *Second Degree Stochastic Dominance*, denoted by $A \underset{SSD}{\geq} B$, if all risk averse individuals having utility functions whose first derivatives are continuous except on a countable subset of $[1, 2]$ prefer A to B. We claim that $A \underset{SSD}{\geq} B$ if and only if

$$E[\tilde{r}_A] = E[\tilde{r}_B] \qquad (2.5.1)$$

and

$$S(y) \equiv \int_0^y (F_A(z) - F_B(z)) dz \leq 0 \quad \forall y \in [0, 1]. \qquad (2.5.2)$$

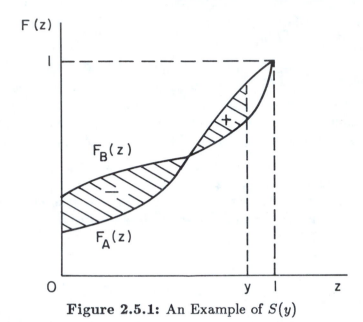

Figure 2.5.1: An Example of $S(y)$

If $F_A(\cdot)$ and $F_B(\cdot)$ are as drawn in Figure 2.5.1, then $S(y)$ is the sum of the two shaded areas, and the signs of the areas are as indicated.

2.6. We will prove the sufficiency part first. From (2.3.1), we have

$$\int_{[0,1]} u(1+z)\, d[F_A(z) - F_B(z)] = -\int_0^1 [F_A(z) - F_B(z)]\, du(1+z).$$

Integration by parts gives

$$-\int_0^1 [F_A(z) - F_B(z)]\, du(1+z) = -\int_0^1 u'(1+z)\, dS(z)$$

$$= -u'(1+z)S(z)\big|_0^1 + \int_0^1 S(z)du'(1+z). \tag{2.6.1}$$

Since

$$S(0) = \int_{[0,0]} (F_A(z) - F_B(z))\, dz$$

$$= 0,$$

and

$$S(1) = \int_{[0,1]} [F_A(z) - F_B(z)]dz$$

$$= \int_0^1 [F_A(z) - F_B(z)]dz$$

$$= (F_A(z) - F_B(z)) \, z|_0^1 - \int_0^1 z \, dF_A(z) + \int_0^1 z \, dF_B(z)$$

$$= \int_0^1 z \, dF_B(z) - \int_0^1 z \, dF_A(z)$$

$$= E[\tilde{r}_B] - E[\tilde{r}_A] = 0, \tag{2.6.2}$$

where the last equality follows from (2.5.1), (2.6.1) can be written as

$$\int_{[0,1]} u(1+z) \, d[F_A(z) - F_B(z)] = \int_0^1 S(z)du'(1+z) \geq 0, \tag{2.6.3}$$

where the inequality follows from (2.5.2) and the fact that u' is decreasing. We have proved the sufficiency part.

2.7. Now we prove the necessity part. Suppose first that $A \; s\overset{\geq}{s}_D \; B$. Since linear utility functions are admissible, we can take a linear strictly increasing utility function and a linear strictly decreasing utility function. Using the definition of $A \; s\overset{\geq}{s}_D \; B$,

$$\int_{[0,1]} z \, dF_A(z) = \int_{[0,1]} z \, dF_B(z),$$

or, equivalently, $E[\tilde{r}_A] = E[\tilde{r}_B]$, which is (2.5.1). Next repeating the integration by parts done in Section 2.6, we get the equality of (2.6.3).

We claim that $S(\cdot)$, which is continuous, is negative. Suppose this is not the case. It then follows from the continuity of $S(\cdot)$ that there must exist an interval $[a, b]$ with $a \neq b$ such that

$$S(z) > 0 \qquad \forall \; z \in [a, b].$$

If we can find a concave utility function whose first derivative is continuous except possibly on a countable set and strictly decreases

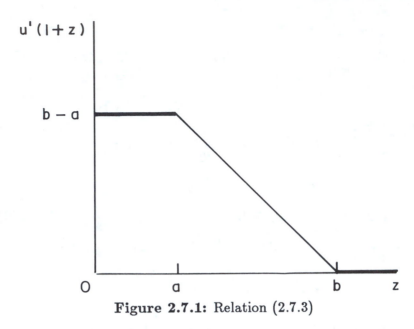

Figure 2.7.1: Relation (2.7.3)

only on $[1 + a, 1 + b]$, then the inequality of (2.6.3) will be violated and thus the hypothesis that $A\ s\overset{\geq}{s}_D B$ will be contradicted. We can accomplish this by defining

$$u(1+z) = \int_0^z \int_y^1 1_{[1+a,1+b]}(1+t)\ dt\ dy \qquad \forall\ z \in [0,1], \quad (2.7.2)$$

which is continuously differentiable and concave with

$$u'(1+z) = \int_z^1 1_{[1+a,1+b]}(1+t)dt. \qquad (2.7.3)$$

This derivative is graphed in Figure 2.7.1.

Thus,

$$\int_{[0,1]} u(1+z)\ d[F_A(z) - F_B(z)] = \int_0^1 S(z)\ du'(1+z)$$

$$= -\int_{[a,b]} S(x)\ dx < 0.$$

This contradicts the hypothesis that $A\ s\overset{\geq}{s}_D B$, Therefore, $A\ s\overset{\geq}{s}_D B$ implies (2.5.2). We have therefore demonstrated that (2.5.1) and (2.5.2) are necessary and sufficient for $A\ s\overset{\geq}{s}_D B$.

2.8. Rothschild and Stiglitz (1970) give another characteriza-
tion of $s\overset{\geq}{s}_D$. They show that $A \; s\overset{\geq}{s}_D \; B$ if and only if:

$$\tilde{r}_B \overset{d}{=} \tilde{r}_A + \tilde{\epsilon}, \quad \text{with } E[\tilde{\epsilon}|\tilde{r}_A] = 0.$$

That is, the rate of return on asset B is equal, *in distribution*, to the
rate of return on asset A plus a noise term. The sufficiency part is
easy. Let $u(\cdot)$ be a concave function. Then:

$$
\begin{aligned}
E[u(\tilde{r}_B)] &= E[u(\tilde{r}_A + \tilde{\epsilon})] \\
&= E\left[E[u(\tilde{r}_A + \tilde{\epsilon})|\tilde{r}_A]\right] \\
&\leq E[u(\tilde{r}_A)],
\end{aligned}
$$

where the first equality follows from the fact that $\tilde{r}_B$ and $\tilde{r}_A + \tilde{\epsilon}$ have
the same distribution, the second equality follows from the law of
iterative expectations, and the inequality follows from the conditional
Jensen's inequality. The necessity part is much more difficult, and we
refer interested readers to Rothschild and Stiglitz (1970) for details.

We have, therefore, three equivalent statements:

1. $A \; s\overset{\geq}{s}_D \; B$;
2. $E[\tilde{r}_A] = E[\tilde{r}_B]$ and $S(z) \leq 0 \; \forall z \in [0,1]$; and
3. $\tilde{r}_B \overset{d}{=} \tilde{r}_A + \tilde{\epsilon}$, with $E[\tilde{\epsilon}|\tilde{r}_A] = 0$.

Denoting by $\text{Var}(\cdot)$ the variance of a random variable and by
$\text{Cov}(\cdot,\cdot)$ the covariance of two random variables, one direct consequence of statement (3) above is that $\text{Var}(\tilde{r}_B) \geq \text{Var}(\tilde{r}_A)$, since
$E[\tilde{\epsilon}|\tilde{r}_A] = 0$ implies $\text{Cov}(\tilde{r}_A, \tilde{\epsilon}) = 0$. Thus if $A s\overset{\geq}{s}_D B$, it must then be
the case that $E[\tilde{r}_A] = E[\tilde{r}_B]$ and $\text{Var}(\tilde{r}_A) \leq \text{Var}(\tilde{r}_B)$. However, the
converse does not hold.

Henceforth, whenever one of the above three conditions is satisfied, we say that asset B is *more risky* than asset A.

2.9. We shall say that risky asset A dominates B in the sense of
second degree stochastic monotonic dominance denoted by $\overset{\geq M}{s_{SD}}$ if all
risk averse and nonsatiable individuals prefer A to B. Given earlier
discussions on first degree and second degree stochastic dominance,
it can be verified that the following three statements are equivalent:

1. $A \overset{\geq M}{\underset{SSD}{}} B$;

2. $E[\tilde{r}_A] \geq E[\tilde{r}_B]$ and $S(z) \leq 0 \ \forall \ z \in [0,1]$;

3. $\tilde{r}_B \overset{d}{=} \tilde{r}_A + \tilde{\epsilon}$, with $E[\tilde{\epsilon}|\tilde{r}_A] \leq 0$.

We will not provide detailed proofs for the equivalence of the above relations. They are minor extensions of the earlier results.

2.10. Rothschild and Stiglitz (1971) present an application of the concepts developed above. Consider a risk averse individual with unit initial wealth to be invested in a risky asset A with a rate of return $\tilde{r}_A$ and a riskless asset with a rate of return r_f. The necessary and sufficient condition for a to be an optimal amount invested in the risky asset is:

$$E[u'((1+r_f) + a(\tilde{r}_A - r_f))(\tilde{r}_A - r_f)] = 0, \qquad (2.10.1)$$

where $u(\cdot)$ is the individual's utility function.

Imagine the following situation. There is another risky asset B that is more risky than asset A in that $A \overset{\geq}{\underset{SSD}{}} B$. We ask the following question. If the same individual is to invest in risky asset B and the riskless asset, is he going to invest less in the risky asset because now the risky asset is more risky? We can render a yes to this question if we have

$$E[u'((1+r_f) + a(\tilde{r}_B - r_f))(\tilde{r}_B - r_f)] \leq 0. \qquad (2.10.2)$$

Relation (2.10.2) indicates that the individual's utility will be improved upon if the amount he invests in the risky asset is less than a.

We shall transform relations (2.10.1) and (2.10.2) to be more in line with the notation of this chapter. Let $F_A(\cdot)$ and $F_B(\cdot)$ be the distribution functions for $\tilde{r}_A$ and $\tilde{r}_B$ with a common support $[0,1]$. Then relations (2.10.1) and (2.10.2) can be written as:

$$\int_{[0,1]} u'[(1+r_f) + a(z - r_f)](z - r_f) \, dF_A(z) = 0 \qquad (2.10.3)$$

and

$$\int_{[0,1]} u'[(1+r_f) + a(z - r_f)](z - r_f) \, dF_B(t) \leq 0. \qquad (2.10.4)$$

Given (2.10.3) and the hypothesis that $A \; s\overset{\geq}{s}_D \; B$, a sufficient condition for (2.10.4) is that $V(z) = u'((1+r_f) + a(z - r_f))(z - r_f)$ is a concave function of z. Differentiating $V(t)$ twice and denoting $1 + r_f + a(z - r_f)$ by z_a, we get

$$V''(t) = a[u'''(z_a)\, a(z - r_f) + 2u''(z_a)]$$

$$= a \left\{ u''(z_a) + \frac{[u''(z_a)]^2 z_a}{u'(z_a)} - \frac{[u''(z_a)]^2}{u'(z_a)} + \frac{[u''(z_a)]^2 - u'''(z_a)u'(z_a)}{u'(z_a)} \right.$$

$$+ \frac{[u'''(z_a)z_a + u''(z_a)]u'(z_a) - [u''(z_a)]^2 z_a}{u'(z_a)} - u'''(z_a)r_f \bigg\}$$

$$= a\{[1 - R_R(z_a) + R_A(z_a)]u''(z_a) + [R'_A(z_a) - R'_R(z_a)]u'(z_a)$$

$$- u'''(z_a)r_f\},$$

$$(2.10.5)$$

where we recall that $R_A(\cdot)$ and $R_R(\cdot)$ are the Arrow–Pratt measures of absolute and relative risk aversion. When $a > 0$, a set of sufficient conditions for $V(\cdot)$ to be concave is that the relative risk aversion is less than one and increasing and that the absolute risk aversion is decreasing. Here we recall from Section 1.21 that nonincreasing absolute risk aversion implies $u''' > 0$.

It is clear from (2.10.5) that $V(\cdot)$ may not be concave. Thus when the riskiness of the risky asset increases, a risk averse individual may well increase his investment in the risky asset!

2.11. In Section 1.26, it is demonstrated that a more risk averse individual will require a higher risk premium on the risky asset for him to invest all his wealth in it than will a less risk averse individual, when there are two assets: one risky and one riskless. Equivalently, a more risk averse individual will never invest more in the risky asset than a less risk averse individual. Recall that individual i is said to be more risk averse than individual k if $R^i_A(z) \geq R^k_A(z) \; \forall \; z$. Unfortunately, this result does not extend to a setting where the two traded assets are both risky. This is illustrated by the example presented below, which is adapted from Ross (1981).

Consider a two asset portfolio problem where $\tilde{r}_A$ and $\tilde{r}_B$ denote the rates of returns on the two risky assets. Denoting $\tilde{z} = \tilde{r}_A - \tilde{r}_B$, we assume that, for every realization of $\tilde{r}_B$, $E[\tilde{z}|\tilde{r}_B] \geq 0$. This implies that asset A is more risky than asset B and also has a higher expected rate of return. In particular, we assume for the time being that $\tilde{z}$ and $\tilde{r}_B$ are independent with

$$\tilde{z} = \begin{cases} 2 & \text{with probability } \frac{1}{2}, \\ -1 & \text{with probability } \frac{1}{2}; \end{cases}$$

$$\tilde{r}_B = \begin{cases} 1 & \text{with probability } \frac{1}{2}, \\ 0 & \text{with probability } \frac{1}{2}. \end{cases}$$

Let $u_k(\cdot)$ be an increasing concave utility function for individual k with

$$u_k'(\frac{5}{2}) = 0, \quad u_k'(\frac{7}{4}) = 2, \quad u_k'(\frac{3}{2}) = 3, \quad u_k'(\frac{3}{4}) = 4.$$

Also let $G(\cdot)$ be a concave function with

$$G'(u_k(\frac{5}{2})) = 0, \ G'(u_k(\frac{7}{4})) = 0, \ G'(u_k(\frac{3}{2})) = 10, \ G'(u_k(\frac{3}{4})) = 10.$$

Now define

$$u_i = G(u_k).$$

From Section 1.25, we know that individual i with utility function u_i is more risk averse than individual k. Assume without loss of generality that both individuals have unit initial wealth. It is easily verified that $a = 1/4$ satisfies the following relation

$$E[u_k'(1 + \tilde{r}_B + a\tilde{z})\tilde{z}] = 0.$$

That is, individual k optimally invests 1/4 units of his wealth in asset A. However

$$E[u_i'(1 + \tilde{r}_B + \frac{1}{4}\tilde{z})\tilde{z}] = E[G'(u_k(1 + \tilde{r}_B + \frac{1}{4}\tilde{z}))\, u_k'(1 + \tilde{r}_B + \frac{1}{4}\tilde{z})\tilde{z}]$$

$$= 5 > 0.$$

This implies that individual i's utility will be increased if he invests strictly more than 1/4 units of wealth in asset A. Even though individual i is more risk averse in the Arrow–Pratt sense than individual k, he will *not* take a less risky position.

2.12. Ross (1981) proposes another measure of risk aversion. Individual i is said to be *strongly more risk averse* than individual k if

$$\inf_z \frac{u_i''(z)}{u_k''(z)} \geq \sup_z \frac{u_i'(z)}{u_k'(z)}. \tag{2.12.1}$$

Relation (2.12.1) implies that for arbitrary z, we have

$$\frac{u_i''(z)}{u_k''(z)} \geq \frac{u_i'(z)}{u_k'(z)}.$$

Rearranging gives

$$-\frac{u_i''(z)}{u_i'(z)} \geq -\frac{u_k''(z)}{u_k'(z)}. \tag{2.12.2}$$

which implies that individual i is more risk averse than individual k in the sense of Arrow–Pratt. The following example shows that (2.12.1) is strictly stronger than (2.12.2).

Let $u_i(z) = -e^{-az}$ and $u_k(z) = -e^{-bz}$, with $a > b$. It is easily verified that i is more risk averse in the sense of Arrow–Pratt than k. However,

$$\frac{u_i'(z_1)}{u_k'(z_1)} = \frac{a}{b} e^{-(a-b)z_1}$$

and

$$\frac{u_i''(z_2)}{u_k''(z_2)} = \left(\frac{a}{b}\right)^2 e^{-(a-b)z_2}$$

imply that when $z_2 - z_1$ is large we will have

$$\frac{u_i''(z_2)}{u_k''(z_2)} < \frac{u_i'(z_1)}{u_k'(z_1)}$$

contradicting (2.12.1). Thus the strong measure of risk aversion is strictly stronger than the Arrow–Pratt measure.

2.13. Now we recall from Section 1.25 that if individual i is more risk averse in the sense of Arrow–Pratt than individual k, then there exists a monotone concave function G such that $u_i = G(u_k)$. When individual i is strongly more risk averse than individual k, we have a similar characterization.

We claim that i is strongly more risk averse than k if and only if there exists a decreasing concave function G and a strictly positive constant λ such that

$$u_i(z) = \lambda u_k(z) + G(z) \quad \forall z. \tag{2.13.1}$$

Consider the sufficiency part. Differentiate (2.13.1) to get

$$u_i'(z) = \lambda u_k'(z) + G'(z) \le \lambda u_k'(z) \quad \forall z$$

and

$$u_i''(z) = \lambda u_k''(z) + G''(z) \le \lambda u_k''(z) \quad \forall z,$$

where the inequalities follow from the fact that G is decreasing and concave. The above two relations imply

$$\frac{u_i''(z)}{u_k''(z)} \ge \lambda \ge \frac{u_i'(z)}{u_k'(z)}. \tag{2.13.2}$$

It is easily seen that (2.13.2) implies (2.12.1). Conversely, let i be strongly more risk averse than k. By the definition of the strong measure of risk aversion, there exists $\lambda > 0$ such that (2.13.2) holds. Define G by (2.13.1). Differentiating we get

$$G'(z) = u_i'(z) - \lambda u_k'(z) \le 0$$

and

$$G''(z) = u_i''(z) - \lambda u_k''(z) \le 0,$$

where the inequalities follow from (2.13.2). Thus we have proved our claim that i is strongly more risk averse than k if and only if (2.13.1) holds.

2.14. Now let us again consider the two risky asset portfolio problem of Section 2.11. Assume that (2.12.1) holds and that individual i is strongly more risk averse than individual k. Let a be such that

$$E[u_k'(1 + \tilde{r}_B + a\tilde{z})\tilde{z}] = 0. \tag{2.14.1}$$

Then a is the amount individual k should optimally invest in asset A. Using (2.13.1) and (2.14.1), we obtain

$$E[u_i'(1 + \tilde{r}_B + a\tilde{z})\tilde{z}] = E[\lambda \ u_k'(1 + \tilde{r}_B + a\tilde{z})\tilde{z} + G'(1 + \tilde{r}_B + a\tilde{z})\tilde{z}]$$
$$= E[G'(1 + \tilde{r}_B + a\tilde{z})\tilde{z}].$$

Using iterative expectations and the definition of covariance, we can rewrite the above relation as:

$$E[G'(1 + \tilde{r}_B + a\tilde{z})\tilde{z}] = E\left[E[G'(1 + \tilde{r}_B + a\tilde{z})\tilde{z}|\tilde{r}_B]\right]$$
$$= E\left[\text{Cov}(G'(1 + \tilde{r}_B + a\tilde{z}), \tilde{z}|\tilde{r}_B)\right.$$
$$\left. + E[G'(1 + \tilde{r}_B + a\tilde{z})|\tilde{r}_B] \ E[\tilde{z}|\tilde{r}_B]\right]$$
$$\leq E[\text{Cov}(G'(1 + \tilde{r}_B + a\tilde{z}), \tilde{z}|\tilde{r}_B)] \leq 0,$$

where the first inequality follows from the hypothesis that $E[\tilde{z}|\tilde{r}_B] \geq 0$ and the fact that $G' \leq 0$, and the second inequality follows from the concavity of G. This implies that individual i's utility can be increased by investing an amount smaller than a in asset A. That is, i will optimally choose a less risky portfolio. Thus the stronger measure of risk aversion gives the *right* comparative statics.

Exercises

2.1. A risky asset A is said to third degree stochastically dominate risky asset B if all investors exhibiting decreasing absolute risk aversion prefer A to B, denoted by $A \ T\overset{\geq}{S}D \ B$. Provide a sufficient condition strictly weaker than that for the second degree stochastic dominance on the distribution functions for $A \ T\overset{\geq}{S}D \ B$.

2.2. Suppose that there are two risky assets with rates of return $\tilde{r}_1$ and $\tilde{r}_2$, which are independent and identically distributed. Show that the equally weighted portfolio is an optimal choice for any risk averse investor.

2.3. Suppose that there are five states of nature denoted by $\omega_n \ n = 1, 2, \ldots, 5$, all of which are of equal probability. Consider two risky assets with rates of returns $\tilde{r}_A$ and $\tilde{r}_B$ as follows:

state	ω_1	ω_2	ω_3	ω_4	ω_5
$\tilde{r}_A$	0.5	0.5	0.7	0.7	0.7
$\tilde{r}_B$	0.9	0.8	0.4	0.3	0.7

Explain which asset a risk averse investor will choose.

2.4. Suppose that there are two risky assets with random rates of returns $\tilde{r}_A$ and $\tilde{r}_B$, respectively. Assume that $\tilde{r}_A$ and $\tilde{r}_B$ are independent and have the same mean. We know further that $\tilde{r}_B \overset{d}{=} \tilde{r}_A + \tilde{\epsilon}$ and that $\tilde{r}_A$ and $\tilde{\epsilon}$ are independent. Does this imply that $\tilde{r}_B$ dominates $\tilde{r}_A$ in the sense of second degree stochastic dominance? Show that if these are the only assets available to a risk averse expected utility–maximizing individual, this individual will invest more in asset A than in asset B.

Remarks. Machina (1982) generalized some of the Ross (1981) results on the stronger measure of risk aversion. Roëll (1983) showed that the comparative statics of Section 2.14. cannot be generalized to a multi–assets case. The sufficiency proofs of $F\overset{\geq}{S}D$ and $s\overset{\geq}{S}D$ are adapted from Hadar and Russel (1969). For a bibliography on the subject of stochastic dominance, see Bawa (1981). Exercise 2.4 was provided to us by Richard Khilstrom.

References

Bawa, V. 1981. Stochastic dominance: A research bibliography. Bell Laboratories Economics Discussion Paper #196.

Hadar, J., and W. Russell. 1969. Rules for ordering uncertain prospects, *American Economic Review* **59**:25–34.

Hanoch, G., and C. Levy. 1969. Efficiency analysis of choices involving risk. *Review of Economic Studies* **36**:335–346.

Machina, M. 1982. A stronger characterization of declining risk aversion. *Econometrica* **50**:1069–1079.

Röell, A. 1983. Risk aversion and wealth effects on portfolios with many independent assets. Mimeo. Johns Hopkins University. Baltimore, Maryland.

Ross, S. 1981. Some stronger measures of risk aversion in the small and large with applications. *Econometrica* **49**:621–638.

Rothschild, M., and J. Stiglitz. 1970. Increasing risk I: A definition. *Journal of Economic Theory* **2**:225–243.

Rothschild, M., and J. Stiglitz. 1971. Increasing risk II: Its economic consequences. *Journal of Economic Theory,* **3**:66–84.

CHAPTER 3
MATHEMATICS OF
THE PORTFOLIO FRONTIER

3.1. In Chapter 2 we demonstrated that when risky asset A second degree stochastically dominates risky asset B, risky asset A must have the same expected rate of return as risky asset B and a lower variance. When there are more than two assets and when portfolios can be formed without restrictions, if there exists a portfolio of assets that second degree stochastically dominates all the portfolios which have the same expected rate of return as it has, then this dominant portfolio must have the minimum variance among all the portfolios. This observation is one of the motivations to characterize those portfolios which have the minimum variance for various levels of expected rate of return.

3.2. The mean–variance model of asset choice has been used extensively in finance since its development by Markowitz (1952) more than two decades ago. A preference for expected return and an aversion to variance is implied by monotonicity and strict concavity of an individual's utility function. However, for arbitrary distributions and utility functions, expected utility cannot be defined over just the expected returns and variances. Nevertheless, the mean–variance model of asset choice is popular because of its analytical tractability and its rich empirical implications. Two technical motivations, besides the one stated in Section 3.1, exist and are briefly reviewed below.

3.3. An individual's utility function may be expanded as a Taylor series around his expected end of period wealth,

$$u(\tilde{W}) = u(E[\tilde{W}]) + u'(E[\tilde{W}])(\tilde{W} - E[\tilde{W}])$$
$$+ \frac{1}{2}u''(E[\tilde{W}])(\tilde{W} - E[\tilde{W}])^2 + R_3,$$

where

$$R_3 = \sum_{n=3}^{\infty} \frac{1}{n!} u^{(n)}(E[\tilde{W}])(\tilde{W} - E[\tilde{W}])^n$$

and where $u^{(n)}$ denotes the n-th derivative of u.

Assuming that the Taylor series converges and that the expectation and summation operations are interchangeable, the individual's expected utility may be expressed as

$$E[u(\tilde{W})] = u(E[\tilde{W}]) + \frac{1}{2!}u''(E[\tilde{W}])\sigma^2(\tilde{W}) + E[R_3], \qquad (3.3.1)$$

where

$$E[R_3] = \sum_{n=3}^{\infty} \frac{1}{n!} u^{(n)}(E[\tilde{W}])m^n(\tilde{W}) \qquad (3.3.2)$$

and where $m^n(\tilde{W})$ denotes the n-th central moment of $\tilde{W}$.

Relation (3.3.1) indicates a preference for expected wealth and an aversion to variance of wealth for an individual having an increasing and strictly concave utility function. However, relation (3.3.2) illustrates that expected utility cannot be defined solely over the expected value and variance of wealth for arbitrary distributions and preferences, as indicated by the remainder term which involves higher order moments.

3.4. For *arbitrary distributions*, the mean–variance model can be motivated by assuming *quadratic utility*. Under quadratic utility, the third and higher order derivatives are zero and, therefore, $E[R_3] = 0$ for arbitrary distributions. Hence, an individual's expected utility is defined over the first two central moments of his end of period wealth, $\tilde{W}$,

$$E[u(\tilde{W})] = E[\tilde{W}] - \frac{b}{2}E[\tilde{W}^2]$$

$$= E[\tilde{W}] - \frac{b}{2}\left((E[\tilde{W}])^2 + \sigma^2(\tilde{W})\right).$$

Thus, when expected rates of return and variances are finite, quadratic utility is sufficient for asset choice to be completely described in terms of a preference relation defined over the mean and variance of expected returns. Unfortunately, quadratic utility displays the undesirable properties of satiation and increasing absolute risk aversion. The satiation property implies that an increase in wealth beyond the satiation point decreases utility. Increasing absolute risk aversion implies that risky assets are inferior goods. Thus, economic conclusions based on the assumption of quadratic utility function are often counter intuitive and are not applicable to individuals who always prefer more wealth to less and who treat risky investments as normal goods.

3.5. For *arbitrary preferences*, the mean–variance model can be motivated by assuming that rates of return on risky assets are *multivariate normally distributed*. The normal distribution is completely described by its mean and variance. Under normality, the third and higher order moments involved in $E[R_3]$ can be expressed as functions of the first two moments, and $E[R_3]$ is, therefore, solely a function of the mean and variance. Normal distributions are also stable under addition; i.e., the rate of return on a portfolio made up of assets having returns that are multivariate normally distributed is also normally distributed. The lognormal distribution is also completely described by its mean and variance; however, it is not stable under addition. That is, a portfolio made up of assets having returns that are multivariate lognormally distributed is *not* lognormally distributed. Thus, for utility functions that are defined over a normally distributed end of period wealth, the assumption that asset returns are multivariate normally distributed implies that demands for risky assets are defined over the mean and variance of portfolio rates of return. However, for other classes of utility functions such as $u(z) = \ln(z)$, expected utility is not defined over non-positive wealth levels. Unfortunately, the normal distribution is unbounded from below, which is inconsistent with limited liability and with economic theory, which attributes no meaning to negative consumption. Fortunately, multivariate normality is only a sufficient distributional condition for all individuals to choose mean–variance efficient portfolios, not a necessary condition.

3.6. Based on the above, the mean–variance model is not a general model of asset choice. Its central role in financial theory can be attributed to its analytical tractability and the richness of its empirical predictions. This chapter develops the analytical relations between the means and the variances of rates of return on feasible portfolios. This will provide the basis for the development of more general conditions for mean–variance asset choice and mean–variance asset pricing models in Chapter 4.

3.7. We suppose that there are $N \geq 2$ risky assets traded in a frictionless economy where unlimited short selling is allowed and that the rates of return on these assets have finite variances and unequal expectations, unless otherwise mentioned. It is also assumed that the random rate of return on any asset cannot be expressed as a linear combination of the rates of return on other assets. Under this assumption, asset returns are said to be linearly independent and their variance covariance matrix $\mathbf{V}$ is nonsingular. The variance-covariance matrix is also symmetric because $\mathrm{Cov}(\tilde{r}_j, \tilde{r}_i) = \mathrm{Cov}(\tilde{r}_i, \tilde{r}_j)$, for all i, j. Such a symmetric matrix is said to be positive definite if for arbitrary N–vector of constants $\mathbf{w}$, with $\mathbf{w} \neq 0$, $\mathbf{w}^\top \mathbf{V} \mathbf{w} > 0$, where $^\top$ denotes "transpose" and where $\mathbf{w} \neq 0$ means there is at least one element of $\mathbf{w}$ that is not zero. $\mathbf{V}$ is a positive definite matrix because $\mathbf{w}^\top \mathbf{V} \mathbf{w}$ is a portfolio variance even when the portfolio weights do not sum to unity and because variances of risky portfolios are strictly positive.

3.8. A portfolio is a *frontier portfolio* if it has the minimum variance among portfolios that have the same expected rate of return. A portfolio p is a frontier portfolio if and only if $\mathbf{w}_p$, the N-vector portfolio weights of p, is the solution to the quadratic program:

$$\min_{\{\mathbf{w}\}} \frac{1}{2} \mathbf{w}^\top \mathbf{V} \mathbf{w} \qquad (3.8.1)$$

s.t.

$$\mathbf{w}^\top \mathbf{e} = E[\tilde{r}_p] \quad \text{and}$$
$$\mathbf{w}^\top \mathbf{1} = 1,$$

where $\mathbf{e}$ denotes the N-vector of expected rates of return on the N risky assets, $E[\tilde{r}_p]$ denotes the expected rate of return on portfolio p, and $\mathbf{1}$ is an N-vector of ones.

The programming problem given in (3.8.1) minimizes the portfolio variance subject to the constraint that the portfolio expected rate of return is equal to $E[r_p]$ and that the portfolio weights sum to unity. Note that short sales (i.e., negative portfolio weights) are permitted. Therefore, the range of expected returns on feasible portfolios is unbounded. (This follows from the assumption that assets do not have identical expected rates of return.)

Forming the Lagrangian, $\mathbf{w}_p$ is the solution to the following:

$$\min_{\{\mathbf{w},\lambda,\gamma\}} L = \frac{1}{2} \mathbf{w}^\top \mathbf{V} \mathbf{w} + \lambda (E[r_p] - \mathbf{w}^\top \mathbf{e}) + \gamma (1 - \mathbf{w}^\top \mathbf{1}), \qquad (3.8.2)$$

where λ and γ are two positive constants. The first order conditions are

$$\frac{\partial L}{\partial \mathbf{w}} = \mathbf{V}\mathbf{w}_p - \lambda \mathbf{e} - \gamma \mathbf{1} = 0, \qquad (3.8.3a)$$

$$\frac{\partial L}{\partial \lambda} = E[\tilde{r}_p] - \mathbf{w}_p^\top \mathbf{e} = 0, \qquad (3.8.3b)$$

$$\frac{\partial L}{\partial \gamma} = 1 - \mathbf{w}_p^\top \mathbf{1} = 0, \qquad (3.8.3c)$$

where 0 is a N vector of zeros. Since $\mathbf{V}$ is a positive definite matrix, it follows that the first order conditions are necessary and sufficient for a global optimum.

3.9. Solving (3.8.3a) for $\mathbf{w}_p$ gives

$$\mathbf{w}_p = \lambda(\mathbf{V}^{-1}\mathbf{e}) + \gamma(\mathbf{V}^{-1}\mathbf{1}). \qquad (3.9.1)$$

Premultiplying both sides of relation (3.9.1) by $\mathbf{e}^\top$ and using (3.8.3b) gives

$$E[\tilde{r}_p] = \lambda(\mathbf{e}^\top\mathbf{V}^{-1}\mathbf{e}) + \gamma(\mathbf{e}^\top\mathbf{V}^{-1}\mathbf{1}). \qquad (3.9.2a)$$

Premultiplying both sides of relation (3.9.1) by $\mathbf{1}^\top$ and using (3.8.3c) gives

$$1 = \lambda(\mathbf{1}^\top\mathbf{V}^{-1}\mathbf{e}) + \gamma(\mathbf{1}^\top\mathbf{V}^{-1}\mathbf{1}). \qquad (3.9.2b)$$

Solving (3.9.2a) and (3.9.2b) for λ and γ gives

$$\lambda = \frac{CE[\tilde{r}_p] - A}{D} \qquad (3.9.3a)$$

$$\gamma = \frac{B - AE[\tilde{r}_p]}{D} \qquad (3.9.3b)$$

where

$$A = \mathbf{1}^\top\mathbf{V}^{-1}\mathbf{e} = \mathbf{e}^\top\mathbf{V}^{-1}\mathbf{1},$$
$$B = \mathbf{e}^\top\mathbf{V}^{-1}\mathbf{e},$$
$$C = \mathbf{1}^\top\mathbf{V}^{-1}\mathbf{1},$$
$$D = BC - A^2.$$

Since the inverse of a positive definite matrix is positive definite, $B > 0$ and $C > 0$. We claim that $D > 0$. To see this, we note that

$$(A\mathbf{e} - B\mathbf{1})^\top\mathbf{V}^{-1}(A\mathbf{e} - B\mathbf{1}) = B(BC - A^2)$$

The left–hand side of the above relation is strictly positive, since $\mathbf{V}^{-1}$ is positive definite. Hence the right–hand side is strictly positive. By the fact that $B > 0$, we have $BC - A^2 > 0$, or, equivalently, $D > 0$.

Substituting for λ and γ in relation (3.9.1) gives the unique set of portfolio weights for the frontier portfolio having an expected rate of return of $E[\tilde{r}_p]$:

$$\mathbf{w}_p = \mathbf{g} + \mathbf{h}E[\tilde{r}_p] \qquad (3.9.4)$$

where

$$\mathbf{g} = \frac{1}{D}[B(\mathbf{V}^{-1}\mathbf{1}) - A(\mathbf{V}^{-1}\mathbf{e})]$$

and

$$\mathbf{h} = \frac{1}{D}[C(\mathbf{V}^{-1}\mathbf{e}) - A(\mathbf{V}^{-1}\mathbf{1})].$$

Note that relations (3.8.3a), (3.8.3b), and (3.8.3c) are necessary and sufficient conditions for $\mathbf{w}_p$ to be the frontier portfolio having an expected rate of return equal to $E[\tilde{r}_p]$. Therefore, any frontier portfolio can be represented by (3.9.4). On the other hand, any portfolio that can be represented by (3.9.4) is a frontier portfolio. The set of all frontier portfolios is called the *portfolio frontier*.

Now we claim that $\mathbf{g}$ is the vector of portfolio weights corresponding to a frontier portfolio having a zero expected rate of return and that $\mathbf{g} + \mathbf{h}$ is the vector of portfolio weights of a frontier portfolio having an expected rate of return equal to 1. To see this, we first substitute zero for $E[\tilde{r}_p]$ of relation (3.9.4) to get

$$\mathbf{w}_p = \mathbf{g} + \mathbf{h} \cdot 0 = \mathbf{g},$$

and then substitute 1 for $E[\tilde{r}_p]$ of (3.9.4) to get

$$\mathbf{w}_p = \mathbf{g} + \mathbf{h} \cdot 1 = \mathbf{g} + \mathbf{h}.$$

Next we claim that the entire portfolio frontier can be *generated* by forming portfolios of the two frontier portfolios $\mathbf{g}$ and $\mathbf{g} + \mathbf{h}$. Let q be a frontier portfolio having an expected rate of return $E[\tilde{r}_q]$. From (3.9.4), we know that

$$\mathbf{w}_q = \mathbf{g} + \mathbf{h}E[\tilde{r}_q].$$

Consider the following portfolio weights on $\mathbf{g}$ and $\mathbf{g} + \mathbf{h}$: $\{1 - E[\tilde{r}_q], E[\tilde{r}_q]\}$, whose portfolio weights on risky assets are

$$(1 - E[\tilde{r}_q])\mathbf{g} + E[\tilde{r}_q](\mathbf{g} + \mathbf{h}) = \mathbf{g} + \mathbf{h}E[\tilde{r}_q] = \mathbf{w}_q.$$

That is, the portfolio $\{1 - E[\tilde{r}_q], E[\tilde{r}_q]\}$ on $\mathbf{g}$ and $\mathbf{g} + \mathbf{h}$ generates the frontier portfolio q. Since the portfolio q is arbitrarily chosen, we have shown that the entire portfolio frontier can be generated by the two frontier portfolios $\mathbf{g}$ and $\mathbf{g} + \mathbf{h}$.

3.10. Note that the arguments in the last section showing that the portfolio frontier is generated by $\mathbf{g}$ and $\mathbf{g} + \mathbf{h}$ only use the fact that the two frontier portfolios g and g + h do *not* have identical expected rates of return. The following much stronger statement is in fact valid: The portfolio frontier can be generated by *any* two distinct frontier portfolios. To see this, let p_1 and p_2 be two distinct frontier portfolios, and let q be *any* frontier portfolio. We want to show that q is a portfolio generated by p_1 and p_2. Since $E[\tilde{r}_{p_1}]$ is not equal to $E[\tilde{r}_{p_2}]$, there exists a unique real number α such that

$$E[\tilde{r}_q] = \alpha E[\tilde{r}_{p_1}] + (1 - \alpha)E[\tilde{r}_{p_2}]. \qquad (3.10.1)$$

Now consider a portfolio of p_1 and p_2 with weights $\{\alpha, (1 - \alpha)\}$. We have

$$\begin{aligned}
\alpha \mathbf{w}_{p_1} + (1 - \alpha)\mathbf{w}_{p_2} &= \alpha(\mathbf{g} + \mathbf{h}E[\tilde{r}_{p_1}]) + (1 - \alpha)(\mathbf{g} + \mathbf{h}E[\tilde{r}_{p_2}]) \\
&= \mathbf{g} + \mathbf{h}(\alpha E[\tilde{r}_{p_1}] + (1 - \alpha)E[\tilde{r}_{p_2}]) \\
&= \mathbf{g} + \mathbf{h}E[\tilde{r}_q] \\
&= \mathbf{w}_q, \qquad (3.10.2)
\end{aligned}$$

where the first equality follows from the fact that p_1 and p_2 are frontier portfolios, the third equality follows from (3.10.1), and the fourth equality follows from the fact that the weights for a frontier portfolio are uniquely determined. Thus, we have demonstrated that the portfolio frontier can be generated by any two distinct frontier portfolios.

3.11. The covariance between the rates of return on any two frontier portfolios p and q is

$$\mathrm{Cov}(\tilde{r}_p, \tilde{r}_q) = \mathbf{w}_p^\top \mathbf{V}\mathbf{w}_q = \frac{C}{D}(E[\tilde{r}_p] - A/C)(E[\tilde{r}_q] - A/C) + 1/C, \qquad (3.11.1)$$

where we have used the definition of covariance and the portfolio weights for a frontier portfolio given in relation (3.9.4).

The definition of the variance of the rate of return of a portfolio and (3.11.1) give

$$\frac{\sigma^2(\tilde{r}_p)}{1/C} - \frac{(E[\tilde{r}_p] - A/C)^2}{D/C^2} = 1, \qquad (3.11.2a)$$

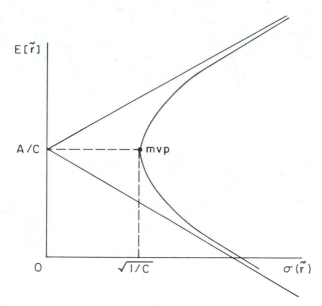

Figure 3.11.1: Portfolio Frontier in the $\sigma(\tilde{r})$–$E[\tilde{r}]$ space

which is a hyperbola in the standard deviation–expected rate of return space with center $(0, A/C)$ and asymptotes $E[\tilde{r}_p] = A/C \pm \sqrt{D/C}\sigma(\tilde{r}_p)$, where $\sigma^2(\tilde{r}_p)$ and $\sigma(\tilde{r}_p)$ denote the variance and the standard deviation of the rate of return on the portfolio p, respectively. Relation (3.11.2a) can equivalently be written as

$$\sigma^2(\tilde{r}_p) = \frac{1}{D}\left(C(E[\tilde{r}_p])^2 - 2AE[\tilde{r}_p] + B\right), \qquad (3.11.2b)$$

which is a parabola in variance–expected rate of return space with vertex $(1/C, A/C)$. The portfolio frontier in mean–standard deviation space is graphed in Figure 3.11.1, and the portfolio frontier in mean–variance space is graphed in Figure 3.11.2. The portfolio having the minimum variance of all possible portfolios, or the *minimum variance portfolio*, is at $(\sqrt{1/C}, A/C)$ in Figure 3.11.1. This follows directly from (3.11.2a).

3.12. The minimum variance portfolio, denoted henceforth by *mvp*, has a special property: The covariance of the rate of return on

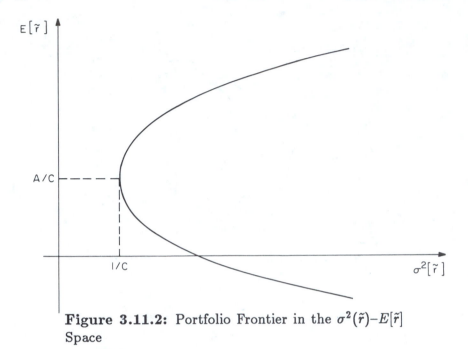

Figure 3.11.2: Portfolio Frontier in the $\sigma^2(\tilde{r})$–$E[\tilde{r}]$
Space

the minimum variance portfolio and that on *any* portfolio (not only
those on the frontier) is always equal to the variance of the rate of
return on the minimum variance portfolio. To see this, let p be any
portfolio. We shall demonstrate below that

$$\text{Cov}(\tilde{r}_p, \tilde{r}_{mvp}) = \text{Var}(\tilde{r}_{mvp}). \qquad (3.12.1)$$

We consider a portfolio of p and mvp with weights a and $1-a$
and with minimum variance. Then, a must be the solution to the
following program:

$$\min_a a^2\sigma^2(\tilde{r}_p) + 2a(1-a)\text{Cov}(\tilde{r}_p, \tilde{r}_{mvp}) + (1-a)^2\sigma^2(\tilde{r}_{mvp}).$$

The first order necessary and sufficient condition for a to be the
solution is:

$$2a\sigma^2(\tilde{r}_p) + 2(1-2a)\text{Cov}(\tilde{r}_p, \tilde{r}_{mvp}) - 2(1-a)\sigma^2(\tilde{r}_{mvp}) = 0. \quad (3.12.2)$$

Since mvp is the minimum variance portfolio, $a = 0$ must satisfy
relation (3.12.2). Thus we have relation (3.12.1). In words, the covariance between the rate of return on *any* portfolio and that on the

minimum variance portfolio is equal to the variance of the rate of return on the minimum variance portfolio. Note that in the arguments proving that relation (3.12.1) holds for any portfolio p, the assumption that risky assets do not have identical expected rates of return is never used. Thus relation (3.12.1) holds even when risky assets have identical expected rates of return.

3.13. Those frontier portfolios which have expected rates of return strictly higher than that of the minimum variance portfolio, A/C, are called *efficient portfolios*. Portfolios that are on the portfolio frontier but are neither efficient nor minimum variance are called *inefficient portfolios*. For each inefficient portfolio there exists an efficient one having the same variance but a higher expected rate of return.

Let $\mathbf{w}_i$, $i = 1, 2, \ldots, m$, be m frontier portfolios and α_i, $i = 1, 2, \ldots, m$, be real numbers such that $\sum_{i=1}^{m} \alpha_i = 1$. Then denoting the expected rate of return on portfolio i by $E[\tilde{r}_i]$ for $i = 1, 2, \ldots, m$, we have

$$\sum_{i=1}^{m} \alpha_i \mathbf{w}_i = \sum_{i=1}^{m} \alpha_i (\mathbf{g} + \mathbf{h} E[\tilde{r}_i])$$

$$= \mathbf{g} + \mathbf{h} \sum_{i=1}^{m} \alpha_i E[\tilde{r}_i].$$

Recalling (3.9.4), the second line of the above expression is a frontier portfolio having an expected rate of return equal to $\sum_{i=1}^{m} \alpha_i E[\tilde{r}_i]$. Thus any linear combination of frontier portfolios is on the frontier.

If portfolios $i = 1, 2, \ldots, m$ are efficient portfolios, and if $\alpha_i, i = 1, 2, \ldots, m$ are nonnegative, then

$$\sum_{i=1}^{m} \alpha_i E[\tilde{r}_i] \geq \sum_{i=1}^{m} \alpha_i \frac{A}{C} = A/C. \tag{3.13.1}$$

Formally stated, any convex combination of efficient portfolios will be an efficient portfolio. The set of efficient portfolios is thus a convex set.

3.14. One important property of the portfolio frontier is that for any portfolio p on the frontier, except for the minimum variance portfolio, there exists a unique frontier portfolio, denoted by $zc(p)$, which has a zero covariance with p.

Setting the covariance between two frontier portfolios p and $zc(p)$, given in relation (3.11.1), equal to zero:

$$\text{Cov}(\tilde{r}_p, \tilde{r}_{zc(p)}) = \frac{C}{D}\left((E[\tilde{r}_p] - A/C)(E[\tilde{r}_{zc(p)}] - A/C) + D/C^2\right) = 0$$

$$(3.14.1)$$

and solving for the expected rate of return on $zc(p)$, we get:

$$E[\tilde{r}_{zc(p)}] = A/C - \frac{D/C^2}{E[\tilde{r}_p] - A/C}. \qquad (3.14.2)$$

In fact, (3.14.2) defines $zc(p)$. The uniqueness assertion follows from the fact that (3.14.2) defines $E[\tilde{r}_{zc(p)}]$ uniquely, which in turn determines $zc(p)$ uniquely by (3.9.4). It is also easily seen from (3.11.1) that the covariance of the minimum variance portfolio and any other frontier portfolio is equal to $1/C$, which is strictly positive. Therefore, there does not exist a frontier portfolio that has zero covariance with the minimum variance portfolio.

3.15. Equation (3.14.2) gives us a clue to the location of $zc(p)$ for p other than the minimum variance portfolio. If p is an efficient portfolio, then (3.14.2) implies that

$$E[\tilde{r}_{zc(p)}] < A/C,$$

thus $zc(p)$ is an inefficient portfolio, and vice versa.

Geometrically $zc(p)$ can be located by the following fact: The intercept on the expected rate of return axis of the line tangent to the portfolio frontier in the standard deviation–expected rate of return space at the point associated with any frontier portfolio p (except the minimum variance portfolio) is $E[\tilde{r}_{zc(p)}]$. Alternatively, in the variance–expected rate of return space, the intercept on the $E[\tilde{r}]$ axis of the line joining any frontier portfolio p and the *mvp* is equal to $E[\tilde{r}_{zc(p)}]$. To see these, we first differentiate (3.11.2a) totally with respect to $\sigma(\tilde{r}_p)$ and $E[\tilde{r}_p]$ to obtain

$$\frac{dE[\tilde{r}_p]}{d\sigma(\tilde{r}_p)} = \frac{\sigma(\tilde{r}_p) \cdot D}{C \cdot E[\tilde{r}_p] - A}, \qquad (3.15.1)$$

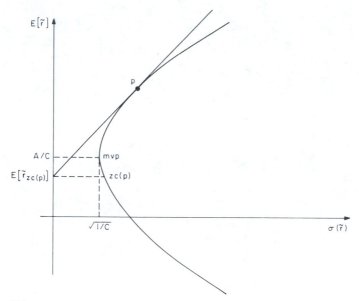

Figure 3.15.1: The Location of a Zero Covariance Portfolio in the $\sigma(\tilde{r})$–$E[\tilde{r}]$ Space

which is the slope of the portfolio frontier at the point $(\sigma(\tilde{r}_p), E[\tilde{r}_p])$. The expected rate of return axis intercept of the tangent line is

$$E[\tilde{r}_p] - \frac{dE[\tilde{r}_p]}{d\sigma(\tilde{r}_p)} \cdot \sigma(\tilde{r}_p) = E[\tilde{r}_p] - \frac{\sigma(\tilde{r}_p) \cdot D}{C \cdot E[\tilde{r}_p] - A} \sigma(\tilde{r}_p)$$

$$= A/C - \frac{D/C^2}{E[\tilde{r}_p] - A/C} \qquad (3.15.2)$$

$$= E[\tilde{r}_{zc(p)}],$$

where the second equality follows from (3.11.2a), and the third equality follows from (3.14.2). The geometric picture of relation (3.15.2) can be seen in Figure 3.15.1.

Next, it is easily seen that the line joining a frontier portfolio p and the *mvp*, in the $\sigma^2(\tilde{r})$–$E[\tilde{r}]$ plane, can be expressed as

$$E[\tilde{r}] = A/C - \frac{D/C^2}{E[\tilde{r}_p] - A/C}$$

$$+ \frac{E[\tilde{r}_p] - A/C}{\sigma^2(\tilde{r}_p) - 1/C} \sigma^2(\tilde{r}). \qquad (3.15.3)$$

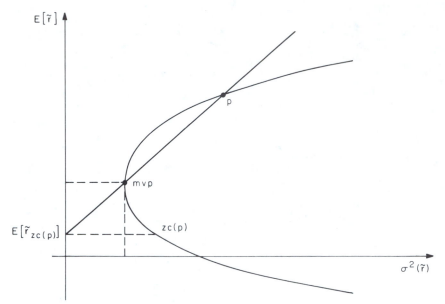

Figure 3.15.2: The Location of a Zero Covariance
Portfolio in the $\sigma^2(\tilde{r}) - E[\tilde{r}]$ Space

Substituting $\sigma^2(\tilde{r}) = 0$ into (3.15.3), we have that the intercept of
the line on the expected rate of return axis is equal to $E[\tilde{r}_{zc(p)}]$. This
result is presented in Figure 3.15.2.

Finally, let p be a portfolio which is not on the portfolio frontier
as depicted in Figure 3.15.3, which we note is in the $\sigma^2(\tilde{r}) - E[\tilde{r}]$ plane.
We claim that the intercept on the expected rate of return axis of
the line joining p and mvp is equal to the expected rate of return
on a portfolio, q, that has zero covariance with p and the minimum
variance among all the zero covariance portfolios with p. To see this,
we note that $\mathbf{w}_q$ is the solution to the following program:

$$\min_{\mathbf{w}_q} \frac{1}{2}\mathbf{w}_q^\top \mathbf{V}\mathbf{w}_q$$
$$\text{s.t. } \mathbf{w}_q^\top \mathbf{V}\mathbf{w}_p = 0, \quad\quad\quad (3.15.4)$$
$$\mathbf{w}_q^\top \mathbf{1} = 1.$$

Using the Lagrangian method, we can easily verify that

$$
\begin{aligned}
\mathbf{w}_q &= \frac{1}{1 - Co^2(\tilde{r}_p)}\mathbf{w}_p - \frac{Co^2(\tilde{r}_p)}{1 - Co^2(\tilde{r}_p)}\frac{\mathbf{V}^{-1}\mathbf{1}}{\mathbf{1}^\mathsf{T}\mathbf{V}^{-1}\mathbf{1}} \\
&= \frac{1}{1 - Co^2(\tilde{r}_p)}\mathbf{w}_p - \frac{Co^2(\tilde{r}_p)}{1 - Co^2(\tilde{r}_p)}\mathbf{w}_{mvp},
\end{aligned}
\tag{3.15.5}
$$

where $\mathbf{w}_{mvp}$ denotes the vector of portfolio weights of the minimum variance portfolio. That is, the minimum variance zero covariance portfolio of p is a linear combination of p and mvp. Since $\sigma^2(\tilde{r}_p) > 1/C$, q is constructed by short selling portfolio p and buying the minimum variance portfolio. The expected rate of return of q is

$$
\begin{aligned}
\mathbf{w}_q^\mathsf{T}\mathbf{e} &= \frac{E[\tilde{r}_p]}{1 - Co^2(\tilde{r}_p)} - \frac{Co^2(\tilde{r}_p)}{1 - Co^2(\tilde{r}_p)}\frac{A}{C} \\
&= \frac{E[\tilde{r}_p] - A\sigma^2(\tilde{r}_p)}{1 - Co^2(\tilde{r}_p)},
\end{aligned}
\tag{3.15.6}
$$

which is easily verified to be the intercept on the expected rate of return axis of the line joining p and mvp in the $\sigma^2(\tilde{r})$–$E[\tilde{r}]$ plane. In Exercise 3.6 we ask the reader to show that the portfolio frontier generated by two assets or portfolios having distinct expected rates of return passes through these two assets or portfolios. Consider the portfolio frontier generated by p and mvp, which is demonstrated graphically in Figure 3.15.3. Note that this portfolio frontier lies inside the portfolio frontier of all assets and touches it at a single point, the mvp. Since any linear combination of two frontier portfolios is on the frontier, any linear combination of p and mvp is on the portfolio frontier generated by p and mvp. It follows that the portfolio q is on the portfolio frontier generated by p and mvp as it is a linear combination of p and mvp by (3.15.5).

3.16. We have demonstrated the existence of a zero covariance portfolio for any frontier portfolio other than the minimum variance portfolio. A characterization of the relationship between the expected rate of return on *any* portfolio q, *not necessarily on the frontier*, and those of the frontier portfolios is given below.

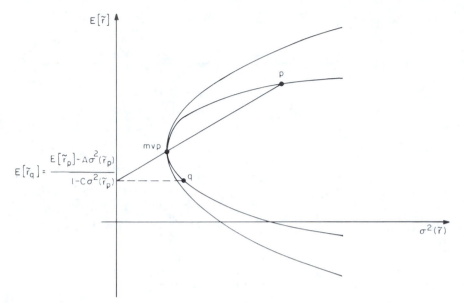

Figure 3.15.3: Minimum Variance Zero Covariance
Portfolio of a Non–frontier Portfolio

Let p be a frontier portfolio other than the minimum variance
portfolio, and let q be any portfolio. The covariance of $\tilde{r}_p$ and $\tilde{r}_q$ is

$$\text{Cov}(\tilde{r}_p, \tilde{r}_q) = \mathbf{w}_p^\top \mathbf{V} \mathbf{w}_q = \lambda \mathbf{e}^\top \mathbf{V}^{-1} \mathbf{V} \mathbf{w}_q + \gamma \mathbf{1}^\top \mathbf{V}^{-1} \mathbf{V} \mathbf{w}_q$$

$$= \lambda \mathbf{e}^\top \mathbf{w}_q + \gamma \mathbf{1}^\top \mathbf{w}_q$$

$$= \lambda E[\tilde{r}_q] + \gamma, \tag{3.16.1}$$

where the second equality follows from the fact that p is a frontier
portfolio and relation (3.9.1), and where the fourth equality follows
from the definition of $E[\tilde{r}_q]$ and the fact that $\mathbf{w}_q$ is a vector of portfolio weights. Substituting (3.9.3a) and (3.9.3b) for λ and γ, respectively, into (3.16.1) we get

$$E[\tilde{r}_q] = \frac{A E[\tilde{r}_p] - B}{C E[\tilde{r}_p] - A} + \text{Cov}(\tilde{r}_q, \tilde{r}_p) \frac{D}{C E[\tilde{r}_p] - A}$$

$$= \frac{A}{C} - \frac{D/C^2}{E[\tilde{r}_p] - A/C}$$

$$+ \frac{\text{Cov}(\tilde{r}_q, \tilde{r}_p)}{\sigma^2(\tilde{r}_p)} \left[\frac{1}{C} + \frac{[E[\tilde{r}_p] - A/C]^2}{D/C} \right] \frac{D}{C E[\tilde{r}_p] - A}$$

$$= E[\tilde{r}_{zc(p)}] + \beta_{qp} \left(E[\tilde{r}_p] - \frac{A}{C} + \frac{D/C^2}{E[\tilde{r}_p] - A/C} \right)$$
$$= E[\tilde{r}_{zc(p)}] + \beta_{qp} \left(E[\tilde{r}_p] - E[\tilde{r}_{zc(p)}] \right)$$
$$= (1 - \beta_{qp}) E[\tilde{r}_{zc(p)}] + \beta_{qp} E[\tilde{r}_p], \qquad (3.16.2)$$

where we have used (3.11.2a) in the second equality, where $\beta_{qp} = \text{Cov}(\tilde{r}_q, \tilde{r}_p)/\sigma^2(\tilde{r}_p)$, and where the fourth equality follows from relation (3.15.2). The expected rate of return on any portfolio q can be written as a linear combination of the expected rates of return on p and on its zero covariance portfolio, with weights β_{qp} and $1 - \beta_{qp}$.

Note that since $zc(zc(p)) = p$ for any frontier portfolio p other than the *mvp*, we can also write (3.16.2) as

$$E[\tilde{r}_q] = \left(1 - \beta_{qzc(p)}\right) E[\tilde{r}_p] + \beta_{qzc(p)} E[\tilde{r}_{zc(p)}]. \qquad (3.16.3)$$

From the fact that $E[\tilde{r}_p] \neq E[\tilde{r}_{zc(p)}]$, there exists a unique number, say α, such that $E[\tilde{r}_q] = \alpha E[\tilde{r}_p] + (1-\alpha) E[\tilde{r}_{zc(p)}]$. Therefore, relations (3.16.2) and (3.16.3) imply that

$$\beta_{qzc(p)} = 1 - \beta_{qp}, \qquad (3.16.4)$$

and we can write

$$E[\tilde{r}_q] = \beta_{qzc(p)} E[\tilde{r}_{zc(p)}] + \beta_{qp} E[\tilde{r}_p]. \qquad (3.16.5)$$

Relations (3.16.2), (3.16.3), and (3.16.5) are equivalent relations.

3.17. The relationship among the three random variables $\tilde{r}_q, \tilde{r}_p$ and $\tilde{r}_{zc(p)}$ can always be written as

$$\tilde{r}_q = \beta_0 + \beta_1 \tilde{r}_{zc(p)} + \beta_2 \tilde{r}_p + \tilde{\epsilon}_q \qquad (3.17.1)$$

with $\text{Cov}(\tilde{r}_p, \tilde{\epsilon}_q) = \text{Cov}(\tilde{r}_{zc(p)}, \tilde{\epsilon}_q) = E[\tilde{\epsilon}_q] = 0$, where $(\beta_0, \beta_1, \beta_2)$ are coefficients from the "multiple regression" of $\tilde{r}_q$ on $\tilde{r}_p$ and $\tilde{r}_{zc(p)}$. Since $\tilde{r}_p$ and $\tilde{r}_{zc(p)}$ are uncorrelated, we have

$$\beta_1 = \beta_{qzc(p)} \qquad \beta_2 = \beta_{qp}. \qquad (3.17.2)$$

It then follows from (3.16.5) that $\beta_0 = 0$, and thus we can always write the return on a portfolio q as:

$$\tilde{r}_q = (1 - \beta_{qp})\tilde{r}_{zc(p)} + \beta_{qp}\tilde{r}_p + \tilde{\epsilon}_q, \qquad (3.17.3)$$

with $\mathrm{Cov}(\tilde{r}_p, \tilde{\epsilon}_q) = \mathrm{Cov}(\tilde{r}_{zc(p)}, \tilde{\epsilon}_q) = E[\tilde{\epsilon}_q] = 0$. This relation will be particularly useful in Chapter 4.

3.18. In previous sections, we have characterized properties of the frontier portfolio when a riskless asset does not exist. When a riskless asset does exist, some simple results follow.

Let p be a frontier portfolio of *all* $N+1$ assets, and let $\mathbf{w}_p$ denote the N-vector portfolio weights of p on risky assets. Then $\mathbf{w}_p$ is the solution to the following program:

$$\min_{\{\mathbf{w}\}} \frac{1}{2}\mathbf{w}^\top \mathbf{V}\mathbf{w}$$

$$\text{s.t.} \qquad \mathbf{w}^\top \mathbf{e} + (1 - \mathbf{w}^\top \mathbf{1})r_f = E[\tilde{r}_p],$$

where we still use $\mathbf{e}$ to denote the N-vector of expected rates of return on risky assets, and r_f is the rate of return on the riskless asset. Forming the Lagrangian, we know that $\mathbf{w}_p$ is the solution to the following:

$$\min_{\{\mathbf{w},\lambda\}} \frac{1}{2}\mathbf{w}^\top \mathbf{V}\mathbf{w} + \lambda(E[\tilde{r}_p] - \mathbf{w}^\top \mathbf{e} - (1 - \mathbf{w}^\top \mathbf{1})r_f).$$

The first order necessary and sufficient conditions for $\mathbf{w}_p$ to be the solution are

$$\mathbf{V}\mathbf{w}_p = \lambda(\mathbf{e} - \mathbf{1}r_f)$$

and

$$r_f + \mathbf{w}_p^\top(\mathbf{e} - \mathbf{1}r_f) = E[\tilde{r}_p].$$

Solving for $\mathbf{w}_p$, we have

$$\mathbf{w}_p = \mathbf{V}^{-1}(\mathbf{e} - r_f\mathbf{1})\frac{E[\tilde{r}_p] - r_f}{H}, \qquad (3.18.1)$$

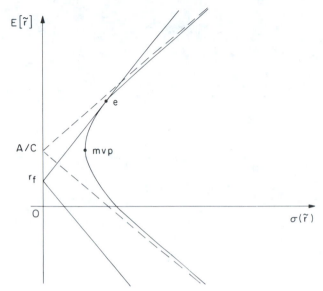

Figure 3.18.1: A Portfolio Frontier when $r_f < A/C$

where $H = (\mathbf{e} - \mathbf{1}r_f)^\top \mathbf{V}^{-1}(\mathbf{e} - \mathbf{1}r_f) = B - 2Ar_f + Cr_f^2$ and A, B, and C are defined as in Section 3.9. It is easily checked that $H > 0$ as $A^2 - BC < 0$. The variance of the rate of return on portfolio p is

$$\sigma^2(\tilde{r}_p) = \mathbf{w}_p^\top \mathbf{V} \mathbf{w}_p = \frac{(E[\tilde{r}_p] - r_f)^2}{H}, \qquad (3.18.2)$$

where the second equality follows from substituting relation (3.18.1). Equivalently, we can write

$$\sigma(\tilde{r}_p) = \begin{cases} \frac{E[\tilde{r}_p] - r_f}{\sqrt{H}} & \text{if } E[\tilde{r}_p] \geq r_f, \\ -\frac{E[\tilde{r}_p] - r_f}{\sqrt{H}} & \text{if } E[\tilde{r}_p] < r_f, \end{cases} \qquad (3.18.3)$$

that is, the portfolio frontier of all assets is composed of two half-lines emanating from the point $(0, r_f)$ in the $\sigma(\tilde{r}_p) - E[\tilde{r}_p]$ plane with slopes $\sqrt{H}$ and $-\sqrt{H}$, respectively.

We now consider some special cases.

Case 1. $r_f < A/C$. This case is presented graphically in Figure 3.18.1, where e is the tangent point of the half line $r_f + \sqrt{H}\sigma(\tilde{r}_p)$ and the portfolio frontier of all risky assets. To verify this, we only

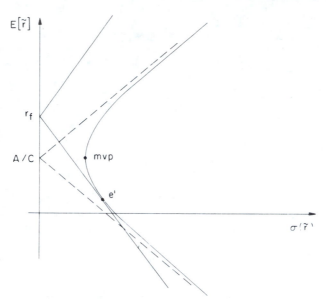

Figure 3.18.2: A Portfolio Frontier when $r_f > A/C$

have to show that

$$\frac{E[\tilde{r}_e] - r_f}{\sigma(\tilde{r}_e)} = \sqrt{H},$$

where we take

$$E[\tilde{r}_e] = A/C - \frac{D/C^2}{r_f - A/C}, \qquad (3.18.4)$$

that is, we use the result in Section 3.15 to conclude that $E[\tilde{r}_{zc(e)}] = r_f$. Now using relations (3.11.2a) and (3.18.4), we get

$$\frac{E[\tilde{r}_e] - r_f}{\sigma(\tilde{r}_e)} = (\frac{A}{C} - \frac{D/C^2}{r_f - A/C} - r_f) \cdot \frac{-C(r_f - A/C)}{\sqrt{H}}$$

$$= \frac{-H}{Cr_f - A} \cdot \frac{Cr_f - A}{\sqrt{H}} = \sqrt{H},$$

which is to be shown.

Any portfolio on the line segment $\overline{r_f e}$ is a convex combination of portfolio e and the riskless asset. Any portfolio on the half line $r_f + \sqrt{H}\sigma(\tilde{r}_p)$ other than those on $\overline{r_f e}$ involves short-selling the riskless asset and investing the proceeds in portfolio e. It can also easily be checked that any portfolio on the half line $r_f - \sqrt{H}\sigma(\tilde{r}_p)$ involves short–selling portfolio e and investing the proceeds in the riskless asset.

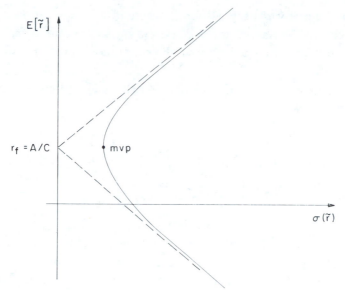

Figure 3.18.3: A Portfolio Frontier when $r_f = A/C$

Case 2. $r_f > A/C$. The story here is a little different. The portfolio frontier of all assets is graphed in Figure 3.18.2. Any portfolio on the half-line $r_f + \sqrt{H}\sigma(\tilde{r}_p)$ involves short-selling portfolio e' and investing the proceeds in the riskless asset. On the other hand, any portfolio on the half-line $r_f - \sqrt{H}\sigma(\tilde{r}_p)$ involves a long position in portfolio e'.

Case 3. $r_f = A/C$. In this case,

$$
\begin{aligned}
H &= B - 2Ar_f + Cr_f{}^2 \\
&= B - 2A\,(A/C) + CA^2/C^2 \\
&= \frac{BC - A^2}{C} = \frac{D}{C} > 0.
\end{aligned}
$$

Recall that $E[\tilde{r}_p] = A/C \pm \sqrt{D/C}\sigma(\tilde{r}_p)$ are the two asymptotes of the portfolio frontier of risky assets. The portfolio frontier of all assets is graphed in Figure 3.18.3.

In the previous two cases it is very clear how the portfolio frontiers of all assets are generated from looking at the figures. Portfolio frontiers are generated by the riskless asset and the "tangency" portfolios e and e', respectively. In the present case, there is no tangency

portfolio. Therefore the portfolio frontier of all assets is *not* generated by the riskless asset and a portfolio on the portfolio frontier of
risky assets. The question is how the portfolio frontier of all assets
is generated.

Substituting $r_f = A/C$ into relation (3.18.1) and premultiplying
$\mathbf{w}_p$ by $\mathbf{1}^T$, we get

$$\mathbf{1}^T\mathbf{w}_p = \mathbf{1}^T\mathbf{V}^{-1}(\mathbf{e} - A/C\mathbf{1})\frac{E[\tilde{r}_p] - r_f}{H}$$

$$= (A - \frac{A}{C}C)\frac{E[\tilde{r}_p] - r_f}{H}$$

$$= 0.$$

Therefore any portfolio on the portfolio frontier of all assets involves
investing everything in the riskless asset and holding an *arbitrage
portfolio* of risky assets – a portfolio whose weights sum to zero.

3.19. When there exists a riskless asset, a relation similar to
(3.17.2) can be derived. Let q be any portfolio, with $\mathbf{w}_q$ the portfolio
weights on the risky assets. Also, let p be a frontier portfolio, with
$\mathbf{w}_p$ the portfolio weights on risky assets. We assume that $E[\tilde{r}_p] \neq r_f$.
Then

$$\text{Cov}(\tilde{r}_q, \tilde{r}_p) = \mathbf{w}_q^T\mathbf{V}\mathbf{w}_p$$

$$= \frac{(E[\tilde{r}_q] - r_f)(E[\tilde{r}_p] - r_f)}{H}.$$

Using (3.18.2), we obtain

$$E[\tilde{r}_q] - r_f = \frac{\text{Cov}(\tilde{r}_q, \tilde{r}_p)}{(E[\tilde{r}_p] - r_f)^2/H} \cdot (E[\tilde{r}_p] - r_f) \qquad (3.19.1)$$

$$= \beta_{qp}(E[\tilde{r}_p] - r_f).$$

This relation holds independent of the relationship between r_f and
A/C.

Given (3.19.1) and Section 3.17, we can readily write

$$\tilde{r}_q = (1 - \beta_{qp})r_f + \beta_{qp}\tilde{r}_p + \tilde{\epsilon}_{qp}, \qquad (3.19.2)$$

with $\text{Cov}(\tilde{r}_p, \tilde{\epsilon}_{qp}) = E[\tilde{\epsilon}_{qp}] = 0$, for any portfolio q and any frontier
portfolio p other than the riskless asset.

Exercises

3.1. Let there be two securities with rates of return $\tilde{r}_j$ and $\tilde{r}_l$. Suppose that these two securities have identical expected rates of return and identical variances. The correlation coefficient between $\tilde{r}_j$ and $\tilde{r}_l$ is ρ. Show that the equally weighted portfolio achieves the minimum variance independently of ρ.

3.2. Suppose that the riskless borrowing rate is higher than the riskless lending rate. Graphically demonstrate the portfolio frontier of all assets. Next suppose that borrowing is not allowed. Graphically demonstrate the portfolio frontier of all assets.

3.3. Let p be a frontier portfolio, and let q be any portfolio having the same expected rate of return. Show that $\text{Cov}(\tilde{r}_p, \tilde{r}_q) = \text{Var}(\tilde{r}_p)$ and, as a consequence, the correlation coefficient of $\tilde{r}_p$ and $\tilde{r}_q$ lies in $(0, 1]$.

3.4. Let f_j, $j = 1, 2, \ldots, n$, be efficient frontier portfolios. Show that if $E[\tilde{r}_p] = \sum_{j=1}^{n} w_i E[\tilde{r}_{f_j}]$, where $\sum_{j=1}^{n} w_j = 1$, then $E[\tilde{r}_{zc(p)}] \neq \sum_{j=1}^{n} w_j E[\tilde{r}_{zc(f_j)}]$, unless all f_j are the same.

3.5. Let f_j, $j = 1, 2, \ldots, n$, be efficient frontier portfolios, and let λ_j be the Lagrangian multiplier of (3.8.2) that is associated with $E[\tilde{r}_{f_j}]$. Show that if $E[\tilde{r}_p] = \sum_{j=1}^{n} w_i E[\tilde{r}_{f_j}]$, where $\sum_{j=1}^{n} w_j = 1$, then $E[\tilde{r}_{zc(p)}] = \frac{1}{\lambda_p} \sum_{j=1}^{n} w_j \lambda_j E[\tilde{r}_{zc(f_j)}]$, where λ_p is the Lagrangian multiplier of (3.8.2) that is associated with $E[\tilde{r}_p]$, where $w_j \geq 0$.

3.6. Show that the portfolio frontier generated by two assets or portfolios having distinct expected rates of return passes through these two assets or portfolios.

Remarks. Most of the discussions in Sections 3.8 through 3.17 are freely adapted from Gonzalez–Gaverra (1973) and Merton (1972). Many results of Gonzalez–Gaverra (1973) were later independently derived by Roll (1977).

Chamberlain (1983) characterizes the complete family of distributions that are necessary and sufficient for the expected utility of final wealth to be a function only of the mean and variance of final wealth or for *mean–variance utility functions*. Epstein (1985) shows that mean–variance utility functions are implied by a set of decreasing absolute risk aversion postulates.

References

Chamberlain, G. 1983. A characterization of the distributions that imply mean–variance utility functions. *Journal of Economic Theory* **29**:185–201.

Epstein, L. 1985. Decreasing risk aversion and mean–variance analysis. *Econometrica* **53**:945–962.

Gonzalez-Gaverra, N. 1973. Inflation and capital asset market prices: Theory and tests. Unpublished PhD dissertation, Stanford University.

Markowitz, H. 1952. Portfolio Selection. *Journal of Finance* **7**:77–91.

Merton, R. 1972. An analytical derivation of the efficient portfolio frontier. *Journal of Financial and Quantitative Analysis* **7**:1851-1872.

Roll, R. 1977. A critique of the asset pricing theory's tests. *Journal of Financial Economics* **4**:129–176.

CHAPTER 4
TWO FUND SEPARATION
AND LINEAR VALUATION

4.1. In Section 3.10 we saw that all portfolios on the portfolio frontier can be generated by any two distinct frontier portfolios. Thus, if individuals prefer frontier portfolios, they can simply hold a linear combination of two frontier portfolios or mutual funds. In that case, given any feasible portfolio, there exists a portfolio of two mutual funds such that individuals prefer at least as much as the original portfolio. This phenomenon is termed *two (mutual) fund separation*.

In the first part of this chapter, we develop conditions on asset returns that are necessary and sufficient for two fund separation given that individuals are risk averse and that variances of asset returns exist. When asset returns exhibit two fund separation, it turns out that the two separating mutual funds must be on the portfolio frontier. It then follows that an individual's optimal portfolio is a frontier portfolio. In equilibrium, markets have to clear. Thus, the market portfolio, a convex combination of individuals' optimal portfolios, is also on the portfolio frontier. As long as the market portfolio is not the minimum variance portfolio, Section 3.16 implies that there exists a linear relation among the expected asset returns with the expected return on the market portfolio as the pivotal variable. This is the Capital Asset Pricing Model – the subject of the second part of this chapter.

Finally, we will turn to the Arbitrage Pricing Model, where a linear relation among expected asset returns holds *approximately* for *most* of the assets in an economy with a large number of assets, when, roughly, there are no *arbitrage opportunities* (in the limit).

4.2. We start our formal discussion by giving a definition. A vector of asset rate of returns $\tilde{r} \equiv (\tilde{r}_j)_{j=1}^{N}$ is said to exhibit *two fund separation* if there exist two mutual funds α_1 and α_2 such that for any portfolio q there exists a scalar λ such that

$$E[u(\lambda \tilde{r}_{\alpha_1} + (1 - \lambda)\tilde{r}_{\alpha_2})] \geq E[u(\tilde{r}_q)] \qquad (4.2.1)$$

for all concave $u(\cdot)$.

We shall assume that all assets are risky, until specified otherwise. Moreover, we assume that asset returns have finite second moments and that no two asset returns are perfectly correlated, which imply that the variance–covariance matrix of asset returns exists and is positive definite. Then portfolio frontier exists, and every frontier portfolio is uniquely determined in that there is a unique set of portfolio weights associated with each frontier portfolio. The above points were discussed in Chapter 3.

Now suppose that the vector of asset rates of return, $\tilde{r}$, exhibits two fund separation. We first claim that the separating mutual funds α_1 and α_2 must be frontier portfolios. To see this, we note that by the definition of two fund separation, for any portfolio q there must exist a scalar λ such that

$$E[u(\lambda \tilde{r}_{\alpha_1} + (1 - \lambda)\tilde{r}_{\alpha_2})] \geq E[u(\tilde{r}_q)] \qquad (4.2.2)$$

for all concave $u(\cdot)$. This is equivalent to

$$\lambda \alpha_1 + (1 - \lambda)\alpha_2 \; \overset{\geq}{_{SSD}} \; q. \qquad (4.2.3)$$

From Section 2.8 we must then have

$$E[\lambda \tilde{r}_{\alpha_1} + (1 - \lambda)\tilde{r}_{\alpha_2}] = E[\tilde{r}_q] \qquad (4.2.4)$$

and

$$\mathrm{Var}[\lambda \tilde{r}_{\alpha_1} + (1 - \lambda)\tilde{r}_{\alpha_2}] \leq \mathrm{Var}(\tilde{r}_q). \qquad (4.2.5)$$

That is, the dominating portfolio $\lambda \alpha_1 + (1 - \lambda)\alpha_2$ must have the same expected rate of return as q and a smaller variance. Suppose, for example, that α_2 is not a frontier portfolio. Then there must exist a portfolio $\hat{\alpha}$ that has a variance strictly smaller than that of any portfolio formed by α_1 and α_2. This contradicts the hypothesis that α_1 and α_2 are separating portfolios. Hence α_1 and α_2 must be on the portfolio frontier.

4.3. Next we observe that because α_1 and α_2 are frontier portfolios, any linear combination of them is also on the frontier. Hence, for any portfolio q, the dominating portfolio formed from two separating portfolios is the frontier portfolio that has the same expected rate of return as portfolio q. As the portfolio weights of any frontier portfolio are uniquely determined and any two distinct frontier portfolios span the whole portfolio frontier, whenever two fund separation obtains, it must be that any two distinct frontier portfolios can be separating portfolios. In particular, we can pick any frontier portfolio, $p \neq mvp$ and its zero covariance portfolio, $zc(p)$, to be the separating portfolios. Sections 3.16 and 3.17 allow us to write, for any portfolio q,

$$\begin{aligned} \tilde{r}_q &= (1 - \beta_{qp})\tilde{r}_{zc(p)} + \beta_{qp}\tilde{r}_p + \tilde{\epsilon}_{qp} \\ &= \tilde{r}_{zc(p)} + \beta_{qp}(\tilde{r}_p - \tilde{r}_{zc(p)}) + \tilde{\epsilon}_{qp}, \end{aligned} \qquad (4.3.1)$$

where $\beta_{qp} = cov(\tilde{r}_q, \tilde{r}_p)/var(\tilde{r}_p)$ and $\tilde{\epsilon}_{qp}$ is such that $E(\tilde{\epsilon}_{qp}) = 0$. Note that

$$\tilde{Q}(\beta_{qp}) \equiv (1 - \beta_{qp})\tilde{r}_{zc(p)} + \beta_{qp}\tilde{r}_p, \qquad (4.3.2)$$

is the rate of return of the dominating portfolio. Next we claim that the necessary and sufficient condition for two fund separation is

$$E[\tilde{\epsilon}_{qp}|\tilde{Q}(\beta_{qp})] = 0 \qquad \forall \; q. \qquad (4.3.3)$$

4.4. First we will demonstrate the necessity of (4.3.3) for two fund separation. We note that as $\tilde{Q}(\beta_{qp})$ is the return on the dominating portfolio, $a = 0$ is a solution of the following program:

$$\max_{\{a\}} \quad E[u(a\tilde{r}_q + (1-a)\tilde{Q}(\beta_{qp}))]$$

A necessary condition for $a = 0$ to be a solution is

$$E[u'(\tilde{Q}(\beta_{qp}))\tilde{\epsilon}_{qp}] = 0 \qquad \forall \text{ concave } u(\cdot). \qquad (4.4.1)$$

Suppose (4.3.3) does not hold for some q. We denote $E[\tilde{\epsilon}_{qp}|\tilde{Q}(\beta_{qp})]$ by $m_q(\tilde{Q})$ and the cumulative distribution function of $\tilde{Q}(\beta_{qp})$ by $F(\cdot)$. As $E[\tilde{\epsilon}_{qp}] = 0$, it follows that there must exist a real number z such that

$$\int_{-\infty}^{z} m_q(\tilde{Q})dF(\tilde{Q}) = -\int_{z}^{+\infty} m_q(\tilde{Q})dF(\tilde{Q}) \neq 0. \qquad (4.4.2)$$

This can be seen as follows. First, the two sides of the equality of (4.4.2) can not be zero for all z, as this will contradict the hypothesis that (4.3.3) does not hold for some q. Second, if the equality of (4.4.2) does not hold for all z, that is,

$$\int_{-\infty}^{z} m_q(\tilde{Q})dF(\tilde{Q}) \neq -\int_{z}^{+\infty} m_q(\tilde{Q})dF(\tilde{Q}),$$

then

$$\begin{aligned} E[\tilde{\epsilon}_{qp}] &= E[E[\tilde{\epsilon}_{qp}|\tilde{Q}(\beta_{qp})]] \\ &= \int_{-\infty}^{+\infty} m_q(\tilde{Q})dF(\tilde{Q}) \\ &= \int_{-\infty}^{z} m_q(\tilde{Q})dF(\tilde{Q}) + \int_{z}^{+\infty} m_q(\tilde{Q})dF(\tilde{Q}) \neq 0, \end{aligned}$$

which contradicts the fact that $E[\tilde{\epsilon}_{qp}] = 0$. Now consider a concave utility function that is piecewise linear:

$$u_1(y) = \begin{cases} K_1\, y & \text{if } y < z; \\ K_1\, z + K_2\,(y - z) & \text{if } y \geq z, \end{cases} \qquad (4.4.3)$$

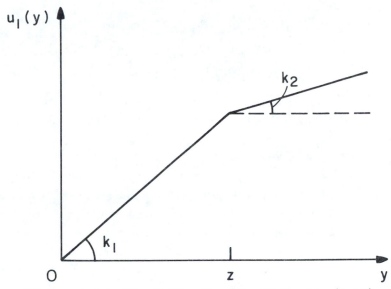

Figure 4.4.1: The Utility Function Defined in (4.4.3)

where $K_1 > K_2$ are strictly positive constants. This utility function is graphed in Figure 4.4.1. Then

$$
\begin{aligned}
E[u_1'(\tilde{Q}(\beta_{qp}))\tilde{\epsilon}_{qp}] &= E[E[u_1'(\tilde{Q}(\beta_{qp}))\tilde{\epsilon}_{qp}|\tilde{Q}(\beta_{qp})]] \\
&= E[u_1'(\tilde{Q}(\beta_{qp}))E[\tilde{\epsilon}_{qp}|\tilde{Q}(\beta_{qp})]] \\
&= K_1 \int_{-\infty}^{z} m_q(\tilde{Q})dF(\tilde{Q}) + K_2 \int_{z}^{+\infty} m_q(\tilde{Q})dF(\tilde{Q}) \\
&= (K_1 - K_2) \int_{-\infty}^{z} m_q(\tilde{Q})dF(\tilde{Q}) \neq 0,
\end{aligned}
$$

which contradicts (4.4.1). Thus (4.3.3) is a necessary condition for two fund separation.

4.5. Now we will show that (4.3.3) is also sufficient for two fund separation. The separating portfolios are p and its zero covariance portfolio. If q is a portfolio, then the dominating portfolio is $(1 - \beta_{qp})\tilde{r}_{zc(p)} + \beta_{qp}\tilde{r}_p$. To see this, let $u(\cdot)$ be any concave utility function.

We have
$$E[u(\tilde{r}_q)] = E[u(\tilde{Q}(\beta_{qp}) + \tilde{\epsilon}_{qp})]$$
$$= E[E[u(\tilde{Q}(\beta_{qp}) + \tilde{\epsilon}_{qp})|\tilde{Q}(\beta_{qp})]]$$
$$\leq E[u(\tilde{Q}(\beta_{qp}))],$$

where the inequality follows from Jensen's inequality because $u(\cdot)$ is concave. Thus, (4.3.3) is sufficient for two fund separation. As we observed earlier, in this case, any two distinct frontier portfolios can be separating portfolios.

Note that the condition for two fund separation can be summarized in words based on (4.3.1) and (4.3.3). The rate of return on any feasible portfolio is equal to the rate of return on a particular portfolio plus a random noise term that has a zero conditional expectation given the rate of return on the particular portfolio. This particular portfolio has the same expected rate of return as the given feasible portfolio and is formed from two fixed mutual funds. As expected rates of return on the two fixed mutual funds are different, portfolios formed from them can have any expected rate of return desired.

4.6. We will say that a vector of asset returns $\tilde{r}$ exhibits *one fund separation* if there exists a (feasible) portfolio α such that every risk averse individual prefers α to any other feasible portfolio. That is, when one fund separation obtains, there must exist a mutual fund α such that for any portfolio q, we have, for all concave $u(\cdot)$,

$$E[u(\tilde{r}_\alpha)] \geq E[u(\tilde{r}_q)].$$

This implies
$$E[\tilde{r}_\alpha] = E[\tilde{r}_q]$$
and
$$\mathrm{Var}(\tilde{r}_\alpha) \leq \mathrm{Var}(\tilde{r}_q)$$

by way of second degree stochastic dominance. As q is arbitrary and α is fixed, all assets must have the same expected rate of return. Furthermore, the separating portfolio must be the minimum variance portfolio. Otherwise, pick q to be the minimum variance portfolio. Then

$$var(\tilde{r}_q) < var(\tilde{r}_\alpha),$$

which violates implications of second degree stochastic dominance. We can, therefore, write

$$\tilde{r}_q = \tilde{r}_\alpha + \tilde{\epsilon}_q \qquad \forall\ q, \tag{4.6.1}$$

with $E[\tilde{\epsilon}_q] = 0$. We claim that the necessary and sufficient condition for one fund separation is

$$E[\tilde{\epsilon}_q | \tilde{r}_\alpha] = 0 \qquad \forall\ q. \tag{4.6.2}$$

The necessity part can easily be demonstrated by reproducing the necessity proof for (4.3.3). Suppose (4.6.2) is not true. We can construct a piecewise linear and concave utility function to show a contradiction. The sufficiency proof is exactly the same as in the two fund separation case.

One fund separation can be viewed as a degenerate case of two fund separation. When all assets have the same expected rate of return, the portfolio frontier degenerates to a single point, the minimum variance portfolio. The portfolio frontier is thus trivially generated by a single mutual fund. A necessary and sufficient condition for one fund separation is given by (4.3.3) with $\beta_{qp} = 1$.

4.7. In this section, we shall give concrete examples of distributions of rates of return that exhibit two fund and one fund separation, respectively.

Let the vector of rates of return be multivariate normally distributed. Suppose that the expected rates of return of risky assets are not identical. We claim that two fund separation obtains. Let p be any frontier portfolio and $zc(p)$ its zero covariance portfolio. As any linear combination of normal random variables is itself normal, it follows that $\tilde{r}_p$ and $\tilde{r}_{zc(p)}$ are bivariate normal random variables. Let q be any portfolio. Relation (4.3.1) implies that $\tilde{\epsilon}_{qp}$ is also a normal random variable. Recall the following from Section 3.17:

$$\text{Cov}(\tilde{\epsilon}_{qp}, \tilde{r}_p) = \text{Cov}(\tilde{\epsilon}_{qp}, \tilde{r}_{zc(p)}) = E[\tilde{\epsilon}_{qp}] = 0. \tag{4.7.1}$$

That is, $\tilde{\epsilon}_{qp}$, $\tilde{r}_p$ and $\tilde{r}_{zc(p)}$ are uncorrelated. Multivariate normality then implies that $\tilde{\epsilon}_{qp}$, $\tilde{r}_p$ and $\tilde{r}_{zc(p)}$ are independent. Consequently, $\tilde{\epsilon}_{qp}$ and $\tilde{Q}(\beta_{qp})$ are independent, and thus

$$E[\tilde{\epsilon}_{qp} | \tilde{Q}(\beta_{qp})] = E[\tilde{\epsilon}_{qp}] = 0. \tag{4.7.2}$$

We have thus shown that two fund separation obtains.

Next, let us suppose that rates of return on assets not only are multivariate normally distributed but also have identical expectations. Let $\tilde{r}_{mvp}$ denote the return on the minimum variance portfolio. For any feasible portfolio q, we can always write

$$\tilde{r}_q = \tilde{r}_{mvp} + \tilde{\epsilon}_q. \qquad (4.7.3)$$

The hypothesis that all assets have identical expected rates of return implies that

$$E[\tilde{\epsilon}_q] = 0.$$

From Section 3.12, we know

$$\mathrm{Cov}(\tilde{r}_q, \tilde{r}_{mvp}) = \mathrm{Var}(\tilde{r}_{mvp}). \qquad (4.7.4)$$

Hence we know $\mathrm{Cov}(\tilde{\epsilon}_q, \tilde{r}_{mvp}) = 0$. Multivariate normality of $\tilde{r}_q, \tilde{r}_{mvp}$ and $\tilde{\epsilon}_q$ then yields

$$E[\tilde{\epsilon}_q | \tilde{r}_{mvp}] = E[\tilde{\epsilon}_q] = 0.$$

This establishes that one fund separation obtains.

In summary, if rates of return are multivariate normally distributed and have nonidentical expectations, two fund separation obtains. On the other hand, when returns have identical expectations, multivariate normality implies one fund separation.

4.8. In the above discussion, we derived the necessary and sufficient condition for two fund separation. In this and the next section, we will show that when two fund separation obtains and markets for risky assets are in equilibrium, a simple linear restriction on asset returns is in effect. That is, the equilibrium relation among asset returns is linear.

We first give a definition of a *market portfolio*. Let $W_0^i > 0$ be individual i's initial wealth, and let w_{ij} be the proportion of the initial wealth invested in the j–th security by individual i. The total wealth in the economy is

$$W_{m0} \equiv \sum_{i=1}^{I} W_0^i,$$

where I is the total number of individuals in the economy. In equilibrium, the total wealth W_{m0} is equal to the total value of securities. Let w_{mj} denote the proportion of the total wealth contributed by the total value of the j–th security. We will call the w_{mj}'s the portfolio weights of the market portfolio. For markets to clear, we must have

$$\sum_{i=1}^{I} w_{ij} W_0^i = w_{mj} W_{m0}. \tag{4.8.1}$$

Dividing both sides of (4.8.1) by W_{m0}, we have

$$\sum_{i=1}^{I} w_{ij} \frac{W_0^i}{W_{m0}} = w_{mj}.$$

That is, the market portfolio weights are a convex combination of the portfolio weights for individuals.

4.9. We claim that when two fund separation obtains, the market portfolio is a frontier portfolio. We have shown in Section 4.2 that when two fund separation holds, the separating portfolios must be frontier portfolios and, indeed, any two distinct frontier portfolios can be the separating portfolios. In that case, each individual will hold a linear combination of the two separating portfolios. Section 3.13 demonstrated that any linear combination of frontier portfolios is on the frontier, which implies that each individual holds a frontier portfolio. Section 4.8 showed that in market equilibrium, the market portfolio is a convex combination of individuals' portfolios. Thus the market portfolio is a convex, and therefore linear, combination of frontier portfolios and is itself on the frontier.

Next we recall from Section 3.16 that if p is a frontier portfolio other than the minimum variance portfolio and q is any feasible portfolio, we have

$$E[\tilde{r}_q] = (1 - \beta_{qp}) E[\tilde{r}_{zc(p)}] + \beta_{qp} E[\tilde{r}_p]. \tag{4.9.1}$$

We have demonstrated above that when two fund separation obtains, the market portfolio is on the portfolio frontier in equilibrium. Hence, if the market portfolio is not the minimum variance portfolio, we get

$$E[\tilde{r}_q] = (1 - \beta_{qm}) E[\tilde{r}_{zc(m)}] + \beta_{qm} E[\tilde{r}_m], \tag{4.9.2}$$

where

$$\tilde{r}_m = \sum_{j=1}^{N} w_{mj}\tilde{r}_j$$

is the rate of return on the market portfolio, and

$$\beta_{qm} = \frac{\text{Cov}(\tilde{r}_q, \tilde{r}_m)}{\text{Var}(\tilde{r}_m)}.$$

Since any risky asset is itself a feasible portfolio, relation (4.9.1) implies that

$$E[\tilde{r}_j] = (1 - \beta_{jm})E[\tilde{r}_{zc(m)}] + \beta_{jm}E[\tilde{r}_m]. \qquad (4.9.3)$$

for all $j = 1, 2, \ldots, N$.

Note that relation (4.9.1), which holds for all frontier portfolios p other than the minimum variance portfolio, is a mathematical fact that follows from the portfolio frontier mathematics without using economic reasoning. Two fund separation plus market clearing allows us, however, to identify that the market portfolio is on the portfolio frontier. If the market portfolio is not of minimum variance, then relation (4.9.3) follows, which places a linear restriction on expected asset returns in equilibrium. Thus the economic content of (4.9.3) lies in the conclusion that the market portfolio is on the portfolio frontier.

4.10. Let us rewrite relation (4.9.3) in the following form:

$$E[\tilde{r}_j] = E[\tilde{r}_{zc(m)}] + \beta_{jm}(E[\tilde{r}_m] - E[\tilde{r}_{zc(m)}]). \qquad (4.10.1)$$

Suppose that the market portfolio is an efficient portfolio. Then $E[\tilde{r}_m] - E[\tilde{r}_{zc(m)}] > 0$, since $zc(m)$ is inefficient. Relation (4.10.1) is drawn in Figure 4.10.1. The higher the β_{jm} for asset j, the higher its equilibrium expected rate of return. The equilibrium expected rate of return on a risky asset depends upon the covariability of its rate of return with the rate of return on the market portfolio. The expected rates of return on all risky assets and on all feasible portfolios lie

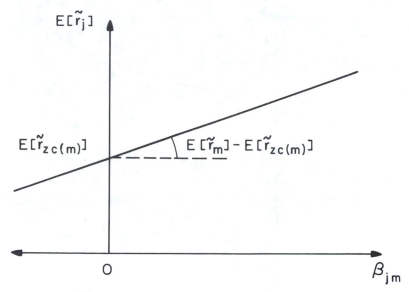

Figure 4.10.1: A Security Market Line

along a line, which is termed the *security market line*, as shown in Figure 4.10.1.

When the market portfolio is an inefficient portfolio, we still have a linear relation between $E[\tilde{r}_j]$ and β_{jm}. However, the slope of the line in the $E[\tilde{r}_j] - \beta_{jm}$ plane is negative. In this case, the higher the covariability between an asset's rate of return with that on the market portfolio, the lower its equilibrium expected rate of return. We can rewrite (4.10.1) as follows:

$$E[\tilde{r}_j] = E[\tilde{r}_m] + \beta_{jzc(m)}(E[\tilde{r}_{zc(m)}] - E[\tilde{r}_m]). \qquad (4.10.2)$$

Then the higher a risky asset return's covariability with the zero covariance portfolio with respect to the market portfolio, the higher its equilibrium expected rate of return will be. Figure 4.10.2 graphs relation (4.10.2) when $E[\tilde{r}_m] - E[\tilde{r}_{zc(m)}] < 0$.

4.11. In the previous two sections, we derived a linear restriction on equilibrium expected rates of return on risky assets when two fund separation obtains. In the analysis, it was assumed that the market portfolio was not the minimum variance portfolio. In

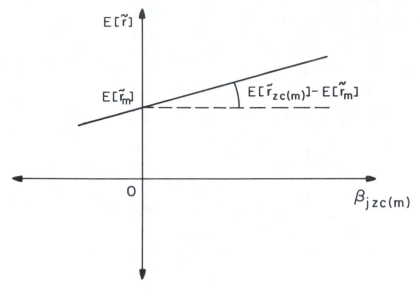

Figure 4.10.2: A Security Market Line

this section, we shall analyze a special case of two fund separation and show that the market portfolio is an efficient portfolio. Thus a relation like (4.10.1) is valid in equilibrium.

Let us assume that individuals' utility functions are increasing and strictly concave. Note that monotonicity and strict concavity imply strict monotonicity. In addition, we assume that the rates of return on assets are multivariate normally distributed. We show first that, under these conditions, each individual will choose to hold an efficient portfolio. We have observed in Section 4.7 that a linear combination of multivariate normal random variables is a normal random variable. Thus the rate of return on any portfolio chosen by an individual is normally distributed. Let p denote the portfolio chosen by individual i. The expected utility of individual i's choice is

$$E[u_i(W_0^i(1 + \tilde{r}_p))] = E[u_i(W_0^i(1 + E[\tilde{r}_p] + \sigma(\tilde{r}_p)\tilde{z}))], \qquad (4.11.1)$$

where $\tilde{z}$ denotes a standard normal random variable. It is clear from relation (4.11.1) that an individual's expected utility can be parameterized by the expected rate of return and standard deviation of the portfolio he chooses to hold. In other word, individuals' preferences can be completely specified by their preferences for expected rates of return and standard deviations of feasible portfolios.

Now we show that strict monotonicity of an individual's utility function implies that he prefers a higher expected rate of return, *ceteris paribus*. Defining

$$V_i(E[\tilde{r}_p], \sigma(\tilde{r}_p)) \equiv E[u_i(W_0^i(1 + E[\tilde{r}_p] + \sigma(\tilde{r}_p)\tilde{z}))]$$

and partially differentiating V_i with respect to $E[\tilde{r}_p]$ gives:

$$\frac{\partial V_i(E[\tilde{r}_p], \sigma(\tilde{r}_p))}{\partial E[\tilde{r}_p]} = E[u_i'(\tilde{W}^i)W_0^i] > 0, \qquad (4.11.2)$$

where

$$\tilde{W}^i \equiv W_0^i(1 + E[\tilde{r}_p] + \sigma(\tilde{r}_p)\tilde{z}) \qquad (4.11.3)$$

and where the strict inequality follows from the strict monotonicity of $u_i(\cdot)$. That is, individual i prefers a higher expected rate of return, *ceteris paribus*.

Next we claim that the strict concavity of an individual's utility function implies that he prefers a portfolio with a lower standard deviation, *ceteris paribus*. To see this, we partially differentiate V_i with respect to $\sigma(\tilde{r}_p)$ to get

$$\frac{\partial V_i(E[\tilde{r}_p], \sigma(\tilde{r}_p))}{\partial \sigma(\tilde{r}_p)} = E[u_i'(\tilde{W}^i)\tilde{z}W_0^i]$$

$$= W_0^i \text{Cov}(u_i'(\tilde{W}^i), \tilde{z}), \qquad (4.11.4)$$

where we have used the definition of covariance to write the second equality. Note that $\tilde{W}^i$ is perfectly correlated with $\tilde{z}$. By the strict concavity of $u_i(\cdot)$, we know that $u_i'(\cdot)$ is strictly decreasing. Hence it follows that $u_i'(\tilde{W}^i)$ and $\tilde{z}$ are strictly negatively correlated, and $\text{Cov}(u_i'(\tilde{W}^i), \tilde{z}) < 0$. So a strictly risk averse individual prefers a portfolio with a lower standard deviation, *ceteris paribus*.

Now we are ready to show that under the conditions postulated above, individuals will choose to hold efficient portfolios. We first demonstrate that individuals' indifference curves in the mean–standard deviation plane are positively sloped. Totally differentiating V_i with respect to $E[\tilde{r}_p]$ and $\sigma(\tilde{r}_p)$ and setting the result equal to zero, we get

$$\frac{dE[\tilde{r}_p]}{d\sigma(\tilde{r}_p)} = -\frac{E[u'(\tilde{W}^i)\tilde{z}]}{E[u'(\tilde{W}^i)]} > 0, \qquad (4.11.5)$$

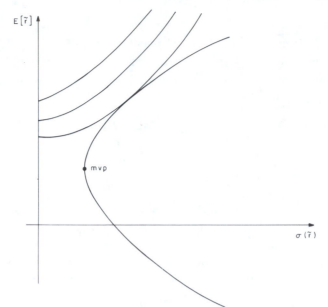

Figure 4.11.1: Indifference Curves when Asset Returns Are Normally Distributed

which was to be shown.

Finally, that individuals will choose to hold efficient portfolios is demonstrated in Figure 4.11.1. The hyperbola in Figure 4.11.1 is the portfolio frontier. The three positively sloped curves are indifference curves. The indifference curves further toward the northwest represent higher utility levels. This follows from the signs of relations (4.11.2) and (4.11.4). Thus an individual will choose to hold a portfolio that is represented by the point of tangency between his indifference curve and the portfolio frontier. Then his strictly positively sloped indifference curves imply that he will choose an efficient portfolio.

Applying the above argument to all individuals, we know that all individuals hold efficient portfolios. Therefore, the market portfolio is an efficient portfolio, since it is a convex combination of individuals' portfolios. Furthermore, we have for any feasible portfolio

$$E[\tilde{r}_q] = E[\tilde{r}_{zc(m)}] + \beta_{qm}(E[\tilde{r}_m] - E[\tilde{r}_{zc(m)}]) \qquad (4.11.6)$$

and

$$E[\tilde{r}_m] - E[\tilde{r}_{zc(m)}] > 0. \qquad (4.11.7)$$

The equilibrium relations among expected rates of return on assets are as described in Figure 4.10.1. Relations (4.11.6) and (4.11.7) are known as the *Zero–Beta Capital Asset Pricing Model* which was developed by Black (1972) and Lintner (1969).

4.12. In carrying out the above analyses, we have assumed that there is no riskless asset. These next three sections are devoted to the case where there is a riskless asset.

Suppose first that the expected rate of return on the minimum variance portfolio exceeds the riskless rate, i.e., $r_f < A/C$. Let e be the tangent portfolio of Figure 3.18.1. From (3.19.2), we know that the rate of return on any feasible portfolio q can be expressed as:

$$\tilde{r}_q = (1 - \beta_{qe})r_f + \beta_{qe}\tilde{r}_e + \tilde{\epsilon}_{qe}, \qquad (4.12.1)$$

with $\text{Cov}(\tilde{r}_e, \tilde{\epsilon}_{qe}) = E[\tilde{\epsilon}_{qe}] = 0$. We claim that

$$E[\tilde{\epsilon}_{je}|\tilde{r}_e] = 0, \qquad j = 1, 2, \ldots, N \qquad (4.12.2)$$

is a necessary and sufficient condition for $\{(\tilde{r}_j)_{j=1}^N, r_f\}$ to exhibit two fund separation.

We prove the necessity part first. Suppose that two fund separation holds. Along the line of arguments of Section 4.2, the two separating portfolios must be frontier portfolios and can be chosen to be portfolio e and the riskless asset. Therefore, when there exists a riskless asset and two fund separation holds, we have two fund monetary separation. Arguments similar to those of Section 4.3 then show that

$$E[\tilde{\epsilon}_{qe}|(1 - \beta_{qe})r_f + \beta_{qe}\tilde{r}_e] = 0, \qquad (4.12.3)$$

for all portfolios q. As r_f is nonstochastic and we can always pick q to be any risky asset j, it follows that

$$E[\tilde{\epsilon}_{je}|\tilde{r}_e] = 0, \qquad j = 1, 2, \ldots, N,$$

is implied by two fund separation when a riskless asset exists.

The sufficiency part follows easily from the arguments of Section 4.4 and the fact that (4.12.2) implies (4.12.3). Thus, $E[\tilde{\epsilon}_{je}|\tilde{r}_e] = 0$ implies two fund separation when a riskless asset exists.

Similar arguments also show that when $r_f > A/C$

$$E[\tilde{\epsilon}_{je'}|\tilde{r}_{e'}] = 0, \qquad j = 1, 2, \ldots, N,$$

is a necessary and sufficient condition for two fund separation, where $(\tilde{\epsilon}_{je'})_{j=1}^{N}$ are such that

$$\tilde{r}_j = (1 - \beta_{je'})r_f + \beta_{je'}\tilde{r}_{e'} + \tilde{\epsilon}_{je'},$$

with $\text{Cov}(\tilde{r}_{e'}, \tilde{\epsilon}_{je'}) = E[\tilde{\epsilon}_{je'}] = 0$ and $\beta_{je'} = \text{Cov}(\tilde{r}_j, \tilde{r}_{e'})/\sigma^2(\tilde{r}_{e'})$.

4.13. We shall assume throughout this section that two fund separation holds. When $r_f \neq A/C$ and risky assets are in strictly positive supply, the tangent portfolios of Figures 3.18.1 and 3.18.2 must be the market portfolios of risky assets in equilibrium. Therefore, in those two cases, the market portfolios of risky assets are on the portfolio frontier. Hence, using (3.19.1), we know

$$E[\tilde{r}_q] - r_f = \beta_{qm}(E[\tilde{r}_m] - r_f) \qquad (4.13.1)$$

for any portfolio q in the market equilibrium. This is the traditional *Capital Asset Pricing Model* (CAPM) independently derived by Lintner (1965), Mossin (1965), and Sharpe (1964).

When $r_f = A/C$, the story is a little different. If this is an equilibrium, we claim that the riskless asset is in strictly positive supply and the risky assets are in zero net supply. To see this we recall that when two fund separation holds, individuals hold frontier portfolios. In addition, Section 3.18 says that when $r_f = A/C$, an individual puts all his wealth into the riskless asset and holds a self-financing portfolio. For markets to clear, it is then necessary that the riskless asset be in strictly positive supply and the risky assets be in zero net supply.

As for equilibrium relations among asset returns, we cannot say much beyond (3.19.1).

4.14. In Section 4.13, we were not able to sign the risk premium of the market portfolio in the presence of two fund separation. We will show in this section that when investors have strictly increasing utility functions, the risk premium of the market portfolio must be strictly positive when the risky assets are in strictly positive supply and (4.12.2) holds.

We first claim that an investor will never choose to hold a portfolio whose expected rate of return is strictly lower than the riskless rate when his utility function $u(\cdot)$ is strictly increasing and concave. Let $\tilde{r}$ be the random return of a portfolio chosen by $u(\cdot)$ such that

$$E[\tilde{r}] < r_f. \tag{4.14.1}$$

Note that

$$
\begin{aligned}
E[u(W_0(1+\tilde{r}))] &\leq u(E[W_0(1+\tilde{r})]) \\
&< u(W_0(1+r_f)),
\end{aligned}
\tag{4.14.2}
$$

where the first inequality follows from the Jensen's inequality and the second inequality follows from the strict monotonicity of u. Relation (4.14.2) contradicts the hypothesis that the individual chooses to hold the portfolio with a random rate of return $\tilde{r}$.

Given that (4.12.2) holds and risky assets are in strictly positive supply, we know from Section 4.13 that $r_f \neq A/C$. Suppose that $r_f > A/C$. Then no investor holds a strictly positive amount of the market portfolio. This is inconsistent with market clearing. Thus in equilibrium, it must be the case that $r_f < A/C$ and the risk premium of the market portfolio is strictly positive. In this event, no individuals hold inefficient portfolios and the half line in the standard deviation–expected rate of return space composed of efficient frontier portfolios and the riskless asset is termed the *Capital Market Line* in the literature.

Before we leave this section, we note that in the above proof when there exists a riskless asset, an investor will never choose to hold a portfolio having an expected rate of return strictly less than the riskless rate we only used the fact that an investor can always invest all his money in the riskless asset. Hence the conclusion holds even when borrowing is not allowed. We ask the reader to show in Exercise 4.6 that in such event, when investors choose to hold efficient frontier portfolios and the riskless asset is in strictly positive supply, (4.11.6) and (4.11.7) are valid and $E[\tilde{r}_{zc(m)}] \geq r_f$. That is,

$$E[\tilde{r}_q] = E[\tilde{r}_{zc(m)}] + \beta_{qm}(E[\tilde{r}_m] - E[\tilde{r}_{zc(m)}]) \tag{4.14.3}$$

for any feasible portfolio and

$$E[\tilde{r}_m] - E[\tilde{r}_{zc(m)}] > 0 \quad \text{and} \quad E[\tilde{r}_{zc(m)}] \geq r_f. \tag{4.14.4}$$

We also ask the reader to work out a similar conclusion when the riskless borrowing is allowed at a rate strictly higher than the riskless lending rate in Exercise 4.7. In that case, we have

$$E[\tilde{r}_q] = E[\tilde{r}_{zc(m)}] + \beta_{qm}(E[\tilde{r}_m] - E[\tilde{r}_{zc(m)}]) \tag{4.14.5}$$

for any feasible portfolio and

$$E[\tilde{r}_m] - E[\tilde{r}_{zc(m)}] > 0 \quad \text{and} \quad r_b \geq E[\tilde{r}_{zc(m)}] \geq r_L, \tag{4.14.6}$$

where r_L and r_b denote the riskless lending rate and borrowing rate, respectively. The versions of the Capital Asset Pricing Model of (4.14.3) and (4.14.4) and (4.14.5) and (4.14.6) will be termed the *constrained borrowing versions* of the CAPM. The constrained borrowing versions of the CAPM are the main subjects of discussion in Chapter 10 when econometrics issues in testing the CAPM are discussed.

4.15. In the above analysis, we derived the traditional CAPM and the zero–beta CAPM by way of two fund separation. The risk premiums of risky assets are related to the risk premium of the market portfolio in a linear fashion. In this and the next section, we will discuss two simple situations where we can explicitly write down how the risk premium of the market portfolio is related to investors' optimal portfolio decisions.

First, suppose that there exists a riskless asset with a rate of return r_f and that the rates of return of risky assets are multivariate normally distributed. Let $\tilde{W}_i$ denote the optimally invested random time–1 wealth for individual i. Section 1.18 shows that

$$E[u_i'(\tilde{W}_i)(\tilde{r}_j - r_f)] = 0 \quad \forall i, j, \tag{4.15.1}$$

where

$$\tilde{W}_i = W_0^i \left(1 + r_f + \sum_{j=1}^{N} w_{ij}(\tilde{r}_j - r_f)\right).$$

Using the definition of a covariance, (4.15.1) can be written as

$$E[u_i'(\tilde{W}_i)]E[\tilde{r}_j - r_f] = -\text{Cov}(u_i'(\tilde{W}_i), \tilde{r}_j). \qquad (4.15.2)$$

Note that $\tilde{W}_i$ and $\tilde{r}_j$ are bivariate normally distributed. We will employ the following mathematical result: Let $\tilde{Y}$ and $\tilde{X}$ be bivariate normally distributed. Then we have

$$\text{Cov}(g(\tilde{X}), \tilde{Y}) = E[g'(\tilde{X})]\text{Cov}(\tilde{X}, \tilde{Y}),$$

provided that g is differentiable and satisfies some regularity conditions. This mathematical result is called the Stein's lemma. Assuming that u_i is twice differentiable and applying the Stein's lemma to (4.15.2), we have

$$E[u_i'(\tilde{W}_i)]E[\tilde{r}_j - r_f] = -E[u_i''(\tilde{W}_i)]\text{Cov}(\tilde{W}_i, \tilde{r}_j). \qquad (4.15.3)$$

Defining the i–th investor's *global absolute risk aversion*

$$\theta_i \equiv \frac{-E[u_i''(\tilde{W}_i)]}{E[u_i'(\tilde{W}_i)]},$$

dividing both sides of (4.15.3) by $E[u_i''(\tilde{W}_i)]$, summing across i, and rearranging gives:

$$E[\tilde{r}_j - r_f] = (\sum_{i=1}^{I} \theta_i^{-1})^{-1}\text{Cov}(\tilde{M}, \tilde{r}_j)$$

$$= W_{m0}(\sum_{i=1}^{I} \theta_i^{-1})^{-1}\text{Cov}(\tilde{r}_m, \tilde{r}_j), \qquad (4.15.4)$$

where

$$\tilde{M} \equiv \sum_{i=1}^{I} \tilde{W}_i = W_{m0}(1 + \tilde{r}_m).$$

Note that $I(\sum_{i=1}^{I} \theta_i^{-1})^{-1}$ is the harmonic mean of individuals' global absolute risk aversion. We can interpret $W_{m0}(\sum_{i=1}^{I} \theta_i^{-1})^{-1}$ to be the *aggregate relative risk aversion* of the economy in equilibrium.

Relation (4.15.4) implies that

$$E[\tilde{r}_m - r_f] = (\sum_{i=1}^{I} \theta_i^{-1})^{-1} W_{m0} \text{Var}(\tilde{r}_m); \qquad (4.15.5)$$

that is, the risk premium on the market portfolio is proportional to the aggregate relative risk aversion of the economy. Thus, the risk premium of the market portfolio is strictly positive when investors' utility functions are increasing and strictly concave. For example, when investors' utility functions are negative exponential, $u_i(z) = -\frac{1}{a_i} \exp\{-a_i z\}$, with $a_i > 0$,

$$(\sum_{i=1}^{I} \theta_i^{-1})^{-1} = (\sum_{i=1}^{I} a_i^{-1})^{-1},$$

a strictly positive constant.

Substituting (4.15.4) into (4.15.3) gives the familiar CAPM relation (4.13.1). However, in the present situation, we have a relation for the market risk premium (4.15.5).

4.16. Now assume instead that utility functions are quadratic:

$$u_i(z) = a_i z - \frac{b_i}{2} z^2 \qquad a_i, b_i > 0. \qquad (4.16.1)$$

Note that individual i reaches satiation when $z \geq a_i/b_i$. We therefore assume that the rates of return of assets and the initial wealth are such that satiation will not be attained.

Substituting (4.16.1) into (4.15.1) and rearranging gives

$$\left(\frac{a_i}{b_i} - E[\tilde{W}_i]\right) E[\tilde{r}_j - r_f] = \text{Cov}(\tilde{W}_i, \tilde{r}_j), \qquad (4.16.2)$$

where we have used the definition of covariance. Note that $(\frac{a_i}{b_i} - E[\tilde{W}_i])^{-1}$ is equal to θ_i, the global risk aversion of investor i with a quadratic utility function. This result does not require the assumption that asset returns are multivariate normally distributed. Summing (4.16.2) over i gives

$$E[\tilde{r}_j - r_f] = \left(\sum_{i=1}^{I} \frac{a_i}{b_i} - E[\tilde{M}]\right)^{-1} W_{m0} \text{Cov}(\tilde{r}_m, \tilde{r}_j), \qquad (4.16.3)$$

where

$$\tilde{M} \equiv \sum_{i=1}^{I} \tilde{W}_i.$$

Relation (4.16.3) implies that

$$E[\tilde{r}_m - r_f] = \left(\sum_{i=1}^{I} \frac{a_i}{b_i} - E[\tilde{M}] \right)^{-1} W_{m0} \text{Var}(\tilde{r}_m). \qquad (4.16.4)$$

Substituting (4.16.4) into (4.16.3) gives the CAPM relation (4.13.1).

4.17. In the context of the CAPM, a risky asset's beta with respect to the market portfolio is a sufficient statistic for its contribution to the the riskiness of an individual's portfolio. Risky assets whose payoffs are positively correlated with those of the market portfolio have positive risk premiums. In such event, the higher the asset beta, the higher the risk premium. The intuition of this relationship can be understood as follows. Consider two assets A and B. Asset A and asset B have the same expected time–1 payoffs. However, asset A's payoffs are positively correlated with the payoffs of the market portfolio, while asset B's payoffs are negatively correlated with that of the market portfolio. That is, asset A has high payoffs when the economy is in relatively prosperous states, while asset B has high payoffs when the economy is in relatively poor states. One unit of the payoff is more valuable in a relatively poor state than in a relative abundant state. Therefore, asset B is more desirable, and its time–0 price will be higher than that of asset A. Since assets A and B have the same expected payoffs, the expected rate of return of asset A will be higher than that for asset B. In other words, asset A's payoff structure is not as attractive as that of asset B. Therefore, it has to yield a higher expected rate of return than asset B to make itself as attractive as asset B in equilibrium.

4.18. Recall from previous analyses that if the rates of return of risky assets satisfy (4.12.1) and (4.12.2), two fund separation implies that there exists a linear relation among expected returns of assets. In equilibrium, the coefficients of the linear relation are identified to be related to the *beta*'s of asset returns with respect to the return on the market portfolio.

Relations (4.12.1) and (4.12.2) may be loosely interpreted as saying that the rate of return on an risky asset is *generated* by a "one factor model" plus a random noise whose conditional expectation given the factor is identically zero. Note however that the residuals from this "one factor model" are not uncorrelated across states. Also, the factor happens to be the rate of return on a portfolio. In such event, the set of portfolios that will be chosen by some risk averse investor is *spanned* by the riskless asset and the factor. We have identified this set to be just the portfolio frontier!

Suppose that (4.12.2) does not hold, but, instead, the $\tilde{\epsilon}_{je}$'s are uncorrelated. Intuitively, the above mentioned *spanning* property may still be true approximately, as long as there are a large number of assets such that the $\tilde{\epsilon}_{ej}$'s can be *diversified away* by forming well–diversified portfolios. Then it may follow that a linear relation among expected asset returns will be valid approximately. The following analyses formalize this intuition and show that a linear relation among expected asset returns will hold for *most* of the assets approximately if there is no arbitrage opportunity (in the limit) and there are a large number of assets.

4.19. We consider a sequence of economies with increasing numbers of assets. In the n–th economy, there are n risky assets and a riskless asset. The rates of return on risky assets are generated by a K–factor model:

$$\tilde{r}_j^n = a_j^n + \sum_{k=1}^{K} \beta_{jk}^n \tilde{\delta}_k^n + \tilde{\epsilon}_j^n, \qquad j = 1, 2, \ldots, n, \qquad (4.19.1)$$

where

$$E[\tilde{\epsilon}_j^n] = 0, \quad j = 1, 2, \ldots, n, \qquad (4.19.2)$$
$$E[\tilde{\epsilon}_j^n \tilde{\epsilon}_l^n] = 0 \quad \text{if } l \neq j, \qquad (4.19.3)$$

and

$$\sigma^2(\tilde{\epsilon}_j^n) \leq \bar{\sigma}^2 \quad j = 1, 2, \ldots, n, \qquad (4.19.4)$$

where $\bar{\sigma}^2$ is a fixed strictly positive real number and β^n_{jk} are real numbers. We also assume that the $\tilde{\delta}^n_k$'s are rates of return on portfolios. Using matrix notation, we can write (4.19.1) as

$$\tilde{\mathbf{r}}^n = \mathbf{a}^n + \mathbf{B}^n \tilde{\boldsymbol{\delta}}^n + \tilde{\boldsymbol{\epsilon}}^n, \tag{4.19.5}$$

where $\mathbf{a}^n$ is an $N \times 1$ vector of a^n_j's, $\mathbf{B}^n$ is an $n \times K$ matrix whose elements are β^n_{jk}, $j = 1, 2, ..., n$, $k = 1, 2, ..., K$, and $\tilde{\boldsymbol{\delta}}^n$ is a K-vector of $\tilde{\delta}^n_k$'s.

To avoid degenerate cases, we will only be interested in economies with more than K risky assets. That is, an implicit assumption to be made henceforth is that $n > K$.

4.20. We first note that if

$$\tilde{\epsilon}^n_j \equiv 0, \quad \forall j \tag{4.20.1}$$

then there exists an exact linear relation among expected rates of return on assets in the n-th economy, if one cannot create something out of nothing. This follows since the returns on risky assets are completely spanned by the K factors (portfolios) and the riskless asset.

Formally, consider a portfolio of the K factors and the riskless asset, $\mathbf{y}^n_j$, with

$$y^n_{j0} = 1 - \sum_{k=1}^{K} \beta^n_{jk},$$
$$y^n_{jk} = \beta^n_{jk}, \quad k = 1, 2, \ldots, K,$$

where y^n_{j0} is the proportion invested in the riskless asset and y^n_{jk} is the proportion invested in the k-th factor. The rate of return on this portfolio is

$$(1 - \sum_{k=1}^{K} \beta^n_{jk}) r_f + \sum_{k=1}^{K} \beta^n_{jk} \tilde{\delta}^n_k.$$

Note that the factor components of the rate of return on $\mathbf{y}^n_j$ replicate those of asset j.

We claim that a_j^n must be equal to $(1 - \sum_{k=1}^{K} \beta_{jk}^n)r_f$. We shall show that if this is not the case, something can be created out of nothing. Suppose that

$$a_j^n < (1 - \sum_{k=1}^{K} \beta_{jk}^n)r_f.$$

We establish a portfolio by investing one dollar in $\mathbf{y}_j^n$ and shorting one dollar's worth of security j. This portfolio costs nothing. Its rate of return, however, is

$$(1 - \sum_{k=1}^{K} \beta_{jk}^n)r_f - a_j^n > 0,$$

which is riskless and strictly positive. Hence something has been created out of nothing, or there exists a *free lunch*.

Barring free lunches and reversing the above arguments for the case $a_j^n > (1 - \sum_{k=1}^{K} \beta_{jk}^n)r_f$, we thus have

$$a_j^n = (1 - \sum_{k=1}^{K} \beta_{jk}^n)r_f. \tag{4.20.2}$$

Substituting (4.20.2) into (4.19.5) and taking expectations, we get

$$E[\tilde{\mathbf{r}}^n] = \mathbf{B}^n E[\tilde{\delta}^n - r_f \mathbf{1}^n], \tag{4.20.3}$$

where $\mathbf{1}^n$ is an $n \times 1$ vector of ones. That is, there exists an exact linear relation among expected asset returns.

4.21. When the $\tilde{\epsilon}_j^n$'s are not zeros, the story is a little complicated. Formally, in economy n, a portfolio of the n risky assets and the riskless asset is an arbitrage portfolio if it costs nothing. An *arbitrage opportunity* (in the limit) is a sequence of arbitrage portfolios whose expected rates of return are bounded below away from zero, while their variances converge to zero.

Roughly, an arbitrage opportunity is a costless portfolio in an economy with a large number of assets such that its expected rate of return is bounded below away from zero while its variance is negligible. That is, it is *almost* a free lunch.

We wish to show that if there is no arbitrage opportunity, then a linear relation among expected asset returns will hold *approximately* for *most* of the assets in a large economy.

We first claim that,

$$a_j^n \approx (1 - \sum_{k=1}^{K} \beta_{jk}^n) r_f \qquad (4.21.1)$$

for most of the asset in large economies, where $\approx$ denotes *approximately equal to*. To see this, we fix $\epsilon > 0$, however small. Let $N(n)$ be the number of assets in the n–th economy such that the absolute value of the difference between the two sides of (4.21.1) is greater than ϵ. Without loss of generality, assume that

$$|a_j^n - (1 - \sum_{k=1}^{K} \beta_{jk}^n) r_f| \geq \epsilon, \quad j = 1, 2, \ldots, N(n). \qquad (4.21.2)$$

If we can show that there exists $\bar{N} < \infty$ such that $N(n) \leq \bar{N}$ for all n, we are done. This follows since there will be at most $\bar{N}$ assets that satisfy (4.21.2) for arbitrarily large n and ϵ can be arbitrarily small. We shall proceed by contraposition.

Suppose that there does not exist a finite $\bar{N}$ such that $N(n) \leq \bar{N}$ for all n. Then there must exist a subsequence of $\{n = K + 2, K + 3, \ldots, \}$, denoted by, $\{n_l\}$, such that $N(n_l) \to \infty$ as $n_l \to \infty$.

We construct a sequence of arbitrage portfolios as follows. First, construct $N(n_l)$ arbitrage portfolios that have no *factor risk* as we did in Section 4.20 for risky assets $j = 1, 2, \ldots, N(n_l)$ in economy n_l. The rate of return for the j–th arbitrage portfolio is

$$|a_j^{n_l} - (1 - \sum_{k=1}^{K} \beta_{jk}^{n_l}) r_f| + s_j^{n_l} \tilde{\epsilon}_j^{n_l}, \qquad (4.21.3)$$

where

$$s_j^{n_l} = \begin{cases} +1 & \text{if } a_j^{n_l} - (1 - \sum_{k=1}^{K} \beta_{jk}^{n_l}) > 0; \\ -1 & \text{if } a_j^{n_l} - (1 - \sum_{k=1}^{K} \beta_{jk}^{n_l}) < 0. \end{cases}$$

Next, form a portfolio of these arbitrage portfolios with a constant weight, $1/N(n_l)$, on each. The resulting portfolio is still an arbitrage portfolio with an expected rate of return

$$\frac{1}{N(n_l)} \sum_{j=1}^{N(n_l)} |a_j^{n_l} - (1 - \sum_{k=1}^{K} \beta_{jk}^{n_l}) r_f| \geq \epsilon > 0, \qquad (4.21.4)$$

and a variance

$$\frac{1}{N^2(n_l)} \sum_{j=1}^{N(n_l)} \sigma^2(\tilde{\epsilon}_j^{n_l}) \leq \frac{\bar{\sigma}^2}{N(n_l)}, \qquad (4.21.5)$$

where we have used (4.19.2), (4.19.3), and (4.19.4).

Since $N(n_l) \to \infty$ as $l \to \infty$, the variances of the sequence of arbitrage portfolios converge to zero, while their expected rates of return are bounded below away from zero by ϵ. Thus there exists an arbitrage opportunity, a contradiction. We hence conclude that there must exists a finite $\bar{N}$ such that $N(n) \leq \bar{N}$ for all n.

4.22. Now using the fact proven above that for a given $\epsilon > 0$, however small, there exist at most $\bar{N}$ risky assets such that

$$|a_j^{n_l} - (1 - \sum_{k=1}^{K} \beta_{jk}^{n_l}) r_f| \geq \epsilon,$$

and (4.19.1), we know

$$|E[\tilde{r}_j^n] - r_f - \sum_{k=1}^{K} \beta_{jk}^n (E[\tilde{\delta}_k^n] - r_f)| \leq \epsilon$$

for all but at most $\bar{N}$ risky assets in any economy. Thus, for economies with the number of assets much larger than $\bar{N}$, a linear relation among expected asset returns holds approximately for most of the assets. This relation is the *Arbitrage Pricing Theory (APT)* originated by Ross (1976).

4.23. In the above derivation of the APT, a linear relation among the expected rates of return on the risky assets holds approximately for most of the assets when the economy is large. On the other hand, for any given asset, the deviation of its expected rate of return from the APT relation might be very large. For the APT to make predictions in an economy with a finite number of assets, we would like to bound the deviation from the APT linear relation for any asset. To achieve this goal, we will make assumptions on the structure of the returns on risky assets that are somewhat different than those used in the above derivation of APT. Equilibrium rather than arbitrage arguments will be used in the following derivation. The resulting relationship among risky assets is sometimes called *equilibrium APT*.

Suppose that there are N risky assets in the economy, indexed by $j = 1, 2, \ldots, N$, and a riskless asset. These risky assets are in strictly positive supply. The rate of return on the riskless asset is r_f, and the rates of return on risky assets are generated by a K–factor model like (4.19.1):

$$\tilde{r}_j = a_j + \sum_{k=1}^{K} \beta_{jk}\tilde{\delta}_k + \tilde{\epsilon}_j, \quad j = 1, 2, \ldots, N, \tag{4.23.1}$$

with

$$E[\tilde{\epsilon}_j] = 0 \quad \text{and} \quad \tilde{\epsilon}_j \geq -1. \tag{4.23.2}$$

We also assume that the random variables

$$(\tilde{\epsilon}_1, \ldots, \tilde{\epsilon}_N, \tilde{\delta}_1, \ldots, \tilde{\delta}_K)$$

are independent and that $\tilde{\delta}_k$ are rates of return on portfolios.

Note that in Section 4.19 we only required that $\tilde{\epsilon}_j$ and $\tilde{\epsilon}_l$ be uncorrelated if $j \neq l$. Here a stronger independence assumption is used. Also, since we are not considering a sequence of economies, we do not need an assumption like (4.19.4).

Agents in the economy have utility functions that are increasing, strictly concave, and three times continuously differentiable, We also assume that agents' Arrow–Pratt measure of absolute risk aversion $A_i(z) \equiv -u_i''(z)/u_i'(z)$ is bounded from above by a constant $\bar{A}$ for all i and that $u_i''' \geq 0$.

Recall from Section 4.20 that, when $\tilde{\epsilon}_j \equiv 0$,

$$a_j = \left(1 - \sum_{k=1}^{K} \beta_{jk}\right) r_f;$$

or equivalently,

$$E[\tilde{r}_j] = r_f + \sum_{k=1}^{K} \beta_{jk}(E[\tilde{\delta}_k] - r_f). \qquad (4.23.3)$$

Our purpose here is to bound the deviation of $E[\tilde{r}_j]$ from the right-hand side of (4.23.3), in market equilibrium, when $\tilde{\epsilon}_j$ is not identically zero.

4.24. Consider a portfolio of the K factors and the riskless asset having a rate of return

$$r_f + \sum_{k=1}^{K} \beta_{jk}(\tilde{\delta}_k - r_f).$$

This portfolio is constructed in the same way as Section 4.20. Next form an arbitrage portfolio by investing one dollar in the above portfolio and shorting one dollar's worth of risky asset j. This arbitrage portfolio has a rate of return

$$\tilde{r} \equiv \left(1 - \sum_{k=1}^{K} \beta_{jk}\right) r_f - a_j - \tilde{\epsilon}_j. \qquad (4.24.1)$$

Let W_{i0} be individual i's initial wealth, and let $\tilde{W}_i$ be individual i's time–1 random wealth. Then $\alpha = 0$ is the unique solution to the following problem:

$$\max_{\alpha} E[u_i(\tilde{W}_i + \alpha \tilde{r})],$$

as $\tilde{W}_i + \alpha \tilde{r}$ is a feasible random wealth for individual i. The first order necessary condition for $\alpha = 0$ to be an optimum is

$$E[u_i'(\tilde{W}_i)\tilde{r}] = 0.$$

Using the definition of covariance, the fact that $E[\tilde{\epsilon}_j] = 0$, and (4.24.1), the above relation can be written as

$$
\begin{aligned}
(1 - \sum_{k=1}^{K} \beta_{jk})r_f - a_j &= \frac{E[u_i'(\tilde{W}_i)\tilde{\epsilon}_j]}{E[u_i'(\tilde{W}_i)]} \\
&= \frac{\text{Cov}(u_i'(\tilde{W}_i), \tilde{\epsilon}_j)}{E[u_i'(\tilde{W}_i)]}.
\end{aligned}
\qquad (4.24.2)
$$

Now we claim that, for all j such that $\tilde{\epsilon}_j \neq 0$,

$$
(1 - \sum_{k=1}^{K} \beta_{jk})r_f - a_j < 0. \qquad (4.24.3)
$$

To see this, we note that risky assets are in strictly positive supply. Therefore, in equilibrium, a risky asset must be held by some individual. Suppose risky asset j with $\tilde{\epsilon}_j \neq 0$ is held in a strictly positive amount in equilibrium by individual i. By the strict concavity of u_i and the assumption that $\tilde{\epsilon}_j$ is independent of all the other random variables, we know that

$$
\text{Cov}(u_i'(\tilde{W}_i), \tilde{\epsilon}_j) < 0. \qquad (4.24.4)
$$

Then (4.24.3) holds for j by the fact that $u_i' > 0$. The above arguments can be applied to all j such that $\tilde{\epsilon}_j \neq 0$. Thus we have that (4.24.3) holds for all such j's.

As a consequence of the above analysis, we can also conclude that if $\tilde{\epsilon}_j \neq 0$, then asset j is held in a strictly positive amount by all individuals. To see this, we note that (4.24.2) holds for all assets and all individuals. If $\tilde{\epsilon}_j \neq 0$, we must have (4.24.3), which in turn implies that (4.24.4) must hold for all i. This is possible only if every individual holds a strictly positive amount of asset j, as $\tilde{\epsilon}_j$ is independent of all the other random variables by assumption.

4.25. Now fix risky asset j with $\tilde{\epsilon}_j \neq 0$. Let α_{ij} be the dollar amount invested in risky asset j by individual i. From Section 4.24, we know that $\alpha_{ij} > 0$. Define

$$
\tilde{W}_i^* \equiv \tilde{W}_i - \alpha_{ij}\tilde{\epsilon}_j.
$$

The Lagrange remainder form of Taylor's expansion gives

$$
\begin{aligned}
&E[u_i'(\tilde{W}_i)\tilde{\epsilon}_j] \\
&= E[u_i'(\tilde{W}_i^*)\tilde{\epsilon}_j] + \alpha_{ij}E[u_i''(\tilde{\xi})\tilde{\epsilon}_j^2] \\
&= E[u_i'(\tilde{W}_i^*)]E[\tilde{\epsilon}_j] + \alpha_{ij}E[u_i''(\tilde{\xi})\tilde{\epsilon}_j^2] \\
&= \alpha_{ij}E[u_i''(\tilde{\xi})\tilde{\epsilon}_j^2],
\end{aligned}
\tag{4.25.1}
$$

where the second equality follows from the assumption that $\tilde{\epsilon}_j$ and all the other random variables are independent and where $\tilde{\xi}$ is a random variable whose value lies between $\tilde{W}_i$ and $\tilde{W}_i^*$. By the assumption that $\tilde{\epsilon}_j \geq -1$, we know

$$
\tilde{\xi} \geq \tilde{W}_i^* - \alpha_{ij}.
$$

Therefore,

$$
|E[u_i''(\tilde{\xi})\tilde{\epsilon}_j^2]| \leq E[\sup_{z \geq \tilde{W}_i^* - \alpha_{ij}} |u_i''(z)|\tilde{\epsilon}_j^2].
\tag{4.25.2}
$$

We claim that

$$
\sup_{z \geq \tilde{W}_i^* - \alpha_{ij}} |u_i''(z)| \leq u_i'(\tilde{W}_i^*)\bar{A}e^{\bar{A}\alpha_{ij}}.
\tag{4.25.3}
$$

To see this, we first note that since $-u_i''(z)/u_i'(z) \leq \bar{A}$,

$$
\begin{aligned}
&\sup_{z \geq \tilde{W}_i^* - \alpha_{ij}} |u_i''(z)| \\
&\leq \bar{A} \sup_{z \geq \tilde{W}_i^* - \alpha_{ij}} u_i'(z) \leq \bar{A}u_i'(\tilde{W}_i^* - \alpha_{ij}),
\end{aligned}
\tag{4.25.4}
$$

where the second inequality follows from the concavity of u_i. Next, we observe that

$$
\begin{aligned}
\ln(u_i'(\tilde{W}_i^* - \alpha_{ij})) &= \ln u_i'(\tilde{W}_i^*) - \int_{\tilde{W}_i^* - \alpha_{ij}}^{\tilde{W}_i^*} u_i''(z)/u_i'(z)dz \\
&\leq \ln u_i'(\tilde{W}_i^*) + \int_{\tilde{W}_i^* - \alpha_{ij}}^{\tilde{W}_i^*} \bar{A}dz \\
&= \ln u_i'(\tilde{W}_i^*) + \bar{A}\alpha_{ij}.
\end{aligned}
$$

Therefore,

$$u_i'(\tilde{W}_i^* - \alpha_{ij}) \leq u_i'(\tilde{W}_i^*)e^{\bar{A}\alpha_{ij}}. \tag{4.25.5}$$

Relations (4.25.4) and (4.25.5) imply (4.25.3).

Now substituting (4.25.3) into (4.25.2) gives

$$\begin{aligned}
|E[u_i''(\tilde{\xi})\tilde{\epsilon}_j^2]| &\leq \bar{A}e^{\bar{A}\alpha_{ij}}E[u_i'(\tilde{W}_i^*)\tilde{\epsilon}_j^2] \\
&\leq \bar{A}e^{\bar{A}\alpha_{ij}}E[u_i'(\tilde{W}_i^*)]\mathrm{Var}(\tilde{\epsilon}_j).
\end{aligned} \tag{4.25.6}$$

Note also that, since $u_i''' \geq 0$, by the law of iterative expectations and the conditional Jensen's inequality, we have

$$\begin{aligned}
E[u_i'(\tilde{W}_i)] &= E[u_i'(\tilde{W}_i^* + \alpha_{ij}\tilde{\epsilon}_j)] \\
&= E[E[u_i'(\tilde{W}_i^* + \alpha_{ij}\tilde{\epsilon}_j)|\tilde{W}_i^*] \\
&\geq E[u_i'(\tilde{W}_i^*)].
\end{aligned} \tag{4.25.7}$$

Finally, substituting (4.25.1), (4.25.6), and (4.25.7) into (4.24.2) gives

$$|a_j - (1 - \sum_{k=1}^{K}\beta_{jk})r_f| \leq \bar{A}e^{\bar{A}\alpha_{ij}}\mathrm{Var}(\tilde{\epsilon}_j)\,\alpha_{ij};$$

or equivalently,

$$|E[\tilde{r}_j] - r_f - \sum_{k=1}^{K}\beta_{jk}(E[\tilde{\delta}_k] - r_f)| \leq \bar{A}e^{\bar{A}\alpha_{ij}}\mathrm{Var}(\tilde{\epsilon}_j)\alpha_{ij}. \tag{4.25.8}$$

Let the total market value of asset j be denoted by S_j. We claim that in equilibrium there exists an i such that $\alpha_{ij} \leq S_j/I$, where I is the number of individuals in the economy. Suppose that this is not true, that is $\alpha_{ij} > S_j/I$ for all i. Then we must have

$$S_j = \sum_{i=1}^{I}\alpha_{ij} > S_j$$

a contradiction. Since (4.25.8) holds for all i, we thus have

$$|E[\tilde{r}_j] - r_f - \sum_{k=1}^{K}\beta_{jk}(E[\tilde{\delta}_k] - r_f)| \leq \bar{A}e^{\bar{A}S_j/I}\mathrm{Var}(\tilde{\epsilon}_j)\,S_j/I. \tag{4.25.9}$$

Relation (4.25.9) gives an explicit bound of the deviation of $E[\tilde{r}_j]$ from the APT relation. The bound is small when S_j/I, $\bar{A}$, or $\text{Var}(\tilde{\epsilon}_j)$ is small, *ceteris paribus*. This bound can be improved by tightening the lower bound of $\tilde{\epsilon}_j$, which readers are asked to do in Exercise 4.9.

Exercises

4.1. Derive the zero–beta CAPM under the assumption that asset returns are multivariate normally distributed. Also derive the zero–beta CAPM under the assumption that investors' utility functions are quadratic.

4.2. Let the random time–1 payoff of a risky security be $\tilde{y}$, and let S_y be its time 0 equilibrium price. Suppose that the CAPM holds and let the security's beta be denoted by β_{ym}. Show that

$$S_y = \frac{E[\tilde{y}]}{1 + r_f + \beta_{ym}(E[\tilde{r}_m] - r_f)}$$
$$= \frac{E[\tilde{y}] - \phi^* \rho_{ym}\sigma(\tilde{y})}{1 + r_f},$$

where

$$\phi^* \equiv \frac{E[\tilde{r}_m] - r_f}{\sigma(\tilde{r}_m)}$$

and

$$\rho_{ym} = \frac{\text{Cov}(\tilde{y}, \tilde{r}_m)}{\sigma(\tilde{y})\sigma(\tilde{r}_m)}.$$

4.3. Suppose that the CAPM holds. Let $\tilde{y}$ and $\tilde{z}$ be the random time 1 payoffs of two securities with time 0 prices S_y and S_z, respectively. Show that the equilibrium price for a security having a time 1 payoff $\tilde{y} + \tilde{z}$ is equal to $S_y + S_z$.

4.4. Consider an economy with N risky assets having independent and identically distributed rates of return. Show that there is one fund separation.

4.5. Suppose that there are five state of the nature denoted by ω_n $n = 1, 2, \ldots, 5$, each of which is of equal probability. Consider two risky assets with rates of returns $\tilde{r}_A$ and $\tilde{r}_B$ as follows:

state	ω_1	ω_2	ω_3	ω_4	ω_5
$\tilde{r}_A$	0.5	0.5	0.7	0.7	0.7
$\tilde{r}_B$	0.9	0.8	0.4	0.3	0.7

Suppose that assets A and B are the only two assets in the economy. Do we have one fund separation? Explain your answer in detail. If your answer is no, how could the numbers in the above table be rearranged to get one fund separation?

4.6. Suppose that there is a riskless asset in strictly positive supply and investors prefer to hold efficient frontier portfolios. Borrowing at the riskless rate r_f is prohibited. Show that (4.11.6) and (4.11.7) hold and $E[\tilde{r}_{zc(m)}] \geq r_f$.

4.7. Suppose that investors in the economy would like to hold efficient frontier portfolios and that the riskless borrowing rate is strictly higher than the riskless lending rate, that is $r_b > r_L$. Describe the viable positions of r_b, r_L, and $E[\tilde{r}_{mvp}]$ in equilibrium. Show that (4.11.6) and (4.11.7) hold and $r_b \geq E[\tilde{r}_{zc(m)}] \geq r_L$.

4.8. Let $K = 1$ in (4.23.1). Under the independence assumption made there, does two fund separation exist?

4.9. In the context of Sections 4.23–4.25, assume instead that $\tilde{\epsilon}_j \geq -1/S_j$, where S_j denotes the total market value of asset j. Show that

$$|E[\tilde{r}_j] - r_f - \sum_{k=1}^{K} \beta_{jk}(E[\tilde{\delta}_k] - r_f)| \leq \bar{A}e^{\bar{A}/I}\text{Var}(\tilde{\epsilon}_j)\,S_j/I.$$

Remarks. For discussions on K–fund separation in general see Ross (1978). Our treatment of two fund separation is taken from Litzenberger and Ramaswamy (1979). Note that (4.3.3) is in general weaker than

$$E[\tilde{\epsilon}_{qp}|\tilde{r}_p, \tilde{r}_{zc(p)}] = 0.$$

Nielsen (1986) has shown that they are equivalent under certain regularity conditions. For the existence of a general equilibrium of the CAPM sort, we refer readers to Nielsen (1985). The discussion in Section 4.14 is adapted from Merton (1982). For a derivation of the

Stein's lemma and its original application to finance, see Rubinstein (1976).

The derivation of the arbitrage pricing relation is different from Ross (1976). We made a simplifying assumption that the factors themselves are portfolios. Also, our definition for an arbitrage opportunity is slightly weaker. Huberman (1983) has a very nice proof of the APT when factors are not portfolios, to which we refer interested readers. For more recent developments of the APT, see Chamberlain and Rothschild (1983), Chamberlain (1983), and Reisman (1987a, 1987b, 1987c). Connor (1984) is the first to discuss APT relation using equilibrium arguments. The discussions on the explicit bound of the pricing deviation in finite economies are a combination of Dybvig (1983) and Grinblatt and Titman (1983). For a review of recent developments of APT, see Connor (1987).

References

Black, F. 1972. Capital market equilibrium with restricted borrowing. *Journal of Business* **45**:444–454.

Chamberlain, G. 1983. Funds, factors, and diversification in arbitrage pricing models. *Econometrica* **50**:1305–1324.

Chamberlain, G., and M. Rothschild. 1983. Arbitrage, factor structure, and mean–variance analysis on large asset markets. *Econometrica* **50**:1281–1304.

Connor, G. 1984. A unified beta pricing theory. *Journal of Economic Theory* **34**:13–31.

Connor, G. 1987. Notes on the arbitrage pricing theory. In *Frontiers of Financial Theory*. Edited by G. Constantinides and S. Bhattacharya. Rowman and Littlefield. Totowa, New Jersey.

Dybvig, P. 1983. An explicit bound on individual assets' deviations from APT pricing in a finite economy. *Journal of Financial Economics* **12**:483–496.

Grinblatt, M., and S. Titman. 1983. Factor pricing in a finite economy. *Journal of Financial Economics* **12**:497–507.

Huberman, G. 1983. A simplified approach to arbitrage pricing theory. *Journal of Economic Theory* **28**:1983–1991.

Lintner, J. 1965. The valuation of risk assets and the selection of risky investments in stock portfolios and capital budgets. *Review of Economics and Statistics* **47**:13–37.

Lintner, J. 1969. The aggregation of investor's diverse judgements and preferences in purely competitive markets. *Journal of Financial and Quantitative Analysis* **4**:346–382.

Litzenberger, R., and K. Ramaswamy. 1979. On distributional restrictions for two fund separation. *TIMS Studies in the Management Science* **11**:99–107.

Merton, R. 1982. On the microeconomic theory of investment under uncertainty. In *Handbook of Mathematical Economics, Vol. II*:601–669. Edited by K. Arrow and M. Intriligator.

Mossin, J. 1966. Equilibrium in a capital asset market. *Econometrica* **35**:768–783.

Nielsen, L. 1985. Risk–taking and capital market equilibrium, Unpublished Ph.D. thesis, Harvard University.

Nielsen, L. 1986. Mutual fund separation, factor structure and robustness, unpublished manuscript, Department of Economics, University of Texas at Austin.

Reisman, H. 1987a. A general approach to the arbitrage pricing theory. Mimeo. Department of Finance, University of Minnesota.

Reisman, H. 1987b. The arbitrage pricing theory with conditional information. Mimeo. Department of Finance, University of Minnesota.

Reisman, H. 1987c. Intertemporal arbitrage pricing theory. Mimeo. Department of Finance, University of Minnesota.

Ross, S. 1976. Arbitrage theory of capital asset pricing. *Journal of Economic Theory* **13**:341–360.

Ross, S. 1978. Mutual fund separation in financial theory: The separation distributions. *Journal of Economic Theory* **17**:254–286.

Rubinstein, M. 1974. An aggregation theorem for securities markets. *Journal of Financial Economics* **1**:225–244.

Sharpe, W. 1964. Capital asset prices: A theory of capital market equilibrium under conditions of risk. *Journal of Finance* **19**:425–442.

CHAPTER 5
ALLOCATIVE EFFICIENCY
AND THE VALUATION OF
STATE CONTINGENT SECURITIES

5.1. In Chapter 4, uncertainty in the economy was characterized by distributions of returns on assets. However, it was noted in
Chapter 1 that the primitive source of uncertainty is the uncertain
states of nature, the collection of which is denoted by Ω with generic
elements ω. Recall that a state of nature is a complete description
of a possible realization of the exogenous uncertain environment.

Very generally, an individual's primitive objects of preference
are consumption in different states of nature. A *state contingent
consumption claim* is a security that pays one unit of the consumption good when one particular state of the world occurs and nothing
otherwise. A state contingent claim is an *elementary claim*. Existing assets, however, may be viewed as complex bundles of elementary
claims. For example, a riskless asset is a bundle of one of each state
contingent claim. In a pure exchange single good economy, the aggregate endowment of the consumption commodity is also a complex
bundle of elementary claims. The first part of this chapter examines

the role of financial markets in allocating resources among individuals
and the types of securities needed to achieve an efficient allocation.

In allocationally efficient financial markets, security prices may
be described in a simple way. We will show that when the allocation of state contingent claims is efficient and individuals have time–
additive state–independent utility functions, prices in the economy
are determined as if there were a single individual in the economy
endowed with the aggregate endowment. This *representative agent*
has a time–additive state–independent utility function. The utility
function of the representative agent will in general depend upon the
distribution of the initial wealth of individuals. As a consequence,
the prices in the economy will in general depend on the distribution
of the initial wealth among individuals. This chapter also examines
the necessary and sufficient conditions on individuals' utility functions for the prices in the economy to be determined independently
of the distribution of initial wealth. Utility functions that exhibit
this property are said to have the *aggregation property*.

5.2. Consider a two-period pure exchange economy under uncertainty with a single perishable consumption good in both periods.
Individuals choose their consumption for today, say time 0, and state
contingent claims on consumption for tomorrow, say time 1. There
is uncertainty about which state of the world will occur at time 1.
Assume that individuals have utility functions for the consumption
good that are strictly increasing, strictly concave, and differentiable.
Without loss of generality, the single consumption good is used as
the numeraire throughout.

5.3. An allocation of state contingent consumption among in-
dividuals, denoted by $\{(c_{i0}, c_{i\omega}, \omega \in \Omega); i = 1, 2, \ldots, I\}$, is *feasible*
if

$$\sum_{i=1}^{I} c_{i0} = C_0$$

and

$$\sum_{i=1}^{I} c_{i\omega} = C_\omega \quad \forall \omega \in \Omega,$$

where c_{i0} denotes individual i's time–0 consumption allocation, $c_{i\omega}$ denotes individual i's time–1 consumption allocation in state ω, C_0 denotes the aggregate time–0 consumption available, and C_ω denotes the aggregate time–1 consumption available in state ω.

An allocation of state contingent consumption claims is said to be *Pareto optimal* or *Pareto efficient* if it is feasible and if there do not exist other allocations which are feasible and can strictly increase at least one individual's utility without decreasing the utilities of others.

For example, an allocation that gives a single individual all the consumption available and others nothing is a Pareto optimal allocation. This example illustrates that Pareto optimality is a weak criterion and does not provide a framework for addressing many social choice issues.

5.4. From the classical second welfare theorem (see, e.g., Varian (1978)), we know that corresponding to every Pareto optimal allocation, there exist a set of non-negative numbers, $\{\lambda_i\}_{i=1}^{I}$, such that the same allocation can be achieved by a social planner maximizing a linear combination of individuals' utility functions using $\{\lambda_i\}_{i=1}^{I}$ as weights, subject to resource constraints:

$$\max_{\{(c_{i0},c_{i\omega})_{i=1}^{I},\omega\in\Omega\}} \sum_{i=1}^{I} \lambda_i \left[\sum_{\omega\in\Omega} \pi_{i\omega} u_{i\omega}(c_{i0}, c_{i\omega}) \right]$$

$$\text{s.t.} \quad \sum_{i=1}^{I} c_{i\omega} = C_\omega \quad \forall \omega \in \Omega$$

and

$$\sum_{i=1}^{I} c_{i0} = C_0,$$

where $\pi_{i\omega}$ is the i-th individual's subjective probability assessment about the occurrence of state ω and $u_{i\omega}(\cdot,\cdot)$ is the i-th individual's utility function for time–0 consumption and for time–1 state–ω consumption. We will only be interested in Pareto optimal allocations that correspond to strictly positive weightings λ_i, so all the λ_i's to appear are strictly positive.

Forming the Lagrangian gives

$$\max_{\{c_{i0}, c_{i\omega}; \omega \in \Omega\}_{i=1}^I} L = \sum_{i=1}^I \lambda_i \left[\sum_{\omega \in \Omega} \pi_{i\omega} u_{i\omega}(c_{i0}, c_{i\omega}) \right]$$

$$+ \phi_0 \left[C_0 - \sum_{i=1}^I c_{i0} \right] + \sum_{\omega \in \Omega} \phi_\omega \left[C_\omega - \sum_{i=1}^I c_{i\omega} \right].$$

By the assumption that utility functions are strictly concave and the fact that the weights, $\{\lambda_i\}_{i=1}^I$, are strictly positive, the first order conditions for the above programming problem are necessary and sufficient for a global optimum. They are

$$\lambda_i \sum_{\omega \in \Omega} \pi_{i\omega} \partial u_{i\omega}(c_{i0}, c_{i\omega}) / \partial c_{i0} = \phi_0 \quad i = 1, \ldots, I, \tag{5.4.1}$$

$$\lambda_i \pi_{i\omega} \partial u_{i\omega}(c_{i0}, c_{i\omega}) / \partial c_{i\omega} = \phi_\omega \quad \omega \in \Omega \; i = 1, \ldots, I. \tag{5.4.2}$$

$$\sum_{i=1}^I c_{i\omega} = C_\omega \quad \forall \omega \in \Omega \tag{5.4.3}$$

and

$$\sum_{i=1}^I c_{i0} = C_0. \tag{5.4.4}$$

Substituting relation (5.4.2) into relation (5.4.1) for the same individual gives

$$\frac{\pi_{i\omega} \partial u_{i\omega}(c_{i0}, c_{i\omega}) / \partial c_{i\omega}}{\sum_{\omega \in \Omega} \pi_{i\omega} \partial u_{i\omega}(c_{i0}, c_{i\omega}) / \partial c_{i0}} = \frac{\phi_\omega}{\phi_0} \quad \omega \in \Omega \; i = 1, \ldots, I. \tag{5.4.5}$$

It follows from (5.4.5) that a feasible allocation of state contingent consumption is Pareto optimal if and only if, for each state, marginal rates of substitution between present consumption and future state contingent consumption are equal across individuals.

5.5. A Pareto optimal allocation can be attained in a competitive economy if there exist a complete set of state contingent consumption claims. To see this, let ϕ_ω denote the price at time 0 of state contingent claim that pays one unit of consumption at time 1 if and only if state ω is the true state.

An individual's problem is

$$\max_{\{c_{i0}, c_{i\omega}, \omega \in \Omega\}} \sum_{\omega \in \Omega} \pi_{i\omega} u_{i\omega}(c_{i0}, c_{i\omega})$$

$$\text{s.t. } c_{i0} + \sum_{\omega \in \Omega} \phi_\omega c_{i\omega} = e_{i0} + \sum_{\omega \in \Omega} \phi_\omega e_{i\omega},$$

where e_{i0} and $e_{i\omega}$ denote individual i's endowments for time–0 consumption and for time–1 state–ω consumption, respectively. We assume that an individual's endowment is such that his wealth at time 0 is strictly positive.

Forming the Lagrangian gives

$$\max_{\{c_{i0}, c_{i\omega}; \omega \in \Omega\}} L = \sum_{\omega \in \Omega} \pi_{i\omega} u_{i\omega}(c_{i0}, c_{i\omega})$$

$$+ \theta_i \left[e_{i0} - c_{i0} + \sum_{\omega \in \Omega} \phi_\omega (e_{i\omega} - c_{i\omega}) \right].$$

The first order conditions, which are necessary and sufficient for an optimum are

$$\sum_{\omega \in \Omega} \pi_{i\omega} \partial u_{i\omega}(c_{i0}, c_{i\omega}) / \partial c_{i0} = \theta_i, \tag{5.5.1}$$

$$\pi_{i\omega} \partial u_{i\omega}(c_{i0}, c_{i\omega}) / \partial c_{i\omega} = \theta_i \phi_\omega \qquad \forall \omega \in \Omega, \tag{5.5.2}$$

and the budget constraint for which θ_i is a shadow price. Note that $\theta_i > 0$, as an individual's utility functions are strictly increasing.

Now substituting (5.5.1) into (5.5.2), we get

$$\frac{\pi_{i\omega} \partial u_{i\omega}(c_{i0}, c_{i\omega}) / \partial c_{i\omega}}{\sum_{\omega \in \Omega} \pi_{i\omega} \partial u_{i\omega}(c_{i0}, c_{i\omega}) / \partial c_{i0}} = \phi_\omega \qquad \omega \in \Omega. \tag{5.5.3}$$

In market equilibrium, (5.4.3) and (5.4.4) are satisfied. Now set ϕ_0 to be 1 and λ_i to be θ_i^{-1} as in Section 5.4. It follows that an allocation in a competitive economy with a complete set of state contingent claims (and a spot market for time–0 consumption) satisfies (5.4.1)–(5.4.4) and thus is Pareto optimal. Conversely, to achieve a Pareto optimal allocation corresponding to a competitive equilibrium allocation, the utility weight that the social planner assigns to individual i, λ_i, is equal to $\theta_i^{-1} > 0$.

When we have a complete set of state contingent claim markets, we say that the markets are *complete*. We sometimes refer to those elementary claim prices to be *state prices*. For example, ϕ_ω is the state price for state ω.

5.6. In actual securities markets, we do not observe state contingent claims but rather a number of *complex securities* such as common stocks of firms. A complex security is a bundle of state contingent claims. The efficiency of an equilibrium in this case for arbitrary preferences depends on whether or not the number of linearly independent securities equals the number of states.

Suppose that we have an economy with one unit each of N (complex) securities indexed by $j = 1, 2, \ldots, N$. Security j pays off $x_{j\omega}$ units of the consumption good at time 1 in state $\omega \in \Omega$. We will sometimes simply use x_j to denote the random time–1 payoffs of security j. Individuals have utility functions as in Sections 5.4 and 5.5, and their endowments are in the form of securities and time–0 consumption. We assume that individual i is endowed with $\widehat{\alpha}_{ij}$ number of shares of security j and e_{i0} unit of time–0 consumption. An individual buys the time–0 consumption good in the spot commodity market and buys future state contingent consumption through the securities markets. We will henceforth refer to this kind of economy as a *securities markets economy*.

Letting α_{ij} and S_j denote the number of shares of security j held by individual i in equilibrium and the price for security j at time 0, respectively, $\{\alpha_{ij}; j = 1, 2, \ldots, N\}$ is the solution to the following program:

$$\max_{\{c_{i0},\alpha_{ij};j=1,2,\ldots,N\}} \sum_{\omega\in\Omega} \pi_{i\omega} u_{i\omega}\left(c_{i0}, \sum_{j=1}^{N} \alpha_{ij} x_{j\omega}\right)$$

$$(5.6.1)$$

$$\text{s.t.} \quad c_{i0} + \sum_{j} \alpha_{ij} S_j = e_{i0} + \sum_{j=1}^{N} \hat{\alpha}_{ij} S_j.$$

The first order conditions, which are necessary and sufficient for individual i's portfolio problem, are

$$\sum_{\omega\in\Omega} \pi_{i\omega} \frac{\partial u_{i\omega}(c_{i0}, c_{i\omega})/\partial c_{i\omega}}{\sum_{\omega\in\Omega} \pi_{i\omega} \partial u_{i\omega}(c_{i0}, c_{i\omega})/\partial c_{i0}} x_{j\omega} = S_j, \qquad j = 1, \ldots, N,$$

$$(5.6.2)$$

where we have used the fact that

$$c_{i\omega} = \sum_{j=1}^{N} \alpha_{ij} x_{j\omega}.$$

Each individual i will adjust his time–0 consumption and security holdings such that (5.6.2) is valid. This does not, however, indicate that marginal rates of substitution between present consumption and state contingent consumption are identical across individuals as required for a Pareto optimal allocation.

5.7. If the number of linearly independent securities is equal to the number of states of nature, then markets are complete because any state contingent claim can be created by forming portfolios of existing securities. To illustrate this, let $|\Omega|$ denote the number of states of nature. Relation (5.6.2) may be written in matrix notation:

$$\begin{pmatrix} x_{1\omega_1}, \ldots, x_{1\omega_{|\Omega|}} \\ x_{2\omega_1}, \ldots, x_{2\omega_{|\Omega|}} \\ \vdots \\ x_{N\omega_1}, \ldots, x_{N\omega_{|\Omega|}} \end{pmatrix} \begin{pmatrix} \pi_{i\omega_1} \dfrac{\partial u_{i\omega}(c_{i0}, c_{i\omega_1})/\partial c_{i\omega_1}}{\sum_{\omega\in\Omega} \pi_{i\omega} \partial u_{i\omega}(c_{i0}, c_{i\omega})/\partial c_{i0}} \\ \pi_{i\omega_2} \dfrac{\partial u_{i\omega}(c_{i0}, c_{i\omega_2})/\partial c_{i\omega_2}}{\sum_{\omega\in\Omega} \pi_{i\omega} \partial u_{i\omega}(c_{i0}, c_{i\omega})/\partial c_{i0}} \\ \vdots \\ \pi_{i\omega_{|\Omega|}} \dfrac{\partial u_{i\omega}(c_{i0}, c_{i\omega_{|\Omega|}})/\partial c_{i\omega_{|\Omega|}}}{\sum_{\omega\in\Omega} \pi_{i\omega} \partial u_{i\omega}(c_{i0}, c_{i\omega})/\partial c_{i0}} \end{pmatrix} = \begin{pmatrix} S_1 \\ S_2 \\ \vdots \\ S_N \end{pmatrix}.$$

$$(5.7.1)$$

If the number of linearly independent securities is equal to the number of states of nature and we include only linearly independent securities in (5.7.1), then the first matrix on the left-hand-side of relation (5.7.1) is invertible. We can therefore invert it and solve for the ratios of marginal utilities between time–1 state–ω and time–0 consumption. Note that the matrix being inverted and the vector on the right-hand-side of (5.7.1) are both independent of individual indices; therefore:

$$\pi_{i\omega} \frac{\partial u_{i\omega}(c_{i0}, c_{i\omega})/\partial c_{i\omega}}{\sum_{\omega \in \Omega} \pi_{i\omega} \partial u_{i\omega}(c_{i0}, c_{i\omega})/\partial c_{i0}} = m_\omega, \quad i = 1, 2, \ldots, I, \quad (5.7.2)$$

for some constants m_ω, $\omega \in \Omega$. The relations in (5.7.2) are the necessary and sufficient conditions for a feasible allocation to be Pareto optimal. Also, it follows from (5.5.3) that m_ω must be equal to ϕ_ω, the state price for state ω. Moreover, state contingent claims can be created by forming portfolios of the complex securities. For example, the state contingent claim that pays one unit of consumption in the first state ω_1 and nothing otherwise is formed by holding α_j shares of security j with

$$(\alpha_1, \alpha_2, \ldots, \alpha_N) = (1, 0, \ldots, 0) \begin{pmatrix} x_{1\omega_1}, & x_{1\omega_2}, & \cdots & , & x_{1\omega_{|\Omega|}} \\ x_{2\omega_1}, & x_{2\omega_2}, & \cdots & , & x_{2\omega_{|\Omega|}} \\ & & \vdots & & \\ x_{N\omega_1}, & x_{N\omega_2}, & \cdots & , & x_{N\omega_{|\Omega|}} \end{pmatrix}^{-1}.$$

$$(5.7.3)$$

The cost of the above portfolio should just be the state price for state 1, which can be easily verified.

From the previous analyses, it should be clear that securities markets in which the number of linearly independent securities is equal to the number of states are complete markets and a Pareto Optimal allocation of state contingent claims is achieved with individuals trading complex securities.

5.8. A common feature of complete markets economies and securities markets economies is that the values of securities are *additive*. That is, if x_ω, y_ω, and z_ω are state–dependent payoffs of three complex securities with $z_\omega = x_\omega + y_\omega$, then the value of z is equal to the sum of the values of x and y. To see this, we note that when there exists a complete set of state contingent claims, a complex security having payoffs x_ω can be viewed as a portfolio of state contingent claims consisting of x_ω shares of the state contingent claim that pays off in state ω. Thus the market value of that security must be equal to the cost of the portfolio that offers the identical state contingent payoffs, which is

$$\sum_{\omega \in \Omega} \phi_\omega x_\omega. \qquad (5.8.1)$$

If relation (5.8.1) were not satisfied, it would be possible to create something out of nothing, which is inconsistent with an economic equilibrium. For example, if the market value of the security were strictly greater than (5.8.1), an individual could short sell the security and purchase x_ω shares of state contingent claim for state ω, for all $\omega \in \Omega$. The payoff of this strategy is identically zero at time 1, while its cost at time 0 is strictly negative! That is, something has been created from nothing. As a consequence, nonsatiated individuals will take unbounded positions in the strategy, and markets cannot clear.

Relation (5.8.1) implies that security values are additive. That is, if x_ω and z_ω are state–dependent payoffs for two complex securities, then the value for $z_\omega \equiv x_\omega + y_\omega$ is equal to the sum of values for x and z:

$$\sum_{\omega \in \Omega} \phi_\omega y_\omega$$
$$= \sum_{\omega \in \Omega} \phi_\omega x_\omega + \sum_{\omega \in \Omega} \phi_\omega z_\omega.$$

Next consider a securities markets economy. Let x, y, and z be three complex securities traded with $z_\omega = x_\omega + y_\omega$. Relation (5.6.2) implies that the value of z, denoted by S_z, is

$$S_z = \sum_{\omega \in \Omega} \pi_{i\omega} \frac{\partial u_{i\omega}(c_{i0}, c_{i\omega})/\partial c_{i\omega}}{\sum_{\omega \in \Omega} \pi_{i\omega} \partial u_{i\omega}(c_{i0}, c_{i\omega})/\partial c_{i0}} z_\omega$$

$$= \sum_{\omega \in \Omega} \pi_{i\omega} \frac{\partial u_{i\omega}(c_{i0}, c_{i\omega})/\partial c_{i\omega}}{\sum_{\omega \in \Omega} \pi_{i\omega} \partial u_{i\omega}(c_{i0}, c_{i\omega})/\partial c_{i0}} x_\omega$$

$$+ \sum_{\omega \in \Omega} \pi_{i\omega} \frac{\partial u_{i\omega}(c_{i0}, c_{i\omega})/\partial c_{i\omega}}{\sum_{\omega \in \Omega} \pi_{i\omega} \partial u_{i\omega}(c_{i0}, c_{i\omega})/\partial c_{i0}} y_\omega$$

$$= S_x + S_y,$$

where we have used S_x and S_y to denote the value of x_ω's and y_ω's, respectively. Hence, values are also additive.

The additivity of values is a consequence of the requirement that in a competitive equilibrium something cannot be created from nothing. If S_z is not equal to $S_x + S_y$, say $S_z > S_x + S_y$, then one can buy complex securities x_ω and y_ω and short sell complex security z_ω. The cost of this investment is equal to $S_x + S_y - S_z$, which is strictly negative. However, the time–1 payoffs of this investment are uniformly zero. Hence something has been created from nothing, which is inconsistent with an economic equilibrium.

5.9. An important application of the above idea is the Modigliani and Miller theorem – the values of firms in the same risk class are determined independently of their capital structure in a frictionless market. Two firms are said to be in the same risk class if their time–1 random payoffs are proportional across states of nature. To see this, consider two firms with time–1 payoffs x_1 and x_2, respectively. Assume that there exists an $\alpha > 0$ such that $\alpha x_{1\omega} = x_{2\omega}$, $\forall \omega \in \Omega$. Firm 1 is 100 percent equity financed and firm 2 is partly financed by, say, debt. We claim that the value of firm 2 is α times the value of firm 1 independent of the capital structure of firm 2. Let the time–1 payoff of the equity of firm 2 be denoted by y and that of the debt be denoted z. We have

$$\alpha x_{1\omega} = x_{2\omega} = y_\omega + z_\omega \quad \forall \omega \in \Omega.$$

The value of firm 2 is just the sum of its equity value and its debt value. It then follows from the arguments of previous paragraphs that $\alpha S_1 = S_2 = S_y + S_z$. Thus the values of firm 1 and firm 2 are proportional – independent of the capitalization of the firms.

Here we note that the Modigliani and Miller theorem does *not* say that the value of a firm will be unchanged after a recapitalization. For example, when markets are incomplete and when a recapitalization of a firm increases the number of linearly independent securities in the economy, the original equilibrium may be upset and new equilibrium prices will form. Under the new set of equilibrium prices, the value of the firm may be different. Even when the recapitalization does not increase the number of linearly independent securities, it may involve buying back some of the existing outstanding equities. This will cause individuals to rebalance their portfolio holdings. Unless there exists a unique equilibrium, the equilibrium prices after the recapitalization may be different and the value of the firm may also be different.

5.10. One can see, by casual empiricism, that in actual securities markets the number of corporate securities is less than the number of the states of nature. Hence we would not in general be able to create a complete set of state contingent claims by forming portfolios of existing corporate securities. Thus, the markets for corporate securities are unlikely to span all state contingent claims. Under some conditions, the corporate securities markets together with markets of options written on corporate securities are sufficient for reaching allocational efficiency for arbitrary preferences.

A European call option written on a common stock is a financial security that gives its holder the right to purchase the underlying stock at a prespecified price on a prespecified date. Similarly, an European put option gives the right to sell the underlying asset at a prespecified price on a prespecified date. The prespecified price is called the *strike price* or the *exercise price*; and the prespecified date is the *expiration date* or *maturity date*.

Assume, for the time being, that there exists a portfolio of corporate securities whose time-1 payoffs, $\{x_\omega; \omega \in \Omega\}$, are strictly positive and *separate states* in that $x_\omega \neq x_{\omega'}$ if $\omega \neq \omega'$. This portfolio will henceforth be referred to as a *state index portfolio*.

For ease of exposition, we assume that $x_{\omega_i} < x_{\omega_j}$ if $i < j$. Since the holder of a call option is not required to exercise, he will do so if and only if the stock price at time 1 is greater than the exercise price. Now consider the payoff matrix of the state index portfolio and $|\Omega| - 1$ European call options written on it with exercise prices equal to $x_{\omega_1}, x_{\omega_2}, \ldots, x_{|\Omega|-1}$:

$$
\begin{pmatrix}
x_{\omega_1} & x_{\omega_2} & x_{\omega_3} & \cdots & x_{\omega_{|\Omega|}} \\
0 & x_{\omega_2} - x_{\omega_1} & x_{\omega_3} - x_{\omega_1} & \cdots & x_{\omega_{|\Omega|}} - x_{\omega_1} \\
0 & 0 & x_{\omega_3} - x_{\omega_2} & \cdots & x_{\omega_{|\Omega|}} - x_{\omega_2} \\
\vdots & \vdots & \vdots & \ddots & \vdots \\
0 & 0 & 0 & \cdots & x_{\omega_{|\Omega|}} - x_{\omega_{|\Omega|-1}}
\end{pmatrix},
$$

where the first row is the payoff structure of the state index portfolio and the n–th row is the payoff structure of the call option with an exercise price $x_{\omega_{n-1}}$. This matrix is of full rank by the fact that x_{ω_1} is nonzero. Hence the common stock and the $|\Omega| - 1$ European call options are $|\Omega|$ linearly independent securities, and the markets are complete.

Similar analysis applies to a common stock and European put options with exercise prices $x_{\omega_2}, x_{\omega_3}, \ldots, x_{\omega_{|\Omega|}}$. The payoff structure of an European stock call/put option with a nontrivial exercise price is a nonlinear function of the payoff of its underlying stock and hence is linearly independent of that of its underlying stock.

When $x_{\omega_1} = 0$, we simply replace the state index portfolio by an European put option with an exercise price equal to any of x_{ω_2}, $x_{\omega_3}, \ldots, x_{\omega_{|\Omega|}}$ in the above payoff matrix to make it of full rank.

5.11. The discussions of Section 5.10 on the optimality of an allocation appear to be very general. Individuals may have different probability beliefs about the states of nature and may have state–dependent and non-time-additive utility functions. To achieve a Pareto optimal allocation for arbitrary preferences and beliefs through securities markets with options, it suffices to have a state index port-folio. The existence of such a portfolio amounts to saying that the realization of the portfolio's time–1 payoff allows us to know the re-alized payoff of any complex security. This is so, because the realized payoff of the state index portfolio reveals the true state of nature. Equivalently, the existence of a state index portfolio implies that the time–1 payoff of any complex security is a function only of that of the state index portfolio. This, however, is unlikely in actual securities markets.

In the following sections, we will restrict our attention to economies where individuals have homogeneous beliefs, $\{\pi_\omega; \omega \in \Omega\}$, and state–independent time-additive utility functions for life–time consumption

$$u_{i\omega}(c_{i0}, c_{i\omega}) = u_{i0}(c_{i0}) + u_i(c_{i\omega}),$$

where $u_{i0}(\cdot)$ and $u_i(\cdot)$ are increasing, strictly concave, and twice differentiable. We will show that a Pareto optimal allocation may be reached without complete markets and without a state index portfolio in this case.

5.12. Fix a Pareto optimal allocation of time–0 consumption, $\{c_{i0}; \ i = 1, 2, \ldots, I\}$, and time–1 consumption $\{c_{i\omega}; \omega \in \Omega, i = 1, 2, \ldots, I\}$ and let $\lambda_i, \ i = 1, 2, \ldots, I$, be the set of strictly positive weights associated with the allocation. As individuals' utility functions are additive across time and states, relations (5.4.1) and (5.4.2) become

$$\lambda_i u_{i0}'(c_{i0}) = \phi_0 \quad i = 1, 2, \ldots, I, \tag{5.12.1}$$

$$\lambda_i \pi_\omega u_i'(c_{i\omega}) = \phi_\omega \quad \omega \in \Omega, \, i = 1, 2, \ldots, I. \tag{5.12.2}$$

As individuals' beliefs are homogeneous, (5.12.1) and (5.12.2) imply

$$\lambda_i u_{i0}'(c_{i0}) = \lambda_k u_{k0}'(c_{k0}) \quad \forall i, k, \tag{5.12.3}$$

and

$$\lambda_i u_i'(c_{i\omega}) = \lambda_k u_k'(c_{k\omega}) \quad \forall i, k, \tag{5.12.4}$$

respectively. Let two states ω and ω' be such that $C_\omega > C_{\omega'}$. We claim that $c_{i\omega} > c_{i\omega'}$ for all i. That is, if the aggregate consumption in state ω is strictly greater than the aggregate consumption in state ω', then the optimal allocation of consumption in state ω for an individual i is strictly greater than that in state ω'. To see this, we note that since $C_\omega > C_{\omega'}$, there must exist an individual k such that $c_{k\omega} > c_{k\omega'}$. By the strict concavity of utility functions, we have

$$\lambda_k u_k'(c_{k\omega}) < \lambda_k u_k'(c_{k\omega'}).$$

Relation (5.12.4) then implies that

$$\lambda_i u_i'(c_{i\omega}) < \lambda_i u_i'(c_{i\omega'}) \quad \forall i.$$

By the strict concavity of u_i, $c_{i\omega} > c_{i\omega'}$ $\forall i$. Hence, for given weights $\lambda_i > 0$, there exists a one–to–one relation between the aggregate consumption in a state and the optimal allocation for an individual in that state. Also, since utility functions are state independent, this one–to–one relation is state independent. In symbols, there are real-valued functions f_i such that we can write

$$\tilde{c}_i = f_i(\tilde{C}), \tag{5.12.5}$$

where for brevity we have used $\tilde{c}_i$ and $\tilde{C}$ for individual i's time–1 random consumption and for time–1 random aggregate endowment, respectively. Note that f_i is strictly increasing. Similar analysis can be carried out for the optimal allocation for time–0 aggregate consumption to show that there exist strictly increasing functions f_{i0} such that $c_{i0} = f_{i0}(C_0)$.

The existence of functions $f_i(\cdot)$ implies that a Pareto optimal allocation must have the characteristic that in states where the aggregate consumption is the same, the allocations are identical. The functions f_{i0}'s and f_i's prescribe the Pareto optimal allocation of time–0 and time–1 aggregate consumption to different individuals. They are called the *Pareto optimal sharing rules*. In the following several sections, we will concentrate on the Pareto optimal sharing rules for time–1 consumption and refer to them as simply the Pareto optimal sharing rules.

5.13. The preceding analysis implies that spot market for time–0 consumption and elementary claims on time–1 aggregate consumption span the set of Pareto optimal allocations. Therefore, a competitive equilibrium allocation in a securities markets economy where markets are complete with respect to the aggregate consumption states will be Pareto optimal. When corporate securities do not span all the time–1 aggregate consumption states, call options written on the time–1 aggregate consumption can be added in the manner discussed in Section 5.10 to *complete* the markets with respect to the time–1 aggregate consumption states.

In Section 5.12, the Pareto optimal sharing rules were shown to be strictly monotonically increasing. They can be nonlinear functions of the time–1 aggregate consumption. When Pareto optimal sharing rules are linear, however, a competitive equilibrium allocation in a securities markets economy is always Pareto efficient if there exists a riskless asset. This is so, because from Section 5.6, in a securities markets economy, individuals are only endowed with time–0 consumption and traded complex securities. To see this, consider a Pareto optimal allocation where individual consumption allocations are linearly related to the aggregate consumption:

$$f_i(\tilde{C}) = a_i + b_i \tilde{C} \quad \forall i. \tag{5.13.1}$$

In a competitive securities markets economy, an individual can first sell his endowments and then allocate his initial wealth according to the following. To achieve the constant term a_i, individual i can purchase a_i shares of the unit riskless discount bond at time 0. The market portfolio of existing securities pays exactly $\tilde{C}$. Hence the stochastic term $b_i \tilde{C}$ can be achieved by purchasing a b_i fraction of the market portfolio. The remaining initial wealth will then be used for consumption at time 0. (Note that the existence of a riskless asset can easily be ensured by creating a riskless borrowing and lending opportunity.)

The following section gives the necessary and sufficient condition on utility functions for Pareto optimal sharing rules to be linear for all strictly positive weightings λ_i's and for all distributions of aggregate consumption.

5.14. Suppose that Pareto optimal sharing rules are linear for all weightings $\lambda = (\lambda_i)_{i=1}^I$:

$$\tilde{c}_i(\lambda) = a_i(\lambda) + b_i(\lambda)\tilde{C} \quad \forall i, \tag{5.14.1}$$

where $\tilde{C}$ is the time–1 aggregate consumption/endowment and where $\tilde{c}_i(\lambda)$ denotes the random time–1 Pareto optimal consumption allocation for individual i associated with the weightings λ. Note that the optimal sharing rules depend upon the weightings and thus the dependence of a_i and b_i on λ. From (5.12.4), we know

$$\lambda_i u_i'(a_i(\lambda) + b_i(\lambda)\tilde{C}) = \lambda_k u_k'(a_k(\lambda) + b_k(\lambda)\tilde{C}) \quad \forall i, k. \tag{5.14.2}$$

Differentiating (5.14.2), with respect to $\tilde{C}$ gives a condition that is necessary for a linear sharing rule to be optimal for a given set of weightings λ:

$$\lambda_i u_i''(\tilde{c}_i(\lambda)) b_i(\lambda) = \lambda_k u_k''(\tilde{c}_k(\lambda)) b_k(\lambda) \qquad \forall \ i, k. \tag{5.14.3}$$

Differentiating (5.14.2) with respect to λ_i gives a condition that is necessary for a linear sharing rule to be Pareto optimal for any arbitrary set of positive weights:

$$\begin{aligned}
u_i'(\tilde{c}_i(\lambda)) + \lambda_i u_i''(\tilde{c}_i(\lambda))(a_{ii}(\lambda) + b_{ii}(\lambda)\tilde{C}) \\
= \lambda_k u_k''(\tilde{c}_k(\lambda))(a_{ki}(\lambda) + b_{ki}(\lambda)\tilde{C}) \quad \forall i, k,
\end{aligned} \tag{5.14.4}$$

where $a_{ki}(\lambda)$ and $b_{ki}(\lambda)$ denote $\partial a_k(\lambda)/\partial \lambda_i$ and $\partial b_k(\lambda)/\partial \lambda_i$, respectively.

Substituting (5.14.3) into (5.14.4) and using (5.14.1) gives

$$-\frac{u_i'(\tilde{c}_i(\lambda))}{u_i''(\tilde{c}_i(\lambda))} = A_i(\lambda) + B_i(\lambda)\tilde{c}_i(\lambda), \tag{5.14.5}$$

Since this is true for all distributions of aggregation consumption, fixing λ and letting the distribution of $\tilde{C}$ to vary gives a differential equation $-u_i'(z)/u_i''(z) = A_i(\lambda) + B_i(\lambda)z$. Since the left-hand side is independent of λ, the right-hand side must also be so. Thus $A_i(\lambda) = A_i$ and $B_i(\lambda) = B_i$ for some constants A_i and B_i. Now we claim that $B_i = B_k$ for all i, k. This follows from the second part of Exercise 5.6. Therefore, we have proved that (5.14.5) with $B_i = B$ for all i is necessary for all Pareto optimal sharing rules to be linear. Note that (5.14.5) must be satisfied for arbitrary weights λ. Therefore, (5.14.5) with $B_i = B$ for all i is equivalent to a differential equation:

$$-\frac{u_i'(z)}{u_i''(z)} = A_i + Bz. \tag{5.14.6}$$

The left-hand side of (5.14.6) is the inverse of the Arrow–Pratt measure of absolute risk aversion and is termed the (Arrow–Pratt measure of absolute) *risk tolerance*, which we denote $T_i(z)$. The derivative of $T_i(z)$ with respect to z is termed the *cautiousness* at z. Using the above terminology, (5.14.6) says that utility functions exhibit linear risk tolerance with identical *cautiousness* B. Note that A_i and B will be appropriately chosen so that the utility functions are increasing and concave. When $B \neq 0$, (5.14.6) is equivalent to

$$u_i'(z) = \rho_i(A_i + Bz)^{-\frac{1}{B}}, \tag{5.14.7}$$

for some strictly positive constant ρ_i. When $B = 0$, however, (5.14.6) is equivalent to

$$u_i'(z) = \rho_i \exp\{-\frac{z}{A_i}\}, \qquad (5.14.8)$$

for some strictly positive constant ρ_i. We can interpret ρ_i to be individual i's time preference parameter.

5.15. Now we will prove that (5.14.6) is also sufficient for all the Pareto optimal sharing rules to be linear. We take cases. Case 1: $B \neq 0$. Using (5.12.4) and (5.14.7) we have

$$\left(\frac{\lambda_i \rho_i}{\lambda_k \rho_k}\right)^{-B} (A_i + B\tilde{c}_i) = (A_k + B\tilde{c}_k) \quad \forall i, k. \qquad (5.15.1)$$

Summing (5.15.1) over k and rearranging gives

$$\tilde{c}_i = \frac{B\tilde{C} + \sum_{k=1}^{I} A_k}{B(\lambda_i \rho_i)^{-B} \sum_{k=1}^{I} (\lambda_k \rho_k)^B} - \frac{A_i}{B} \quad i = 1, 2, \ldots, I, \qquad (5.15.2)$$

which is clearly linear in $\tilde{C}$. Case 2: $B = 0$. Relation (5.12.3) and (5.14.8) imply

$$\tilde{c}_i = A_i \ln(\lambda_i \rho_i) - \frac{A_i \sum_{k=1}^{I} A_k \ln(\lambda_k \rho_k)}{\sum_{k=1}^{I} A_k} + \frac{A_i}{\sum_{k=1}^{I} A_k} \tilde{C}, \quad \forall i,$$

which is also linear in $\tilde{C}$. Hence (5.14.6) is sufficient for Pareto optimal sharing rules to be linear for all weightings.

Note that when utility functions for time–1 consumption satisfy (5.14.6) and when there exists a riskless security in zero net supply, an equilibrium in a securities markets economy involves *two fund separation* in that an individual in equilibrium holds a fraction of the market portfolio and certain amount of the riskless asset. Readers can compare the results reported here and those of Sections 1.27 and 1.28. There we discussed necessary and sufficient conditions on utility functions for an individual's optimal portfolios, for all levels of initial wealth, to be composed of linear combinations of two funds. Those necessary and sufficient conditions are identical to (5.14.6) except that B is allowed to vary across different individuals. Here changing weights is equivalent to varying initial wealth as in Sections 1.27 and 1.28. For individuals to hold the same risky fund, we also require here that B_i be equal for all i. Finally, the resource constraint that the sharing rules must satisfy necessitates that the separating risky fund is the market portfolio.

5.16. As a consequence of the fact that a Pareto optimal allocation does not vary across states in which the aggregate consumption is the same, the state prices in complete markets have a special structure. This special structure enables us to value risky payoffs without knowing a complete set of state prices.

First we shall fix some notation. Let Ω_k denote the subset of Ω such that $C_\omega = k$ if $\omega \in \Omega_k$, let $\phi(k)$ denote the price at time 0 of an elementary claim on aggregate time–1 consumption that pays one unit of the consumption at time 1 if and only if $\tilde{C} = k$, and let $\pi(k)$ be the probability that $\tilde{C} = k$. The time-additivity and state-independence of utility functions simplify (5.5.3) to be

$$\phi_\omega = \frac{\pi_\omega u_i'(c_{i\omega})}{u_{i0}'(c_{i0})} \quad \forall \omega \in \Omega. \tag{5.16.1}$$

To rule out arbitrage, we must have

$$\begin{aligned}
\phi(k) &= \sum_{\omega \in \Omega_k} \phi_\omega \\
&= \frac{u_i'(f_i(k))}{u_{i0}'(c_{i0})} \sum_{\omega \in \Omega_k} \pi_\omega \\
&= \frac{u_i'(f_i(k))}{u_{i0}'(c_{i0})} \pi(k),
\end{aligned} \tag{5.16.2}$$

where the second equality follows from (5.12.5) and the third equality follows from the definition of $\pi(k)$.

Now let x be the random payoff of a complex security. Its value at time zero, denoted by S_x, is

$$
\begin{aligned}
S_x &= \sum_{\omega \in \Omega} \phi_\omega x_\omega = \sum_k \sum_{\omega \in \Omega_k} \phi_\omega x_\omega \\
&= \sum_k \frac{u_i'(f_i(k))}{u_{i0}'(c_{i0})} \sum_{\omega \in \Omega_k} \pi_\omega x_\omega \\
&= \sum_k \phi(k) \sum_{\omega \in \Omega_k} \frac{\pi_\omega}{\pi(k)} x_\omega \\
&= \sum_k \phi(k) E[\tilde{x} | \tilde{C} = k],
\end{aligned}
\qquad (5.16.3)
$$

where the third equality follows from (5.12.5) and (5.16.1), the fourth equality follows from (5.16.2), and the fifth equality follows from the definition of conditional expectation, and $E[\cdot]$ denotes the expectation with respect to π_ω's.

From (5.16.3), the price of any complex security can be computed using just its expected payoffs conditional on aggregate consumption states and the prices for the elementary claims on aggregate consumption.

5.17. Recall from Section 5.10 that state prices can be computed from prices of put and call options on a state index portfolio. It then follows that elementary claim prices for the aggregate consumption states can be computed from put and call option prices on the time–1 aggregate consumption. Or equivalently, elementary claims on aggregate consumption states can be *manufactured* by forming portfolios of put and call options written on time–1 aggregate consumption.

Under certain conditions on the possible values of time–1 aggregate consumption, we will show in Section 5.18 that an elementary claim on an aggregate consumption state can be constructed by a *butterfly spread* of call options. When the time–1 aggregate consumption has a continuous distribution and when the price for a call option on aggregate consumption is twice differentiable with respect to its exercise price, the price for an elementary claim on aggregate consumption states is related to the second derivative of the option's price with respect to its exercise price.

	$x(0)$	x(1)	x(2)
$\tilde{C} = 1$	1	0	0
$\tilde{C} = 2$	2	1	0
$\tilde{C} = 3$	3	2	1
.	.	.	.
.	.	.	.
.	.	.	.
$\tilde{C} = L$	L	L-1	L-2

Table 5.18.1: Payoffs for Call Options on the Aggregate Consumption

5.18. Initially, suppose that time–1 aggregate consumption has possible values: $1, 2, \ldots, L$. Denote the vector of payoffs of an European call option on aggregate consumption with one period to maturity and an exercise price of k as $x(k)$; its time–0 price will be denoted by $p(k)$. For calls with exercise prices of 0, 1, and 2 units of consumption, the state-contingent payoffs $x(k)$ are as shown in Table 5.18.1.

Note that as the exercise price of a call option is increased from k to $k+1$, two changes in the payoff vector occur: (1) the payoff in the set of states with $\tilde{C} = k+1$ becomes zero, and (2) the payoffs in all states with $\tilde{C} \geq k+2$ are reduced by the change in the exercise price. Therefore, in this example, $x(k) - x(k+1)$ gives a payoff of one unit of consumption in every state with $\tilde{C} \geq k+1$, and $x(k+1) - x(k+2)$ gives a payoff of one unit consumption in every state for which $\tilde{C} \geq k+2$.

A security having a payoff of one unit consumption if and only if $\tilde{C} = 1$ may be constructed as $[x(0) - x(1)] - [x(1) - x(2)]$, since this combination of calls would have a payoff vector of

$$\begin{pmatrix} 1 \\ 1 \\ 1 \\ \vdots \\ 1 \end{pmatrix} - \begin{pmatrix} 0 \\ 1 \\ 1 \\ \vdots \\ 1 \end{pmatrix} = \begin{pmatrix} 1 \\ 0 \\ 0 \\ \vdots \\ 0 \end{pmatrix}$$

An elementary claim for any given level of time–1 aggregate consumption can be constructed in a similar manner. Given the call prices, $p(k)$, prices of elementary claims on aggregate consumption must be those computed from the replicating portfolio of call options. The portfolio yielding one unit of consumption if and only if time–1 aggregate consumption is k consists of buying one call with an exercise price $k - 1$, buying one call with an exercise price $k + 1$, and selling two calls with an exercise price k, which is a *butterfly spread*. For example, if $L = 3$ and the prices of calls are $p(0) = 1.7$, $p(1) = 0.8$, and $p(2) = 0.1$, then the respective prices for elementary-claims on aggregate consumption are $\phi(1) = 0.2$, $\phi(2) = 0.6$, and $\phi(3) = 0.1$. Note that $p(3) = 0$ because $L = 3$. The price of a one period riskless discount bond paying one unit of consumption in all states would be $\phi(1) + \phi(2) + \phi(3) = 0.9$. The riskless rate of interest would be 11.1%; i.e. $1/.9 - 1 = 0.111$.

5.19. In general, if the step size between potential levels of aggregate consumption is Δ, then, letting k be a possible value of the time–1 aggregate consumption, $x(k) - x(k+\Delta)$ has a payoff vector with zeroes for aggregate consumption $\tilde{C} \le k$, and Δ for all levels of aggregate consumption greater than or equal to $k + \Delta$. Therefore, the portfolio of call options that produces a payment of one unit of consumption if the aggregate consumption is k and zero otherwise is:

$$\frac{1}{\Delta}(x(k - \Delta) - x(k)) - (x(k) - x(k + \Delta)),$$

where the coefficient of $x(k)$ in this expression is the number of calls with exercise price of k that should be held in the portfolio.

Since the portfolio of calls gives a payoff of 1 if $\tilde{C} = k$ in period 1, the cost of the call portfolio is $\phi(k)$. Now note the following: With step size of Δ, $\phi(k)$ divided by the step size may be written as

$$\frac{\phi(k)}{\Delta} = \frac{[p(k + \Delta) - p(k)] - [p(k) - p(k - \Delta)]}{\Delta^2}. \qquad (5.19.1)$$

Suppose that the time–1 aggregate consumption has a continuous distribution and that the prices for call options on the time–1 aggregate consumption are twice differentiable with respect to their exercise prices. Then as Δ approaches zero in (5.19.1), we get

$$\frac{\phi(k)}{dk} \equiv \lim_{\Delta \to 0} \frac{[p(k+\Delta) - p(k)] - [p(k) - p(k-\Delta)]}{\Delta^2}$$
$$= \frac{\partial^2 p(k)}{\partial k^2}.$$

(5.19.2)

From differential calculus, the finiteness of $\partial^2 p(k)/\partial k^2$ implies that the elementary claim price for any particular level of the time–1 aggregate consumption is zero. We thus interpret (5.19.2) to be the *pricing density* for elementary claims on aggregate consumption states in that a complex security that pays one unit of consumption if and only if the time–1 aggregate consumption lies in a subset A of the real line has a price:

$$\int_A \frac{\phi(k)}{dk} dk = \int_A \frac{\partial^2 p(k)}{\partial k^2} dk.$$

Moreover, as a generalization of (5.16.3), the price for a complex security having payoffs x is

$$S_x = \int \frac{\phi(k)}{dk} E[\tilde{x}|\tilde{C} = k] dk.$$

(5.19.3)

Hence (5.19.1) gives the pricing function for an elementary claim on $\tilde{C}$ maturing in one period in the discrete case, and (5.19.2) gives the pricing density when $\tilde{C}$ has a continuous distribution and $\frac{\partial^2 p(k)}{\partial k^2}$ exists and is finite. Note from (5.19.2) that the positivity of elementary claim prices implies strict convexity of call option's price in its exercise price.

5.20. The economies considered in this chapter are two pe-riod economies. By the strict monotonicity of their utility functions, individuals will consume all their wealth at time 1. As the single consumption good is the numeraire, by the market clearing condi-tion in an economic equilibrium, the aggregate time–1 wealth is the aggregate time–1 consumption which in turn is the aggregate time–1 endowment. Note that the aggregate wealth is just the market portfolio that we discussed in detail in Chapter 4. Thus all the conclusions above about time–1 aggregate consumption apply to the market portfolio. For instance, $\phi(k)$ can be computed from prices for put and call options written on the market portfolio maturing at time 1. Also, (5.16.3) can be written as

$$S_x = \sum_k \phi(k) E[\tilde{x} | \tilde{M} = k],$$

where, as usual, we have used $\tilde{M}$ to denote the time–1 value of the market portfolio.

Note that the equivalence of time–1 aggregate consumption and aggregate wealth holds true only in a two period economy. When the economy lasts for more than two periods, say times 0, 1, and 2, time–1 aggregate consumption is only a fraction of the aggregate wealth at that time. The aggregate wealth at time 1 is composed not only of the aggregate time–1 consumption/endowment but also of the value of the time–2 aggregate consumption/endowment. We will come back to this point later in Chapter 7.

5.21. Now let $\{\phi_\omega; \omega \in \Omega\}$ be the state prices in a competitive economy with complete markets where individuals have homogeneous beliefs and time–additive, state–independent utility functions that are increasing, strictly concave, and differentiable. We claim that $\{\phi_\omega; \omega \in \Omega\}$ will be the state prices in an otherwise identical economy except that there is only one representative agent who is endowed with the aggregate endowment $(C_0, C_\omega; \omega \in \Omega)$. We will prove our claim through construction – construct a representative agent, endow him with $(C_0, C_\omega; \omega \in \Omega)$, and show that equilibrium prices for state contingent claims are $\{\phi_\omega; \omega \in \Omega\}$.

5.22. Consider the competitive complete markets economy equilibrium prices of elementary claims $\{\phi_\omega; \omega \in \Omega\}$ and equilibrium allocation $\{c_{i0}, c_{i\omega}; \omega \in \Omega, i = 1, \ldots, I\}$ in Section 5.5. Let λ_i be the inverse of the Lagrangian multiplier of individual i's maximization problem, that is, $\lambda_i = \theta_i^{-1}$, where we recall that the θ_i's are strictly positive. Now define functions u_0 and u_1 as follows:

$$u_0(z) \equiv \max_{(z_i)_{i=1}^I \in \Re^I} \sum_{i=1}^I \lambda_i u_{i0}(z_i)$$

$$\text{s.t. } \sum_{i=1}^I z_i = z,$$

(5.22.1)

and

$$u_1(z) \equiv \max_{(z_i)_{i=1}^I \in \Re^I} \sum_{i=1}^I \lambda_i u_i(z_i)$$

$$\text{s.t. } \sum_{i=1}^I z_i = z.$$

(5.22.2)

It can be verified that u_0 and u_1 are increasing and strictly concave. An immediate consequence of the definitions of u_0 and u_1 is that

$$u_0'(C_0) = \sum_{i=1}^I \lambda_i u_{i0}'(c_{i0}) \frac{dc_{i0}}{dC_0}$$

$$= \sum_{i=1}^I \frac{dc_{i0}}{dC_0} = 1,$$

(5.22.3)

and

$$u_1'(C_\omega) = \sum_{i=1}^I \lambda_i u_{i1}'(c_{i\omega}) \frac{dc_{i\omega}}{dC_\omega}$$

$$= \frac{\phi_\omega}{\pi_\omega} \sum_{i=1}^I \frac{dc_{i\omega}}{dC_\omega} = \frac{\phi_\omega}{\pi_\omega},$$

(5.22.4)

where we have used the resources constraints

$$\sum_{i=1}^I c_{i0} = C_0$$

and

$$\sum_{i=1}^I c_{i\omega} = C_\omega \quad \forall \omega \in \Omega$$

to conclude that

$$\sum_{i=1}^{I} \frac{dc_{i0}}{dC_0} = 1 \qquad (5.22.5)$$

and

$$\sum_{i=1}^{I} \frac{dc_{i\omega}}{dC_\omega} = 1 \quad \forall \omega \in \Omega. \qquad (5.22.6)$$

5.23. Now consider an economy with a representative agent, whose time–additive and state–independent utility functions are u_0 and u_1, whose probability beliefs are $\{\pi_\omega; \omega \in \Omega\}$, and whose endowments of time–0 and time–1 consumptions are $(C_0, C_\omega; \omega \in \Omega\}$. We claim that the prices for elementary consumption claims in this economy, using the single consumption good as the numeraire, must be $\{\phi_\omega; \omega \in \Omega\}$.

Observe that in this single individual economy, for the markets to clear, the prices must be set so that the representative individual's optimal consumption choice is to hold his endowment. Therefore, using the time–0 consumption good as the numeraire, the state price for state ω must be equal to the representative individual's marginal rate of substitution between time–0 consumption and time–1 state–ω consumption, which is

$$\frac{\pi_\omega u_1'(C_\omega)}{u_0'(C_0)}. \qquad (5.23.1)$$

Substituting (5.22.3) and (5.22.4) into (5.23.1) gives

$$\begin{aligned}
&\frac{\pi_\omega u_1'(C_\omega)}{u_0'(C_0)} \\
&= \frac{\pi_\omega \phi_\omega}{\pi_\omega} = \phi_\omega.
\end{aligned} \qquad (5.23.2)$$

Thus, for the market to clear, it is necessary that the price for state–ω contingent claim be ϕ_ω. It is also straightforward to show that $\{\phi_\omega; \omega \in \Omega\}$ are indeed equilibrium prices in the economy with the representative agent.

5.24. The utility functions for the representative individual we constructed in Section 5.22 depend on the weightings λ_i. The representative individual's utility functions will be affected when we change the relative magnitudes of those weightings. Recall from Section 5.5 that the λ_i is just the inverse of individual i's Lagrangian multiplier in his maximization and depends upon his initial endowment. Therefore, the relative magnitudes of the λ_i's are determined by the distribution of initial endowments of individuals. As a consequence, the prices in the economy will be affected by the distribution of initial endowments across individuals.

We say that an economy with heterogeneous agents satisfies the *aggregation property* if the equilibrium prices are determined independently of the distribution of initial endowments. We will demonstrate below that a sufficient condition for the aggregation property is that utility functions of individuals exhibit linear risk tolerance with identical cautiousness and have the same time preferences. Note that this condition is a little stronger than (5.14.6), the necessary and sufficient condition for all Pareto optimal sharing rules to be linear. For (5.14.6) to hold, it is not necessary that individuals' time preference parameters be identical.

The solutions of (5.14.6) include power functions

$$u_i(z) = \frac{1}{B-1}(A_i + Bz)^{1-\frac{1}{B}}$$

and negative exponential functions:

$$u_i(z) = -A_i \exp\{-\frac{z}{A_i}\},$$

where we understand the power function to be $\ln(A_i + Bz)$ when $B = 1$.

5.25. Suppose first that individuals' utility functions are power functions with $B \neq 1$ and the same time preference ρ:

$$u_{i0}(z_0) + u_i(z_1)$$
$$= \frac{1}{B-1}(A_i + Bz_0)^{1-\frac{1}{B}} + \rho\frac{1}{B-1}(A_i + Bz_1)^{1-\frac{1}{B}}.$$

Fix a set of weightings (λ_i). Define u_0 and u_1 as in (5.22.1) and (5.22.2). We can compute u_0 and u_1 explicitly. The first order conditions for (5.22.1) are

$$(A_i + By_i)^{-\frac{1}{B}} = \frac{\theta}{\lambda_i} \quad i = 1, 2, \ldots, I, \quad (5.25.1)$$

$$\sum_{i=1}^{I} y_i = y, \quad (5.25.2)$$

where θ is the Lagrangian multiplier for the resource constraint. Now raising (5.25.1) to the $-B$ power and summing over i gives

$$\sum_{i=1}^{I} A_i + By = (\theta)^{-B} \sum_{i=1}^{I} \lambda_i^B. \quad (5.25.3)$$

Solving for θ from (5.25.3) and substituting it into (5.25.1) gives

$$\lambda_i \frac{1}{B-1} (A_i + By_i)^{1-\frac{1}{B}}$$
$$= \frac{1}{B-1} (\sum_{k=1}^{I} A_k + By)^{-\frac{1}{B}} (\sum_{k=1}^{I} \lambda_k^B)^{\frac{1}{B}} (A_i + By_i).$$

Summing the above relation over i gives

$$u_0(y) = \frac{1}{B-1} \sum_{i=1}^{I} \lambda_i (A_i + By_i)^{1-\frac{1}{B}}$$

$$= \frac{1}{B-1} (\sum_{i=1}^{I} \lambda_i^B)^{\frac{1}{B}} (\sum_{i=1}^{I} A_i + By)^{1-\frac{1}{B}}. \quad (5.25.4)$$

Similarly, for u_1 we have

$$u_1(y) = \frac{1}{B-1} \rho \sum_{i=1}^{I} \lambda_i (A_i + By_i)^{1-\frac{1}{B}}$$

$$= \frac{1}{B-1} \rho (\sum_{i=1}^{I} \lambda_i^B)^{\frac{1}{B}} (\sum_{i=1}^{I} A_i + By)^{1-\frac{1}{B}}. \quad (5.25.5)$$

From (5.23.2), the prices for elementary securities are

$$\phi_\omega = \frac{\pi_\omega \rho (\sum_{i=1}^{I} A_i + BC_\omega)^{-\frac{1}{B}}}{(\sum_{i=1}^{I} A_i + BC_0)^{-\frac{1}{B}}}, \quad \forall \omega \in \Omega \qquad (5.25.6),$$

which are independent of the weightings! Prices are determined independently of the distribution of initial endowments.

We leave verification of the aggregation property when $B = 1$ for readers in Exercise 5.4.

5.26. When the utility functions are negative exponential, we can prove a bit more. In the above construction of a representative individual, we assumed that individuals have homogeneous beliefs and time preferences. The representative individual naturally inherits these beliefs and time preferences. In the negative exponential case, we can allow heterogeneous beliefs and time preferences in the construction of the representative agent, and his beliefs and time preference will be *composites* of individuals' beliefs and time preferences.

Consider the following maximization:

$$\max_{\{y_{i\omega}; \omega \in \Omega, i=1,2,\ldots,I\}} \sum_{i=1}^{I} \lambda_i \rho_i \sum_{\omega \in \Omega} \pi_{i\omega} (-A_i \exp\{\frac{-y_{i\omega}}{A_i}\})$$

$$(5.26.1)$$

$$\text{s.t.} \sum_{i=1}^{I} y_{i\omega} = y_\omega \quad \forall \omega \in \Omega.$$

The first order necessary and sufficient conditions are

$$\lambda_i \rho_i \pi_{i\omega} \exp\{\frac{-y_{i\omega}}{A_i}\} = \theta_\omega \quad \forall \omega \in \Omega, \, i = 1, 2, \ldots, I \qquad (5.26.2)$$

$$\sum_{i=1}^{I} y_{i\omega} = y_\omega \quad \forall \omega \in \Omega, \qquad (5.26.3)$$

where θ_ω is the Lagrangian multiplier for the resource constraint in state ω. The first order conditions imply

$$\theta_\omega = \prod_{i=1}^{I} (\lambda_i \rho_i \pi_{i\omega})^{\frac{A_i}{\sum_{k=1}^{I} A_k}} \exp\{-\frac{y_\omega}{\sum_{k=1}^{I} A_k}\}, \qquad (5.26.4)$$

where $\prod$ is the product sign. It then follows from (5.26.2) and (5.26.4) that the maximand of (5.26.1) is

$$\prod_{i=1}^{I}(\lambda_i \rho_i)^{\overline{\sum_{k=1}^{I} A_k}} \sum_{\omega \in \Omega} \left(\prod_{i=1}^{I}(\pi_{i\omega})^{\overline{\sum_{k=1}^{I} A_k}}\right)\left(-\sum_{i=1}^{I} A_i\right)\exp\{-\frac{y_\omega}{\sum_{i=1}^{I} A_i}\}$$

(5.26.5)

We interpret

$$\prod_{i=1}^{I}(\rho_i)^{\overline{\sum_{k=1}^{I} A_k}}$$

(5.26.6)

to be the time preference of the representative individual,

$$\prod_{i=1}^{I}(\pi_{i\omega})^{\overline{\sum_{k=1}^{I} A_k}} \quad \forall \omega \in \Omega$$

(5.26.7)

to be his probability beliefs, and

$$u_1(y) = \left(\prod_{i=1}^{I}(\lambda_i)^{\overline{\sum_{k=1}^{I} A_k}}\right)\left(-\sum_{i=1}^{I} A_i\right)\exp\{-\frac{y}{\sum_{i=1}^{I} A_i}\} \quad (5.26.8)$$

to be his utility function for time–1 consumption. Here let us note that (5.26.7) may not be probabilities as they may not sum to one. That constitutes no problem, as we can always normalize to get probabilities.

Taking $\rho_i = 1$ and $\pi_{i\omega} = 1$ in (5.26.5), we get

$$u_0(y) = \left(\prod_{i=1}^{I}(\lambda_i)^{\overline{\sum_{k=1}^{I} A_k}}\right)\left(-\sum_{i=1}^{I} A_i\right)\exp\{-\frac{y}{\sum_{i=1}^{I} A_i}\}. \quad (5.26.9)$$

The prices for elementary claims in an economy with this representative individual and with aggregate endowments $(C_0, C_\omega; \omega \in \Omega)$ are, $\forall \omega \in \Omega$,

$$\phi_\omega = \frac{\left(\prod_{i=1}^{I}(\rho_i)^{\overline{\sum_{k=1}^{I} A_k}}\right)\left(\prod_{i=1}^{I}(\pi_{i\omega})^{\overline{\sum_{k=1}^{I} A_k}}\right)\exp\{-\frac{C_\omega}{\sum_{i=1}^{I} A_i}\}}{\exp\{-\frac{C_0}{\sum_{i=1}^{I} A_i}\}},$$

(5.26.10)

which are independent of the weightings. We will ask you to verify in Exercise 5.5 that (5.26.10) gives prices for elementary claims in a complete markets economy with individuals having negative exponential utility functions. Hence negative exponential utility functions are sufficient for aggregation.

Exercises

5.1. Verify that the u_0 and u_1 defined in (5.22.1) and (5.22.2) are strictly increasing and concave.

5.2. Solve (5.14.6) to verify that the solutions include power functions and negative exponential functions.

5.3. Verify that negative exponential utility functions imply linear Pareto optimal sharing rules.

5.4. Derive equilibrium prices for elementary claims in a complete markets economy when individuals have log utility functions.

5.5. Verify that (5.26.10) gives equilibrium prices for elementary claims in a complete markets economy where individuals have negative exponential utility functions with different coefficients of the Arrow–Pratt measure of absolute risk aversion.

5.6. Fix a Pareto optimal allocation and the sharing rules for this allocation, f_i. Let $T_i(z) = -u_i'(z)/u_i''(z)$ be the risk tolerance function for individual i. Show that

$$f_i'(z) = \frac{T_i(f_i(z))}{\sum_{k=1}^{I} T_k(f_k(z))}.$$

The *cautiousness* for individual i at z, denoted by $\sigma_i(z)$, is $T_i'(z)$. Show that for the f_i's to be linear, it is necessary and sufficient that

$$\sigma_i(f_i(z)) = \sigma_k(f_k(z)) \quad \forall i, k, \forall z.$$

That is, individuals' cautiousness must be identical *along* the optimal schedule, although their cautiousness may not be a constant across individuals.

5.7. Let f_{i0} and f_i be Pareto optimal sharing rules for individual i for a set of weightings λ. Define $u_0'(z) \equiv \lambda_i u_{i0}'(f_{i0}(z))$ and $u_1'(z) \equiv \lambda_i u_i'(f_i(z))$. Show that u_0 and u_i are strictly increasing and concave and can be utility functions for a representative agent as discussed in Section 5.22 and Section 5.23.

5.8. Suppose that all the individuals' utility functions exhibit decreasing absolute risk aversion. Show that the representative agent's utility functions as defined in Section 5.22 also exhibit decreasing absolute risk aversion.

Remarks. The general framework of this chapter is due to Arrow (1964) and Debreu (1959). For more discussion on the issues related to recapitalization and the Modigliani and Miller theorem, see Litzenberger and Sosin (1977). The discussions on the allocational role of stock options follow Breeden and Litzenberger (1978) and Ross (1976). The construction of a representative agent is taken from Breeden and Litzenberger (1978), Constantinides (1982), and Wilson (1968). The discussions on the aggregation property of prices and the Pareto optimal sharing rules are freely adapted from Amershi and Stoeckenius (1983), Rubinstein (1974), and Wilson (1968). For an extensive review of the literature on equilibrium under uncertainty, see Radner (1982). Exercise 5.8 is taken from Kraus and Litzenberger (1983).

References

Amershi, A., and J. Stoeckenius. 1983. The theory of syndicates and linear sharing rules. *Econometrica* **51**:1407–1416.

Arrow, K. 1964. The role of securities in the optimal allocation of risk–bearing. *Review of Economic Studies* **31**:91–96.

Breeden, D., and R. Litzenberger. 1978. State contingent prices implicit in option prices, *Journal of Business* **51**:621–651.

Constantinides, G. 1982. Intertemporal asset pricing with heterogeneous consumers and without demand aggregation. *Journal of Business* **55**:253–267.

Debreu, G. 1959. *Theory of Value.* Yale University Press, New Haven.

Kraus, A., and R. Litzenberger. 1983. On the distributional conditions for a consumption–oriented three moment CAPM. *Journal of Finance* **38**:1381–1391.

Litzenberger, R., and H. Sosin. 1977. The theory of recapitalizations and the evidence of dual purpose funds. *Journal of Finance* **32**:1433–1455.

Modigliani, F., and M. Miller. 1958. The cost of capital, corporate finance and the theory of corporation finance. *American Economic Review* **48**:261–297.

Radner, R. 1982. Equilibrium under uncertainty. In *Handbook of Mathematical Economics, Vol II*:923–1006. Edited by K. Arrow and M. Intriligator. North–Holland Publishing Co, New York.

Ross, S. 1976. Options and efficiency. *Quarterly Journal of Economics* **90**:75–89.

Rubinstein, M. 1974. An aggregation theorem for securities markets. *Journal of Financial Economics* **1**:225–244.

Varian, H. 1978. *Microeconomic Analysis.* W.W. Norton & Company, Inc., New York.

Wilson, R. 1968. The theory of syndicates, *Econometrica* **36**:119–131.

CHAPTER 6
VALUATION OF COMPLEX SECURITIES AND OPTIONS WITH PREFERENCE RESTRICTIONS

6.1. In Chapter 4, we made assumptions on the return distributions in order to derive linear valuation relations. In this chapter, we will first discuss valuation principles for complex securities in the framework of Chapter 5 without special assumptions on either the return distributions or individuals' utility functions. We will then derive explicit valuation expressions for risky assets under preference and distribution restrictions. In particular, the price of a European call option written on a stock when individuals' utility functions exhibit constant relative risk aversion and the option's underlying asset has a payoff structure that is jointly lognormally distributed with the aggregate consumption is explicitly computed. We also apply the pricing formula for a European call option to study the pricing of risky corporate debt. In the last section of this chapter, we derive a pricing relation similar to the CAPM for a particular class of risky assets.

The pricing relations derived in this chapter provide additional testable propositions concerning the pricing of complex securities such as common stocks and options. Some of these propositions will be empirically examined in Chapter 10.

6.2. Assume that individuals have homogeneous beliefs π_ω and utility functions that are time–additive and state–independent, denoted by u_{i0} and u_i, and assume that these utility functions are increasing, strictly concave, and differentiable. There are $N + 1$ securities traded, indexed by $j = 0, 1, \ldots, N$. Individuals' time–0 endowments are units of time–0 consumption good and shares of traded securities. Security j is represented by its state dependent payoff structure $x_{j\omega}$. The 0–th security is a riskless discount bond with $x_{0\omega} = 1$ for all $\omega \in \Omega$.

We assume that the equilibrium allocation is Pareto optimal. We recall from Chapter 5 that under this condition, a representative agent with increasing and strictly concave utility functions u_0 and u_1 can be constructed, and the price of a primitive state contingent claim can be expressed as

$$\phi_\omega = \frac{\pi_\omega u_1'(C_\omega)}{u_0'(C_0)} \quad \forall \omega \in \Omega, \qquad (6.2.1)$$

where ϕ_ω is the state price for state ω. A complex security may be viewed as a portfolio of elementary state contingent claims. Thus the price for security j is

$$S_j = \sum_{\omega \in \Omega} \phi_\omega x_{j\omega}. \qquad (6.2.2)$$

Substituting (6.2.1) into (6.2.2) for ϕ_ω gives

$$S_j = E\left[\frac{u_1'(\tilde{C})}{u_0'(C_0)} \tilde{x}_j \right], \qquad (6.2.3)$$

where we have used $\tilde{x}_j$ to denote the random time–1 payoff of security j. For the case of a riskless unit discount bond – a complex security that pays one unit of consumption at time 1 in all states, we have

$$S_0 = E\left[\frac{u_1'(\tilde{C})}{u_0'(C_0)} \right]. \qquad (6.2.4)$$

As S_0 is the price of a unit discount bond, the riskless interest rate r_f is

$$r_f = \frac{1}{S_0} - 1. \qquad (6.2.5)$$

By the strict monotonicity of the utility functions, $S_0 > 0$. This implies that $r_f > -1$. Substituting (6.2.5) into (6.2.4) gives

$$\frac{1}{1 + r_f} = E\left[\frac{u_1'(\tilde{C})}{u_0'(C_0)}\right]. \qquad (6.2.6)$$

Dividing both sides of (6.2.3) by S_j and using the definition of covariance, we can write

$$E[\tilde{r}_j - r_f] = -\left(E\left[\frac{u_1'(\tilde{C})}{u_0'(C_0)}\right]\right)^{-1} \mathrm{Cov}(\tilde{r}_j, u_1'(\tilde{C})/u_0'(C_0)), \qquad (6.2.7)$$

where $\tilde{r}_j \equiv \tilde{x}_j/S_j - 1$ is the rate of return of security j. Substituting (6.2.6) into (6.2.7) gives an equilibrium relation for the risk premiums on securities:

$$E[\tilde{r}_j - r_f] = -(1 + r_f)\mathrm{Cov}(\tilde{r}_j, u_1'(\tilde{C})/u_0'(C_0)). \qquad (6.2.8)$$

By the fact that u_1 is strictly concave, the risk premium of a security is positive if and only if its random payoff at time 1 is positively correlated with the time–1 aggregate consumption. Note that in a two–period (period 0 and period 1) economy, by the strict monotonicity of utility functions, the time–1 aggregate consumption $\tilde{C}$ is equal to the time–1 aggregate endowment, which in turn is equal to time–1 aggregate wealth $\tilde{M}$. Therefore, (6.2.8) can be written as

$$E[\tilde{r}_j - r_f] = -(1 + r_f)\mathrm{Cov}(\tilde{r}_j, u_1'(\tilde{M})/u_0'(C_0)). \qquad (6.2.9)$$

That is, the risk premium of a security is positive if and only if its time–1 random payoff is positively correlated with the time-1 aggregate wealth. The intuition behind this result is the same as that of the Capital Asset Pricing Model. One unit of consumption in a state where the aggregate resource is abundant is less valuable than one unit of consumption in a state where the aggregate resource is scarce. Therefore, a security that pays more in states where the aggregate consumption/wealth is low is more valuable than a security that pays more in states where the aggregate consumption/wealth is high, *ceteris paribus*. As a result, the price for the former will be higher than that for the latter, and the rate of return on the former will be lower than that on the latter.

The market portfolio is a portfolio of traded securities. Thus its rate of return $\tilde{r}_m$ must also satisfy (6.2.9):

$$E[\tilde{r}_m - r_f] = -(1 + r_f)\text{Cov}(\tilde{r}_m, u_1'(\tilde{M})/u_0'(C_0)). \qquad (6.2.10)$$

Relation (6.2.10) implies that the risk premium on the market portfolio must be strictly positive, as $r_f > -1$ and u_1' is strictly decreasing so that $\text{Cov}(\tilde{r}_m, u_1'(\tilde{M}))$ is strictly negative. (Readers should compare this with the result of Section 4.14.) Substituting (6.2.10) into (6.2.9) gives

$$E[\tilde{r}_j - r_f] = \frac{\text{Cov}(\tilde{r}_j, u_1'(\tilde{M}))}{\text{Cov}(\tilde{r}_m, u_1'(\tilde{M}))} E[\tilde{r}_m - r_f]. \qquad (6.2.11)$$

In equilibrium, the risk premium of security j is proportional to that of the market portfolio. The proportionality is equal to the ratio of the covariance of $\tilde{r}_j$ and $u_1'(\tilde{M})$ and the covariance of $\tilde{r}_m$ and $u_1'(\tilde{M})$.

6.3. We will now specialize the pricing relation of (6.2.11) by considering a class of utility functions. Assume that individuals' utility functions for time–1 consumption are power functions:

$$u_i(z) = \frac{1}{B-1}(A_i + Bz)^{1-\frac{1}{B}} \qquad (6.3.1)$$

and that there is a riskless asset. Note that B is assumed to be constant across individuals. We also assume that the u_i's are increasing and strictly concave over the relevant region. Recall from Chapter 5 that the Pareto optimal sharing rules for time–1 consumption are linear in this case and can be attained if there is a riskless asset and if all assets are traded. Therefore, by the assumption that individuals are endowed only with holdings of shares of traded securities and time–0 consumption good in a securities markets economy, the equilibrium allocation is Pareto optimal. Moreover, Chapter 5 also shows that there exists a representative agent whose utility function for time–1 consumption is a power function with the same B:

$$u_1(z) = \frac{1}{B-1}(A + Bz)^{1-\frac{1}{B}}, \tag{6.3.2}$$

where $A \equiv \sum_{i=1}^{I} A_i$. Hence (6.2.11) becomes

$$E[\tilde{r}_j - r_f] = \frac{\mathrm{Cov}(\tilde{r}_j, (A + B\tilde{M})^{-\frac{1}{B}})}{\mathrm{Cov}(\tilde{r}_m, (A + B\tilde{M})^{-\frac{1}{B}})} E[\tilde{r}_m - r_f]. \tag{6.3.3}$$

Note that when $B = -1$, individuals' utility functions are quadratic and (6.3.3) becomes the familiar CAPM relation. When $B = -1/2$, the representative agent's utility function for time–1 consumption is a cubic function:

$$u_1(z) = -\frac{2}{3}\left(A - \frac{1}{2}z\right)^3.$$

The marginal utility in this case is

$$u_1'(z) = \left(A - \frac{1}{2}z\right)^2,$$

so u_1 is increasing and strictly concave for $z < 2A$. Thus if $\tilde{M} < 2A$, (6.3.3) becomes

$$E[\tilde{r}_j - r_f] = \frac{\mathrm{Cov}(\tilde{r}_j, (A - \tilde{M}/2)^2)}{\mathrm{Cov}(\tilde{r}_m, (A - \tilde{M}/2)^2)} E[\tilde{r}_m - r_f]$$

$$= \frac{(A - W_{m0})\mathrm{Cov}(\tilde{r}_j, \tilde{r}_m)W_{m0} - \frac{1}{4}\mathrm{Cov}(\tilde{r}_j, \tilde{r}_m^2)W_{m0}^2}{(A - W_{m0})\mathrm{Var}(\tilde{r}_m)W_{m0} - \frac{1}{4}\mathrm{Cov}(\tilde{r}_m, \tilde{r}_m^2)W_{m0}^2} E[\tilde{r}_m - r_f],$$

$$\tag{6.3.4}$$

where W_{m0} is the time–0 total value of traded securities. From (6.3.4) we notice that the risk premium of risky asset j depends not only upon the covariance of its return with the return on the market portfolio but also upon $\mathrm{Cov}(\tilde{r}_j, \tilde{r}_m^2)$, which we term *coskewness*. The risk premium on asset j is higher the higher the covariance $\mathrm{Cov}(\tilde{r}_j, r_m)$ and the lower the *coskewness* with the market portfolio. The latter of these two effects is a consequence of the fact that a cubic utility function exhibits preference towards the skewness of time–1 random consumption. The higher the coskewness of a security's return with that of the market portfolio, the more attractive it is to the individuals, *ceteris paribus*. Therefore, it will sell for a higher price and thus will have a lower expected rate of return.

6.4. Chapter 5 showed that call options help to achieve nonlinear sharing rules. Moreover, the prices of call options on aggregate consumption are sufficient to price *any* complex security in an allocationally efficient securities market where individuals' preferences are represented by time–additive, increasing, and strictly concave von Neumann–Morgenstern utility functions. In Sections 6.5 through 6.8, we will discuss certain properties of option prices that can be established by using purely arbitrage arguments. Section 6.9 gives some comparative statics of option prices as functions of their underlying asset prices and exercise prices. In later sections, an option pricing formula will be derived under the assumption that the payoff of the option's underlying asset and time–1 aggregate consumption are jointly lognormally distributed and that the representative agent's utility functions exhibit constant relative risk aversion.

6.5. Recall that a European call option is a security that gives its holder the right to purchase a share of its underlying security at a fixed exercise price on the maturity date of the option. Let $\tilde{x}_j(k)$ be the time–1 payoff from a European call on one share of the j–th security maturing at time 1 with an exercise price of k, and let $p_j(S_j, k)$ be the price of this call at time 0 when its underlying stock price is S_j. Since an option gives its holder the right but not the obligation to exercise on the maturity date,

$$\tilde{x}_j(k) = \begin{cases} \tilde{x}_j - k & \text{if } \tilde{x}_j - k > 0, \\ 0 & \text{otherwise,} \end{cases}$$

where $\tilde{x}_j$ is the random payoff of a share of the j–th security.

We claim that

$$p_j(S_j, k) \geq \max[S_j - k/(1 + r_f), 0], \tag{6.5.1}$$

independent of individuals' utility functions and payoff distributions. The inequality will be strict if the probability that the option will be exercised is strictly between 0 and 1. We will prove now the strict inequality. Consider the following strategy: short sell one share of security j, buy one European call written on security j with an exercise price k maturing at time 1 and lend $k/(1+r_f)$ dollars at the riskless rate. This strategy has an initial cost equal to $p_j(S_j, k) - S_j + k/(1+r_f)$ and has a time-1 payoff:

$$
\begin{cases}
\tilde{x}_j - k - \tilde{x}_j + k = 0 & \text{if } \tilde{x}_j \geq k, \\
-\tilde{x}_j + k > 0 & \text{if } \tilde{x}_j < k.
\end{cases}
$$

The time-1 payoff of this strategy is nonnegative and is strictly positive with a strictly positive probability, since there is a strictly positive probability that $\tilde{x}_j < k$. Therefore, its initial cost must be strictly positive to prevent something being created from nothing. That is, we must have

$$p_j(S_j, k) - S_j + k/(1+r_f) > 0,$$

which is equivalent to

$$p_j(S_j, k) > S_j - k/(1+r_f). \tag{6.5.2}$$

Lastly, since a holder of the option only has the right and not the obligation to buy a share of its underlying security at the exercise price, the price of the option must be nonnegative. Moreover, by assumption there exists a strictly positive probability that the option will be exercised. Therefore, $p_j(S_j, k) > 0$. This observation together with (6.5.2) gives

$$p_j(S_j, k) > \max[S_j - k/(1+r_f), 0].$$

which was to be shown. The intuition behind this inequality is as follows. The present value of an obligation to buy a share of security j at time 1 at a price k is $S_j - k/(1+r_f)$. When there exists a strictly positive probability that $\tilde{x}_j$ will be strictly less than k, the option *not* to buy has a strictly positive value. Thus the call option must be worth strictly more than $S_j - k/(1+r_f)$. On the other hand, there exists a strictly positive probability that the option will be exercised. Hence, $p_j(S_j, k) > 0$.

6.6. In Section 5.19, by assuming that an option price is a twice differentiable function of its exercise price, we showed that an option price is a convex function of its exercise price. This property, as it turns out, holds more generally.

We want to show that

$$\alpha p_j(S_j, k) + (1 - \alpha)p_j(S_j, \hat{k}) \geq p_j(S_j, \bar{k}), \qquad (6.6.1)$$

where $\bar{k} = \alpha k + (1 - \alpha)\hat{k}$ and $\alpha \in (0, 1)$. Consider the strategy of buying α shares of the call option with an exercise price k and $(1 - \alpha)$ shares of the call option with an exercise price $\hat{k}$, and short selling a share of call option with an exercise price $\bar{k}$. Without loss of generality, assume that $\hat{k} > k$. The time–1 payoff of this strategy is

$$\begin{cases} 0 & \text{if } \tilde{x}_j \leq k, \\ \alpha(\tilde{x}_j - k) > 0 & \text{if } k < \tilde{x}_j \leq \bar{k}, \\ (1 - \alpha)(\hat{k} - \tilde{x}_j) > 0 & \text{if } \bar{k} < \tilde{x}_j \leq \hat{k}, \\ 0 & \text{if } \tilde{x}_j > \hat{k}, \end{cases}$$

which is nonnegative. Thus,

$$\alpha p_j(S_j, k) + (1 - \alpha)p_j(S_j, \hat{k}) - p_j(S_j, \bar{k}) \geq 0,$$

which is just (6.6.1). When there is a strictly positive probability that $\tilde{x}_j \in (k, \hat{k}]$, the weak inequality becomes a strict inequality.

You are asked to prove in Exercise 6.2 that $p_j(S_j, k)$ is a decreasing function of k. Hence $p_j(S_j, k)$ is a decreasing and convex function of its exercise price.

In a frictionless market, buying an option on two shares of security j with an exercise $2k$ should be equal to buying two options with an exercise price k on security j. To see this, we simply note that the random payoffs of the former are identical to those of the latter.

6.7. An option on a positively weighted portfolio of securities with an exercise price k is less valuable than a positively weighted portfolio of options with equal exercise prices k. Consider a positively weighted portfolio of securities with weights α_j, $j = 1, \ldots, N$, where α_j denotes the portfolio weight on security j. Note that

$$\sum_{j=1}^{N} \alpha_j = 1 \quad \alpha_j \geq 0.$$

The time–0 cost and time–1 random payoff of this portfolio are

$$S^* \equiv \sum_{j=1}^{N} \alpha_j S_j$$

and

$$\tilde{x}^* \equiv \sum_{j=1}^{N} \alpha_j \tilde{x}_j,$$

respectively. Let $p^*(S^*, k)$ be the price of a European call written on the portfolio of securities with an exercise price k that expires at time 1. The time–1 random payoff of this option is

$$\max[\sum_{j=1}^{N} \alpha_j \tilde{x}_j - k, 0].$$

Since $\max[z, 0]$ is a convex function of z, by the Jensen's inequality we have

$$\max[\sum_{j=1}^{N} \alpha_j \tilde{x}_j - k, 0] \leq \sum_{j=1}^{N} \alpha_j \max[\tilde{x}_j - k, 0].$$

Note that the right–hand side of the inequality is the time–1 random payoff of a portfolio of call options on individual securities with identical exercise prices k. Thus

$$p^*(S^*, k) \leq \sum_{j=1}^{N} \alpha_j p_j(S_j, k),$$

where the inequality is strict if and only if there exist some j and j' such that $\tilde{x}_j < k < \tilde{x}_{j'}$ with a strictly positive probability. Suppose that all securities have payoffs such that all individual options with an exercise price k will be optimally exercised simultaneously. Then a positively weighted portfolio of options on individual securities with an exercise price k will be worth just as much as an option on a portfolio of securities with the same exercise price and using the same weights. Suppose on the other hand that some options on individual securities will not be optimally exercised simultaneously. A portfolio of options, unlike an option on a portfolio of securities, gives its holder an "option" to exercise different options individually. Thus a positively weighted portfolio of call options is strictly more valuable than a call option on a portfolio of securities with the same weights.

6.8. The holder of a European put option has the right to sell its underlying security at the exercise price on the maturity date. Let $P_j(S_j, k)$ be the time–0 price of a European put written on security j with exercise price k and maturity date 1, when the current price of security j is S_j. The time–1 payoff of this put option is

$$\begin{cases} k - \tilde{x}_j > 0 & \text{if } \tilde{x}_j < k, \\ 0 & \text{if } \tilde{x}_j \geq k. \end{cases}$$

The price of a European put can be computed from the prices of its underlying security and its European call counterpart through a relation called *put–call parity*.

We claim that $P_j(S_j, k) = k/(1+r_f) - S_j + p_j(S_j, k)$. To see this, consider the following strategy: lend $k/(1 + r_f)$ at the riskless rate, short sell one share of security j, and buy one share of the European call with exercise price k. The time–1 payoff of this strategy is

$$\begin{cases} k - \tilde{x}_j & \text{if } \tilde{x}_j < k, \\ 0 & \text{if } k \leq \tilde{x}_j, \end{cases}$$

which is clearly the payoff of a European put with exercise price k. To rule out arbitrage opportunities, two packages of financial assets having the same payoffs must sell for the same price. Hence our assertion follows. It is easy to see that $P_j(S_j, k)$ is an increasing function of k. Also, using arguments similar to those of Section 6.5, we can get

$$P_j(S_j, k) \geq \max[k/(1 + r_f) - S_j, 0].$$

You will be asked to verify these two relations in Exercise 6.3.

Given put–call parity and the facts that the price of a call is a decreasing function of its exercise price and that the price of a put is an increasing function of its exercise price, we have

$$\frac{\partial p_j(S_j, k)}{\partial k} \geq -\frac{1}{1 + r_f} \quad \text{and} \quad \frac{\partial P_j(S_j, k)}{\partial k} \leq \frac{1}{1 + r_f},$$

when $p_j(S_j, k)$ and $P_j(S_j, k)$ are differentiable functions of k. Moreover, $P_j(S_j, k)$ is also a convex function of k by put–call parity.

6.9. In the previous two sections, we have seen that a call price is a decreasing and convex function of its exercise price. We will show in this section that, fixing a return distribution on the underlying asset, the price of a call option is an increasing and convex function of the price of its underlying asset. Readers are cautioned to note that this relation is a comparative statics result and is not an arbitrage relation, since different stock prices can not prevail contemporaneously.

Consider $p_j(S_j, k)$. Assume the distribution of $\tilde{x}_j / S_j$ is invariant with respect to changes in S_j. For example, if we increase S_j to S_j', then $\tilde{x}_j$ changes to $S_j' \tilde{x}_j / S_j$. We claim first that $p_j(S_j, k)$ is increasing in S_j and is strictly so if the probability that $\tilde{x}_j > k$ is strictly positive. By the assumption that return distribution is held fixed, we have

$$p_j(S_j', k) = \frac{S_j'}{S_j} p_j(S_j, kS_j / S_j') \tag{6.9.1}$$

$$\geq \frac{S_j'}{S_j} p_j(S_j, k) \geq p_j(S_j, k). \tag{6.9.2}$$

Relation (6.9.1) follows since, given that the return distribution is invariant to changes in S_j, the time–1 payoff of a call on security–j with an exercise price k when security–j's price is S_j' is equivalent to the time–1 payoff of S_j' / S_j shares of call options with an exercise price kS_j / S_j' when security j's price is S_j. Note that (6.9.1) amounts to saying that the function $p_j(S_j, k)$ is *homogeneous of degree one* in S_j and k. The first inequality of (6.9.2) follows since the call option price is a decreasing function of its exercise price. Finally, the second inequality of (6.9.2) follows because $S_j'/S_j > 1$ by assumption and $p_j(S_j, k) \geq 0$. The second inequality of (6.9.2) is strict if there is a strictly positive probability that $\tilde{x}_j > k$, as then $p_j(S_j, k) > 0$.

Next we want to show that $p_j(S_j, k)$ is a convex function of S_j. Let

$$\hat{S}_j \equiv \alpha S_j + (1 - \alpha)S_j' \quad \text{where } \alpha \in (0, 1).$$

To prove convexity, we must show that

$$\alpha p_j(S_j, k) + (1 - \alpha)p_j(S_j', k) \geq p_j(\hat{S}_j, k).$$

From the fact that $p_j(S_j, k)$ is a convex function of k for all possible S_j,

$$\gamma p_j(1, k_1) + (1 - \gamma)p_j(1, k_2) \geq p_j(1, k_3) \quad \forall \gamma \in (0, 1), \qquad (6.9.3)$$

where $k_3 \equiv \gamma k_1 + (1 - \gamma)k_2$. Now take $\gamma \equiv \alpha S_j/\hat{S}_j$, $k_1 \equiv k/S_j$, and $k_2 \equiv k/S_j'$. Multiplying both sides of (6.9.3) by $\hat{S}_j$ and recalling from (6.9.1) that $p_j(S_j, k)$ is homogeneous of degree one in S_j and k,

$$\alpha p_j(S_j, S_j k_1) + (1 - \alpha)p_j(S_j', S_j' k_2) \geq p_j(\hat{S}_j, \hat{S}_j k_3).$$

Using the definitions of $\hat{S}_j$, γ, k_1, k_2, and k_3, this inequality can be written as

$$\alpha p_j(S_j, k) + (1 - \alpha)p_j(S_j', k) \geq p_j(\hat{S}_j, k). \qquad (6.9.4)$$

The weak inequality of (6.9.4) will be strict if that of (6.9.3) is strict. From Section 6.6, we know that (6.9.3) is a strict inequality if there exists a strictly positive probability that $\tilde{x}_j$ lies between k_1 and k_2 or equivalently between k/S_j and k/S_j'.

Figure 6.9.1 illustrates the general shape that a call option price should have as a function of its underlying security price and its exercise price, while holding constant the return distribution of its underlying asset. Note that we have used (6.5.1) in Figure 6.9.1.

6.10. In this section, a pricing formula for a European call is derived under conditions on individuals' preferences and on the joint

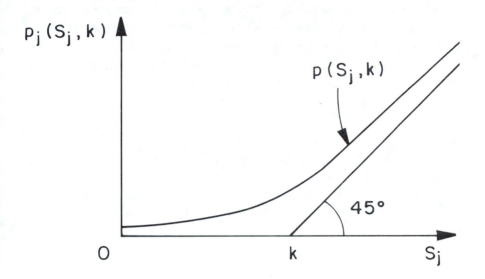

Figure 6.9.1: Call Option Price as a Function of Its Underlying Stock Price

distribution of the time–1 aggregate consumption and the payoffs of the option's underlying asset.

Consider a two–period securities markets economy. Individuals' utility functions are time–additive extended power functions with identical cautiousness as in (6.3.1). Moreover, assume that $\sum_{i=1}^{I} A_i = 0$. Recall that in a securities markets economy, an individual is endowed with time–0 consumption and shares of traded securities. From Sections 5.14 and 5.15, we know that the equilibrium allocation will be Pareto optimal, since optimal sharing rules are linear. Thus, a representative agent can be constructed with power utility functions:

$$u_0(z_0) + u_1(z_1) = \frac{1}{1-B} z_0^{1-B} + \rho \frac{1}{1-B} z_1^{1-B},$$

where ρ is the time preference parameter. Then (6.2.3) implies that

$$p_j(S_j, k) = \rho E \left[\max[\tilde{x}_j - k, 0] \left(\frac{\tilde{C}}{C_0} \right)^{-B} \right]. \tag{6.10.1}$$

We will further assume that $\tilde{x}_j$ and $\tilde{C}$ are bivariate lognormally distributed, that is, $\ln \tilde{x}_j$ and $\ln \tilde{C}$ are bivariate normally distributed with means $(\hat{\mu}_j, \hat{\mu}_c)$ and variance–covariance matrix:

$$\begin{pmatrix} \sigma_j^2 & \kappa \sigma_j \hat{\sigma}_c \\ \kappa \sigma_j \hat{\sigma}_c & \hat{\sigma}_c^2 \end{pmatrix},$$

where κ is the correlation coefficient of $\ln \tilde{x}_j$ and $\ln \tilde{C}$. This assumption implies that $\ln(\tilde{x}_j/S_j)$ and $\ln \rho(\tilde{C}/C_0)^{-B}$ are bivariate normally distributed with means

$$(\mu_j, \mu_c) \equiv (\hat{\mu}_j - \ln S_j, \ -B\hat{\mu}_c + \ln \rho + B \ln C_0)$$

and variance–covariance matrix

$$\begin{pmatrix} \sigma_j^2 & \kappa \sigma_j \sigma_c \\ \kappa \sigma_j \sigma_c & \sigma_c^2 \end{pmatrix} \equiv \begin{pmatrix} \sigma_j^2 & -B\kappa \sigma_j \hat{\sigma}_c \\ -B\kappa \sigma_j \hat{\sigma}_c & B^2 \hat{\sigma}_c^2 \end{pmatrix}.$$

Given the above distributional assumption, (6.10.1) can be written as

$$p_j(S_j, k) = S_j \int_{-\infty}^{+\infty} \int_{\ln(k/S_j)}^{+\infty} (e^z - k/S_j) e^y f(z, y) dz dy, \quad (6.10.2)$$

where $f(z, y)$ is the joint density function for $\tilde{z} \equiv \ln(\tilde{x}_j/S_j)$ and $\tilde{y} \equiv \ln \rho(\tilde{C}/C_0)^{-B}$. Relation (6.10.2) may be rewritten as the difference between two integrals

$$\begin{aligned} p_j(S_j, k) = S_j &\int_{-\infty}^{+\infty} \int_{\ln(k/S_j)}^{+\infty} e^{z+y} f(z, y) dz dy \\ &- k \int_{-\infty}^{+\infty} \int_{\ln(k/S_j)}^{+\infty} e^y f(z, y) dz dy. \end{aligned} \quad (6.10.3)$$

In the next section the two integrals are evaluated and the following relations are obtained:

$$\int_{-\infty}^{\infty} \int_a^{\infty} e^y f(z, y) dz dy = (e^{\mu_c + \sigma_c^2/2}) \ N(\frac{-a + \mu_j}{\sigma_j} + \kappa \sigma_c), \quad (6.10.4)$$

and

$$\int_{-\infty}^{\infty} \int_{a}^{\infty} e^{z+y} f(z,y) dz dy$$

$$= \left(e^{\mu_j + \mu_c + (\sigma_j^2 + 2\kappa\sigma_j\sigma_c + \sigma_c^2)/2}\right) N\left(\frac{-a + \mu_j}{\sigma_j} + \kappa\sigma_c + \sigma_j\right),$$

(6.10.5)

where $N(\cdot)$ is the distribution function of a standard normal random variable:

$$N(z) \equiv \frac{1}{\sqrt{2\pi}} \int_{-\infty}^{z} e^{-v^2/2} dv,$$

and

$$n(z) \equiv \frac{1}{\sqrt{2\pi}} e^{-z^2/2}$$

is the standard normal density function. By setting $a = \ln(k/S_j)$, (6.10.4) may be used to evaluate the second integral on the right–hand side of (6.10.3), and (6.10.5) may be used to evaluate the first integral on the right side of (6.10.3) by setting $a = \ln(k/S_j)$.

It is easily verified that

$$E\left[\rho(\tilde{C}/C_0)^{-B}\right] = e^{\mu_c + \frac{1}{2}\sigma_c^2},$$

(6.10.6)

and that

$$E\left[\frac{\tilde{x}_j}{S_j}\rho\left(\frac{\tilde{C}}{C_0}\right)^{-B}\right] = e^{\mu_j + \mu_c + (\sigma_j^2 + 2\kappa\sigma_j\sigma_c + \sigma_c^2)/2}.$$

(6.10.7)

The left–hand side of (6.10.6) is equal to $(1+r_f)^{-1}$, since it gives the present value of one unit of time–1 consumption in all states. Hence,

$$e^{\mu_c + \frac{1}{2}\sigma_c^2} = (1+r_f)^{-1}.$$

(6.10.8)

Also, (6.2.3) implies that the left–hand side of (6.10.7) is equal to 1. Thus

$$e^{\mu_j + \mu_c + (\sigma_j^2 + 2\kappa\sigma_j\sigma_c + \sigma_c^2)/2} = 1.$$

(6.10.9)

Now substituting (6.10.4), (6.10.5), (6.10.8), and (6.10.9) into (6.10.3) gives

$$p_j(S_j, k) = S_j N(Z_k + \sigma_j) - (1+r_f)^{-1} k N(Z_k),$$

(6.10.10)

where

$$Z_k \equiv \frac{\ln(S_j/k) + (\mu_j + \kappa\sigma_j\sigma_c)}{\sigma_j}.$$ (6.10.11)

Relations (6.10.8) and (6.10.9) also imply that

$$\mu_j + \kappa\sigma_j\sigma_c = \ln(1 + r_f) - \frac{1}{2}\sigma_j^2.$$ (6.10.12)

Thus (6.10.11) can be written as

$$Z_k = \frac{\ln(S_j/k) + \ln(1 + r_f)}{\sigma_j} - \frac{1}{2}\sigma_j$$ (6.10.13)

Relations (6.10.10) and (6.10.13) are the well known *Black–Scholes option pricing formula* that was originally derived by an arbitrage argument in a continuous time economy under the assumption that the stock price follows a geometric Brownian Motion and the instantaneous riskless interest rate is a known constant. Here we derived this formula in a discrete time economy by making joint conditions on the distributions as well as on the individuals' preferences.

6.11. The derivations of (6.10.4) and (6.10.5) will be presented in this section, which are adapted from the appendix of Rubinstein (1976). Readers can skip this section without loss of continuity. The derivations of these relations require evaluations of other indefinite integrals over the marginal and conditional normal density functions. The first relation to be derived is

$$\int_a^\infty f(z)dz = N(\frac{-a + \mu_j}{\sigma_j}),$$ (6.11.1)

where $f(z)$ is the marginal density function for $\ln(\tilde{x}_j/S_j)$. The first step in deriving relation (6.11.1) involves converting $f(z)$ into standard normal density function and exchanging the limits of integration, which is a valid procedure since the density function of a standard normal random variable is symmetric around zero:

$$\int_a^{+\infty} f(z)dz = \int_{\frac{a-\mu_j}{\sigma_j}}^\infty n(v)dv = \int_{-\infty}^{-\frac{a-\mu_j}{\sigma_j}} n(v)dv = N(\frac{-a + \mu_j}{\sigma_j}).$$

The second evaluation is

$$\int_a^{+\infty} e^z f(z)dz = \int_a^{+\infty} \frac{1}{\sigma_j\sqrt{2\pi}} \exp\{\frac{-1}{2\sigma_j^2}(z-\mu_j)^2 + z\}dz$$

$$=(e^{\mu_j+\sigma_j^2/2}) \int_a^{+\infty} \frac{1}{\sigma_j\sqrt{2\pi}} \exp\{\frac{-1}{2\sigma_j^2}(z-(\mu_j+\sigma_j^2))^2\}dz$$

$$=(e^{\mu_j+\sigma_j^2/2}) N(\frac{-a+\mu_j}{\sigma_j}+\sigma_j).$$

$$(6.11.2)$$

The third evaluation is

$$\int_{-\infty}^{+\infty} e^y f(y|z)dy = \exp\{\mu_c + \kappa\frac{\sigma_c}{\sigma_j}(z-\mu_j) + \frac{1}{2}(1-\kappa^2)\sigma_c^2\}, \quad (6.11.3)$$

where $f(y|z)$ is the conditional density of $\ln\rho(\tilde{C}/C_0)^{-B}$ given that $\ln(\tilde{x}_j/S_j) = z$. Note that the conditional distribution of $\ln\rho(\tilde{C}/C_0)^{-B}$ given that $\ln(\tilde{x}_j/S_j) = z$ is a normal distribution with mean $\mu_c + \kappa(\sigma_c/\sigma_j)(z-\mu_j)$ and variance $(1-\kappa^2)\sigma_c^2$. Then the evaluation of the left–hand side of (6.11.3) is equivalent to that of (6.11.2) by taking $a = -\infty$ and by appropriate parameter change.

Now we are prepared to derive (6.10.4). From (6.11.3) we can write

$$\int_{-\infty}^{+\infty}\int_a^{+\infty} e^y f(z,y)dzdy = \int_a^{+\infty} f(z)\int_{-\infty}^{+\infty} e^y f(y|z)dydz$$

$$=\int_a^{+\infty} e^{\mu_c+\kappa\frac{\sigma_c}{\sigma_j}(z-\mu_j)+(1-\kappa^2)\sigma_c^2/2} f(z)dz$$

$$=(e^{\mu_c+\sigma_c^2/2}) \int_a^{+\infty} \frac{1}{\sigma_j\sqrt{2\pi}} \exp\{\frac{-1}{2\sigma_j^2}(z-(\mu_j+\kappa\sigma_j\sigma_c))^2\}dz,$$

where $f(z)$ is the marginal density function for $\ln(\tilde{x}_j/S_j)$. Relation (6.10.4) follows by converting the density in the integral on the right–hand side of the third equality to a standard normal density and changing the limits of integration accordingly.

Finally, we are prepared to derive relation (6.10.5). From (6.11.3)

$$\int_{-\infty}^{+\infty} \int_{a}^{+\infty} e^{z} e^{y} f(z, y) dz dy = \int_{a}^{+\infty} e^{z} f(z) \int_{-\infty}^{+\infty} e^{y} f(y|z) dy dz$$

$$= \int_{a}^{+\infty} e^{\mu_c + \kappa \frac{\sigma_c}{\sigma_j}(z - \mu_j) + (1 - \kappa^2)\sigma_c^2/2} e^{z} f(z) dz$$

$$= e^{\mu_j + \mu_c + (\sigma_j^2 + 2\kappa\sigma_j\sigma_c + \sigma_c^2)/2} \int_{a}^{+\infty} \frac{1}{\sigma_j\sqrt{2\pi}} e^{-\frac{1}{2\sigma_j^2}(z - \mu_j - \kappa\sigma_j\sigma_c - \sigma_j^2)^2} dz.$$

Relation (6.10.5) is then obtained by converting the density in the integral on the right–hand side of the third equality into a standard normal density and changing the limits of the integration accordingly.

6.12. The option pricing formula in Section 6.10 is derived in an economy where individuals' utility functions exhibit linear risk tolerance with identical cautiousness and where individuals are only endowed with traded securities. In equilibrium, every individual holds a linear combination of the market portfolio and the riskless asset and a Pareto optimal allocation is achieved. Therefore, if a call option written on a security is introduced into the economy, no individual will demand it in equilibrium. Equivalently, if the economy is in equilibrium when a call option is introduced, as long as the option is priced according to (6.10.10) and (6.10.13), the original equilibrium will not be upset. The option is priced so that no individual will demand it in equilibrium. In this context, an option has no allocational role in equilibrium and is sometimes said to be a *redundant asset*. Note that the above discussion applies not only to options but also to any financial asset that is in zero net supply.

6.13. From (6.10.10) and (6.10.13), $p_j(S_j, k)$ depends upon the time–0 price of its underlying asset S_j, the exercise price k, the riskless interest rate r_f, and the variance of $\ln(\tilde{x}_j/S_j)$. It does not depend upon the mean of $\ln(\tilde{x}_j/S_j)$, however. You will be asked in Exercise 6.4 to verify the following comparative statics of $p_j(S_j, k)$ with respect to S_j, k, r_f, and σ_j:

$$\frac{\partial p_j(S_j, k)}{\partial k} = -(1 + r_f)^{-1} N(Z_k) < 0, \qquad (6.13.1)$$

$$\frac{\partial p_j(S_j, k)}{\partial S_j} = N(Z_k + \sigma_j) > 0, \tag{6.13.2}$$

$$\frac{\partial p_j(S_j, k)}{\partial \sigma_j} = k(1 + r_f)^{-1} n(Z_k) > 0, \tag{6.13.3}$$

$$\frac{\partial p_j(S_j, k)}{\partial r_f} = (1 + r_f)^{-2} k N(Z_k) > 0. \tag{6.13.4}$$

Relations (6.13.1) and (6.13.2) are confirmations of the general discussions in Sections 6.6 and 6.9. Note that in computing (6.13.2), we have assumed that the distribution of $\ln(\tilde{x}_j/S_j)$ is unchanged when we vary S_j. Relation (6.13.3) says that the higher the variance of $\ln(\tilde{x}_j/S_j)$, the more valuable the option is. This is so because an option holder does not have an obligation to exercise – he only has the right to do so. Hence, a higher σ_j allows a higher upside potential for an option. Finally, the higher the riskless interest rate, the lower the present value of the exercise price in the event of exercising at time 1, thus the more valuable the option is.

From (6.13.1), we can also get

$$\frac{\partial^2 p_j(S_j, k)}{\partial k^2} = ((1 + r_f)\sigma_j k)^{-1} n(Z_k) > 0. \tag{6.13.5}$$

That is, $p_j(S_j, k)$ is a convex function of the exercise price, which is a general property of call options proved earlier using an arbitrage argument. From Section 5.19, we can interpret the right–hand side of (6.13.5) to be the *price density* for a security that pays one unit of consumption at time 1 if and only if the payoff of security j is equal to k at that time. This price density is always strictly positive.

6.14. The option pricing formula derived above can be applied to study the pricing of risky corporate debt. Consider the economy in Section 6.10. Suppose that firm j has one share of common stock and a discount bond with face value k outstanding, with prices S_j and D_j, respectively. The discount bond matures at time 1. The total time–1 earning of firm j is $\tilde{x}_j$, which is assumed to be joint lognormally distributed with $\tilde{C}$, the time–1 aggregate consumption, with parameters as in Section 6.10. The present value of $\tilde{x}_j$ is the total value of the firm at time 0 and is denoted by V_j. Note that

$V_j = S_j + D_j$. The time–1 random payoff of the discount bond is $\min[\tilde{x}_j, k]$. When the firm is solvent at time 1, that is, when $\tilde{x}_j \geq k$, the bond holders receive the face value of the discount bond; otherwise, the firm goes bankrupt, and the bond holders take over the firm and get $\tilde{x}_j$. One way to compute D_j is to use (6.2.3):

$$D_j = \rho E \left[\min[\tilde{x}_j, k] \left(\frac{\tilde{C}}{C_0} \right)^{-B} \right]. \qquad (6.14.1)$$

We can, however, use the Black–Scholes option pricing formula to compute D_j in a direct and straightforward way. Note that the time–1 payoff to the equity holders is $\max[\tilde{x}_j - k, 0]$. When the firm is solvent at time 1, the equity holders pay off the bond holders and get the residual value of the firm, which is $\tilde{x}_j - k$; otherwise, the bond holders take over the firm, and the equity holders get zero. Therefore, the equity holders are holding a European call on the total value of the firm with an exercise price k maturing at time 1. The value of the equity is

$$S_j = V_j N(Z_k + \sigma_j) - (1 + r_f)^{-1} k N(Z_k)$$
$$\text{where} \quad Z_k \equiv \frac{\ln(V_j/k) + \ln(1 + r_f)}{\sigma_j} - \frac{1}{2}\sigma_j. \qquad (6.14.2)$$

From the comparative statics of Section 6.13, we know that, *ceteris paribus*, the value of the equity decreases as the face value of the bond increases, and increases as σ_j increases, that is, as the total time–1 earning of the firm becomes more volatile. When the total value of the firm V_j is fixed, the increase in σ_j shifts value from the debt holders to the equity holders.

The value of the discount bond is

$$D_j = V_j - S_j$$
$$= V_j(1 - N(Z_k + \sigma_j)) + (1 + r_f)^{-1} k N(Z_k). \qquad (6.14.3)$$

It increases as its face value increases and decreases as the earnings of the firm become more volatile.

We give two interpretations of a risky debt. The time–1 random payoff of the debt can be written as

$$\min[\tilde{x}_j, k] = \tilde{x}_j - \max[\tilde{x}_j - k, 0] \qquad (6.14.4)$$
$$= k - \max[k - \tilde{x}_j, 0]. \qquad (6.14.5)$$

Using (6.14.4), the bond holders can be viewed as holding the firm while selling a European call option on the value of the firm with an exercise price equal to the face value of the debt to the equity holders. We used this interpretation to compute (6.14.3). On the other hand, (6.14.5) implies that the bond holders are holding a riskless discount bond with a face value k, while at the same time selling a European put option on the value of the firm with an exercise price k. In the event that the firm's time–1 earnings are strictly less than k, the equity holders will *sell* the firm to the bond holders at a price k. Since $\tilde{x}_j$ is lognormally distributed and there, therefore, exists a strictly positive probability that the firm will default on the debt, the put option of (6.14.5) is not worthless, and the debt is risky. Therefore, the discount bond will sell at a price strictly less than $k/(1+r_f)$ and has a strictly positive risk premium.

6.15. Not all securities in strictly positive supply can have payoffs that are jointly lognormally distributed with time–1 aggregate consumption, since the sum of lognormally distributed random variables is not lognormally distributed. Under the conditions of Section 6.10, however, we can always use (6.10.10) and (6.10.13) to price European call options on the aggregate consumption/wealth. Recall from Section 5.19 that these option prices can, in turn, be used to price any complex securities.

Let $p_c(k)$ denote the price of a European call on aggregate consumption with an exercise price k maturing at time 1. Then

$$p_c(k) = S_c N(Z_k + \hat{\sigma}_c) - (1+r_f)^{-1} k\, N(Z_k), \qquad (6.15.1)$$

where

$$Z_k \equiv \frac{\ln(S_c/k) + \ln(1+r_f)}{\hat{\sigma}_c} - \frac{1}{2}\hat{\sigma}_c, \qquad (6.15.2)$$

$$\hat{\sigma}_c^2 = \mathrm{Var}(\ln(\tilde{C})), \qquad (6.15.3)$$

and

$$S_c = \rho E\left[\tilde{C}\left(\frac{\tilde{C}}{C_0}\right)^{-B}\right] \qquad (6.15.4)$$

is the present value of the time–1 aggregate consumption.

The price for one unit of consumption paid in states where the time 1 aggregate consumption is equal to k is

$$\Phi_c(k) = \frac{\partial^2 p_c(k)}{\partial k^2} dk = ((1 + r_f)\hat{\sigma}_c k)^{-1} n(Z_k) dk. \qquad (6.15.5)$$

Since the probability that time-1 aggregate consumption will be equal to any fixed k is formally equal to zero, $\Phi_c(k)$ is equal to zero. (Mathematically, dk is treated as zero.) The *pricing density* $\phi_c(k) \equiv \Phi_c(k)/dk$, is strictly positive, however.

We can do a comparative statics analysis of $\phi_c(k)$. The elasticity of $\phi_c(k)$ with respect to an increase in the value of S_c is analyzed holding the distribution of $(\tilde{C}/S_c)$ constant thereby implying a proportional change in $\tilde{C}$. The resulting increase in probabilities of "high" levels of $\tilde{C}$ and decrease in probability of "low" levels of $\tilde{C}$ increase and decrease, respectively, their elementary claim prices. This elasticity is

$$\frac{\partial \ln \phi_c(k)}{\partial \ln S_c} = -\frac{Z_k}{\hat{\sigma}_c}. \qquad (6.15.6)$$

Note that Z_k is a strictly decreasing function of k and

$$\lim_{k \to 0} Z_k = \infty, \qquad \lim_{k \to \infty} Z_k = -\infty.$$

Therefore, (6.15.6) is positive for high k and negative for low k.

The elasticity of $\phi_c(k)$ with respect to the standard deviation, $\hat{\sigma}_c$, is

$$\frac{\partial \ln \phi_c(k)}{\partial \ln \hat{\sigma}_c} = (Z_k + \hat{\sigma}_c)Z_k - 1 \qquad (6.15.7)$$

This elasticity will be positive for very large and very small k and will be negative for k near $E(\tilde{C})$, because an increase in variance increases the probability of extreme observations relative to the probability of central observations.

The elasticity of the elementary claim price with respect to the riskless bond price, $(1 + r_f)^{-1}$, is

$$\frac{\partial \ln \phi_c(k)}{\partial \ln(1 + r_f)^{-1}} = 1 + \frac{Z_k}{\hat{\sigma}_c} \qquad (6.15.8)$$

Thus, an increase in the riskless bond price lowers the prices of claims that pay off when the level of $\tilde{C}$ is high and raise the prices of claims that pay off when the level of $\tilde{C}$ is low. However, since $(1+r_f)^{-1} = \int_0^{+\infty} \phi_c(k)dk$, an increase in $(1+r_f)^{-1}$ must increase the average elementary claim price. From (6.10.6) and (6.10.8), a change in the bond price may be associated with either a change in the expected growth rate of aggregate consumption and/or a change in relative risk aversion. Both these possibilities would provide an intuitive explanation for the resulting impact on elementary claim prices

6.16. We analyzed the comparative statics of $\phi_c(k)$ with respect to the parameters of the economy in the previous section. We can also extract some information on the structure of $\phi_c(k)$ for different levels of k. The elasticity of $\phi_c(k)$ with respect to the level of consumption on which it is contingent is

$$\frac{\partial \ln \phi_c(k)}{\partial \ln k} = \frac{Z_k}{\hat{\sigma}_c} - 1. \qquad (6.16.1)$$

For levels of k far below $E(\tilde{C})$, the elasticity will be positive because the probability density for $\tilde{C}$ increases as k increases. For k well above $E(\tilde{C})$, the elasticity will be negative due to the combined effects of the decreasing probability density of the level of consumption on which the elementary claim is contingent and of decreasing marginal utility of consumption.

6.17. Previous analyses demonstrated that lognormally distributed aggregate time–1 consumption and constant relative risk aversion utility functions for the representative agent are sufficient conditions for the Black–Scholes option pricing formula to price European options on aggregate consumption correctly. Given that time–1 aggregate consumption is lognormally distributed, a constant relative risk aversion utility function for time–1 consumption for the representative agent turns out to be also necessary for the Black–Scholes formula to price European options correctly. Recall that the pricing density of an elementary claim on aggregate consumption divided by the probability density of occurrence of that level of aggregate consumption is the marginal rate of substitution between present consumption and future consumption for the representative agent. The elasticity of this ratio with respect to aggregate consumption is constant if and only if the representative agent's utility function for time–1 consumption exhibits constant relative risk aversion. The probability density of a given level of aggregate consumption k, given S_c, is

$$\pi_c(k) = \frac{(2\pi\hat{\sigma}_c^2)^{-1/2}}{k} \exp\left\{ \frac{-1}{2\hat{\sigma}_c^2}[\ln(\frac{k}{S_c}) - (\mu - \hat{\sigma}_c^2/2)]^2 \right\}; \quad (6.17.1)$$

Therefore, the price density of an elementary claim on aggregate consumption divided by the probability density of the occurrence of that level of aggregate consumption is

$$\frac{\phi_c(k)}{\pi_c(k)} = \frac{\exp\left[\frac{\mu-\ln(1+r_f)}{\hat{\sigma}_c^2}\ln(S_c/k) + \frac{(\mu-\ln(1+r_f))(\mu+\ln(1+r_f)-\hat{\sigma}_c^2)}{2\hat{\sigma}_c^2} \right]}{(1+r_f)}.$$

$$(6.17.2)$$

The elasticity of (6.17.2) with respect to k is

$$\frac{\partial \ln(\phi_c(k)/\pi_c(k))}{\partial \ln k} = -\frac{\mu - \ln(1+r_f)}{\hat{\sigma}_c^2} < 0, \quad (6.17.3)$$

which is a constant. Exercise 6.5 will ask the reader to show that the negative of the above elasticity is the coefficient of relative risk aversion for the representative agent's utility function for time 1 consumption. Thus, using the Black–Scholes formula to price options on aggregate consumption is implicitly assuming that individuals' utility functions for time–1 consumption aggregate to a constant relative risk aversion utility function.

Exercises

6.1. Derive a pricing relation similar to (6.3.3) when individuals have log utility functions.

6.2. Show that the price of a European call option is a decreasing function of its exercise price, and find the conditions under which it is a strictly decreasing function of its exercise price.

6.3. Let $P_j(S_j, k)$ be the price of a European put on security j with an exercise price k maturing at time 1. Show that P_j is an increasing function of k and that, when the probability that $\tilde{x}_j < k$ lies strictly between 0 and 1,

$$P_j(S_j, k) > \max[k/(1 + r_f) - S_j, 0].$$

6.4. Verify relations (6.13.1) to (6.13.5).

6.5. Prove that (6.17.3) is the relative risk aversion of the representative agent's utility function for time–1 consumption.

6.6. We derived the Black–Scholes option pricing formula by assuming that the representative agent's utility functions for time–0 as well as for time–1 consumption are of constant relative risk aversion. Derive a similar pricing formula by assuming only that the representative agent's utility function for time–1 consumption exhibits constant relative risk aversion.

Remarks. The discussion on skewness preferences follows Kraus and Litzenberger (1976, 1983). Discussions in Sections 6.5–6.9 are taken from Merton (1973), in which readers can also find a host of related subjects. Our derivation of the Black–Scholes option pricing formula is from Rubinstein (1976). Unlike the original Black–Scholes derivation, Rubinstein's derivation uses equilibrium arguments. Black and Scholes (1973) use arbitrage arguments and derive their formula in a continuous time economy. Merton (1973) formalizes and extends the Black–Scholes results. Cox, Ross, and Rubinstein (1979) also use arbitrage arguments to derive an option pricing formula in a discrete time economy by assuming that risky stock prices follow a binomial random walk. This subject is covered in Chapter 8. They show that their formula converges to the Black–Scholes formula when the trading intervals shrink to zero and when appropriate limits of their price system are taken. The application of the Black–Scholes option pricing formula to the pricing of corporate risky debt is adapted from Merton (1974). The discussions in Sections 6.15–6.18 are taken from Breeden and Litzenberger (1978). An option pricing formula under the assumptions that individuals have negative exponential utility functions and that asset returns are multivariate normally distributed is derived by Brennan (1979). For a review of the recent developments in option pricing theory and its applications see Cox and Huang (1987).

References

Black, F., and M. Scholes. 1973. The pricing of options and corporate liabilities. *Journal of Political Economy* **81**:637–654.

Breeden, D., and R. Litzenberger. 1978. Prices of state–contingent claims implicit in option prices. *Journal of Business* **51**:621–651.

Brennan, M. 1979. The pricing of contingent claims in discrete time models. *Journal of Finance* **34**:53–68.

Cox, J., and C. Huang. 1987. Option pricing theory and its applications. In *Frontiers of Financial Theory*. Edited by G. Constantinides and S. Bhattacharya. Rowman and Littlefield. Totowa, New Jersey.

Cox, J., S. Ross, and M. Rubinstein. 1979. Option pricing: A simplified approach. *Journal of Financial Economics* **7**:229–263.

Kraus, A., and R. Litzenberger. 1976. Skewness preference and the valuation of risk assets. *Journal of Finance* **31**:1085–1100.

Kraus, A., and R. Litzenberger. 1983. On the distributional conditions for a consumption–oriented three moment CAPM. *Journal of Finance* **38**:1381–1391.

Merton, R. 1973. Theory of rational option pricing. *Bell Journal of Economics and Management Science* **4**:141–183.

Merton, R. 1974. On the pricing of corporate debt: The risk structure of interest rates. *Journal of Finance* **29**:449–470.

Rubinstein, M. 1976. The valuation of uncertain income streams and the pricing of options. *Bell Journal of Economics* **7**:407–425.

References

Black, F., and M. Scholes. 1973. The pricing of options and corporate liabilities. *Journal of Political Economy* **81**:637–654.

Breeden, D., and R. Litzenberger. 1978. Prices of state–contingent claims implicit in option prices. *Journal of Business* **51**:621–651.

Brennan, M. 1979. The pricing of contingent claims in discrete time models. *Journal of Finance* **34**:53–68.

Cox, J., and C. Huang. 1987. Option pricing theory and its applications. In *Frontiers of Financial Theory*. Edited by G. Constantinides and S. Bhattacharya. Rowman and Littlefield. Totowa, New Jersey.

Cox, J., S. Ross, and M. Rubinstein. 1979. Option pricing: A simplified approach. *Journal of Financial Economics* **7**:229–263.

Kraus, A., and R. Litzenberger. 1976. Skewness preference and the valuation of risk assets. *Journal of Finance* **31**:1085–1100.

Kraus, A., and R. Litzenberger. 1983. On the distributional conditions for a consumption–oriented three moment CAPM. *Journal of Finance* **38**:1381–1391.

Merton, R. 1973. Theory of rational option pricing. *Bell Journal of Economics and Management Science* **4**:141–183.

Merton, R. 1974. On the pricing of corporate debt: The risk structure of interest rates. *Journal of Finance* **29**:449–470.

Rubinstein, M. 1976. The valuation of uncertain income streams and the pricing of options. *Bell Journal of Economics* **7**:407–425.

CHAPTER 7
MULTIPERIOD
SECURITIES MARKETS I:
EQUILIBRIUM VALUATION

7.1. In Chapters 5 and 6, we discussed allocational efficiency and general pricing principles in two period economies. Most of the results there can be generalized in a straightforward manner to economies with more than two periods. In two–period economies with a single consumption good, individuals trade only at time 0. In a multiperiod economy with reconvening markets, there exists the possibility of trade after time 0. Therefore, individuals' expectations of future prices become an indispensable part of an economic equilibrium. This leads to the notion of a *rational expectations equilibrium*, in which individuals' ex ante expectations about future prices are fulfilled ex post. One of the most important features of a multiperiod economy is that the number of securities needed to complete the markets is in general much smaller than the number of states, since individuals can revise their portfolio compositions at each trading date. That is, all the state contingent claims can be manufactured dynamically by trading in a limited number of long–lived complex securities – securities that are available for trading at every trading date. Thus, the equilibrium allocation will be Pareto optimal. In allocationally efficient securities markets, we can then follow the arguments in Chapter 5 to construct a representative agent for pricing purposes. The sign of the risk premium of a risky security depends upon the covariability of its return with the aggregate consumption process. Only in very special cases can the aggregate wealth process, or the market portfolio, play the role of the aggregate consumption process. These are the subjects to which we now turn.

7.2. Consider a multiperiod pure exchange economy under uncertainty that has $T + 1$ trading dates indexed by $t = 0, 1, \ldots, T$. There is a single perishable consumption good available for consumption at each trading date. Any possible complete history of the exogenous uncertain environment from time 0 to time T is a state of nature and is denoted by ω. We as before use Ω to denote the collection of all possible states of nature. In a two–period economy with time 0 and time 1, individuals at time 0 only know that the true state of nature is one of Ω, which will be revealed at time 1. In a multiperiod economy, we will assume that the true state of nature is partially revealed to individuals over time and is completely revealed at the final date of the economy, T. The revelation of the true state of nature over time is best represented by an *event tree*, which we will term an *information structure*. Figure 7.2.1 illustrates an information structure when there are five possible states and three trading dates. The five possible states are denoted by $\omega_1, \ldots, \omega_5$. At time 0, the only information is that the true state is one of $\{\omega_1, \ldots, \omega_5\}$. At time 1, individuals learn that the true state of nature is either one of $\{\omega_1, \omega_2, \omega_3\}$ or one of $\{\omega_4, \omega_5\}$. At time 2, the true state of nature is revealed. For example, suppose that the true state of nature is ω_3. Then at time 1, it will be learned that the true state is one among the first three possible states and is neither ω_4 nor ω_5. At time 2, state ω_3 is known to be the true state.

Before we proceed, we first fix some terminology and notation. An *event* is a subset of Ω. For example, $\{\omega_1, \omega_2, \omega_3\}$ is an event. In Figure 7.2.1, this event simply says that the true state is one member of $\{\omega_1, \omega_2, \omega_3\}$. Two events are said to be disjoint if they have an

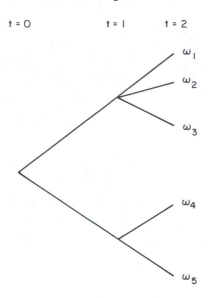

Figure 7.2.1: An Information Structure

empty intersection, that is, if we know the true state is in one event, it cannot be in another. A *partition* of Ω is a collection of events $\{A_1, \ldots, A_n\}$ such that the union of these events is equal to Ω and the pairwise intersections of these events are empty. A given partition is said to be *finer* than another if any event in the latter partition is a union of some events in the former. In Figure 7.2.1, the event Ω forms a partition at time 0. At time 1, the two events $\{\omega_1, \omega_2, \omega_3\}$ and $\{\omega_4, \omega_5\}$ form a partition. At time 2, the five individual states form a partition. The information revelation represented by an event tree can be described by a family of partitions of Ω, indexed by time, that become finer and finer.

We will use $\mathbf{F} = \{\mathcal{F}_t; t = 0, 1, \ldots, T\}$ to denote the common *information structure* with which individuals are endowed, where each $\mathcal{F}_t$ is a partition of Ω with the property that $\mathcal{F}_t$ is finer than $\mathcal{F}_s$ if $t \geq s$. We will always assume that $\mathcal{F}_0 = \{\Omega\}$ and $\mathcal{F}_T$ is the partition generated by all the individual states. This simply means that individuals know at time 0 that the true state is in Ω and they learn the true state by time T.

A *time–event contingent claim* is a security that pays one unit of consumption at a trading date $t \geq 1$ in an event $a_t \in \mathcal{F}_t$ and nothing otherwise.

There are I individuals in the economy indexed by $i = 1, 2, \ldots, I$. To simplify notation, we assume that individuals have homogeneous beliefs about the possible states of nature denoted by π_ω, $\omega \in \Omega$. As usual, we assume also that $\pi_\omega > 0$, $\forall \omega \in \Omega$. These probabilities induce probabilities about events. For an event $a_t \in \mathcal{F}_t$, the probability of its occurrence is

$$\pi_{a_t} \equiv \sum_{\omega \in a_t} \pi_\omega. \tag{7.2.1}$$

Individual i has preferences for time–event contingent claims that are represented by time–additive and state independent von Neumann–Morgenstern utility functions that are increasing, strictly concave, and differentiable:

$$u_{i0}(z_0) + \sum_{t=1}^{T} \sum_{a_t \in \mathcal{F}_t} \pi_{a_t} u_{it}(z_{a_t}). \tag{7.2.2}$$

Implicit in the assumption that an individual's preferences are defined on the time–event contingent claims is the requirement that he can not consume different amounts of consumption across the states that comprise the event $a_t \in \mathcal{F}_t$ at time t. This is a natural informational constraint – as an individual at time t cannot distinguish among different states in any $a_t \in \mathcal{F}_t$, his consumption choice cannot therefore depend upon different states in an event in $\mathcal{F}_t$. We also assume that an individual has a nonnegative endowment of time–0 consumption and time–event contingent claims denoted by

$$\{e_0^i, e_{a_t}^i, a_t \in \mathcal{F}_t; t = 1, \ldots, T\}.$$

To avoid degeneracy, we assume that there exists a t and an event $a_t \in \mathcal{F}_t$ such that $e_{a_t}^i > 0$.

Before we leave this section, we remark that the conclusions of Sections 7.3 to 7.14 are valid when individuals have heterogeneous probability beliefs, as long as their probability beliefs all assign a strictly positive probability to each state $\omega \in \Omega$. Readers can draw on the analogy between the discussions of Sections 5.4 to 5.10 and those of Sections 7.3 to 7.14. The former do not depend upon individuals having homogeneous probability beliefs. We leave it for interested readers to show that the latter do not either.

7.3. An allocation of time–0 consumption and the time–event contingent claims is said to be Pareto optimal if there does not exist another allocation that increases at least one individual's expected utility without decreasing any other individual's expected utility. As in Chapter 5, a Pareto optimal allocation

$$\{c_0^i, c_{a_t}^i, a_t \in \mathcal{F}_t, t = 1, \ldots, T, i = 1, 2, \ldots, I\}$$

is the solution to the following maximization problem for a set of positive weightings $(\lambda_i)_{i=1}^I$:

$$\max_{\left\{\substack{z_0^i, z_{a_t}^i, a_t \in \mathcal{F}_t, \\ t=1,\ldots,T, i=1,2,\ldots,I}\right\}} \sum_{i=1}^I \lambda_i \left(u_{i0}(z_0^i) + \sum_{t=1}^T \sum_{a_t \in \mathcal{F}_t} \pi_{a_t} u_{it}(z_{a_t}^i) \right)$$

$$\text{s.t.} \sum_{i=1}^I z_0^i = \sum_{i=1}^I e_0^i \tag{7.3.1}$$

$$\sum_{i=1}^I z_{a_t}^i = \sum_{i=1}^I e_{a_t}^i \quad \forall a_t \in \mathcal{F}_t \; \forall t.$$

We shall be interested only in Pareto optimal allocations that correspond to strictly positive λ_i's. The first order conditions that are necessary and sufficient for $(c_0^i, c_{a_t}^i, a_t \in \mathcal{F}_t, t = 1, \ldots, T)_{i=1}^I$ to be a solution to (7.3.1) with strictly positive λ's are

$$\lambda_i u_{i0}'(c_0^i) = \phi_0 \quad \forall i \tag{7.3.2}$$

$$\lambda_i \pi_{a_t} u_{it}'(c_{a_t}^i) = \phi_{a_t} \quad \forall i, \forall a_t \in \mathcal{F}_t, \forall t, \tag{7.3.3}$$

for some strictly positive constants ϕ_0 and ϕ_{a_t} and the resource constraint of (7.3.1), where ϕ_0 and ϕ_{a_t} are Lagrangian multipliers for the resource constraints at time 0 and for event a_t at time t, respectively. Substituting (7.3.2) into (7.3.3) gives

$$\frac{\pi_{a_t} u_{it}'(c_{a_t}^i)}{u_{i0}'(c_0^i)} = \frac{\phi_{a_t}}{\phi_0} \quad \forall i, \forall a_t \in \mathcal{F}_t \; \forall t. \tag{7.3.4}$$

Note that the right–hand side of (7.3.4) is independent of i, the index of individuals. That is, in a Pareto optimal allocation, the ratios of marginal utilities between any event–a_t consumption and time–0 consumption are equalized across individuals.

A Pareto optimal allocation can be achieved in a competitive economy with a spot market of time–0 consumption and a complete set of time–event contingent claims markets. To see this, let ϕ_0 and ϕ_{a_t} be the prices at time 0 for the time–0 consumption good and for a share of the time–event contingent claim paying off at time t in event a_t. Suppose also that markets for these time–event contingent claims are open only at time 0. In such an economy, individual i's equilibrium allocation $\{c_0^i, c_{a_t}^i\}$ must be a solution to the following program:

$$\max_{\{z_0^i, z_{a_t}^i\}} u_{i0}(z_0^i) + \sum_{t=1}^{T} \sum_{a_t \in \mathcal{F}_t} \pi_{a_t} u_{it}(z_{a_t}^i)$$

$$\text{s.t. } \phi_0 z_0^i + \sum_{t=1}^{T} \sum_{a_t \in \mathcal{F}_t} \phi_{a_t} z_{a_t}^i = \phi_0 e_0^i + \sum_{t=1}^{T} \sum_{a_t \in \mathcal{F}_t} \phi_{a_t} e_{a_t}^i. \tag{7.3.5}$$

The first order necessary conditions for $\{c_0^i, c_{a_t}^i\}$ to be a solution to (7.3.5) are

$$u_{i0}'(c_0^i) = \gamma_i \phi_0 \tag{7.3.6}$$

$$\pi_{a_t} u_{it}'(c_{a_t}^i) = \gamma_i \phi_{a_t} \quad \forall a_t \in \mathcal{F}_t, \forall t, \tag{7.3.7}$$

for some strictly positive constant γ_i, and the budget constraint, for which γ_i is the Lagrangian multiplier. In equilibrium, we also know that markets must clear:

$$\sum_{i=1}^{I} c_0^i = \sum_{i=1}^{I} e_0^i$$

$$\sum_{i}^{I} c_{a_t}^i = \sum_{i}^{I} e_{a_t}^i \quad \forall a_t \in \mathcal{F}_t, \forall t. \tag{7.3.8}$$

Comparing (7.3.6), (7.3.7), and (7.3.8) with (7.3.2), (7.3.3), and the resource constraints of (7.3.1), one can easily see that the solutions to (7.3.5) for all individuals correspond to the solution to (7.3.1) when we take $\lambda_i = \gamma_i^{-1}$. Therefore, the equilibrium allocation corresponds to a Pareto optimal allocation if there exists a complete set of time–event contingent claims or when *markets are complete*. An equilibrium of this kind will henceforth be referred to as a *complete markets competitive equilibrium*.

7.4. Note that we have assumed in the competitive economy of Section 7.3 that markets for the time–event contingent claims do not reopen after time 0. Therefore, in the specification of an equilibrium there are no prices for the *trading dates* $t = 1, 2, \ldots, T$ and no expectations about these prices held by individuals. When markets for the time–event contingent claims open at each trading date, an equilibrium requires a specification of individuals' expectations about prices for securities in each event at each trading date. The market clearing condition will have to hold for each trading date. An equilibrium is a *rational expectations equilibrium* if individuals' expectations are fulfilled ex post.

In the following section, we will show that a rational expectations equilibrium exists and has the same allocation as a complete markets competitive equilibrium. Moreover, although markets reopen after time 0, there is no trading in equilibrium after time 0.

7.5. We will first introduce some notation. Let $\phi_{a_s}(a_t)$ be the ex–dividend (ex–payoff) price at time t in the event a_t for the time–event contingent claim paying off at time s in event a_s. It is clear that in any equilibrium we must have

$$\phi_{a_s}(a_t) = \begin{cases} 0 & \text{if } t \geq s; \\ 0 & \text{if } t < s \text{ and } a_s \not\subseteq a_t. \end{cases} \qquad (7.5.1)$$

When $t = s$, the first case follows since prices are ex-dividend. If $t < s$ and $a_s \not\subseteq a_t$, in event a_t, it will be learned that event a_s will not occur. Thus, the time–event contingent security paying off in event a_s will be worthless.

For $t < s$, let $\pi_{a_s}(a_t)$ be the probability of event a_s when at time

t event a_t occurs. By Bayes rule, we have

$$\pi_{a_s}(a_t) = \begin{cases} 0 & \text{if } a_s \not\subseteq a_t; \\ \frac{\pi_{a_s}}{\pi_{a_t}} & \text{if } a_s \subseteq a_t. \end{cases} \tag{7.5.2}$$

We will now construct a rational expectations equilibrium. Define $\phi_{a_s}(a_t)$ according to (7.5.1) and

$$\phi_{a_s}(a_t) = \frac{\phi_{a_s}}{\phi_{a_t}} \quad \text{if } t < s \text{ and } a_s \subseteq a_t. \tag{7.5.3}$$

We claim that the prices defined in (7.5.1) and (7.5.3) and the complete markets competitive equilibrium allocation $\{c_0^i, c_{a_t}^i; a_t \in \mathcal{F}_t, \forall t = 1, \ldots, T\}$ are a rational expectations equilibrium in which trading takes place only at time 0. Individuals have rational expectations in the sense that they believe that prices will evolve according to (7.5.1) and (7.5.3).

To prove our claim, it suffices to show that at any time t and in any event $a_t \in \mathcal{F}_t$, $\{c_{a_s}^i, a_s \in \mathcal{F}_s, a_s \subseteq a_t, s \geq t\}$ is a solution to the program:

$$\max_{\substack{\{z_{a_s}^i, a_s \in \mathcal{F}_s \\ a_s \subseteq a_t, s \geq t\}}} u_{it}(z_{a_t}^i) + \sum_{s=t+1}^{T} \sum_{\substack{\{a_s \in \mathcal{F}_s \\ a_s \subseteq a_t\}}} \pi_{a_s}(a_t) u_{is}(z_{a_s}^i)$$

$$\text{s.t. } z_{a_t}^i + \sum_{s=t+1}^{T} \sum_{\substack{\{a_s \in \mathcal{F}_s \\ a_s \subseteq a_t\}}} \phi_{a_s}(a_t) z_{a_s}^i = c_{a_t}^i + \sum_{s=t+1}^{T} \sum_{\substack{\{a_s \in \mathcal{F}_s \\ a_s \subseteq a_t\}}} \phi_{a_s}(a_t) c_{a_s}^i.$$

$$\tag{7.5.4}$$

That is, at each trading date t, given his expectations of future prices, an individual is content to hold his competitive equilibrium allocation of the time–event contingent claims. First note that $\{c_{a_s}^i, a_s \in \mathcal{F}_s, a_s \subseteq a_t\}$ is feasible for (7.5.4), because the budget constraint is satisfied. Next, from the Lagrangian theory, as utility functions are concave, it is sufficient to demonstrate the existence of a constant $\gamma_{a_t}^i$, the Lagrangian multiplier for the budget constraint of (7.5.4), such that

$$u_{it}'(c_{a_t}^i) = \gamma_{a_t}^i$$
$$\pi_{a_s}(a_t) u_{is}'(c_{a_s}^i) = \gamma_{a_t}^i \phi_{a_s}(a_t), \tag{7.5.5}$$

for all $a_s \in \mathcal{F}_s$, $a_s \subset a_t$, and $s > t$, for $\{c^i_{a_s}, a_s \in \mathcal{F}_s, a_s \subseteq a_t\}$ to be a solution to (7.5.4). Now let

$$\gamma^i_{a_t} = \gamma_i \frac{\phi_{a_t}}{\pi_{a_t}}, \qquad (7.5.6)$$

where γ_i is the Lagrangian multiplier for the program (7.3.5). Substituting (7.5.6) into (7.3.6) and (7.3.7), and using (7.5.2) and (7.5.3), we immediately get (7.5.5). That is, there exists a constant $\gamma^i_{a_t}$, as defined in (7.5.6), such that (7.5.5.) is satisfied. We thus conclude that individual i will be content to hold his allocation in a competitive complete markets equilibrium at any time t and in any event a_t even when he has the opportunity to retrade. Therefore, there exists a rational expectations equilibrium with complete markets such that the equilibrium allocation is identical to that in a complete market competitive equilibrium. Note that in this rational expectations equilibrium, trading only occurs at time 0.

7.6. An individual's optimal consumption and portfolio decisions in a multiperiod economy are simple when he has rational expectations and when there exists a complete set of time–event contingent claims markets at time 0. This is so because he only has to solve (7.3.5) at time 0. After time 0, there is no need to adjust portfolio holdings of the time–event contingent claims; and, as a consequence, there is no value in markets reopening after time 0. When there does not exist a complete set of the time–event contingent securities, however, there may be value for the markets to remain open after time 0, and an individual's optimal consumption and portfolio problem becomes more complicated. The following several sections are devoted to an analysis of multiperiod securities markets which lack a complete set of time–event contingent claims. The most important lesson to be learned is that, with reconvening markets, the markets can be completed by dynamically managing a portfolio of *long–lived securities*, in number far fewer than the number of time–events.

7.7. Before we proceed, we will first revise some definitions which were used before in two–period economies. A *complex security* is composed of units of time–0 consumption good and a bundle of time–event contingent claims and is represented by $x = \{x_0, x_{a_t}; a_t \in \mathcal{F}_t, t = 1, \ldots, T\}$, where x_0 and x_{a_t} are the *dividends* paid at time 0 and at time t in event a_t, respectively, in units of the consumption good. A *long–lived security* is a complex security that is available for trading at all trading dates. A real world example of a long–lived security is a common stock traded on a stock exchange. A *multiperiod securities markets economy* or simply a *securities markets economy* is composed of a finite number of long–lived securities in strictly positive supply represented by their dividend processes x_j, $j = 0, 1, \ldots, N$, and a finite number of individuals indexed by $i = 1, 2, \ldots, I$. Assume that the dividend process x_j is nonnegative and is strictly positive at some time t in some event $a_t \in \mathcal{F}_t$. Instead of being endowed with the time–0 consumption good and time–event contingent claims, individual i is endowed with shares of the long–lived securities. Let $\bar{\theta}_j^i(0)$ denote the numbers of shares of security j with which individual i is endowed. To avoid degeneracy, assume that $\bar{\theta}_j^i(0) \geq 0$ and, for every i, there exists some j such that $\bar{\theta}_j^i(0) > 0$. We also assume without loss of generality that the total number of shares of each security is one. Thus

$$\sum_{i=1}^{I} \bar{\theta}_j^i(0) = 1 \quad \forall j = 0, 1, \ldots, N.$$

As the total supply of a long–lived security is one share, the number of shares held by an individual can be interpreted as the proportion of the total supply held.

The ex-dividend price of security j at time t is a random variable denoted by $S_j(t)$. It is natural to require that $S_j(T) = 0$, for all j. Being a random variable, realizations of $S_j(t)$ depend on the state of nature. So, formally, a realization of $S_j(t)$ can be denoted by $S_j(\omega, t)$. As individuals at time t cannot distinguish among states of nature in an event $a_t \in \mathcal{F}_t$, a natural informational constraint of $S_j(t)$ is that its realizations not vary across states in an event $a_t \in \mathcal{F}_t$. In mathematical terminology, this property is usually termed the *measurability* of $S_j(t)$ with respect to $\mathcal{F}_t$. Individuals are assumed to have *rational expectations* in that they agree on the mappings $S_j(\omega, t)$, $j = 0, 1, \ldots, N$.

A *process* is a collection of random variables indexed by t. For example, S_j is a process. If $S_j(t)$ is measurable with respect to $\mathcal{F}_t$ for all t, then we say that the *price process* S_j is *adapted* to **F**. Using this terminology, a long–lived security is represented by a *dividend process* adapted to **F**.

As there does not exist a complete set of the time–event contingent securities, individuals may not be able to trade to a Pareto optimal allocation at time 0. As a consequence, there may exist incentives for them to trade after time 0. Therefore, we must have a way of describing the manner in which individuals' portfolio compositions are adjusted over time. To this end, we introduce the notion of a trading strategy.

A trading strategy θ is an $N+1$–dimensional process

$$\theta = \{\theta_j(t); j = 0, 1, 2, \ldots, N; t = 1, \ldots, T\},$$

where $\theta_j(t)$ is the number of shares of security j held from time $t-1$ to t before trading takes place at time t. Therefore, the values of $\theta_j(t)$ are determined at time $t-1$, and a natural informational constraint is that $\theta_j(t)$ be measurable with respect to $\mathcal{F}_{t-1}$. In mathematical terminology, the process θ_j is then said to be *predictable* with respect to **F**, or simply *predictable* when there is no ambiguity about the information structure **F**. Note that a predictable process is certainly adapted.

We shall denote $(\theta_0(t), \ldots, \theta_N(t))^\top$ by $\theta(t)$, where as before $^\top$ denotes the *transpose*.

A consumption plan c is a process adapted to **F**:

$$c = \{c(t); t = 0, 1, \ldots, T\},$$

where $c(t)$ is the random consumption at time t, in units of the single consumption good. A trading strategy θ is said to be *admissible* if it is predictable and there exists a consumption plan c such that, $\forall t$,

$$\theta(t+1)^\top S(t) = \theta(t)^\top (S(t) + X(t)) - c(t), \qquad (7.7.1)$$

where $S(t) = (S_0(t), \ldots, S_N(t))^\top$, and $X(t) = (x_0(t), \ldots, x_N(t))^\top$. Note that in (7.7.1), we have used the convention that when $t = T$, the left–hand side is 0, since $S_j(T) = 0$ for all j. Thus, at $t = T$, (7.7.1) is just

$$\theta(T)^\top X(T) = c(T). \tag{7.7.2}$$

Relation (7.7.1) is a natural budget constraint. The left–hand side of (7.7.1) is the value of the portfolio at time t *after* trading and consumption, while the right–hand side is the value of the portfolio at time t before trading plus dividends received net of consumption. At the final date of the economy, consumption is equal to the total value of the dividends, which is natural because of the assumption that utility functions are strictly increasing. The consumption plan of (7.7.1) is said to be *financed* by the trading strategy θ. The space of admissible strategies will be denoted by H.

Individual i's problem is to maximize his expected utility of consumption by choosing a consumption plan financed by an admissible strategy. Formally, individual i's problem is

$$\max_{\theta \in H} u_{i0}(c(0)) + E\left[\sum_{t=1}^{T} u_{it}(c(t))\right] \tag{7.7.3}$$
$$\text{s.t. } \theta(0) = \bar{\theta}^i(0)$$
$$\text{and } \{c(t)\} \text{ is financed by } \theta.$$

A *rational expectations equilibrium* for the securities markets is composed of I pairs of admissible strategies and consumption plans $\{\theta^i, c^i; i = 1, 2, \ldots, I\}$ and price processes for the long–lived securities $\{S(t); t = 0, 1, \ldots, T\}$ such that θ^i solves (7.7.3), c^i is financed by θ^i, and markets clear at all times:

$$\sum_{i=1}^{I} \theta_j^i(t) = 1$$

for all $t = 1, 2, \ldots, T$ and all $j = 0, \ldots, N$.

In a securities markets economy, the source of consumption is the dividends paid by long–lived securities, in units of the consumption good. Therefore, in equilibrium, Walras law implies that, for all $t = 0, 1, \ldots, T$,

$$\sum_{i=1}^{I} c^i(t) = \sum_{j=0}^{N} x_j(t). \tag{7.7.4}$$

7.8. In the above definition of a rational expectations equilibrium, each individual maximizes his life–time expected utility of consumption at time 0. As markets are open and individuals are able to retrade at each trading date, for the above definition to make sense, it must be an equilibrium property that at each trading time t, there does not exist another consumption plan financed by a trading strategy admissible from t onward that strictly improves the welfare of any individual. We prove this property by contraposition. The idea is that if there exists such an improvement at time $t \geq 1$, then the expected utility of life–time consumption computed at time 0 can be strictly improved upon. This is a contradiction.

Formally, suppose that there exists a trading date t with $0 < t < T$, an event $a_t \in \mathcal{F}_t$, a trading strategy θ, and a consumption plan c starting at time t such that, for every state in the event a_t and $\forall k = 1, 2, \ldots, T - t$,

$$\theta(t+1)^\top S(t) = \theta^i(t)^\top (S(t) + X(t)) - c(t),$$
$$\theta(t+k+1)^\top S(t+k) = \theta(t+k)^\top (S(t+k) + X(t+k)) - c(t+k),$$
$$(7.8.1)$$

and

$$\sum_{s=t}^{T} \sum_{a_s \subseteq a_t} \pi_{a_s}(a_t) u_{is}(c_{a_s}) > \sum_{s=t}^{T} \sum_{a_s \subseteq a_t} \pi_{a_s}(a_t) u_{is}(c_{a_s}^i). \qquad (7.8.2)$$

Define a trading strategy and a consumption plan starting at time 0:

$$\hat{\theta}(s) = \begin{cases} \theta^i(s) & \text{if } s \leq t; \\ \theta^i(s) & \text{if } s > t \text{ and in the events } a_s \nsubseteq a_t; \\ \theta(s) & \text{if } s > t \text{ and in the events } a_s \subseteq a_t; \end{cases}$$

$$\hat{c}(s) = \begin{cases} c^i(s) & \text{if } s < t; \\ c^i(s) & \text{if } s \geq t \text{ and in the events } a_s \nsubseteq a_t; \\ c(s) & \text{if } s \geq t \text{ and in the events } a_s \subseteq a_t. \end{cases}$$

It is easily verified that $\hat{\theta}$ is an admissible trading strategy and finances the consumption plan $\hat{c}$. We claim that the consumption plan $\hat{c}$ yields a strictly higher expected utility at time 0 than does c^i. Denoting the conditional expectation at time t by $E[\cdot | \mathcal{F}_t]$, relation

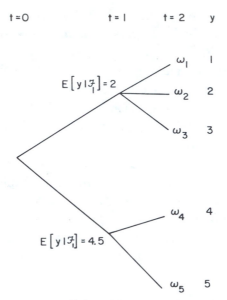

Figure 7.8.1: Conditional Expectation of a Random Variable

(7.8.2) implies that

$$E\left[\sum_{s=t}^{T} u_{is}(\hat{c}(s))|\mathcal{F}_t\right] \geq E\left[\sum_{s=t}^{T} u_{is}(c^i(s))|\mathcal{F}_t\right], \qquad (7.8.3)$$

with the strict inequality holding in the event a_t. Here we note that the conditional expectation at each time $t > 0$ is a random variable measurable with respect to $\mathcal{F}_t$. For example, consider the information structure depicted in Figure 7.2.1 and redrawn here in Figure 7.8.1. The numbers at time $t = 2$ are possible realizations of a random variable y. Assume that each branch is equally likely. Then the expectation of y conditional on $\mathcal{F}_1$ is a random variable:

$$E[y|\mathcal{F}_1] = \begin{cases} 2 & \text{if the true state is a member of } \{\omega_1, \omega_2, \omega_3\}; \\ 4.5 & \text{if the true state is a member of } \{\omega_4, \omega_5\}. \end{cases}$$

That is, at time 1, if the upper node is realized, the conditional expectation of y is equal to 2; while if the lower node realizes, the conditional expectation of y is equal to 4.5. These two numbers are recorded in Figure 7.8.1 on the nodes at time 1.

Taking expectation on both sides of (7.8.3) gives

$$E\left[\sum_{s=t}^{T} u_{is}(\hat{c}(s))\right] > E\left[\sum_{s=t}^{T} u_{is}(c^i(s))\right]. \qquad (7.8.4)$$

By the definition of $\hat{c}$, we know that

$$E\left[\sum_{s=0}^{t-1} u_{is}(\hat{c}(s))\right] = E\left[\sum_{s=0}^{t-1} u_{is}(c^i(s))\right]. \qquad (7.8.5)$$

Adding (7.8.4) and (7.8.5) yields

$$E\left[\sum_{s=0}^{T} u_{is}(\hat{c}(s))\right] > E\left[\sum_{s=0}^{T} u_{is}(c^i(s))\right]. \qquad (7.8.6)$$

This contradicts the fact that c^i is a solution to (7.7.3). Therefore, in a rational expectations equilibrium, there is no incentive for individuals to deviate from the strategies chosen at time 0.

7.9. Optimal consumption policies and trading strategies in a multiperiod securities markets economy are traditionally characterized by *dynamic programming*. This procedure starts at time $T-1$ with one period remaining. For notational simplicity, we will drop individual indices in this section and Section 7.10 and use $u_t(\cdot)$ to denote the utility function for some individual at time t. Naturally, $u_t(\cdot)$ is increasing, strictly concave, and differentiable. The problem faced by the individual at time $T-1$ is

$$\max_{\{c(T-1),\theta(T)\}} u_{T-1}(c(T-1)) + E[u_T(c(T))|\mathcal{F}_{T-1}]$$

$$\text{s.t. } c(T-1) + \theta(T)^\top S(T-1)$$
$$= \theta(T-1)^\top(S(T-1) + X(T-1)) \qquad (7.9.1)$$
$$\text{and } c(T) = \theta(T)^\top X(T),$$

where $\theta(T-1)$ is the vector of shares of long–lived securities that are held from $T-2$ to $T-1$ and is $\mathcal{F}_{T-2}$ measurable. We note that

$c(T-1)$ and $\theta(T)$ are random variables measurable with respect to $\mathcal{F}_{T-1}$.

Denote the maximand of (7.9.1) by $V(\theta(T-1); \mathcal{F}_{T-1})$, which we term the *indirect utility function* at time $T - 1$. Embodied in this notation is the fact that, given $\theta(T-1)$ and $\mathcal{F}_{T-1}$, the individual's maximization problem is well-defined and thus so is $V(\theta(T-1); \mathcal{F}_{T-1})$. Given $\mathcal{F}_{T-1}$, the individual knows at which "node" along the event tree representing $\mathbf{F}$ he is at time $T - 1$ and thus has "correct" expectations about the $X(T)$ to be realized at time T. Knowing $\theta(T-1)$, the portfolio that the individual holds from time $T - 2$ to time $T - 1$, allows him to know the value of his portfolio and to meet his budget constraint at time $T - 1$.

Now go to time $T - 2$. The problem facing the individual is

$$
\max_{\left\{\substack{(c(t))_{t=T-2}^{T-1} \\ (\theta(t))_{t=T-1}^{T}}\right\}} u_{T-2}(c(T-2)) + E[\sum_{t=T-1}^{T} u_t(c(t))|\mathcal{F}_{T-2}]
$$

$$
\text{s.t.} \quad c(t-1) + \theta(t)^\top S(t-1)
$$
$$
= \theta(t-1)^\top (S(t-1) + X(t-1)), \, t = T-1, T,
$$
$$
\text{and} \quad c(T) = \theta(T)^\top X(T).
$$

(7.9.2)

We similarly define the maximand of (7.9.2) to be $V(\theta(T-2); \mathcal{F}_{T-2})$, the indirect utility function at time $T - 2$. Using the arguments of Section 7.8, it is easily seen that the optimal consumption plan and trading strategy chosen at time $T - 2$ must remain optimal at time $T - 1$. This implies that once decisions about $c(T-2)$ and $\theta(T-1)$ are made, the maximal expected utility at time $T - 1$ (for future consumption) conditional on $\mathcal{F}_{T-1}$ is $V(\theta(T-1); \mathcal{F}_{T-1})$. Thus (7.9.2) is equivalent to

$$
\max_{\{c(T-2), \theta(T-1)\}} u_{T-2}(c(T-2)) + E[V(\theta(T-1); \mathcal{F}_{T-1})|\mathcal{F}_{T-2}]
$$
$$
\text{s.t. } c(T-2) + \theta(T-1)^\top S(T-2)
$$
$$
= \theta(T-2)^\top (S(T-2) + X(T-2)).
$$

(7.9.3)

In general, at any time $t = 0, 1, \ldots, T-1$, the individual solves the following program:

$$\max_{\{c(t),\theta(t+1)\}} u_t(c(t)) + E[V(\theta(t+1); \mathcal{F}_{t+1})|\mathcal{F}_t]$$

$$\text{s.t. } c(t) + \theta(t+1)^\top S(t) = \theta(t)^\top (S(t) + X(t)), \qquad (7.9.4)$$

where $V(\theta(t+1); \mathcal{F}_{t+1})$ is the indirect utility function at time $t+1$. That is, the dynamic problem the individual faces is equivalent to a sequence of two–period problems: At every time $t < T$, the individual chooses a consumption $c(t)$ and a portfolio strategy $\theta(t+1)$ to maximize his consumption preferences for $c(t)$ and his preferences for the random wealth at time $t+1$. Note that the random wealth at time $t+1$ can be computed if we know $\theta(t+1)$ and $S(t+1)$. Moreover, an individual has rational expectations, therefore, he has the correct expectation about $S(t+1)$ given $\mathcal{F}_t$. This explains the dependence of V on $\theta(t+1)$ and $\mathcal{F}_t$. The preferences for the time $t+1$ random wealth are represented by the indirect utility function $V(\theta(t+1); \mathcal{F}_{t+1})$, which represents the maximal expected utility for future consumption conditional on $\mathcal{F}_{t+1}$ when the random wealth at time $t+1$ is equal to $\theta(t+1)^\top(S(t+1) + X(t+1))$.

7.10. Now we derive a property of an optimal consumption plan which will be useful later in this chapter. Suppose throughout this section that (c, θ) is optimal. As mentioned in Section 7.9, the wealth of the individual at time t is

$$W(t) \equiv \theta(t)^\top (S(t) + X(t)). \qquad (7.10.1)$$

It is clear from (7.9.1) and (7.9.2) that, at any time t, the role of $\theta(t)$ is to allow the individual to satisfy his or her budget constraint:

$$c(t) + \theta(t+1)^\top S(t) = \theta(t)^\top (S(t) + X(t)) = W(t). \qquad (7.10.2)$$

Therefore, the indirect utility function at time t can equally well be written as $V(W(t); \mathcal{F}_t)$. Then (7.9.4) implies that, along the optimal solution,

$$V(W(t); \mathcal{F}_t) = u_t(c(t)) + E[V(W(t+1); \mathcal{F}_{t+1})|\mathcal{F}_t]. \qquad (7.10.3)$$

Exercise 7.3 asks the reader to show that $V(W(t); \mathcal{F}_t)$ is increasing and strictly concave in $W(t)$. We shall assume that V is differentiable in $W(t)$.

Differentiating both sides of (7.10.3) with respect to $W(t)$ while noting (7.10.2) gives

$$V_W(W(t); \mathcal{F}_t) = u_t'(c(t)), \qquad (7.10.4)$$

where V_W denotes the partial derivative of V with respect to $W(t)$. That is, along the optimal solution and at any time t, the marginal utility of wealth must be equal to the marginal utility of consumption – this is the so-called *envelope condition*. By strict concavity, u_t' and V_W are strictly decreasing. Thus, there exists a function g, depending on $\mathcal{F}_t$, such that

$$c(t) = g(W(t); \mathcal{F}_t) \qquad (7.10.5)$$

and g is strictly increasing in $W(t)$. The dependence of g on $\mathcal{F}_t$ signifies the possibility that $c(t)$ is not a deterministic function of $W(t)$ and may well depend also on the events in $\mathcal{F}_t$. Relation (7.10.5) formalizes the intuitive notion that the higher the wealth an individual has at any time, the higher the consumption chosen at that time will be, *ceteris paribus*.

7.11. In the complete market rational expectations equilibrium discussed in Section 7.5, the number of time–event contingent claims available for trading at time 0 is equal to

$$\sum_{t=1}^{T} \#(\mathcal{F}_t),$$

where $\#(\mathcal{F}_t)$ is the number of disjoint events in $\mathcal{F}_t$. This number is equal to the total number of nodes, excluding the node at zero, in the event tree that represents the information structure **F**. With these time–event contingent claims, the equilibrium allocation is Pareto optimal.

In the securities markets of Sections 7.6 and 7.7, there does not exist a complete set of time–event contingent securities. Thus, the markets are not complete at time 0, and individuals may not achieve

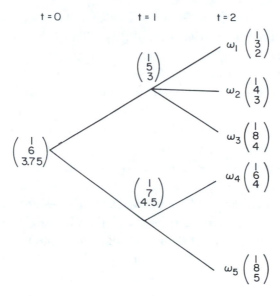

Figure 7.12.1: An Example of a Securities Market

their optimal allocation of time–event contingent consumption by simply trading once at time 0. However, the opportunity to trade after time 0 may allow individuals to reach a Pareto optimal allocation even without a complete set of the time–event contingent securities. Helped by the discussion of Section 5.7 about market completion by complex securities in a two–period economy, our intuition suggests that markets can be completed by dynamic trading in long–lived securities if, at every node on the event tree representing the information structure, the markets are complete for the subsequent nodes. In a two–period economy, market completion by complex securities can be ensured by having complex securities, equal in number to the number of states of nature, that have linearly independent time–1 random payoffs. In a multiperiod economy, however, the market completion of a two–period sub–economy will depend upon the endogenous prices of the long–lived securities. This is a major distinction between a two–period economy and a multiperiod economy. This point will be made clear by the example discussed in the next section.

7.12. Consider the event tree in Figure 7.12.1. We will not specify probabilities for different states of nature except that each state is of a strictly positive probability. The following analysis is valid for all probability specifications that assign a strictly positive probability to every state.

Excluding the node at time 0, there are seven nodes. That is, in a complete markets competitive equilibrium, we need seven time–event contingent securities. Suppose now that in a securities markets economy, there are three long–lived securities that do not pay dividends until time 2. Security 0 pays one unit of consumption at time 2 in all states and has unit price before time 2. Securities $j = 1, 2$ are risky, and their prices at each time–event before time 2 and their dividends paid at time 2 are listed along the event tree. For example, if the true state is one of $\{\omega_1, \omega_2, \omega_3\}$ at time 1, the price for security 1 is 5 and that for security 2 is 3. The prices and dividends specified are certainly adapted to the information structure represented by the event tree.

One question immediately comes to mind. Are the prices specified for the long–lived securities reasonable? For example, do they admit arbitrage opportunities? We will have a complete answer to this question in Chapter 8. For now, we just say that these prices do not admit any arbitrage opportunities and withhold the reasoning until Chapter 8.

We claim that any time–event contingent claim can be created by dynamically managing a portfolio of the three long–lived securities. We shall demonstrate how to design a trading strategy to replicate the payoff of the time–event contingent security that pays one unit of consumption at time 2 if and only if ω_1 is the true state. Other time–event contingent claims can be replicated by analogy. We use the idea of dynamic programming and work backwards. Suppose that the true state is one of $\{\omega_1, \omega_2, \omega_3\}$. Then we will be at the upper node at time 1. The task to be accomplished is to design a portfolio having a payoff equal to 1 at time 2 if ω_1 is the true state and nothing otherwise. Let x be the number of shares of the riskless asset held, and let y_j be the number of shares of security $j = 1, 2$ held to create a payoff of 1 at time 2 if and only if ω_1 is the true state. Then (x, y_1, y_2) must satisfy the following:

$$x + 3y_1 + 2y_2 = 1,$$
$$x + 4y_1 + 3y_2 = 0, \tag{7.12.1}$$
$$x + 8y_1 + 4y_2 = 0.$$

The unique solution of (7.12.1) is

$$(x, y_1, y_2) = (8/3, 1/3, -4/3). \tag{7.12.2}$$

That is, buying 8/3 shares of the riskless asset, 1/3 shares of security 1, and short selling 4/3 shares of security 2 at time 1 if the upper node is reached creates a payoff of 1 at time 2 if w_1 is the true state and nothing otherwise. If, on the other hand, the true state is either w_4 or w_5, at time 1, we will be at the lower node. Since the payoff we are replicating is the time–event contingent security that pays off only at time 2 in state w_1, we do nothing at the lower node. Thus, the payoff at time 2 will be zero in states w_4 and w_5.

We go back one period to time 0. From the previous calculation, we learn that to replicate the time–event contingent claim paying off at time 2 in state w_1, at time 1 we need to follow the strategy specified in (7.12.2) at the upper node and take no position in the securities at the lower node. To implement this strategy at time 1, we need 1/3 units of the consumption good at the upper node and 0 units of the consumption good at the lower node. Thus the question at time 0 is what portfolio to purchase in order to have, at time 1, a payoff of 1/3 at the upper node and 0 at the lower node. Again let (x, y_1, y_2) denote the number of shares of long–lived securities. We must solve

$$x + 5y_1 + 3y_2 = 1/3,$$
$$x + 7y_1 + 4.5y_2 = 0. \tag{7.12.3}$$

There exist many solutions to (7.12.3). One of the solutions is

$$(x, y_1, y_2) = (7/6, -1/6, 0). \tag{7.12.4}$$

The cost of this strategy at time 0 is

$$\frac{7}{6} - 6 \left(\frac{1}{6} \right) = \frac{1}{6}.$$

One can also verify that *all* solutions of (7.12.3) have the same cost.

Now we are ready to state the trading strategy that replicates the time–event contingent claim under consideration. At time 0, purchase 7/6 shares of the riskless security and short sell 1/6 shares of security 1. This costs 1/6 units of the consumption good. At time 1, if we are at the upper node, the portfolio constructed at time 0 will have a value equal to 1/3 units of the consumption good. We adjust our portfolio composition according to (7.12.2), which costs exactly 1/3. The portfolio of (7.12.2) has a payoff of 1 at time 2 if and only if ω_1 is the true state. If the lower node is realized at time 1, the portfolio purchased at time 0 is worthless and we close out our position and do nothing. The dynamic strategy specified in (7.12.2) and (7.12.4) replicates the time–event contingent claim that pays off at time 2 in state ω_1.

7.13. In the example considered in the previous section, the number of time–event contingent claims is equal to *seven* – the total number of nodes in the event tree of Figure 7.12.1, excluding the node at time 0. However, markets can be completed in a securities markets economy by dynamically trading only *three* long–lived securities. Note that the three long–lived securities of Section 7.11 *dynamically complete* the markets; because, for every node on the event tree of Figure 7.12.1, the prices of the three securities at the subsequent nodes form a matrix whose rank is equal to the number of subsequent nodes. That is, markets are complete for every one period sub-economy. For example, if the true state is ω_1, we will be at the upper node at time 1. The prices for the three long–lived securities at the subsequent three nodes form a 3×3 matrix

$$\begin{pmatrix} 1 & 1 & 1 \\ 3 & 4 & 8 \\ 2 & 3 & 4 \end{pmatrix},$$

which is of rank 3.

Certainly, dynamic completion of markets depends on the price processes of the three long–lived securities. Consider a trivial example in which all long–lived securities have proportional dividend processes. Their prices at every node will simply be proportional, and dynamic trading does not provide the investors with more *spanning* than does trading once at time 0. On the other hand, for the markets to be *dynamically complete*, the number of long–lived securities traded must be no less than the maximum number of branches leaving each node on the event tree representing the information structure. In the example presented in Figure 7.12.1, this number is three. Suppose that the number of traded long–lived securities is strictly less than three. If the upper node is realized at time 1, the spanning property fails for the subsequent nodes, because the number of securities is strictly less than the number of states that will possibly be realized at time 2.

Therefore, the number of long–lived securities being no less than the maximum number of branches leaving each node is a necessary but not sufficient condition for the dynamic completion of markets. It is a sufficient condition in a generic sense, however. This is the subject to which we now turn.

7.14. In the rational expectations complete markets equilibrium of Section 7.5, the arguments of Section 5.8 can be used to show that the ex–dividend price of a complex security or a long–lived security x at time t in event $a_t \in \mathcal{F}_t$ is

$$S_x(a_t, t) = \sum_{s=t+1}^{T} \sum_{\substack{a_s \in \mathcal{F}_s \\ a_s \subseteq a_t}} \phi_{a_s}(a_t) x_{a_s} \tag{7.14.1}$$

$$= \sum_{s=t+1}^{T} \sum_{\substack{a_s \in \mathcal{F}_s \\ a_s \subseteq a_t}} \frac{\pi_{a_s}(a_t) u'_{is}(c^i_{a_s})}{u'_{it}(c^i_{a_t})} x_{a_s}, \tag{7.14.2}$$

$$= \sum_{\substack{a_{t+1} \in \mathcal{F}_{t+1} \\ a_{t+1} \subseteq a_t}} \frac{\pi_{a_{t+1}}(a_t) u'_{i,t+1}(c^i_{a_{t+1}})}{u'_{it}(c^i_{a_t})} (x_{a_{t+1}} + S_x(a_{t+1}, t+1)), \tag{7.14.3}$$

where the third equality follows from the definition of $S_x(a_{t+1}, t+1)$.

Recall that $\pi_{a_s}(a_t)$ is the conditional probability of event a_s at time t given that the true state is in a_t. Let $S_x(t)$ denote the random ex–dividend price for the complex security x at time t. Then (7.14.2) and (7.14.3) can be rewritten as

$$S_x(t) = E\left[\sum_{s=t+1}^{T} \frac{u'_{is}(c^i(s))}{u'_{it}(c^i(t))} x(s)\Big|\mathcal{F}_t\right] \tag{7.14.4}$$

$$= E\left[\frac{u'_{i,t+1}(c^i(t+1))}{u'_{it}(c^i(t))}(x(t+1) + S(t+1))\Big|\mathcal{F}_t\right] ,\tag{7.14.5}$$

where $x(t)$ is the random dividend paid by security x at time t.

A securities markets rational expectations equilibrium is said to *implement* a complete market rational expectations equilibrium if the following three conditions are met: First, the prices for the long–lived securities in the securities markets equilibrium are the same as those in the rational expectations complete markets equilibrium determined according to (7.14.4) and (7.14.5). Second, the markets are dynamically complete in the securities markets rational expectations equilibrium. Third, the equilibrium allocations under the two market structures are identical.

Now let N be the maximum number of branches leaving each node of the event tree representing the information structure, and let $\mathbf{X}$ denote the collection of all the possible long–lived securities. The generic sense of sufficiency referred to at the end of Section 7.13. is as follows: Fix a complete market rational expectations equilibrium. If we randomly pick N long–lived securities from $\mathbf{X}$ and assign their prices at each node using the time–event prices of the complete markets rational expectations equilibrium, then, with probability one, the N long–lived securities dynamically complete the markets. In this probability one event, it is easily verified that there exists a securities markets rational expectations equilibrium having the same equilibrium allocation as the complete markets rational expectations equilibrium. That is, with probability one, a complete markets rational expectations equilibrium can be implemented in a securities markets rational expectations equilibrium by randomly selecting N long–lived securities. Conversely, it is also easily seen that every securities markets rational expectations equilibrium with dynamically complete markets corresponds to a complete markets rational expectations equilibrium, as the complete set of time–event contingent claims can be manufactured by dynamic trading of the long–lived securities.

The proof for the above *generic implementability* is rather technical, and we refer interested readers to Kreps (1982) for complete details.

7.15. From the previous discussion, the number of long–lived securities required to complete the markets dynamically in a securities markets equilibrium is no larger than the number of distinct time–events and may be much smaller. The minimum number of long–lived securities needed is determined completely by the way information is revealed over time or by the *temporal resolution of uncertainty*. If uncertainty is resolved gradually, that is, there are few branches leaving each node and thus the *amount* of information to be revealed the *next period* is small, the minimum number of long–lived securities needed is small. On the other hand, if, at some node, the amount of information to be revealed is large, the minimum number of long–lived securities needed is large. Intuitively, at each node, for every possible independent source of uncertainty to be resolved the next period, there should be a security or a portfolio of securities having payoffs contingent upon that uncertainty.

Here we note that the ideas discussed in Sections 5.10–5.19 can be generalized in a straightforward manner to multiperiod economies. For example, since we have assumed in this chapter that individuals have time–additive state–independent utility functions and homogeneous beliefs, it can be shown that an individual's Pareto optimal allocation of time–t consumption is a strictly increasing function of the time–t aggregate consumption/endowment. Thus as long as securities markets are dynamically complete with respect to the aggregate consumption "events", a Pareto optimal allocation will be achieved. Other generalizations are left for the readers.

Henceforth, we will only consider securities markets economies with dynamically complete markets unless we specify otherwise.

7.16. Recall from Sections 5.21 and 5.23 that in a two–period competitive equilibrium with complete markets, when individuals have homogeneous beliefs and state–independent and time–additive

utility functions, a representative agent with the same probability beliefs and with a state–independent and time–additive utility function
can be constructed to support equilibrium prices by consuming the
aggregate endowment. In our securities markets economy, the same
conclusion holds. That is, a representative agent can be constructed
in equilibrium so that equilibrium price processes can be supported
by this representative agent endowed with all the long–lived securities. The optimal trading strategy of this representative agent is to
hold the aggregate supply of long–lived securities throughout without trading, and the optimal consumption plan is simply to consume
the aggregate dividends paid at each date and in each event.

The representative agent's utility function can be constructed
as follows. First we note that, as markets are dynamically complete
in equilibrium, we can compute the complete set of time–event contingent claim prices, denoted by ϕ_{a_t}. The equilibrium consumption
plan of individual i, c^i, must be a solution to (7.3.5). Let γ_i be the
Lagrangian multiplier for the budget constraint. Putting $\lambda_i = \gamma_i^{-1}$,
we define

$$u_t(z) \equiv \max_{(z_i)_{i=1}^I} \sum_{i=1}^I \lambda_i u_{it}(z_i)$$

$$\text{s.t.} \sum_{i=1}^I z_i = z,$$

$\hspace{8cm}$ (7.16.1)

for all $t = 0, 1, \ldots, T$. Using the same arguments as in Section 5.22,
it is straightforward to show that equilibrium prices in the securities
markets economy are supported by an agent with the utility functions
defined in (7.16.1), probability beliefs π_{a_t}, and endowment of the
total supply of long–lived securities.

Employing (7.14.5), the price process for a long–lived security j
can then be written as

$$S_j(t-1) = E\left[\frac{u_t'(\tilde{C}_t)}{u_{t-1}'(\tilde{C}_{t-1})}(x_j(t) + S_j(t))|\mathcal{F}_{t-1}\right],$$

$\hspace{8cm}$ (7.16.2)

where

$$\tilde{C}_t \equiv \sum_{i=1}^I c^i(t) = \sum_{j=0}^N x_j(t)$$

is the random aggregate consumption at time t. Defining

$$\tilde{r}_{jt} \equiv \frac{x_j(t) + S_j(t)}{S_j(t-1)} - 1,$$

the rate of return for holding one share of security j from time $t-1$ to time t, (7.16.2) implies that

$$1 = E\left[\frac{u_t'(\tilde{C}_t)}{u_{t-1}'(\tilde{C}_{t-1})}(1 + \tilde{r}_{jt})|\mathcal{F}_{t-1}\right]$$

$$= \text{Cov}_{t-1}\left(\frac{u_t'(\tilde{C}_t)}{u_{t-1}'(\tilde{C}_{t-1})}, 1 + \tilde{r}_{jt}\right) + E\left[\frac{u_t'(\tilde{C}_t)}{u_{t-1}'(\tilde{C}_{t-1})}|\mathcal{F}_{t-1}\right]E[1 + \tilde{r}_{jt}|\mathcal{F}_{t-1}],$$

$$(7.16.3)$$

where $\text{Cov}_t(\cdot, \cdot)$ denotes the conditional covariance operator given the information at time t.

To facilitate our analysis, we will assume that the 0–th long–lived security is riskless in that it does not pay dividends until time T and its price at time $t < T$ is

$$S_0(t) = \Pi_{s=1}^t(1 + r_{fs}),$$

where r_{fs} is the riskless interest rate from time $s-1$ to time s. Note that r_{ft} can be stochastic, provided that the value of r_{ft} is known at time $t-1$. The dividend paid at time T by security 0 is

$$x_0(T) = \Pi_{s=1}^T(1 + r_{fs}).$$

Then (7.16.2) implies

$$E\left[\frac{u_t'(\tilde{C}_t)}{u_{t-1}'(\tilde{C}_{t-1})}|\mathcal{F}_{t-1}\right] = \frac{1}{1 + r_{ft}}. \qquad (7.16.4)$$

Now we can proceed as in Section 6.2 by substituting (7.16.4) into (7.16.3) to get

$$E[\tilde{r}_{jt}|\mathcal{F}_{t-1}] - r_{ft} = -(1 + r_{ft})\text{Cov}_{t-1}(\tilde{r}_{jt}, u_t'(\tilde{C}_t)/u_{t-1}'(\tilde{C}_{t-1})).$$

$$(7.16.5).$$

In equilibrium, the risk premium of security j at time $t-1$ is positive if its resale value plus its dividend at time t is positively correlated with the time t aggregate consumption, and vice versa. The intuition for (7.16.5) is the same as for (6.2.8).

Note that in Section 6.2, we used the observation that in a two–period economy, time–1 aggregate consumption is equal to time–1 aggregate wealth to substitute aggregate wealth for aggregate consumption in a relation like (7.16.5). In a multiperiod securities markets economy, there are more than two dates in the economy. Hence, the above observation is only valid at the final date of the economy. At any time before time T, aggregate consumption is only a fraction of the aggregate wealth. The aggregate wealth at any time t is composed of the aggregate consumption or the aggregate dividends at that time and the ex-dividend values of all the long–lived securities. As long as the aggregate ex-dividend value of long–lived securities is not zero, aggregate consumption will not be equal to aggregate wealth.

Even though aggregate consumption is not equal to aggregate wealth, there exists a functional relation between the two. Consider the representative agent in the dynamic programming context of Sections 7.9 and 7.10. Relation (7.10.5) implies that there exists a function $g(\cdot; \mathcal{F}_t)$ such that

$$\tilde{C}_t = g(\tilde{M}_t; \mathcal{F}_t), \tag{7.16.6}$$

where $\tilde{M}_t$ denotes aggregate wealth at time t. Substituting (7.16.6) into (7.16.5) gives

$$E[\tilde{r}_{jt}|\mathcal{F}_{t-1}] - r_{ft}$$
$$= -(1+r_{ft})\mathrm{Cov}_{t-1}(\tilde{r}_{jt}, u_t'(g(\tilde{M}_t; \mathcal{F}_t)))/u_{t-1}'(g(\tilde{M}_{t-1}; \mathcal{F}_{t-1})). \tag{7.16.7}$$

As g may not be a deterministic function of just $\tilde{M}$ and t, the sign of the covariance of (7.16.7) may not be determined by just the sign of $\mathrm{Cov}_{t-1}(\tilde{r}_{jt}, \tilde{M}_t)$. Hence, there may not be a market–based pricing relation. Under a set of very restrictive conditions, however, the relationship between $\tilde{C}_t$ and $\tilde{M}_t$ is deterministic – independent of the events in $\mathcal{F}_t$. As a consequence, a market–based asset pricing relation holds. This is the subject to be covered in Section 7.22.

7.17. Explicit pricing formulae can be derived by making assumptions on individuals' utility functions, as in Section 6.3, and utilizing (7.16.5). For example, suppose that the representative agent's utility functions are quadratic

$$u_t(z) = \rho^t\left(a_t z - \frac{b_t}{2}z^2\right) \quad a_t, b_t > 0, \tag{7.17.1}$$

where ρ represents the time preference. As in Section 4.16, we note that individual i reaches satiation at time t when $z \geq a_t/b_t$. We therefore assume that aggregate consumption at all times is such that satiation will not be attained. Substituting (7.17.1) into (7.16.5), we get

$$E[\tilde{r}_{jt}|\mathcal{F}_{t-1}] - r_{ft}$$
$$= -(1+r_{ft})\text{Cov}_{t-1}\left(\tilde{r}_{jt}, \frac{\rho^t(a_t - b_t\tilde{C}_t)}{\rho^{t-1}(a_{t-1} - b_{t-1}\tilde{C}_{t-1})}\right). \tag{7.17.2}$$

In the arguments in Sections 4.16 and 6.2, we also utilized the fact that in a two period securities markets economy there exists a portfolio of securities whose time–1 payoff is perfectly correlated with that of the aggregate consumption/wealth, namely the market portfolio itself. Therefore, the risk premia of risky securities can be expressed in terms of their *betas* with respect to the market portfolio and the risk premium on the market portfolio. In a multiperiod securities markets economy, however, there is no guarantee that there exists a portfolio of securities whose payoff is perfectly correlated with the aggregate consumption process. We therefore choose a dynamically rebalanced portfolio of securities whose rates of return over time are most highly correlated with the aggregate consumption process. Denote the rate of return of this portfolio at time t by $\tilde{r}_{ct}$. As $\tilde{r}_{ct}$ is the rate of return on a feasible portfolio, it must also satisfy (7.17.2):

$$E[\tilde{r}_{ct}|\mathcal{F}_{t-1}] - r_{ft}$$
$$= -(1+r_{ft})\text{Cov}_{t-1}\left(\tilde{r}_{ct}, \frac{\rho^t(a_t - b_t\tilde{C}_t)}{\rho^{t-1}(a_{t-1} - b_{t-1}\tilde{C}_{t-1})}\right). \tag{7.17.3}$$

Substituting (7.17.3) into (7.17.2) gives

$$E[\tilde{r}_{jt}|\mathcal{F}_{t-1}] - r_{ft} = \frac{\text{Cov}_{t-1}(\tilde{r}_{jt}, \tilde{C}_t)}{\text{Cov}_{t-1}(\tilde{r}_{ct}, \tilde{C}_t)}(E[\tilde{r}_{ct}|\mathcal{F}_{t-1}] - r_{ft}). \qquad (7.17.4)$$

Now define the *consumption beta* at time $t-1$ of security j to be

$$\beta_{jct-1} \equiv \frac{\text{Cov}_{t-1}(\tilde{r}_{jt}, \tilde{C}_t)}{\text{Var}_{t-1}(\tilde{C}_t)}, \qquad (7.17.5)$$

where $\text{Var}_t(\cdot)$ is the conditional variance at time t. Dividing $\text{Var}_{t-1}(\tilde{C}_t)$ into the numerator and the denominator of the right–hand side of (7.17.4) gives

$$E[\tilde{r}_{jt}|\mathcal{F}_{t-1}] - r_{ft} = \frac{\beta_{jct-1}}{\beta_{cct-1}}(E[\tilde{r}_{ct}|\mathcal{F}_{t-1}] - r_{ft}). \qquad (7.17.6)$$

This is the *Consumption Capital Asset Pricing Model*, abbreviated henceforth as CCAPM. Other pricing relations for different utility functions can be derived. We leave them to readers.

    7.18. As a historical note, a consumption–based asset pricing model of the form (7.16.5) was first derived by Rubinstein (1976) in a discrete time single agent economy. Later, Breeden and Litzenberger (1978) derived a similar relation in a complete markets competitive equilibrium with many heterogeneous individuals. Breeden (1979) shows that the CCAPM relation (7.17.6) is valid in general in a continuous time securities markets economy where local changes of the prices of long–lived securities and the optimal individual consumption are small. We will give a heuristic derivation of Breeden's result. Recall from calculus that

$$u'_{it}(c^i(t)) \approx u'_{it}(c^i(t-\Delta)) + u''_{it}(c^i(t-\Delta))\Delta c^i(t), \qquad (7.18.1)$$

if $\Delta c^i(t)$ is small, where

$$\Delta c^i(t) \equiv c^i(t) - c^i(t-\Delta).$$

Using (7.14.5) and the arguments used in deriving (7.16.5), we have

$$E[\tilde{r}_{jt}|\mathcal{F}_{t-\Delta}] - r_{ft} = -(1 + r_{ft})\text{Cov}_{t-\Delta}\left(\tilde{r}_{jt}, \frac{u'_{it}(c^i(t))}{u'_{it-\Delta}(c^i(t-\Delta))}\right),$$

(7.18.2)

where $\tilde{r}_{jt}$ and r_{ft} now denote the rate of return on security j and the riskless rate from time $t - \Delta$ to time t, respectively. Substituting (7.18.1) into (7.18.2) gives

$$E[\tilde{r}_{jt}|\mathcal{F}_{t-\Delta}] - r_{ft}$$

$$\approx -(1 + r_{ft})\text{Cov}_{t-\Delta}\left(\tilde{r}_{jt}, \frac{u'_{it}(c^i(t-\Delta)) + u''_{it}(c^i(t-\Delta))\Delta c^i(t)}{u'_{it-\Delta}(c^i(t-\Delta))}\right)$$

$$= -(1 + r_{ft})\frac{u''_{it}(c^i(t-\Delta))}{u'_{it-\Delta}(c^i(t-\Delta))}\text{Cov}_{t-\Delta}(\tilde{r}_{jt}, \Delta c^i(t)),$$

(7.18.3)

where the second equality follows because $c^i(t - \Delta)$ is known at time $t - \Delta$.

Dividing both sides of (7.18.3) by $-u''_{it}(c^i(t-\Delta))/u'_{it-\Delta}(c^i(t-\Delta))$ and summing across i gives

$$E[\tilde{r}_{jt}|\mathcal{F}_{t-\Delta}] - r_{ft} \approx \frac{1 + r_{ft}}{\sum_{i=1}^{I}\frac{-u'_{it-\Delta}(c^i(t-\Delta))}{u''_{it}(c^i(t-\Delta))}}\text{Cov}_{t-\Delta}(\tilde{r}_{jt}, \Delta\tilde{C}_t)$$

$$= \frac{1 + r_{ft}}{\sum_{i=1}^{I}\frac{-u'_{it-\Delta}(c^i(t-\Delta))}{u''_{it}(c^i(t-\Delta))}}\text{Cov}_{t-\Delta}(\tilde{r}_{jt}, \tilde{C}_t),$$

(7.18.4)

where

$$\Delta\tilde{C}_t \equiv \sum_{i=1}^{I}\Delta c^i(t) = \tilde{C}_t - \tilde{C}_{t-\Delta}$$

and the equality follows from the facts that $\tilde{C}_t = \tilde{C}_{t-\Delta} + \Delta\tilde{C}_t$ and that $\tilde{C}_{t-\Delta}$ is known at time $t - \Delta$. Let the rate of return from time $t - \Delta$ to t of a portfolio of securities whose rate of return is most highly correlated with the aggregate consumption be denoted by $\tilde{r}_{ct}$. This rate of return must also satisfy (7.18.4):

$$E[\tilde{r}_{ct}|\mathcal{F}_{t-\Delta}] - r_{ft} \approx \frac{1 + r_{ft}}{\sum_{i=1}^{I}\frac{-u'_{it-\Delta}(c^i(t-\Delta))}{u''_{it}(c^i(t-\Delta))}}\text{Cov}_{t-\Delta}(\tilde{r}_{ct}, \tilde{C}_t). \quad (7.18.5)$$

Substituting (7.18.5) into (7.18.4) and dividing by $\text{Var}_{t-\Delta}(\tilde{C}_t)$, we get

$$E[\tilde{r}_{jt}|\mathcal{F}_{t-\Delta}] - r_{ft} \approx \frac{\beta_{jc_{t-\Delta}}}{\beta_{cc_{t-\Delta}}}(E[\tilde{r}_{ct}|\mathcal{F}_{t-\Delta}] - r_{ft}). \qquad (7.18.6)$$

That is, the CCAPM holds approximately over the short time interval $[t - \Delta, t]$. Note that in the above derivation, we require neither that markets be (dynamically) complete nor that utility functions be quadratic.

Breeden (1979) shows that (7.18.6) holds exactly in a continuous time economy. His derivation uses stochastic calculus, which is outside the scope of this book. Interested readers should consult his paper for details.

7.19. In Section 7.16, we argued that in a multiperiod economy the aggregate consumption is not equal to the aggregate wealth except at the final date of the economy. Therefore, asset pricing relations depend upon the aggregate consumption process except at $T-1$. At any time $t \leq T-1$, however, there should be some relation between consumption and wealth. If this relation is nonstochastic and one–to–one, then consumption at any time can be expressed as a nonstochastic function of wealth. As a consequence, we can have a pricing relation that gives the risk premia of risky securities in terms of the stochastic properties of the market portfolio.

In the remaining sections of this chapter, we will formalize the ideas in the previous paragraph and give sufficient conditions under which there exists a one–to–one nonstochastic relation between consumption and wealth at each trading date. As the reader will see, these sufficient conditions essentially make a multiperiod problem into a sequence of almost disconnected single period problems. The only connections between adjacent periods are the wealth dynamics. Thus, there exists a nonstochastic relation between consumption and wealth when the multiperiod economy essentially lacks any intertemporal flavor. As an interim result, we will also derive an approximate *multi–beta* asset pricing relation in Section 7.21.

7.20. To avoid technical complexity, we will assume that there is a single representative individual in the multiperiod securities markets economy with utility functions $u_t(z)$ for time t consumption, which are increasing, strictly concave, and differentiable. Let $Y(t)$ denote an M–vector of random variables that are observable at time t. A possible realization of this vector of random variables from time 0 to time t is a *state of nature*, or an ω in the state space Ω. Thus, an observation of the realization of Y from time 0 to any time t tells us which states are possible and which states are not. When $Y(t)$ can only take a finite number of values, as we will assume, all the possible realizations of Y from time 0 to any time t generate a partition, $\mathcal{F}_t$, of the state space. The sequence $\{\mathcal{F}_t; t = 0, 1, \ldots, T\}$ is then an information structure. We assume that the single individual is endowed with the information structure constructed above. We will call the vector Y the vector of state variables and $Y(t)$ the vector of state variables at time t. We also assume that $Y(0)$ is a vector of known constants, so that $\mathcal{F}_0$ is just $\{\Omega\}$.

   To begin with, we will put some mild structure on Y. Fix $t < T$. Let z be a random variable, whose value depends upon $\{Y(t + 1), \ldots, Y(T)\}$. We assume that

$$E[z|\mathcal{F}_t] = E[z|Y(t)]. \qquad (7.20.1)$$

That is, the conditional expectation of z given the information conveyed by $\{Y(0), \ldots, Y(t)\}$ is equivalent to the expectation at time t of z conditional only upon $Y(t)$. That is, the historical realizations of Y strictly before time t are irrelevant for the conditional expectation of a random variable whose value depends only upon the possible realizations of Y after t. This kind of *memorylessness* property is known as the *Markov property*.

   Assume that the dividend paid by long–lived security j at time t depends only on $Y(t)$ and t. That is, $x_j(t) = x_j(Y(t), t)$. The total supply of any long–lived security is one share. The single individual is endowed with the total supply of long–lived securities. The aggregate consumption at time t is thus

$$C(Y(t), t) = \sum_{j=0}^{N} x_j(Y(t), t).$$

In this single individual economy, it is straightforward to identify a rational expectations equilibrium for the securities markets. Define

$$
\begin{aligned}
S_j(Y(t),t) &\equiv E\left[\sum_{s=t+1}^{T} \frac{u_s'(C(Y(s),s))}{u_t'(C(Y(t),t))} x_j(Y(s),s) \Big| \mathcal{F}_t\right] \\
&= E\left[\sum_{s=t+1}^{T} \frac{u_s'(C(Y(s),s))}{u_t'(C(Y(t),t))} x_j(Y(s),s) \Big| Y(t)\right],
\end{aligned}
\tag{7.20.2}
$$

where the second equality follows from the Markov property. You are asked in Exercise 7.6 to verify that the prices defined in (7.20.2), the consumption plan $C(Y(t),t)$, and trading strategy $\theta_j(t) = 1$ for all j comprise a rational expectations equilibrium for the securities markets.

7.21. In the rational expectations equilibrium established in Section 7.20, (7.16.5) is certainly valid. Thus, a consumption–based asset pricing relation holds approximately in the framework of Section 7.18. With a Markov structure, however, another linear asset pricing relation also holds approximately. This relation has more than one "beta."

Formally, we assume that aggregate consumption, $C(Y(t),t)$, is a differentiable function of $Y(t)$ and t. We will denote the partial derivatives of $C(Y(t),t)$ with respect to $Y(t)$ and t by $C_Y(t)$ and $C_t(t)$, respectively. Note the C_Y is an M–dimensional vector. Calculus implies that

$$
\begin{aligned}
C(t) &\approx C(t-\Delta) + C_Y(t-\Delta)^\top \Delta Y(t) \\
&\quad + C_{t-\Delta}(t-\Delta)\Delta t,
\end{aligned}
\tag{7.21.1}
$$

and

$$
u_t'(C(t)) \approx u_t'(C(t-\Delta)) + u_t''(C(t-\Delta))\Delta C(t), \tag{7.21.2}
$$

when $\Delta C(t)$, $\Delta Y(t)$, and Δt are small, where

$$
\begin{aligned}
\Delta Y(t) &\equiv Y(t) - Y(t-\Delta), \\
\Delta C(t) &\equiv C(t) - C(t-\Delta),
\end{aligned}
$$

and we have suppressed the dependence of $C(Y(t), t)$ on $Y(t)$. Substituting (7.21.2) into (7.21.1) gives

$$u_t'(C(t)) \approx u_t'(C(t-\Delta)) + u_t''(C(t-\Delta))\Big(C_Y(t-\Delta)^\top \Delta Y(t)$$
$$+ C_{t-\Delta}(t-\Delta)\Delta t\Big).$$
(7.21.3)

Now substituting (7.21.3) into (7.18.2) and using the Markov property gives

$$E[\tilde{r}_{jt}|Y(t-\Delta)] - r_{ft}$$
$$\approx -(1+r_{ft})\frac{u_t''(C(t-\Delta))C_Y(t-\Delta)^\top}{u_{t-\Delta}'(C(t-\Delta))}\text{Cov}_{t-\Delta}(\tilde{r}_{jt}, \Delta Y(t)), \quad \forall j.$$
(7.21.4)

Writing (7.21.4) in matrix notation gives

$$E[\tilde{\mathbf{r}}_t|Y(t-\Delta)] - r_{ft}\mathbf{1}$$
$$\approx -(1+r_{ft})\frac{u_t''(C(t-\Delta))}{u_{t-\Delta}'(C(t-\Delta))}\mathbf{V}_{xy}(t-\Delta)C_Y(t-\Delta),$$
(7.21.5)

where $\mathbf{1}$ is an N–vector of 1's, $\tilde{\mathbf{r}}_t$ is an N–vector of asset returns from time $t-\Delta$ to t, and $\mathbf{V}_{xy}(t-\Delta)$ is the $N \times M$ matrix of the variance–covariance matrix of $\tilde{\mathbf{r}}_t$ and $Y(t)$, conditional on $Y(t-\Delta)$.

Next, let $\tilde{r}_{z_k t}$ denote the rate of return, from time $t-\Delta$ to t, on a portfolio whose rates of return over time are most highly correlated with y_k, the k–th state variable. We denote $(\tilde{r}_{z_1 t}, \ldots, \tilde{r}_{z_M t})^\top$ by $\tilde{\mathbf{r}}_{zt}$. Each $\tilde{r}_{z_k t}$ satisfies (7.21.4), and in matrix notation we have

$$E[\tilde{\mathbf{r}}_{zt}|Y(t-\Delta)] - r_{ft}\mathbf{1}$$
$$\approx -(1+r_{ft})\frac{u_t''(C(t-\Delta))}{u_{t-\Delta}'(C(t-\Delta))}\mathbf{V}_{zy}(t-\Delta)C_Y(t-\Delta),$$
(7.21.6)

where $\mathbf{V}_{zy}(t-\Delta)$ denotes the $M \times M$ variance–covariance matrix of $\tilde{\mathbf{r}}_{zt}$ and $Y(t)$, conditional on $Y(t-\Delta)$. Substituting (7.21.6) into

(7.21.5) gives

$$
\begin{aligned}
&E[\tilde{\mathbf{r}}_t|Y(t-\triangle)] - r_{ft}\mathbf{1} \\
&\approx \mathbf{V}_{zy}(t-\triangle)\mathbf{V}_{zy}(t-\triangle)^{-1}\left(E[\tilde{\mathbf{r}}_{zt}|Y(t-\triangle)] - r_{ft}\mathbf{1}\right) \\
&= \mathbf{V}_{zy}(t-\triangle)\mathbf{V}_{yy}(t-\triangle)^{-1}\left(\mathbf{V}_{zy}(t-\triangle)\mathbf{V}_{yy}(t-\triangle)^{-1}\right)^{-1} \\
&\qquad\qquad \left(E[\tilde{\mathbf{r}}_{zt}|Y(t-\triangle)] - r_{ft}\mathbf{1}\right) \\
&\equiv \mathbf{B}_{zy}(t-\triangle)\mathbf{B}_{zy}(t-\triangle)^{-1}\left(E[\tilde{\mathbf{r}}_{zt}|Y(t-\triangle)] - r_{ft}\mathbf{1}\right),
\end{aligned}
\tag{7.21.7}
$$

where $\mathbf{V}_{yy}(t-\triangle)$ denotes the $M \times M$ variance–covariance matrix of $Y(t)$ conditional on $Y(t-\triangle)$ and $\mathbf{V}_{yy}(t-\triangle)^{-1}$ denotes the inverse of $\mathbf{V}_{yy}(t-\triangle)$. Note that the j-th row of $\mathbf{B}_{zy}(t-\triangle)$ and the the k-th row of $\mathbf{B}_{zy}(t-\triangle)$ contain the "multiple regression coefficients" of $\tilde{r}_{jt}$ and $\tilde{r}_{z_k t}$ on $Y(t)$ conditional on $Y(t-\triangle)$, respectively. That is, as an approximation, expected rates of return on risky assets are related to the rates of returns on M portfolios in a linear way.

Merton (1973) derives an exact multi–beta asset pricing relation in a continuous time economy. Relation (7.21.7) is an approximation.

7.22. The wealth of the single individual at time t is denoted by $W(t)$. It is equal to the sum of the ex–dividend values of the long–lived securities and the total dividends, at time t:

$$
W(t) = \sum_{j=0}^{N}(S_j(Y(t),t) + x_j(Y(t),t)).
\tag{7.22.1}
$$

The right–hand side of (7.22.1) depends only on $Y(t)$ and t. Thus we can write $W(t) = W(Y(t),t)$. Defining

$$
\eta(Y(t),t) \equiv \frac{C(Y(t),t)}{W(Y(t),t)},
$$

we can write

$$
C(Y(t),t) = \eta(Y(t),t)W(t).
\tag{7.22.2}
$$

That is, at each time t, the equilibrium consumption is a stochastic fraction of the wealth, which depends on the realization of the state variables. Note that (7.22.2) is just a special case of (7.10.5). Substituting (7.22.2) into (7.16.5) gives

$$
E[\tilde{r}_{jt}|\mathcal{F}_{t-1}] - r_{ft}
$$
$$
= -(1 + r_{ft})\text{Cov}_{t-1}\left(\tilde{r}_{jt}, \frac{u'_t(\eta(Y(t), t)W(t))}{u'_{t-1}(\eta(Y(t-1), t-1)W(t-1))}\right),
$$
$$
(7.22.3).
$$

so the wealth $W(t)$ does appear in the pricing relation. Unfortunately, the dependence of $\eta(t)$ on $Y(t)$ may be nontrivial. Thus the covariance term on the right–hand side of (7.22.3) may depend not only on $W(t)$ but also on some part of $Y(t)$, and the covariability between the rate of return on a security and that on the market portfolio alone cannot determine the sign of the risk premium.

Now we will provide a sufficient condition for consumption at each time to be a nonstochastic function of wealth so that the co-variability between $\tilde{r}_{jt}$ and $W(t)$ alone determines the sign of the risk premium for security j at time $t - 1$. Let us assume that $\{Y(1), Y(2), \ldots, Y(T)\}$ is a sequence of independent random variables, that is, any partial observation of the sequence has no effect on the probabilities of its future realizations. More formally, let z be a random variable whose value depends upon $\{Y(t+1), \ldots, Y(T)\}$. Then

$$
E[z|\mathcal{F}_t] = E[z].
$$

Using this independence assumption, (7.20.2) becomes

$$
S_j(t) \equiv E\left[\sum_{s=t+1}^{T} \frac{u'_s(C(Y(s), s))}{u'_t(C(Y(t), t))} x_j(Y(s), s)|\mathcal{F}_t\right]
$$
$$
= \frac{E[\sum_{s=t+1}^{T} u'_s(C(Y(s), s))x_j(Y(s), s)]}{u'_t(C(Y(t), t))}, \qquad (7.22.4)
$$

Note that the numerator of (7.22.4) depends only on the calendar time t. The denominator, however, is a strictly decreasing function of $C(t)$, because utility functions are strictly concave. Therefore, we can write $S_j(t) = S_j(C(t), t)$. Moreover, we know that $S_j(C(t), t)$ is a strictly increasing function of $C(t)$. Rewrite (7.22.1) as

$$W(t) = \sum_{j=0}^{N} (S_j(Y(t), t) + x_j(Y(t), t))$$

$$= \sum_{j=0}^{N} S_j(C(t), t) + \sum_{j=0}^{N} x_j(Y(t), t)$$

$$= \sum_{j=0}^{N} S_j(C(t), t) + C(Y(t), t).$$

It is easily seen that the wealth at time t can be written as $W(t) = W(C(t), t)$ and is a strictly increasing function of $C(t)$. As a consequence, there exists a function g such that $g(W(t), t) = C(t)$ and g is strictly increasing in $W(t)$. Substituting $C(t) = g(W(t), t)$ into (7.16.5) and using the Markov property gives

$$E[\tilde{r}_{jt}|Y(t-1)] - r_{ft}$$
$$= -(1 + r_{ft})\text{Cov}_{t-1}\left(\tilde{r}_{jt}, \frac{u'_t(g(W(t), t))}{u'_{t-1}(g(W(t-1), t-1))}\right). \qquad (7.22.5).$$

Risky security j has a positive risk premium at time $t-1$ if and only if its rate of return at time t is positively correlated with $W(t)$, the aggregate wealth at t, and vice versa. We have thus recovered a single period result by making an assumption strong enough to make a multiperiod problem into, essentially, a sequence of disconnected single period problems in the sense that the realization of the state variables before time t conveys no information about the stochastic properties of Y after t. Moreover, using a local approximation argument on (7.22.5) as in Section 7.21, we will get a single–beta linear asset pricing relation with the rate of return on the market portfolio as the pivotal variable. We leave this for the reader in Exercise 7.10.

Exercises

7.1. Let the consumption plan c be financed by a trading strategy θ. Show that

$$\theta(t)^\top S(t) = \theta(0)^\top S(0) + \sum_{s=1}^{t} \theta(s)^\top [S(s) - S(s-1)]$$

$$+ \sum_{s=0}^{t-1} \theta(s)^\top X(s) - \sum_{s=0}^{t-1} c(s).$$

7.2. Show that if (7.5.3) is violated, there exists an arbitrage opportunity in a rational expectations competitive economy.

7.3. Show that the indirect utility function of Section 7.10 is increasing and strictly concave in wealth.

7.4. Consider a multiperiod securities markets economy with dynamically complete markets. Show that the indirect utility function, as a function of wealth for an individual with time–additive utility functions;

$$u_t(z) = \rho^t \frac{1}{1-b} z^{1-b},$$

has the following form,

$$V(W(t); \mathcal{F}_t) = f(t; \mathcal{F}_t) W(t)^{1-b} + h(t; \mathcal{F}_t),$$

where f and h are possibly stochastic functions depending on events in $\mathcal{F}_t$.

7.5. Show in the context of Exercise 7.4 that when $u_t(z) = \rho^t \ln z$, the indirect utility function has the form

$$V(W(t); \mathcal{F}_t) = f(t) \ln W(t) + h(t; \mathcal{F}_t),$$

where we note that f is a deterministic function of time.

7.6. In Figure 7.12.1, we listed prices for two long–lived securities along the event tree. Besides these two securities, there also exists a riskless security as described in Section 7.12. Show that the prices of these three long–lived securities do not admit arbitrage opportunities. That is, there do not exist trading strategies that cost nothing at time 0 and finance consumption plans that are nonnegative and strictly positive at at least one node on the event tree.

7.7. In the context of Section 7.11, determine the price of a complex security that pays \$5 at time 1 if and only if the upper node is realized and pays \$10 at time 2 if and only if ω_5 is the true state. Also, describe the dynamic strategy that manufactures this complex security.

7.8. Show that the utility functions defined in (7.16.1) are utility functions for a representative agent in the sense of Chapter 5.

7.9. Verify that the prices defined in (7.20.2) can be supported in a rational expectations equilibrium for the securities markets considered in Section 7.20.

7.10. Use a local approximation argument on (7.22.5) as in Section 7.21 to get a single–beta linear asset pricing relation with the rate of return on the market portfolio as the pivotal variable.

Remarks. Sections 7.2 to 7.5 are freely adapted from Arrow (1964) and Debreu (1959). Note that if individuals do not have rational expectations and if markets remain open after time 0, there may exist speculation. A good reference for this is Svensson (1981). When utility functions are not time–additive, there exist situations where there are incentives to trade after time 0 in a complete markets competitive economy. Interested readers should consult Donaldson, Rossman and Selden (1980) and Donaldson and Selden (1981). The discussions on the issues relating to dynamically completing markets are borrowed from Kreps (1982). Our heuristic derivation of the CCAPM in continuous time is from Bhattacharya (1980). Interested readers should consult Breeden's (1979) derivation. Recently, Duffie and Zam (1987) rederived the CCAPM more rigorously. There now exists a growing literature on the existence of an equilibrium when there are an infinite number of states of nature. Interested readers can consult Mas-Colell (1986), Mas-Colell and Richard (1987), and Zam (1987), for example.

Duffie and Huang (1985) discuss dynamic spanning when there are infinitely many states of nature in continuous time economies. The Markov economy constructed in Section 7.19 is adapted from Lucas (1978) and Prescott and Mehra (1980), although the method of analysis is different. For generalizations of Lucas' model in exchange as well as production economies, see Brock (1982), Cox, Ingersoll, and Ross (1985) and Huang (1987). Constantinides (1980, 1982) gives various conditions under which a single market beta asset pricing model is valid in exchange as well as production economies. Chamberlain (1987) derives a single market beta asset pricing model under conditions more general than those in Section 7.22. Hansen and Richard (1987) discuss the role of conditioning information in dynamic asset pricing models. For a recent overview of asset pricing theories, see Constantinides (1987).

In many places in this and earlier chapters, we assert without proof that $\text{Cov}(f(\tilde{X}), \tilde{Y})$ and $\text{Cov}(\tilde{X}, \tilde{Y})$ have opposite signs when $f(\cdot)$ is positive and monotone decreasing. This is in general not true. It is true, however, when $\tilde{X} = a + \tilde{Y} + \tilde{\varepsilon}$ with $\tilde{Y}$ and $\tilde{\varepsilon}$ independent. For example, (4.24.4) on p. 111 is true.

References

Arrow, K. 1964. The role of securities in the optimal allocation of risk–bearing. *Review of Economic Studies* **31**:91–96.

Bhattacharya, S. 1981. Notes on multiperiod valuation and the pricing of options. *Journal of Finance* **36**:163–180.

Breeden, D. 1979. An intertemporal capital pricing model with stochastic investment opportunities. *Journal of Financial Economics* **7**: 265–296.

Breeden, D., and R. Litzenberger. 1978. State contingent prices implicit in option prices, *Journal of Business* **51**:621–651.

Brock, W. 1982. Asset prices in a production economy. In *The Economics of Uncertainty and Information*. Edited by J. McCall. University of Chicago Press. Chicago.

Chamberlain, G. 1987. Asset pricing in multiperiod securities markets. Mimeo. Department of Economics, University of Wisconsin–Madison.

Constantinides, G. 1980. Admissible uncertainty in the intertemporal asset pricing model. *Journal of Financial Economics* **8**:71–86.

Constantinides, G. 1982. Intertemporal asset pricing with heterogeneous consumers and without demand aggregation. *Journal of Business* **55**:253–267.

Constantinides, G. 1987. Theory of valuation: Overview and recent developments. In *Frontiers of Financial Theory*. Edited by G. Constantinides and S. Bhattacharya. Rowman and Littlefield. Totowa, New Jersey.

Cox, J., J. Ingersoll, and S. Ross. 1985. An intertemporal general equilibrium model of asset prices. *Econometrica* **53**:363–384.

Debreu, G. 1959. *Theory of Value*. Yale University Press, New Haven and London.

Donaldson, J., M. Rossman, and L. Selden. 1980. On the need to revise dynamic consumption strategies in the presence of unchanging Arrow–Debreu preferences. Mimeo. Columbia University.

Donaldson, J., and L. Selden. 1981. Arrow–Debreu preferences and the reopening of contingent claims markets. *Economic Letters* **8**:209–216.

Duffie, D., and C. Huang. 1985. Implementing Arrow–Debreu equilibria by continuous trading of few long–lived securities. *Econometrica* **53**:1337–1356.

Duffie, D., and W. Zam. 1987. The consumption–based capital asset pricing model. GSB Research Paper #922, Stanford University.

Hansen, L., and S. Richard. 1987. The role of conditioning information in deducing testable restrictions implied by dynamic asset pricing models. *Econometrica* **55**:587–614.

Huang, C. 1987. An intertemporal general equilibrium asset pricing model: The case of diffusion information. *Econometrica* **55**:117–142.

Kreps, D. 1982. Multiperiod securities and the efficient allocation of risk: A comment on the Black–Scholes option pricing model. In *The Economics of Uncertainty and Information*. Edited by J. McCall. University of Chicago Press. Chicago.

Lucas, R. 1978. Asset prices in an exchange economy. *Econometrica* **46**:1426–1446.

Mas–Colell, A. 1986. The price equilibrium existence problem in topological vector lattices. *Econometrica* **54**:1039–1053.

Mas–Colell, A., and S. Richard. 1987. A new approach to the existence of equilibria in vector lattices. Mimeo. Economics Department, Harvard University.

Merton, R. 1973. An intertemporal capital asset pricing model. *Econometrica* **41**:867–887.

Prescott, E., and R. Mehra. 1980. Recursive competitive equilibrium: The case of homogeneous households. *Econometrica* 48:1365–1379.

Radner, R. 1972. Existence of equilibrium of plans, prices and price expectations in a sequence of markets. *Econometrica* 40:289–303.

Svensson, L. 1981. Efficiency and speculation in a model with price–contingent contracts. *Econometrica* 49:131–151.

Rubinstein, M. 1976. The valuation of uncertain income streams and the pricing of options. *Bell Journal of Economics* 7:407–425.

Zam, W. 1985. Competitive equilibria in production economies with an infinite dimensional commodity space. Mimeo. Department of Mathematics, State University of New York at Buffalo.

CHAPTER 8
MULTIPERIOD
SECURITIES MARKETS II:
VALUATION BY ARBITRAGE

8.1. In Chapter 7, we discussed equilibrium asset valuations in multiperiod economies. In this chapter, we will focus our attention on issues related to the pricing of derivative securities. Derivative securities are long–lived securities whose payoffs depend on the price processes of other long–lived securities. For example, a call option written on a common stock is a derivative security. In many situations, pricing of derivative securities does not rely on equilibrium arguments – a derivative security may be priced by arbitrage arguments in the sense that if securities markets do not admit arbitrage opportunities, the price of the derivative security can be determined completely by the price processes of other long–lived securities. When we price by arbitrage, we normally take the price processes of a set of long–lived securities as given and price derivative assets. There is one question that naturally needs to be resolved, namely how do we know that the price processes we take as given do not admit any arbitrage opportunities?

The necessary and sufficient condition for price processes not to admit arbitrage opportunities is that they are related to martingales, to be defined, through a normalization and change of probability. This martingale connection also provides a direct way to compute price processes of derivative assets that can be priced by arbitrage. As an application, we use this method to price a call option when the price process of the underlying stock follows a binomial random walk.

8.2. In this chapter we consider a multiperiod securities markets economy with a single perishable consumption good. We fix, until further notice, a state space Ω with a finite number of states of nature and an information structure $\mathbf{F} = \{\mathcal{F}_t; t = 0, 1, \ldots, T\}$. As in Chapter 7, we assume that the true state will be learned by time T and $\mathcal{F}_0 = \{\Omega\}$. There are $N + 1$ long–lived securities traded, indexed by $j = 0, 1, \ldots, N$. As in Chapter 7, long–lived security j is characterized by its dividend process $x_j = \{x_j(t); t = 0, 1, 2, \ldots, T\}$, where $x_j(t)$ is the random dividend paid at time t, in units of the consumption good. Dividend processes are adapted to $\mathbf{F}$. To simplify the analyses that follow, we assume that the 0–th long–lived security does not pay dividends until time T, at which time it pays one unit of the consumption good in all states. The 0–th long–lived security is just a T–period discount bond with a face value equal to one unit of the consumption good.

We depart a little from the notation and setup used in Chapter 7. The ex–dividend price of the 0–th security at time t is denoted by $B(t)$; while the ex–dividend price of security $j \geq 1$ at time t is denoted by $S_j(t)$. As the price processes are ex–dividend, $S_j(T) = 0$ and $B(T) = 0$. Naturally, $B(t)$, and $S_j(t)$ are random variables measurable with respect to $\mathcal{F}_t$. Since only relative prices are determined in an economic equilibrium, we assume without loss of generality that prices of long–lived securities are in units of the single consumption good. That is, the spot price of the consumption good is unity throughout.

Individuals in the economy, indexed by $i = 1, 2, \ldots, I$, have time–additive von Neumann–Morgenstern utility functions $u_{it}(\cdot)$ that are increasing, strictly concave, and differentiable. For ease of exposition, we assume that $u'_{it}(0) = \infty$. This will ensure that individuals always choose strictly positive consumption, which is a plausible economic condition. Individual i is endowed with a probability belief $\pi^i = \{\pi^i_\omega; \omega \in \Omega\}$ about the states of nature and with shares of long–lived securities $(\bar{\alpha}^i(0), \bar{\theta}^i(0))$. Since $B(t)$ and $S(t)$ are random variables and depend on the states of nature, so they are functions of ω and t. We assume that individuals have *rational expectations* in that they agree on the mappings $B(\omega, t)$ and $S_j(\omega, t)$. We assume that, for every i, π^i assigns a strictly positive probability to every state.

A trading strategy is denoted by $\{\alpha(t), \theta(t) = (\theta_j(t))_{j=1}^N\}$, where $\alpha(t)$ and $\theta_j(t)$ are the random number of shares of the 0–th and the j–th security, respectively, held from time $t - 1$ to time t, before trading occurs at time t. A trading strategy is a predictable process. A consumption plan $c = \{c(t); t = 0, 1, \ldots, T\}$ is a process adapted to $\mathbf{F}$, where $c(t)$ denotes the random units of time–t consumption. A trading strategy (α, θ) is said to be admissible if there exists a consumption plan c such that, $\forall t$,

$$\alpha(t+1)B(t) + \theta(t+1)^\top S(t) = \alpha(t)B(t) + \theta(t)^\top (S(t) + X(t)) - c(t),$$
$$(8.2.1)$$

where $S(t) = (S_1(t), \ldots, S_N(t))^\top$, $X(t) = (x_1(t), \ldots, x_N(t))^\top$, and $\theta(t) = (\theta_1(t), \ldots, \theta_N(t))^\top$. Note that in (8.2.1) we have used the convention that the left–hand side is identically equal to 0 when $t = T$. Thus, at $t = T$, (8.2.1) becomes

$$\alpha(T) + \theta(T)^\top X(T) = c(T). \qquad (8.2.2)$$

The consumption plan of (8.2.1) is then said to be *financed* by (α, θ). Alternatively, a consumption plan is said to be *marketed* if it is *financed* by an admissible trading strategy.

Note that the definition of a marketed consumption plan does not depend upon any of the individuals' probability beliefs π^i. They will certainly agree whether a consumption plan is marketed and whether a consumption plan is financed by an admissible trading strategy.

8.3. As we mentioned in Section 8.1, one of the major purposes of this chapter is to price derivative securities while taking a price system (B, S) as given. Therefore, our first order of business is to give conditions on (B, S) such that it forms a "reasonable" price system. As the weaker our requirement of reasonableness is, the stronger the implications of our requirement will be, we would like to impose as weak a condition on (B, S) as possible. Ideally, the requirement should be a necessary condition for any equilibrium price system so that its implications would apply to all equilibrium price systems.

As individuals in the economy strictly prefer more to less, it follows that a necessary condition for a price system to be an equilibrium price system is that it cannot admit the possibility of something being created from nothing, or admit the existence of *arbitrage opportunities*. This necessary condition of an equilibrium price system will be our requirement for a reasonable price system.

Formally, an arbitrage opportunity is a consumption plan c financed by an admissible trading strategy (α, θ) with the following properties: c is nonnegative and there at least exists a t and an event $a_t \in \mathcal{F}_t$ such that $c(a_t, t)$ is strictly positive, and $\alpha(0)B(0) + \theta(0)^\top (S(0) + X(0)) \leq 0$, where $c(a_t, t)$ denotes consumption at time t in event a_t. That is, an arbitrage opportunity is a consumption plan that is nonnegative always and strictly positive in at least one event, and has a nonpositive initial cost. A price system that admits arbitrage opportunities can *never* be an equilibrium price system, because nonsatiated individuals will take unbounded positions in an arbitrage opportunity so that markets cannot clear. Here we remark that the definition of an arbitrage opportunity does *not* involve any of the individuals' possibly diverse probability beliefs π^i's.

We will show in Sections 8.4 and 8.5 that when no arbitrage opportunities are present, a long–lived security price process and its accumulated dividends, in units of the 0–th long–lived security, have the property that at any time t, the conditional expectation of their sum at any future date must be equal to the sum of their values at time t, where the expectation is taken under a (pseudo) probability $\pi^* = \{\pi^*_\omega; \omega \in \Omega\}$ not necessarily equal to any of the individuals' endowed beliefs π^i's. Equivalently, the price of a long–lived security plus its accumulated dividends, in units of the 0–th long–lived security, must form a *martingale* under a probability π^*. Like all of the π^i's, this probability π^* also assigns a strictly positive probability to every state $\omega \in \Omega$. Since the absence of arbitrage opportunities is a necessary condition for an economic equilibrium, it then follows that *every* equilibrium price system must have this *martingale property*. It turns out that this martingale property is also sufficient for a price system not to admit any arbitrage opportunities.

Before we leave this section, we will give a formal definition of a martingale. A process $Y = \{Y(t); t = 0, 1, \ldots, T\}$ is a martingale adapted to $\mathbf{F}$ under a probability π if

$$E[Y(s)|\mathcal{F}_t] = Y(t) \quad \forall s \geq t,$$

where $E[\cdot|\mathcal{F}_t]$ is the expectation under π conditional on $\mathcal{F}_t$. All the martingales will be adapted to $\mathbf{F}$.

8.4. We will prove first that the no arbitrage condition implies the martingale property. Suppose that (B, S) admits no arbitrage opportunities. Note that an individual i in this economy solves the following problem:

$$\max_{(\alpha, \theta)} E_i[\sum_{t=0}^{T} u_{it}(c(t))]$$

$$\text{s.t. } c \text{ is financed by } (\alpha, \theta) \tag{8.4.1}$$

$$\text{and } (\alpha(0), \theta(0)) = (\bar{\alpha}^i(0), \bar{\theta}^i(0)),$$

where $E_i[\cdot]$ denotes the expectation under π^i. As there are only a finite number of time–events, there are no arbitrage opportunities, and individuals only choose nonnegative consumption plans, mathematical arguments show that there always exists a solution to (8.4.1), denoted by (α^i, θ^i). Let c^i be the consumption plan financed by (α^i, θ^i). The reader is asked in Exercise 8.1 to show that, $\forall t < T$,

$$S_j(t) = E_i\left[\frac{u'_{i,t+1}(c^i(t+1))}{u'_{it}(c^i(t))}(S_j(t+1) + x_j(t+1))|\mathcal{F}_t\right]. \tag{8.4.2}$$

As $u'_{it}(c^i(t))$ is known at time t, relation (8.4.2) is equivalent to

$$u'_{it}(c^i(t))S_j(t) = E_i\left[u'_{i,t+1}(c^i(t+1))(S_j(t+1) + x_j(t+1))|\mathcal{F}_t\right]. \tag{8.4.3}$$

Relation (8.4.3) can be understood as follows. The left–hand side of (8.4.3) is the marginal utility at time t of one fewer share of security j, and the right–hand side is the marginal utility at time t of one additional share of security j. In the optimal solution, there should be no incentive to deviate. Thus it is necessary that the left–hand side of (8.4.3) be equal to the right–hand side. The reader should compare (8.4.2) with (5.6.2) and (7.14.5).

The discount bond prices satisfy a relation similar to (8.4.2):

$$B(t) = \begin{cases} E_i \left[\frac{u'_{i,t+1}(c^i(t+1))}{u'_{it}(c^i(t))} B(t+1) | \mathcal{F}_t \right] & \text{if } t \leq T - 2; \\ E_i \left[\frac{u'_{i,t+1}(c^i(t+1))}{u'_{it}(c^i(t))} | \mathcal{F}_t \right] & \text{if } t = T - 1. \end{cases}$$

By repeated substitution of the above relation into itself, we have

$$B(t) = \begin{cases} E_i \left[\frac{u'_{is}(c^i(s))}{u'_{it}(c^i(t))} B(s) | \mathcal{F}_t \right] & \text{if } t \leq s \leq T - 1; \\ E_i \left[\frac{u'_{is}(c^i(s))}{u'_{it}(c^i(t))} | \mathcal{F}_t \right] & \text{if } s = T. \end{cases} \tag{8.4.4}$$

Price processes of long–lived securities are in general not martingales under any of the π^i's, as is evident from (8.4.2) and (8.4.4). One sufficient condition for price processes plus accumulated dividends to be martingales under some individual's probability belief is that there exists at least one risk neutral individual who does not exhibit any time preference. In such an event, (8.4.2) must apply for this risk neutral individual under his probability belief, say π. Since he is risk neutral and does not have any time preference,

$$u'_{is}(c^i(s)) = u'_{it}(c^i(t)) = \text{constant} \quad \forall s, t.$$

Thus (8.4.2) and (8.4.4) become, $\forall t < T$,

$$S_j(t) = E[S_j(t+1) + x_j(t+1) | \mathcal{F}_t] \tag{8.4.5}$$
$$B(t) = 1, \tag{8.4.6}$$

where we have used $E[\cdot | \mathcal{F}_t]$ to denote the expectation under π conditional on $\mathcal{F}_t$. From (8.4.6), interest rates are zero throughout.

Define the accumulated dividend process for security j to be

$$D_j(t) = \sum_{s=0}^{t} x_j(s), \quad \forall t = 0, 1, \ldots, T.$$

Now adding $D_j(t)$ to both sides of (8.4.5) gives

$$S_j(t) + D_j(t) = E\left[S_j(t+1) + D_j(t+1)|\mathcal{F}_t\right] \qquad (8.4.7)$$
$$= E\left[S_j(s) + D_j(s)|\mathcal{F}_t\right], \quad \forall s > t, \qquad (8.4.8)$$

where (8.4.8) follows from repeated substitution of (8.4.7) into itself. Thus prices plus accumulated dividends are martingales under π.

When no individual is risk neutral, prices of long–lived securities plus accumulated dividends are still connected to martingales through a normalization and change of probability. The process of normalization makes interest rates in units of a long–lived security equal to zero throughout. The change of probability subsumes risk aversion. This is the subject to which we now turn.

8.5. We proceed by first defining a *normalized* or *discounted price system* and accumulated dividend processes,

$$S_j^*(t) \equiv \begin{cases} \frac{S_j(t)}{B(t)} & \text{if } t \neq T; \\ 0 & \text{if } t = T; \end{cases}$$

$$B^*(t) \equiv \begin{cases} 1 & \text{if } t \neq T; \\ 0 & \text{if } t = T; \end{cases}$$

$$D_j^*(t) \equiv \sum_{s=0}^{t} x_j^*(s),$$

where

$$x_j^*(t) \equiv \begin{cases} \frac{x_j(t)}{B(t)} & \text{if } t \neq T; \\ x_j(t) & \text{if } t = T. \end{cases}$$

We note here that $B(t)$ must be strictly positive for all $t < T$, or else there is an arbitrage opportunity which is buying the bond when its price reaches zero and holding it to time T.

Next, define a probability π^* as follows

$$\pi_\omega^* \equiv \frac{u'_{iT}(c^i(\omega,T))}{u'_{i0}(c^i(0))} \frac{\pi_\omega^i}{B(0)} \qquad \forall \omega \in \Omega. \qquad (8.5.1)$$

To verify that π^* is a probability defined on Ω we have to check two defining properties of a probability: $\pi_\omega^* \geq 0$ and $\sum_{\omega \in \Omega} \pi_\omega^* = 1$. The first property follows from the fact that utility functions are strictly increasing, $B(0) > 0$, and the assumption that $\pi_\omega^i > 0$, $\forall \omega$. In fact, $\pi_\omega^* > 0$, $\forall \omega$. Next note that

$$\sum_{\omega \in \Omega} \pi_\omega^* = \sum_{\omega \in \Omega} \frac{u'_{iT}(c^i(\omega,T))}{u'_{i0}(c^i(0))} \frac{\pi_\omega^i}{B(0)}$$

$$= E_i \left[\frac{u'_{iT}(c^i(T))}{u'_{i0}(c^i(0))} \right] / B(0)$$

$$= B(0)/B(0) = 1,$$

where the third equality follows from (8.4.4).

Now we want to show that $S_j^* + D_j^*$ is a martingale under π^*. First we observe that the conditional probability under π^* of an event $a_s \in \mathcal{F}_s$ given an event $a_t \in \mathcal{F}_t$ with $s \geq t$, denoted by $\pi_{a_s}^*(a_t)$, is

$$\pi_{a_s}^*(a_t) = \begin{cases} \dfrac{\sum_{\omega \in a_s} \pi_\omega^*}{\sum_{\omega \in a_t} \pi_\omega^*} & \text{if } a_s \subseteq a_t; \\ 0 & \text{if } a_s \not\subseteq a_t. \end{cases} \qquad (8.5.2)$$

Similarly, we can define $\pi_{a_s}^i(a_t)$, the probability under π^i of a_s conditional on a_t. When $a_s \subseteq a_t$, we have

$$\pi_{a_s}^*(a_t) = \frac{\sum_{\omega \in a_s} \pi_\omega^*}{\sum_{\omega \in a_t} \pi_\omega^*} = \frac{\sum_{\omega \in a_s} \pi_\omega^i u'_{iT}(c^i(\omega,T))}{\sum_{\omega \in a_t} \pi_\omega^i u'_{iT}(c^i(\omega,T))}$$

$$= \frac{\pi_{a_s}^i u'_{is}(c^i(a_s,s)) \sum_{\omega \in a_s} \frac{\pi_\omega^i u'_{iT}(c^i(\omega,T))}{\pi_{a_s}^i u'_{is}(c^i(a_s,s))}}{\pi_{a_t}^i u'_{it}(c^i(a_t,t)) \sum_{\omega \in a_t} \frac{\pi_\omega^i u'_{iT}(c^i(\omega,T))}{\pi_{a_t}^i u'_{it}(c^i(a_t,t))}}, \qquad (8.5.3)$$

where $c^i(a_t,t)$ denotes individual i's optimal consumption at time t in event a_t, and $\pi_{a_t}^i$ is the probability of a_t under π^i. Relation (8.4.4) implies that

$$\sum_{\omega \in a_t} \frac{\pi_\omega^i u'_{iT}(c^i(\omega,T))}{\pi_{a_t}^i u'_{it}(c^i(a_t,t))} = B(a_t,t), \forall t \leq T-1, \qquad (8.5.4)$$

where $B(a_t, t)$ denotes the bond price at time t in event a_t. Substituting (8.5.4) into (8.5.3) gives

$$
\pi^*_{a_s}(a_t) = \begin{cases}
\dfrac{B(a_s, s)}{B(a_t, t)} \dfrac{\pi^i_{a_s}(a_t) u'_{is}(c^i(a_s, s))}{u'_{it}(c^i(a_t, t))} & \text{if } s \leq T - 1; \\[3mm]
\dfrac{1}{B(a_t, t)} \dfrac{\pi^i_{a_s}(a_t) u'_{is}(c^i(a_s, s))}{u'_{it}(c^i(a_t, t))} & \text{if } s = T.
\end{cases}
\tag{8.5.5}
$$

We are now ready to prove the first main result of this chapter. Substituting (8.5.5) into (8.4.2) gives, for all $t \leq T - 1$,

$$
\begin{aligned}
S_j(t) &= E_i \left[\frac{u'_{i,t+1}(c^i(t+1))}{u'_{it}(c^i(t))} (S_j(t+1) + x_j(t+1)) \Big| \mathcal{F}_t \right] \\
&= B(t) E^* \left[S^*_j(t+1) + x^*_j(t+1) | \mathcal{F}_t \right],
\end{aligned}
\tag{8.5.6}
$$

where $E^*[\cdot | \mathcal{F}_t]$ is the expectation operator with respect to π^* conditional on $\mathcal{F}_t$. Rearranging (8.5.6) gives, for all $t \leq T - 1$,

$$
S^*_j(t) = E^*[S^*_j(t+1) + x^*_j(t+1) | \mathcal{F}_t].
\tag{8.5.7}
$$

The reader should compare (8.5.7) with (8.4.5). These two relations have the same form, except that one is in units of the consumption good and the expectation is taken with respect to π and one is in units of the discount bond and the expectation is taken with respect to π^*. Following the same line of arguments used in deriving (8.4.7) from (8.4.5), we easily get

$$
\begin{aligned}
S^*_j(t) + D^*_j(t) &= E^*[S^*(s) + D^*_j(s) | \mathcal{F}_t] \quad \forall s \geq t, \\
&= E^*[D^*_j(T) | \mathcal{F}_t].
\end{aligned}
\tag{8.5.8}
$$

That is, $S^*_j + D^*_j$ is a martingale under π^*. As for the discount bond, $B^*(t) + D^*_0(t) = 1$, $\forall t$, and is certainly a martingale under π^*.

In summary, we have proved that if a price system admits no arbitrage opportunities, then, after a normalization, there must exist a probability π^* that assigns a strictly positive probability to every state of nature such that price processes plus the accumulated dividends are martingales under π^*. A probability having the above property is termed *an equivalent martingale measure*.

Before we leave this section, we make one remark. We constructed an equivalent martingale measure by using an individual's probability belief π^i and his marginal utilities. Under the martingale measure, however, the normalized price processes plus normalized accumulated dividends form martingales for *all* individuals.

8.6. We now proceed to prove the converse part of the martingale property: if $B(t) > 0$ for all $t < T$ and if there exists an equivalent martingale measure, π^*, for $S_j^* + D_j^*$, then (B, S) admits no arbitrage opportunities.

We will prove the assertion by contraposition. Let there be an arbitrage opportunity c financed by an admissible trading strategy (α, θ). That is, $c \geq 0$, $c \neq 0$, and $\alpha(0)B(0)+\theta(0)^\top(S(0)+X(0)) \leq 0$.

Recall from Exercise 7.1 that if c is financed by (α, θ), we have

$$
\begin{aligned}
\alpha(T) + \theta(T)^\top X(T) = {} & \alpha(0)B(0) + \theta(0)^\top(S(0) + X(0)) \\
& - \sum_{s=0}^{T-1} c(s) + \sum_{s=1}^{T} \alpha(s)(B(s) - B(s-1) + x_0(s)) \\
& + \sum_{s=1}^{T} \theta(s)^\top (S(s) - S(s-1) + X(s)).
\end{aligned}
\tag{8.6.1}
$$

Relation (8.6.1) follows from the self–financing budget constraint. The left–hand side of (8.6.1) is the value of the strategy (α, θ) at time T. The right–hand side of (8.6.1) is the initial value of the strategy plus accumulated gains or losses from trading in the long–lived securities from time 0 to time T minus the accumulated consumption withdrawals from time 0 to time $T - 1$.

Similar arguments show that in discounted units,

$$
\begin{aligned}
\alpha(T) + \theta(T)^\top X^*(T) = {} & \alpha(0) + \theta(0)^\top(S^*(0) + X^*(0)) \\
& + \sum_{s=1}^{T} \theta(s)^\top (S^*(s) - S^*(s-1) + X^*(s)) - \sum_{s=0}^{T-1} c^*(s),
\end{aligned}
\tag{8.6.2}
$$

where $X^*(t) = (x_1^*(t), \ldots, x_N^*(t))^\top$ and

$$
c^*(t) \equiv \begin{cases} c(t)/B(t) & \text{if } t \leq T - 1; \\ c(t) & \text{if } t = T. \end{cases}
$$

Denoting $(D_1^*(t), \ldots, D_N^*(t))^\top$ by $D^*(t)$, we have

$$X^*(t) = D^*(t) - D^*(t-1). \tag{8.6.3}$$

Substituting (8.6.3) into (8.6.2), noting that

$$c^*(T) = \alpha(T) + \theta(T)^\top X^*(T),$$

and rearranging gives

$$\sum_{t=0}^{T} c^*(t) = \alpha(0) + \theta(0)^\top (S^*(0) + X^*(0))$$

$$+ \sum_{t=1}^{T} \theta(t)^\top (S^*(t) + D^*(t) - S^*(t-1) - D^*(t-1)). \tag{8.6.4}$$

Recall that $\theta_j(t)$ is predictable and its value is thus known at time $t-1$. It follows that

$$\begin{aligned} &E^*[\theta(t)^\top (S^*(t) + D^*(t) - S^*(t-1) - D^*(t-1))|\mathcal{F}_{t-1}] \\ =\, &\theta(t)^\top E^*[S^*(t) + D^*(t) - S^*(t-1) - D^*(t-1)|\mathcal{F}_{t-1}] \\ =\, &\theta(t)^\top (E^*[S^*(t) + D^*(t)|\mathcal{F}_{t-1}] - S^*(t-1) - D^*(t-1)) \\ =\, &0, \end{aligned} \tag{8.6.5}$$

where the third equality follows from the hypothesis that $S^* + D^*$ is a martingale under π^*.

Now we the take expectation of (8.6.4) under π^* and use the law of iterative expectations to obtain

$$E^* \left[\sum_{t=0}^{T} c^*(t) \right] = \alpha(0) + \theta(0)^\top (S^*(0) + X^*(0))$$

$$+ E^* \left[\sum_{t=1}^{T} \theta(t)^\top (S^*(t) + D^*(t) - S^*(t-1) - D^*(t-1)) \right]$$

$$= \alpha(0) + \theta(0)^\top (S^*(0) + X^*(0))$$

$$+ E^* \left[\sum_{t=1}^{T} E^*[\theta(t)^\top (S^*(t) + D^*(t) - S^*(t-1) - D^*(t-1))|\mathcal{F}_{t-1}] \right]$$

$$= \alpha(0) + \theta(0)^\top (S^*(0) + X^*(0)), \tag{8.6.6}$$

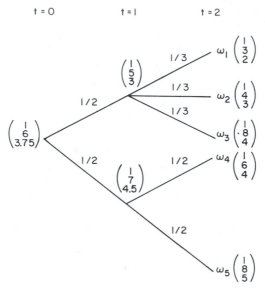

Figure 8.7.1: An Example of a Securities Market

where the third equality follows from (8.6.5).

Note the following. If c is an arbitrage opportunity, it must be nonnegative and be strictly positive in at least one event $a_t \in \mathcal{F}_t$. By the assumption that $B(t) > 0$, $c^*(a_t, t) > 0$. The probability π^* is an equivalent martingale measure and thus assigns a strictly positive probability to a_t. It follows that the left–hand side of (8.6.6) must be strictly positive. On the other hand, because c is financed by (α, θ) and is an arbitrage opportunity,

$$\alpha(0)B(0) + \theta(0)^\top (S(0) + X(0)) \le 0.$$

As $B(0) > 0$, this implies that

$$\alpha(0) + \theta(0)^\top (S^*(0) + X^*(0)) \le 0,$$

which is a contradiction to (8.6.6). Therefore, there are no arbitrage opportunities. We have thus shown that the existence of an equivalent martingale measure is a necessary and sufficient condition for (B, S) not to admit any arbitrage opportunities.

8.7. As a sufficient condition, the martingale property makes it convenient to make sure that a given price system admits no arbitrage opportunities. For example, the prices and dividends for the three long–lived securities considered in Section 7.12, shown here again in Figure 8.7.1, admit no arbitrage opportunities, because there exists an equivalent martingale measure. (Recall that these three securities do not pay dividends until time 3 and the numbers shown at that time are the dividends paid. Also, every branch in the event tree is of a strictly positive probability.) To see this, we will construct an equivalent martingale measure explicitly. We do this recursively by dynamic programming.

At time 1 at the upper node, let p_1, p_2 and p_3 be the conditional probabilities for ω_1, ω_2, and ω_3, respectively. As the price process plus accumulated dividends for the 0–th security is unity throughout, the *discounted price system* is equivalent to the original price system. If there exists a martingale measure, then p_1, p_2, and p_3 must satisfy the following linear equations:

$$p_1 + p_2 + p_3 = 1,$$
$$3p_1 + 4p_2 + 8p_3 = 5, \qquad (8.7.1)$$
$$2p_1 + 3p_2 + 4p_3 = 3.$$

The unique solution to (8.7.1) is

$$\begin{pmatrix} p_1 \\ p_2 \\ p_3 \end{pmatrix} = \begin{pmatrix} 1/3 \\ 1/3 \\ 1/3 \end{pmatrix}$$

and is written along the three top branches in Figure 8.7.1. Repeating the above procedure, we solve for all the conditional probabilities and write them along the branches. The reader can verify that those conditional probabilities are the *unique* set that makes prices plus accumulated dividends a vector of martingales. Note that the conditional probabilities are all strictly positive.

Given the conditional probabilities written along the branches, it is then straightforward to compute the martingale measure π^*, which is simply the unconditional probabilities implied by the conditional

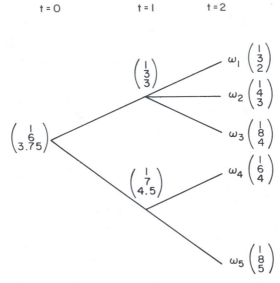

Figure 8.7.2: An Arbitrage Opportunity

probabilities:

$$
\begin{pmatrix} \pi^*(\omega_1) \\ \pi^*(\omega_2) \\ \pi^*(\omega_3) \\ \pi^*(\omega_4) \\ \pi^*(\omega_5) \end{pmatrix} = \begin{pmatrix} 1/6 \\ 1/6 \\ 1/6 \\ 1/4 \\ 1/4 \end{pmatrix}, \tag{8.7.2}
$$

which is equivalent to π. Thus there are no arbitrage opportunities.

Conversely, the failure of the martingale property at any node implies that an arbitrage opportunity can be constructed there. To see this, we change the prices at time 1 at the upper node to be those written on the event tree in Figure 8.7.2. The price at that node for security 2 is changed to 3. It is easily seen that there does not exist an equivalent martingale measure. The unique conditional probability that makes the prices plus accumulated dividends for security 2 a martingale assigns probability one to state ω_1 and probability zero to states ω_2 and ω_3. Any unconditional probability implied by this conditional probability cannot assign a strictly positive probability to every branch. Moreover, this conditional probability does not make the martingale property hold for security 3. A casual observation immediately reveals why an equivalent martingale measure does not exist and where the arbitrage opportunity is. The price for the second security at time $t = 1$ at the upper node is equal to 3, while its dividends in the three possible states at time 2 are all greater than 3. Indeed, the dividends in state ω_2 and ω_3 are strictly greater than 3. At this node, the second long–lived security dominates the riskless security and the third long–lived security in that its total returns in all states following the upper node are greater than those of the other two securities and are strictly greater in at least one state. An arbitrage opportunity is, for example, short selling security 1 and buying in security 2 . The reader will be asked in Exercise 8.2 to supply the details in constructing an arbitrage opportunity.

8.8. Besides pinpointing the existence of arbitrage opportunities, the martingale property, as a necessary condition, has important implications. It allows us to compute the prices of a complex long–lived security over time in a simple way, when the price of the complex security is well–defined over time. Recall that a long–lived security is characterized by its payoffs in each time–event. Thus, a long–lived security is equivalent to a consumption plan and we will use these two terms interchangeably. We will show in this section that when there are no arbitrage opportunities, it is precisely those marketed consumption plans/long–lived securities that have well–defined prices over time. A derivative security is just a consumption plan/long–lived security, so it has well–defined prices over time when it is marketed and when no arbitrage opportunities exist. In such an event, we say that a derivative security is *priced by arbitrage*.

We now show that a consumption plan has well defined prices over time when it is *marketed* and there are no arbitrage opportunities. First, we show that a marketed consumption plan has a unique *cum–dividend* price at time 0. Let c be marketed and financed by (α, θ). From (8.2.1), we see that an initial cost for c, by dynamic trading, is

$$\alpha(0)B(0) + \theta(0)^\top (S(0) + X(0)).$$

This is a cum–dividend price for c at time 0. We claim that when there are no arbitrage opportunities, this price is unique. Suppose this is not the case. Then there must exist another admissible trading strategy $(\hat{\alpha}, \hat{\theta})$ that finances c with a different initial cost. Without loss of generality, assume that

$$\alpha(0)B(0) + \theta(0)^\top(S(0) + X(0)) > \hat{\alpha}(0)B(0) + \hat{\theta}(0)^\top(S(0) + X(0)).$$

It can be verified that $(\hat{\alpha} - \alpha, \hat{\theta} - \theta)$ is an admissible trading strategy that finances a consumption plan which is zero throughout and has a strictly negative initial cost. It is then easy to turn this into an arbitrage opportunity and a contradiction. The reader will be asked to provide a construction of an arbitrage opportunity in Exercise 8.4. Therefore, the cum–dividend price at time 0 for any marketed consumption plan is unique. This conclusion also extends to the ex–dividend price at time 0 by subtraction of the time 0 dividend/consumption from the cum–dividend price.

Next, we want to show that any marketed consumption plan has a unique price at any time t. We will work with the ex–dividend prices. An ex–dividend price for a marketed consumption plan at any time t is the number of units of time-t consumption good needed to begin a dynamic strategy that replicates the consumption plan *after* time t. From (8.2.1), we know that if c is financed by (α, θ) then a price for $\{c(s); s = t+1, \ldots, T\}$ at time t is

$$\alpha(t+1)B(t) + \theta(t+1)^\top S(t).$$

The fact that this cost is unique when there are no arbitrage opportunities follows from the same arguments as above. We can thus define unambiguously *the* ex–dividend price of the consumption plan c at time t as

$$S_c(t) \equiv \alpha(t+1)B(t) + \theta(t+1)^\top S(t). \qquad (8.8.1)$$

Similarly, we define the *discounted* prices over time for c as follows

$$
\begin{aligned}
S_c^*(t) &\equiv \begin{cases} \frac{S_c(t)}{B(t)} & \text{if } t \le T-1 \\ 0 & \text{if } t = T \end{cases} \\
&= \alpha(t+1) + \theta(t+1)^\top S^*(t), \\
&= \alpha(t) + \theta(t)(S^*(t) + X^*(t)) - c^*(t),
\end{aligned}
\qquad (8.8.2)
$$

where the last equality follows from (8.2.1). Let π^* be an equivalent martingale measure, which we know exists because (B, S) does not admit arbitrage opportunities by assumption. We claim that $S_c^*(t) + \sum_{s=0}^{t} c^*(s)$ is a martingale under the equivalent martingale measure π^*. This claim follows from arguments similar to those used in deriving (8.6.6). To see this, we know from Exercise 7.1 and from (8.8.2) that

$$\alpha(t+1) + \theta(t+1)^\top S^*(t) = \alpha(0) + \theta(0)^\top (S^*(0) + X^*(0))$$

$$+ \sum_{s=1}^{t} \theta(s)^\top (S^*(s) - S^*(s-1) + X^*(s)) - \sum_{s=0}^{t} c^*(s).$$

$$(8.8.3)$$

Substituting (8.8.3) into (8.6.4) gives

$$\sum_{s=t+1}^{T} c^*(s) = \alpha(t+1) + \theta(t+1)^\top S^*(t)$$

$$(8.8.4)$$

$$+ \sum_{s=t+1}^{T} \theta(s)^\top (S^*(s) + D^*(s) - S^*(s-1) - D^*(s-1)).$$

Taking expectations of both sides of (8.8.4) with respect to π^* conditional on $\mathcal{F}_t$ and using the law of iterative expectations gives

$$E^*[\sum_{s=t+1}^{T} c^*(s)|\mathcal{F}_t] = \alpha(t+1) + \theta(t+1)^\top S^*(t)$$

$$+ E^* \left[\sum_{s=t+1}^{T} E^*[\theta(s)^\top (S^*(s) + D^*(s) - S^*(s-1) - D^*(s-1))|\mathcal{F}_{s-1}]|\mathcal{F}_t \right]$$

$$= \alpha(t+1) + \theta(t+1)^\top S^*(t) = S_c^*(t).$$

$$(8.8.5)$$

That is, the discounted ex–dividend price for the consumption plan c at time t is the conditional expectation under π^* of the sum of discounted future consumption.

Note that adding $\sum_{s=0}^{t} c^*(s)$ to both sides of (8.8.5) immediately yields

$$S_c^*(t) + \sum_{s=0}^{t} c^*(s) = E^* \left[\sum_{s=0}^{T} c^*(s)|\mathcal{F}_t \right] \quad \forall t, \qquad (8.8.6)$$

which is equivalent to saying that $S_c^*(t) + \sum_{s=0}^{t} c^*(s)$ is a martingale under π^*; because by the law of iterative expectations, $\forall s \geq t$,

$$E^*[S_c^*(s) + \sum_{v=0}^{s} c^*(v)|\mathcal{F}_t]$$

$$= E^* \left[E^* \left[\sum_{v=0}^{T} c^*(v)|\mathcal{F}_s \right] |\mathcal{F}_t \right]$$

$$= E^* \left[\sum_{v=0}^{T} c^*(v)|\mathcal{F}_t \right] \tag{8.8.7}$$

$$= S_c^*(t) + \sum_{s=0}^{t} c^*(s).$$

We have thus shown that if (B, S) admits no arbitrage opportunities, not only the prices of the long–lived securities but also the prices of marketed consumption plans have the martingale property. Given an equivalent martingale measure, the prices over time of any marketed consumption plan can be computed by evaluating a conditional expectation under this martingale measure. Although individuals' probability beliefs about the states of nature may differ, they nevertheless agree on the price processes of marketed consumption plans. This follows since the price processes of marketed consumption plans are determined by the no arbitrage condition and since the definition of an arbitrage opportunity does not involve any of the individuals' probabilities π^i's.

8.9. Consider the price system for the three long–lived securities represented in Figure 8.7.1. The unique equivalent martingale measure is defined in (8.7.2), and the implied conditional probabilities are recorded along the branches in Figure 8.7.1. The three trading/consumption dates are $t = 0, 1, 2$. The first security is a discount bond. As its price is unity at time 0 and time 1, the interest rate is zero throughout. Recall from Sections 7.12 and 7.13 that the securities market with the three long–lived securities is dynamically complete. Therefore, any consumption plan can be manufactured dynamically, or is marketed, and has well–defined prices over time.

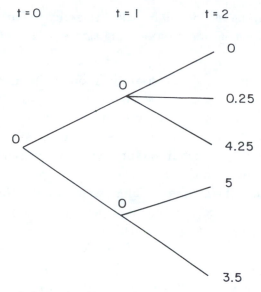

Figure 8.9.1: An Example of a Consumption Plan

Now consider the consumption plan c depicted in Figure 8.9.1. In this consumption plan, individuals consume only at time 2. The prices for this consumption plan before time 2 can be determined by finding a trading strategy that replicates it through dynamic trading as we did in Section 7.12. Alternatively, because an equivalent martingale measure has been computed, we can use (8.8.6) to compute the prices in a straightforward fashion. Note first that because $B(t) = 1$, $\forall t \leq T - 1$, the *discounted* price system is equivalent to the undiscounted one. Thus

$$S_c(0) = \left(\frac{1}{6}\right) 0 + \left(\frac{1}{6}\right) 0.25 + \left(\frac{1}{6}\right) 4.25 + \left(\frac{1}{4}\right) 1.5 + \left(\frac{1}{4}\right) 3.5$$
$$= 2,$$

$$S_c(\omega_n, 1) = \begin{cases} \left(\frac{1}{3}\right) 0 + \left(\frac{1}{3}\right) 0.25 + \left(\frac{1}{3}\right) 4.25 = 1.5 & \text{if } n = 1, 2, 3, \\ \frac{1}{2} 1.5 + \frac{1}{2} 3.5 = 2.5 & \text{if } n = 4, 5. \end{cases}$$
$$(8.9.1)$$

In Exercise 8.5, the reader will be asked to verify the prices computed in (8.9.1) by constructing a replicating strategy.

8.10. Before we discuss an application of the martingale property in pricing stock options, we digress slightly on some aspects of the theory developed here as they relate to Chapter 7.

In Chapter 7, we discussed dynamically complete markets. A necessary and sufficient condition for markets to be dynamically complete is that at every node on the event tree representing the information structure, the number of long–lived securities having linearly independent random returns the next period is equal to the number of branches leaving the node. We will show in this section that, given a price system that admits no arbitrage opportunities, markets are dynamically complete if and only if there exists a unique equivalent martingale measure. We will see that this conclusion follows easily from elementary algebra.

We fix price system (B, S) that admits no arbitrage opportunities, so that there exists an equivalent martingale measure π^*. Let $a_{t-1} \in \mathcal{F}_{t-1}$ for some $t \leq T$ and let $\{a_{s_1}, \ldots, a_{s_m}\}$ be such that $a_{s_k} \in \mathcal{F}_t$, $a_{s_k} \subseteq a_{t-1}$ for $k = 1, 2, \ldots, m$, and $\bigcup_{k=1}^{m} a_{s_k} = a_{t-1}$. Note that m is the number of branches leaving the node a_{t-1}. Consider the following system of linear equations:

$$
\begin{pmatrix}
1 & \cdots & 1 \\
S_1^*(a_{s_1},t)+D_1^*(a_{s_1},t) & \cdots & S_1^*(a_{s_m},t)+D_1^*(a_{s_m},t) \\
S_2^*(a_{s_1},t)+D_2^*(a_{s_1},t) & \cdots & S_2^*(a_{s_m},t)+D_2^*(a_{s_m},t) \\
\vdots & \ddots & \vdots \\
S_N^*(a_{s_1},t)+D_N^*(a_{s_1},t) & \cdots & S_N^*(a_{s_m},t)+D_N^*(a_{s_m},t)
\end{pmatrix}
\begin{pmatrix}
p_{a_{s_1}} \\
p_{a_{s_2}} \\
\vdots \\
p_{a_{s_m}}
\end{pmatrix}
$$

$$
=
\begin{pmatrix}
1 \\
S_1^*(a_{t-1},t-1)+D_1^*(a_{t-1},t-1) \\
S_2^*(a_{t-1},t-1)+D_2^*(a_{t-1},t-1) \\
\vdots \\
S_N^*(a_{t-1},t-1)+D_N^*(a_{t-1},t-1).
\end{pmatrix}
$$

$$(8.10.1)$$

The unknowns in this system are $p \equiv \{p_{a_{s_k}}, k = 1, 2, \ldots, m\}$. A strictly positive solution to the system is a conditional probability for $\{a_{s_k}; k = 1, \ldots, m\}$ given the event a_{t-1}, because the first linear equation in the system requires that the solutions, $p'_{a_{s_k}}s$, sum to one. The other linear equations will simply turn $S^* + D^*$ into a martingale from the node a_{t-1} to its subsequent nodes under the conditional probability $\{p_{a_{s_k}}; k = 1, \ldots, m\}$.

Note that we have m unknowns and $N + 1$ linear equations in the system, where m is the number of branches leaving node a_{t-1}. By the hypothesis that there exists an equivalent martingale measure π^*, there exists a strictly positive solution to (8.10.1). This strictly positive solution is the conditional probability induced by π^* conditional on a_{t-1}. If the matrix on the left–hand side of (8.10.1) has m linearly independent rows, the solution induced by π^* is unique.

We can carry out the above analysis for each node in the event tree representing the information structure **F** and conclude that if there are as many linearly independent long–lived securities at each node as the number of branches leaving the node, that is, if markets are dynamically complete, there exists a unique equivalent martingale measure.

Conversely, suppose that the conditional probability induced by π^* on a_{t-1} is the unique strictly positive solution to (8.10.1). We claim that the matrix on the left–hand side of (8.10.1) must have m linearly independent rows. Here we note that m is the maximum number of linearly independent rows the matrix can have, because it has m columns. Suppose this is not the case, that is, the number of linearly independent rows is strictly less than m. By the hypothesis that (B, S) admits no arbitrage opportunities, we know that there exists a strictly positive solution, p, to (8.10.1). From linear algebra, we then know that there exists a continuum of solutions to (8.10.1) but not all solutions to (8.10.1) will be strictly positive. Now take any solution $p' = \{p'_{a_{s_1}}, \ldots, p'_{a_{s_m}}\}$. As p is strictly positive, there exists $\lambda \in [0, 1]$ such that $\hat{p} \equiv \lambda p + (1 - \lambda)p'$ is strictly positive. It is easily checked that $\hat{p}$ is also a solution to (8.10.1). Thus π^* is not the unique equivalent martingale measure, a contradiction. It then follows that at every node, the number of long–lived securities that have linearly independent returns in the subsequent nodes must be equal to the number of branches leaving that node. This implies that the markets are dynamically complete. We have thus shown that the uniqueness of an equivalent martingale measure is equivalent to dynamic market completeness.

Before we end this section, we make one final remark. The equivalent martingale measure of (8.5.1) is constructed by using an individual's ratios of marginal utilities weighted by his probability belief π^i. When markets are dynamically complete, those ratios weighted by π^i's are equal across individuals, and thus the equivalent martingale measure is unique.

8.11. Recall from Chapter 7 that for every equilibrium in a competitive economy with a complete set of time–event contingent claims where markets open only at time 0, there exists a rational expectations equilibrium with reconvening securities markets that has the same allocation, when a set of long–lived securities is appropriately chosen. With the aid of the discussion in Section 8.9, we can prove a very general converse of the above statement. We will show that for every price system (B, S) admitting no arbitrage opportunities, there exists a competitive economy where markets open only at time 0 such that every individual optimally trades, in this static setting, to his allocation in the rational expectations long–lived securities markets economy. The price system (B, S) does not have to be an equilibrium price system, and the markets are not necessarily complete. Moreover, any solution to an individual's maximization problem in the static economy is also a solution in the dynamic economy.

Formally, let (B, S) be a price system that does not admit arbitrage opportunities, and let $\mathcal{M}$ be the space of marketed consumption plans. From (8.8.6) we know that

$$S_c^*(0) + c^*(0) = E^* \left[\sum_{s=0}^{T} c^*(s) \right] \quad \forall c \in \mathcal{M}, \tag{8.11.1}$$

where the expectation is taken under an equivalent martingale measure. Take any individual in the economy, say individual i. Let c^i be his optimal consumption plan in the dynamic economy. Consider the following static problem:

$$\max_{c \in M} E_i \left[\sum_{t=0}^{T} u_{it}(c(t)) \right]$$

$$\text{s.t. } E^* \left[\sum_{t=0}^{T} c^*(t) \right] = \bar{\alpha}^i(0) + \bar{\theta}^i(0)^\top (S^*(0) + X^*(0)).$$

(8.11.2)

This static problem can be understood as follows. At time 0, individual i can choose a consumption plan from those that are marketed. The price of a marketed consumption plan is exactly equal to its initial cost in a dynamic long–lived securities markets economy.

We claim that c^i is also a solution to (8.11.2). To see this, we note that because c^i is a solution in the dynamic economy, it must be marketed. Relation (8.8.6) implies that

$$E^* \left[\sum_{t=0}^{T} c_i^*(t) \right] = \bar{\alpha}^i(0) + \bar{\theta}^i(0)^\top (S^*(0) + X^*(0)).$$

(8.11.3)

Thus, c^i is budget feasible for (8.11.2). Suppose that c^i is not a solution to (8.11.2). Then, there must exist a $\hat{c} \in M$ satisfying the budget constraint of (8.11.2) such that

$$E_i \left[\sum_{t=0}^{T} u_{it}(\hat{c}(t)) \right] > E_i \left[\sum_{t=0}^{T} u_{it}(c^i(t)) \right].$$

(8.11.4)

As $\hat{c} \in M$ and has an initial cost equal to $\alpha^i(0)B(0) + \theta^i(0)^\top (S(0) + X(0))$, it must also be feasible for individual i in the dynamic economy. This contradicts the fact that c^i is a solution in the dynamic economy.

Conversely, let c^i be a solution to (8.11.2). We want to show that it is also a solution in the dynamic economy. First, c^i is feasible in the dynamic economy because it is marketed and has an initial cost equal to $\bar{\alpha}^i(0)B(0) + \bar{\theta}^i(0)^\top (S(0) + X(0))$. Suppose that c^i is not a solution in the dynamic economy. Then there must exist a consumption plan $\hat{c} \in M$ financed by (α, θ) with $(\alpha(0), \theta(0)) = (\bar{\alpha}^i(0), \bar{\theta}^i(0))$ such that (8.11.4) is true. Relation (8.8.6) implies that $\hat{c}$ satisfies (8.11.3) and is thus feasible for (8.11.2). This contradicts the hypothesis that c^i is a solution to (8.11.2).

Finally we note that, using the same arguments as in Section 7.8, we can show that in the dynamic economy, an individual has no incentive to deviate from the consumption plan that is optimal in the static economy.

8.12. The correspondence between a dynamic economy and a static economy makes some analyses in a dynamic economy easier. We will give an example here. In the remarks at the end of this chapter, the reader can find references for other applications. The power of this correspondence is most pronounced in a continuous time continuous state model.

We consider the consumption–portfolio problem for an individual i posed in (8.4.1). Suppose that (B, S) admits a *unique* equivalent martingale measure π^*. From Section 8.10, we know that markets are dynamically complete. Thus the space of marketed consumption plans $\mathcal{M}$ is composed of *all* the possible consumption plans. Then (8.11.2) becomes

$$\max_c E_i \left[\sum_{t=0}^{T} u_{it}(c(t)) \right]$$

$$\text{s.t. } E^* \left[\sum_{t=0}^{T} c^*(t) \right] = \bar{\alpha}^i(0) + \bar{\theta}^i(0)^\top (S^*(0) + X^*(0)), \tag{8.12.1}$$

where $E^*[\cdot]$ is the expectation under π^*. Standard mathematical arguments show that there always exists a solution to (8.12.1), because there is a finite number of states of nature and $u'_{it}(0) = \infty$. Denote this solution by c^i. It then follows from Section 8.11 that there exists a solution to the dynamic problem.

Next we want to characterize the optimal consumption and portfolio policies. We can rewrite the budget constraint in (8.12.1) as follows:

$$E^* \left[\sum_{t=0}^{T} \frac{c(t)}{B(t) + D_0(t)} \right]$$

$$= \sum_{\omega \in \Omega} \pi_\omega^i \frac{\pi_\omega^*}{\pi_\omega^i} \sum_{t=0}^{T} \frac{c(\omega, t)}{B(\omega, t) + D_0(\omega, t)}$$

$$= E_i \left[\frac{\tilde{\pi}^*}{\tilde{\pi}^i} \sum_{t=0}^{T} \frac{c(t)}{B(t) + D_0(t)} \right] \qquad (8.12.2)$$

$$= E_i \left[\sum_{t=0}^{T} E_i \left[\frac{\tilde{\pi}^*}{\tilde{\pi}^i} \frac{c(t)}{B(t) + D_0(t)} | \mathcal{F}_t \right] \right]$$

$$= E_i \left[\sum_{t=0}^{T} \eta(t) \frac{c(t)}{B(t) + D_0(t)} \right],$$

where $\tilde{\pi}^*/\tilde{\pi}^i$ denotes the random ratio of $\pi_\omega^*/\pi_\omega^i$, and

$$\eta(t) \equiv E_i \left[\frac{\pi^*}{\pi} | \mathcal{F}_t \right].$$

Forming the Lagrangian yields

$$\max_{c, \gamma_i} L = E_i \left[\sum_{t=0}^{T} u_{it}(c(t)) \right]$$

$$+ \gamma_i \left(\bar{\alpha}^i(0) + \bar{\theta}^i(0)^\top (S^*(0) + X^*(0)) - E_i \left[\sum_{t=0}^{T} \eta(t) \frac{c(t)}{B(t) + D_0(t)} \right] \right),$$

where γ_i is a strictly positive Lagrangian multiplier. The first order conditions, which are necessary and sufficient for c^i to be an optimum, are

$$u'_{it}(c^i(t)) = \gamma_i \frac{\eta(t)}{B(t) + D_0(t)} \qquad \forall t, \qquad (8.12.3)$$

and the budget constraint. Relation (8.12.3) can be written more explicitly as

$$u'_{it}(c^i(a_t, t)) = \gamma_i \frac{\eta(a_t, t)}{B(a_t, t) + D_0(a_t, t)} \qquad \forall a_t \in \mathcal{F}_t, \forall t. \qquad (8.12.4)$$

The reader is asked in Exercise 8.6 to verify that

$$\frac{\pi^i_{a_t}\eta(a_t,t)}{B(a_t,t)+D_0(a_t,t)}$$

is the time–0 price of a time–event contingent claim for the time–event (t,a_t). Then (8.12.3) corresponds to (7.3.7).

Relation (8.12.3) completely characterizes the optimal consumption policy. The one remaining task is to compute the optimal portfolio strategy. As we know the optimal consumption plan already, this is then a standard practice of finding a replicating strategy as demonstrated in Section 7.12.

Utilizing the correspondence between a static economy and a dynamic economy allows us to decompose an individual's optimal consumption and portfolio problem into two parts. First, find an optimal consumption plan in a static economy through the standard Lagrangian method. Second, implement this optimal consumption plan in the dynamic economy through a replicating strategy.

8.13. In the rest of this chapter, we will use the martingale property developed in the earlier parts to discuss a discrete time option pricing theory due to Cox, Ross, and Rubinstein (1979).

Consider a multiperiod securities market with two long–lived securities, a risky common stock and a riskless bond. The economy has a long time horizon. However, we only look at a piece of it, say the trading dates $t = 0,1,\ldots,T$. The risky asset does not pay dividends from time 0 to time T and has prices over time following the binomial random walk depicted in Figure 8.13.1. At time 0, the stock price is $S(0) > 0$. At time 1, the stock price will be either $uS(0)$ or $dS(0)$, with $u > d$, and so on and so forth. That is, at every trading date, the return on the common stock next period will either be u or d. We will assume that $u > 1$ and $d < 1$ and interpret the stock price movement from $S(t)$ to $uS(t)$ to be moving up and that to $dS(t)$ to be moving down. Note that if $S(0) > 0$, the stock price will never reach zero. The riskless asset, the bond, does not pay dividends and earns a constant return R. Equivalently, let the bond price at time t be R^t.

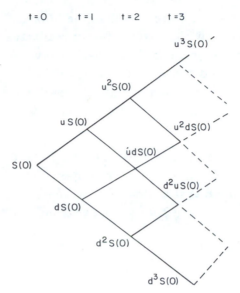

Figure 8.13.1: A Binomial Random Walk

We assume that the information structure an individual has is the information *generated* by the stock price. By this we mean that a state of nature is a complete realization of the risky stock price from time 0 to time T. For example, when $T = 3$, a possible complete realization of the stock price is

$$S(0), \ S(1) = uS(0), \ S(2) = udS(0), \ S(3) = u^2 dS(0).$$

In this realization, the stock price moves up at time 1, moves down at time 2, and moves up again at time 3. Thus the state space Ω is composed of all the possible complete realizations of the stock price from time 0 to time T. The event tree representing the information structure is just that depicted in Figure 8.13.1. At time 0, an individual knows that the state of nature is one complete realization of the stock price from time 0 to time T. Thus $\mathcal{F}_0 = \{\Omega\}$. At time 1, the partition $\mathcal{F}_1$ has two events. The first (second) event is composed of all the realizations of stock prices from 0 to T such that the stock moves up (down) at time 1. The other $\mathcal{F}_t$'s can be understood similarly. Note that, for every node on the event tree of Figure 8.13.1 before time T, there are only two branches leaving the node. More formally, for every $a_t \in \mathcal{F}_t$ with $t < T$, there are two elements of $\mathcal{F}_{t+1}$

that are subsets of a_t. Note also that the information an individual has at time t is simply the historical price realizations of the common stock. The riskless asset does not generate any information, because its return is purely deterministic over time.

Finally, we assume that individuals' possibly heterogeneous probability beliefs assign strictly positive probabilities to all states.

8.14. Now we want to make sure that the prices presented in Section 8.13 do not admit arbitrage opportunities. We recall from Sections 8.5 and 8.6 that a necessary and sufficient condition for no arbitrage opportunities is that there exists an equivalent martingale measure.

As usual, we define

$$S^*(t) \equiv S(t)R^{-t}$$
$$B^*(t) \equiv R^t R^{-t} = 1.$$

We want to find a probability that assigns to every state of nature a strictly positive probability such that

$$E^*[S^*(t+1)|\mathcal{F}_t] = S^*(t) \quad \forall t < T. \tag{8.14.1}$$

As $S^*(t)$ is strictly positive, (8.14.1) is equivalent to

$$E^*\left[\frac{S^*(t+1)}{S^*(t)}|\mathcal{F}_t\right] = 1 \quad \forall t < T. \tag{8.14.2}$$

That is, under the martingale measure, the risky stock is expected to earn a rate of return, in number of the bond, equal to zero. Given the price dynamics, there are two branches leaving each node before time T; and, on the two subsequent nodes, $S^*(t+1)/S^*(t)$ has values uR^{-1} and dR^{-1}, which we note are two constants independent of time t and of the node at time t. For (8.14.2) to hold, the conditional probabilities at any node on the event tree at time $t < T$ for the subsequent two nodes, induced by the equivalent martingale measure, denoted by π and $1 - \pi$ must solve the following linear equation:

$$\pi uR^{-1} + (1 - \pi)dR^{-1} = 1. \tag{8.14.3}$$

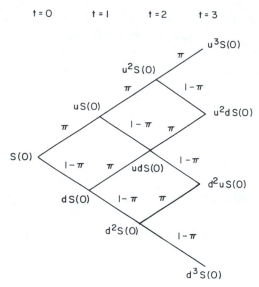

Figure 8.14.1: The Equivalent Martingale Measure

The unique solution to (8.14.3) is

$$\pi = \frac{R - d}{u - d}. \tag{8.14.4}$$

As π and $1 - \pi$ are conditional probabilities induced by an equivalent martingale measure, π must lie in $(0, 1)$. The necessary and sufficient condition for π to be in $(0, 1)$ is

$$d < R < u. \tag{8.14.5}$$

Let us assume henceforth that (8.14.5) is true. Then there exists an equivalent martingale measure. Moreover, since π is the unique solution to (8.14.3), the equivalent martingale measure is unique. The conditional probability induced by the equivalent martingale measure at each node for time $t < T$ assigns probability π to the stock's subsequent upward move and probability $1 - \pi$ to the stock's subsequent downward move; see Figure 8.14.1. It is easily seen that the probability, under the martingale measure, for a state of nature is completely determined by the number of upward moves of the stock price. For example, the probability, under the martingale measure, for a complete realization of the stock prices that has n upward moves is $\pi^n(1-\pi)^{T-n}$. Two complete realizations that have the same number of upward moves but differ in the timing of those upward moves are of the same probability under the martingale measure.

By simple combinatorial mathematics, there are

$$\binom{T}{n} \equiv \frac{T!}{n!(T-n)!}$$

number of complete realizations that have exactly n upward moves. In addition, the final stock price for each of these complete realizations is equal to $S(0)u^n d^{T-n}$. Similarly, given $S(t)$ at time t, the conditional probability, under the equivalent martingale measure, that there will be $n \leq T - t$ upward moves in the future and, therefore, the stock price at time T is $S(t)u^n d^{T-t-n}$ is

$$\binom{T-t}{n} \pi^n(1-\pi)^{T-t-n}. \tag{8.14.6}$$

8.15. Now we are ready to price an European call option written on the common stock. First, we note that because there exists a unique equivalent martingale measure, the markets are dynamically complete. Thus *any* consumption plan is marketed and has well–defined prices over time or is *priced by arbitrage*.

Consider a European call option written on the common stock with exercise price k and expiration date T. The payoff at time T of this call option is

$$\max[S(T) - k, 0].$$

From (8.8.6) and (8.14.6), we know that the price of this call option at time t is

$$E^* \left[\max[S(T) - k, 0] R^{-(T-t)} | \mathcal{F}_t \right]$$

$$= R^{-(T-t)} \sum_{n=0}^{T-t} \binom{T-t}{n} \pi^n(1-\pi)^{T-t-n} \max[S(t)u^n d^{T-t-n} - k, 0].$$

$$\tag{8.15.1}$$

This clearly depends only on $S(t)$, the exercise price k, and the time t. Thus we can write the option price at time t as $p(S(t), t; k)$.

Let j be the minimum number of upward moves such that

$$S(t)u^j d^{T-t-j} \geq k.$$

That is, j is the minimum positive integer such that

$$j \geq \frac{\ln \frac{k}{S(t)d^{T-t}}}{\ln \frac{u}{d}}. \tag{8.15.2}$$

Then (8.15.1) becomes

$$
\begin{aligned}
&p(S(t), t; k) \\
&= R^{-(T-t)} \sum_{n=j}^{T-t} \binom{T-t}{n} \pi^n (1-\pi)^{T-t-n} (S(t)u^n d^{T-t-n} - k) \\
&= S(t) \sum_{n=j}^{T-t} \binom{T-t}{n} \left(\frac{\pi u}{R}\right)^n \left(\frac{(1-\pi)d}{R}\right)^{T-t-n} \\
&\quad - kR^{-(T-t)} \sum_{n=j}^{T-t} \binom{T-t}{n} \pi^n (1-\pi)^{T-t-n},
\end{aligned}
$$

$$\tag{8.15.3}$$

where we have used the convention that if $j > T - t$, the summation is equal to zero.

Now note the following: In a series of $T - t$ independent trials of an experiment whose success rate is π and whose failure rate is $1 - \pi$, the probability that there will be at least $j \geq 0$ successes is

$$\Phi(j; T - t, \pi) \equiv \sum_{n=j}^{T-t} \binom{T-t}{n} \pi^n (1-\pi)^{T-t-n}. \tag{8.15.4}$$

This is termed the *complementary binomial distribution function* with parameters j, $T - t$, and π. The *binomial distribution function* is equal to 1 minus the complementary binomial distribution function, and gives the probability that the number of successes is strictly less than j. The trials are termed *Bernoulli* trials. Substituting (8.15.4) into (8.15.3) gives

$$p(S(t), t; k) = S(t)\Phi(j; T - t, \pi') - kR^{-(T-t)}\Phi(j; T - t, \pi), \quad (8.15.5)$$

where j is defined in (8.15.2) and where

$$\pi' \equiv \frac{u}{R}\pi \quad \text{and} \quad 1 - \pi' = \frac{d}{R}(1 - \pi).$$

This is the *binomial option pricing formula* due to Cox, Ross, and Rubinstein (1979).

Finally, we note that as the number of independent trials increases to infinity, the *central limit theorem* from probability theory shows that the binomial distribution function converges to the standard normal distribution function after a suitable normalization. Cox, Ross, and Rubinstein make use of this observation and show that if we allow trading to occur more and more frequently while keeping the time interval $[0, T]$ fixed, then the binomial option pricing formula converges to the Black–Scholes formula if we choose appropriate parameters of the price processes in the process of taking limits. The limiting formula is

$$p(S, t; k) = SN(x_t) - ke^{-r(T-t)}N(x_t - \sigma\sqrt{T - t}),$$

where

$$x_t \equiv \frac{\ln(S/ke^{-r(T-t)})}{\sigma\sqrt{T - t}} + \frac{1}{2}\sigma\sqrt{T - t},$$

and the two constants r and σ are the continuously compounded riskless interest rate per unit time and the standard deviation of the rate of return on the common stock per unit time, respectively. To use this formula, we first fix the unit of measure of time. Suppose that t is in units of a month, for example. R is one plus the monthly riskless interest rate, define $r \equiv \ln R$, and take σ to be the standard deviation of the monthly return on the stock.

We will not present here the limiting procedure mentioned above. Cox and Rubinstein (1985, pp.196–208) is an excellent source for this procedure, which we encourage the reader to consult.

Exercises

8.1. Prove relation (8.4.2).

8.2. Given the prices depicted in Figure 8.7.2, demonstrate an arbitrage opportunity.

8.3. Suppose that the 0–th long–lived security also pays dividends $x_0(t) > 0$, $\forall t$. Prove that the martingale property is still true with a suitable normalization.

8.4. Show that if a consumption plan is financed by two admissible trading strategies with different initial costs, there exists an arbitrage opportunity.

8.5. Verify the prices computed in (8.9.1) by constructing a dynamic replicating strategy.

8.6. Verify that, in the context of Section 8.12,

$$\frac{\pi^i_{a_t}\,\eta(a_t,t)}{B(a_t,t) + D_0(a_t,t)}$$

is the time–0 price of a time–event contingent claim for the time–event (t, a_t).

8.7. In the context of the binomial model, price a security that gives the right to its holder to purchase at time T a share of the common stock at the minimum price that the stock has reached from time 0 to time T.

Remarks. The martingale characterization of a price system that admits no arbitrage opportunities was pioneered by Harrison and Kreps (1979). Their paper, in turn, was motivated by an observation made by Cox and Ross (1976) in an option pricing context. In deriving the martingale property, we assume that individuals' preferences have expected utility representations. This is far more restrictive than necessary. In a finite state model, the only condition needed is that individuals' preferences are strictly increasing. In an infinite states model, some other technical conditions are needed; see Kreps (1981). The martingale property assumes its full power in a continuous time continuous–states model. Interested readers should consult Duffie and Huang (1985), Duffie (1985), Harrison and Pliska (1981), and Huang (1985a, 1985b).

A good reference for the correspondence between a dynamic and a static economy is Kreps (1979). Cox and Huang (1986, 1987), Pagès (1987), and Pliska (1986) apply this idea to solve an optimal consumption and portfolio problem in a continuous time model. Our brief discussion on the convergence of the binomial option pricing formula to the Black–Scholes formula is taken directly from Cox and Rubinstein (1985).

References

Black, F., and M. Scholes. 1973. The pricing of options and corporate liabilities. *Journal of Political Economy* **81**:637–654.

Cox, J., and C. Huang. 1986. A variational problem arising in financial economics with an application to a portfolio turnpike theorem. Working Paper #1751–86. Sloan School of Management, Massachusetts Institute of Technology.

Cox, J., and C. Huang. 1987. Optimal consumption and portfolio policies when asset prices follow a diffusion process. Working Paper #1926–87. Sloan School of management, Massachusetts Institute of Technology.

Cox, J., and S. Ross. 1976. The valuation of options for alternative stochastic processes. *Journal of Financial Economics* **3**, 145–166.

Cox, J., S. Ross, and M. Rubinstein. 1979. Option pricing: A simplified approach. *Journal of Financial Economics* **7**:229–263.

Cox, J., and M. Rubinstein. 1985. *Options Markets*. Prentice–Hall, Inc., New Jersey.

Duffie, D., and C. Huang. 1985. Implementing Arrow–Debreu equilibria by continuous trading of few long–lived securities. *Econometrica* **53**, 1337–1356.

Duffie, D. 1985. Stochastic equilibria: Existence, spanning number, and the "no expected gain from trade" hypothesis. *Econometrica* **54**:1161–1184.

Harrison, M., and D. Kreps. 1979. Martingales and arbitrage in multiperiod securities markets. *Journal of Economic Theory* **20**,

381–408.

Harrison, M., and S. Pliska. 1981. Martingales and stochastic integrals in the theory of continuous trading. *Stochastic Processes and Their Applications* **11**, 261–271.

Huang, C. 1985a. Information structure and equilibrium asset prices. *Journal of Economic Theory* **35**, 33–71.

Huang, C. 1985b. Information structure and viable price systems. *Journal of Mathematical Economics* **13**, 215–240.

Kreps, D. 1979. Three essays on capital markets. Mimeo. Graduate School of Business, Stanford University.

Kreps, D. 1981. Arbitrage and equilibrium in economies with infinitely many commodities. *Journal of Mathematical Economics* **8**, 15–35.

Pagès, H. 1987. Optimal consumption and portfolio policies when markets are incomplete. Working Paper #1883–86. Sloan School of Management, Massachusetts Institute of Technology.

Pliska, S. 1986. A stochastic calculus model of continuous trading: Optimal portfolios. *Mathematics of Operations Research* **11**, 371–382.

CHAPTER 9
FINANCIAL MARKETS WITH DIFFERENTIAL INFORMATION

9.1.   In our previous discussions, it was assumed either implicitly or explicitly that individuals had homogeneous information. Differential information among individuals is, however, an important aspect of financial markets. Regulations on insider trading provide evidence for this claim. Many mutual fund managers claim to trade on the basis of superior information. In addition, the existence of active markets for information, such as advisory services and newsletters, signifies the possibility that individuals are differentially informed *a priori*. The first part of this chapter will develop a model of financial markets that incorporates the heterogeneity of information among individuals. The focus of this discussion will be on how private information of individuals gets transmitted to the public through prices and on the appropriate equilibrium concepts.

The idea that individuals may be differentially informed is plausible, and it is even more plausible that the managers of a firm have private information about the firm that is not shared with outside investors. In the the second part of this chapter, we consider an entrepreneur seeking outside investors to finance his project. The entrepreneur is privately informed about the quality of the project, which he can only credibly reveal by taking some observable action. This action is termed a *signal*. We will introduce the notion of a *signalling equilibrium*, in which an entrepreneur takes certain actions that would not have been taken were there not information asymmetry.

9.2. We will first discuss in general how differential information among individuals can be modeled. In the course of this discussion, we will make extensive use of certain set theoretic notions developed in Section 7.2.

Our attention will be limited to two–period economies where trades occur at time 0 and consumption of a single good occurs at time 1. We assume that before trading occurs at time 0, each individual receives a piece of *private signal* conveying to him some information about the state of nature that will be realized at time 1. Recall from Chapters 7 and 8 that information revelation over time can be modeled by finer and finer partitions of the possible states of nature. In this context, it is natural to say that two individuals are differentially informed if their information structures are not identical. In a two period economy, we can therefore model a signal that an individual receives before trading to be a partition of the state space.

Formally, we fix a state space Ω, each element, ω, of which is a possible state of nature. Assume for now that Ω has a finite number of elements. Individuals are endowed with a common information structure at time 0, denoted by $\mathbf{F} = \{\mathcal{F}_0, \mathcal{F}_1\}$, where $\mathcal{F}_0$ and $\mathcal{F}_1$ are partitions of Ω. Assume that $\mathcal{F}_0 = \{\Omega\}$ and that $\mathcal{F}_1$ is the partition in which each state is an event. Recall that the latter condition simply says that the true state of nature will be revealed at time 1 to all individuals. Individuals' prior beliefs are such that every state of nature is of strictly positive probability. Before trading at time 0, however, individual i receives a private signal represented by a partition $\mathcal{F}_0^i$. For example, suppose that $\Omega = \{\omega_1, \ldots, \omega_5\}$ and that $\mathcal{F}_0^i = \{\{\omega_1, \omega_2, \omega_3\}, \{\omega_4, \omega_5\}\}$. If, for example, ω_3 is the state of nature that will be realized at time 1, then individual i learns from his signal that the state to be realized at time 1 is one of $\{\omega_1, \omega_2, \omega_3\}$. Equivalently, a private signal for individual i can also be represented by a random variable $\tilde{Y}_i$ defined on Ω. For instance, the random variable

$$Y_i(\omega) = \begin{cases} 1 & \text{if } \omega \in \{\omega_1, \omega_2, \omega_3\}, \\ 2 & \text{if } \omega \in \{\omega_4, \omega_5\}, \end{cases}$$

conveys the same information as the partition $\mathcal{F}_0^i$ of the example above, where we note that $Y_i(\omega)$ is the realization of $\tilde{Y}_i$ when the state of nature is ω. If $\tilde{Y}_i = 1$, individual i learns that the true state of nature is one of $\{\omega_1, \omega_2, \omega_3\}$, and if $\tilde{Y} = 2$, individual i learns that the true state of nature is one of $\{\omega_4, \omega_5\}$. That is, a realization of $\tilde{Y}_i$ tells individual i whether the true state is one of $\{\omega_1, \omega_2, \omega_3\}$ or one of $\{\omega_4, \omega_5\}$. In this sense, we can say that $\tilde{Y}_i$ *generates* the partition $\mathcal{F}_0^i$.

As usual, we assume throughout that individuals strictly prefer more to less. Now we claim that in the current context, there does *not* exist a competitive equilibrium with complete markets when there exist some nonsatiated individuals i and k such that $\mathcal{F}_0^i \neq \mathcal{F}_0^k$. (Here we remark that prices in a competitive equilibrium have only one function, namely to determine an individual's budget constraint.) To see this, it suffices to consider an example. We take the state space and individual i's signal to be the same as those considered in the last paragraph. Let there be another individual k with signal represented as $\mathcal{F}_0^k = \{\{\omega_1, \omega_2\}, \{\omega_3, \omega_4, \omega_5\}\}$. Suppose to begin with that either ω_1 or ω_2 is the state that will be realized at time 1. Then, after receiving his signal, individual i learns that the true state is one of $\{\omega_1, \omega_2, \omega_3\}$. On the other hand, individual k learns that the true state of nature is one of $\{\omega_1, \omega_2\}$.

Since markets are complete, a competitive equilibrium must assign a price to each state contingent claim. Consider the state contingent claim that pays off in state ω_3. After receiving his signal, individual k learns that ω_3 is not the true state. However, even after receiving his signal, individual i still believes that ω_3 may be the true state. If the state contingent price for state ω_3 is strictly positive, by the hypothesis that utility functions are strictly increasing, individual k will short sell an infinite amount of the state–ω_3 contingent claim and use the proceeds to buy state contingent claims paying off in states ω_1 and ω_2. As a consequence, the market for the state–ω_3 contingent claim cannot clear. On the other hand, if the state contingent price for state ω_3 is nonpositive, individual i will purchase an infinite amount and the market for it cannot clear. Thus, there does not exist a competitive equilibrium when the true state is either ω_1 or ω_2.

Arguments similar to those in the last paragraph show that there cannot exist a competitive equilibrium with complete markets if the true state is any of $\{\omega_1, \ldots, \omega_5\}$. Thus, there does not exist a competitive equilibrium with complete markets.

9.3. A casual examination of the nonexistence result of the last section reveals the reason why an equilibrium does not exist: the individuals do not learn from observing prices. For example, when ω_1 is the true state, a zero price for the state contingent claim paying off in state ω_3 would be the *equilibrium price* if individual i concluded that the true state must not be state ω_3 when he observed that the price for state ω_3 was 0. In this case, an equilibrium can be constructed as follows when individuals i and k are the only two individuals in the economy: Use Bayes rule to compute the two individuals' posterior probability assessments about the states of nature conditional upon the knowledge that the true state is one of $\{\omega_1, \omega_2\}$. There exists, under standard conditions, a competitive equilibrium given these posterior probability assessments. The competitive equilibrium price system must assign zero prices to states ω_3, ω_4, and ω_5. This competitive equilibrium price system is an equilibrium price system for our economy with differential information, when individuals *learn* from observing equilibrium prices and the true state is either ω_1 or ω_2. Note that in this equilibrium, both individuals know that the true state is one of $\{\omega_1, \omega_2\}$ and do *not* know which is the true state. That is, the difference in the information conveyed by the signals they received is symmetrized by the equilibrium prices.

One can apply the same arguments to cases where the true state of nature is any of $\{\omega_3, \omega_4, \omega_5\}$ and determine that the conclusion reached in the last paragraph is valid in all cases. Moreover, this conclusion is not limited to the special case of two individuals and five states considered and is valid in general. The reader will be asked to show in Exercise 9.1 that, in fact, a necessary characteristic for a price system to be an equilibrium price system when markets are complete and individuals learn from observing the price system is that the price system symmetrizes information among individuals.

9.4. Note that in the construction of an equilibrium in Section 9.3, unlike in a competitive equilibrium, a price system has two roles: first, determining an individual's budget constraint as in a competitive equilibrium; second, conveying information. An equilibrium where a price system plays these two roles will be termed a *rational expectations equilibrium*. This term is the same as was used in Chapters 7 and 8 but applies in a different context. In Chapters 7 and 8, individuals are endowed with the same information structure. They are said to have rational expectations if they agree on the mapping from (ω, t) to the price system $S(\omega, t)$. Here, individuals are endowed with different information structures. We will not give a general definition of a rational expectations equilibrium, because it would involve some mathematical concepts that are unnecessary for our purposes here. We will examine, however, a class of models with differential information among individuals and give a formal definition of a rational expectations equilibrium in this context. Readers interested in general discussions of rational expectations equilibria can find references in the remarks at the end of this chapter.

Analyses in previous sections and Exercise 9.1 show that when markets are complete and individuals have differential information before trading occurs, it is necessary that individuals have rational expectations for an equilibrium to exist. In addition, in *any* rational expectations equilibrium with complete markets, the price system must symmetrize the difference in information among individuals. In such event, the price system is said to be *fully revealing*. Moreover, a fully revealing rational expectations equilibrium with complete markets always exists under standard conditions. Thus, observationally, there is no distinction between a rational expectations equilibrium and a competitive equilibrium in a corresponding *artificial economy* that is identical in every aspect except that individuals are endowed with the common information held in the rational expectations equilibrium.

Note that although our previous discussion is based on an economy with a finite number of states of nature, all our conclusions hold, with some additional regularity conditions, in economies with infinitely many states of nature.

9.5. Now we turn our attention to economies with incomplete markets. Unlike the complete markets case, a rational expectations equilibrium need not exist and a competitive equilibrium can exist. We will present an example to show the former result in this section and present another example to demonstrate the latter result in the next two sections.

We consider an economy with two groups of individuals which are equal in number, the *informed* and the *uninformed*. The state space is denoted by Ω. There is a single consumption good available only at time 1, whose spot price at time 1 is a random variable denoted by $\tilde{q}$, which we assume to be normally distributed. An individual, informed or uninformed, has a negative exponential utility function defined on time–1 random wealth, $-\exp\{-a\tilde{W}\}$. At time 0, an individual can trade on the futures contract of the single consumption commodity, whose unit price, the futures price, is denoted by F. Note that a futures contract is a financial asset that promises to deliver a unit of the consumption good at time 1 for a price F, the futures price, determined at time 0. No resources need be committed at time 0 for the purchase of a futures contract. The accounts are settled at time 1.

The markets are obviously incomplete, since there exist infinitely many states and only one security, the futures contract. Note that the structure of this economy is a little different from our usual setup. The single consumption good is not taken to be the numeraire, and the utility function is defined on wealth rather than on consumption. The reader can think of our model here as only a "slice" of an economy with multiple consumption goods where the numeraire is not the consumption good discussed in the "slice."

Before trading at time 0, an informed individual receives a private signal denoted by $\tilde{Y}$. This private signal takes on two possible values

$$\tilde{Y} = \begin{cases} 1 & \text{if } \omega \in \Omega_1; \\ 2 & \text{if } \omega \in \Omega_2; \end{cases}$$

where $\{\Omega_1, \Omega_2\}$ is a partition of Ω. Assume that Ω_1 and Ω_2 are of equal probability. Conditional on $\tilde{Y} = n$, $n = 1, 2$, $\tilde{q}$ is normally distributed with mean m_n and variance σ^2. Assume that $m_1 \neq m_2$.

Conditional on $\tilde{Y} = n$, an uninformed individual is endowed with $k_n > 0$ units of time–1 consumption, with $n = 1, 2$. Assume that $k_1 \neq k_2$. An informed individual, however, is endowed with a constant $k > 0$ units of time–1 consumption. An uninformed individual does not receive any private signal before trading takes place at time 0 and his prior beliefs about $\tilde{q}$ are, therefore, an even mixture of two normal random variables, which is generally not a normal random variable.

The price at time 0 of the futures contract F may depend upon the realization of the signal received by the informed individuals. If $F(\tilde{Y} = 1)$ is not equal to $F(\tilde{Y} = 2)$, an uninformed individual can infer the private signal received by an informed individual from the futures price. In such event, the equilibrium price for the futures contract is *fully revealing*.

Conditional on $\tilde{Y} = n$, an informed individual i solves the following problem:

$$\max_{\theta_i} E[-\exp\{-a\tilde{W}\} | \tilde{Y} = n] \tag{9.5.1}$$

$$\text{s.t. } \tilde{W} = \theta_i(\tilde{q} - F) + \tilde{q}k,$$

where θ_i is the number of futures contracts purchased by individual i at time 0. Conditional on $\tilde{Y} = n$, $\tilde{W}$ is normally distributed with mean and variance:

$$E[\tilde{W} | \tilde{Y} = n] = (\theta_i + k)m_n - \theta_i F,$$

$$\text{Var}(\tilde{W} | \tilde{Y} = n) = (\theta_i + k)^2 \sigma^2.$$

Note that the conditional variance is independent of the realization of $\tilde{Y}$, which is a general property of normal random variables. The distribution of $\exp\{-a\tilde{W}\}$ conditional on $\tilde{Y} = n$ is lognormal. Direct computation yields

$$E[-\exp\{-a\tilde{W}\} | \tilde{Y} = n]$$

$$= -\exp\{-a[(\theta_i + k)m_n - \theta_i F] + \frac{1}{2}a^2(\theta_i + k)^2 \sigma^2\}.$$

As an exponential function is strictly increasing in its exponent, (9.5.1) becomes

$$\max_{\theta_i} a[(\theta_i + k)m_n - \theta_i F] - \frac{1}{2}a^2(\theta_i + k)^2\sigma^2. \qquad (9.5.2)$$

This is a strictly concave program, and its unique solution is characterized by the first order condition:

$$\theta_i = \frac{m_n - F}{a\sigma^2} - k. \qquad (9.5.3)$$

Suppose there exists a rational expectations equilibrium with a *price functional* $F(\tilde{Y})$. We first claim that $F(\tilde{Y})$ must be fully revealing. Suppose this is not the case. That is, there exists a rational expectations equilibrium price functional $F(\tilde{Y})$ with $F(\tilde{Y} = 1) = F(\tilde{Y}=2)$. From (9.5.3), we know that the optimal demand for the futures contract for an informed individual when $\tilde{Y} = 1$ is different from that when $\tilde{Y}=2$, since $m_1 \neq m_2$. By the hypothesis that the futures price does not vary across two possible realizations of an informed individual's private signal, an uninformed individual maximizes expected utility according to his prior beliefs about $\tilde{q}$. Thus his optimal demand for the futures contract does not vary across the realizations of $\tilde{Y}$. It then follows that the markets for the futures contract cannot clear so that a rational expectations equilibrium, when one exists, must be fully revealing.

Next let $F(\tilde{Y})$ be a price functional for the futures contract such that $F(\tilde{Y} = 1) \neq F(\tilde{Y} = 2)$. Facing the price functional $F(\tilde{Y})$, an uninformed individual learns the realization of $\tilde{Y}$ received by an informed individual. Conditional on $\tilde{Y} = n$, an uninformed individual j's optimal demand for the futures contract is a solution to the following problem

$$\max_{\theta_j} E[-\exp\{-a\tilde{W}\}|\tilde{Y} = n] \qquad (9.5.4)$$

$$\text{s.t. } \tilde{W} = \theta_j(\tilde{q} - F) + \tilde{q}k_n,$$

where θ_j denotes the number of futures contracts purchased by individual j. Using identical arguments as in the analysis of (9.5.1) we get, conditional on $\tilde{Y} = n$,

$$\theta_j = \frac{m_n - F}{a\sigma^2} - k_n. \qquad (9.5.5)$$

The equilibrium futures price, conditional on $\tilde{Y} = n$, is determined by the market clearing condition

$$\theta_i + \theta_j = 0.$$

It is

$$F(\tilde{Y} = n) = m_n - (k + k_n)\frac{a\sigma^2}{2}. \qquad (9.5.6)$$

Consider the following data: $m_1 = 3$, $m_2 = 4$, $a = 1$, $\sigma^2 = 1$, $k = 2$, $k_1 = 3$, and $k_2 = 5$. Then

$$F(\tilde{Y} = n) = 0.5, \quad n = 1, 2.$$

This contradicts the fact that $F(\tilde{Y})$ is fully revealing. Thus there does not exist a rational expectations equilibrium!

Note that the above example is not robust in that with a slight change of data there can exist a rational expectations equilibrium. For example, consider the same data as above except that $m_2 = 5$. Then

$$F(\tilde{Y} = n) = \begin{cases} 0.5 & \text{if } n = 1; \\ 1.5 & \text{if } n = 2; \end{cases}$$

and is a fully revealing rational expectations equilibrium price functional. The crux of the matter, however, is that a rational expectations equilibrium may not exist for a given specification of the parameters of the economy.

9.6. In the previous section, we discussed an example of nonexistence of a rational expectations equilibrium when markets are incomplete. Recall from Section 9.2 that when markets are complete and individuals are asymmetrically informed, there does not exist a competitive equilibrium. We now demonstrate, through an example, that there can exist a competitive equilibrium when markets are incomplete. In this competitive equilibrium, however, individuals ignore the informational content of a price system.

Consider the following model of financial markets. There are two periods, time 0 and time 1. At time 0, individuals trade in one risky and one riskless asset. At time 1, individuals consume and the economy ends. One share of the risky asset pays $\tilde{X}$ units of the single consumption good at time 1, where $\tilde{X}$ is a random variable. The risky asset has a total supply of one share. The riskless asset is in zero net supply and pays one unit of the single consumption good for sure at time 1. There are I individuals in the economy, indexed by $i = 1, 2, \ldots, I$. Individual i is characterized by his utility function $u_i(z) = -\exp\{-a_i z\}$ on time 1 consumption and his endowment of a number of shares of the risky asset, denoted by $\bar{\theta}_i$. Individuals are not endowed with the riskless asset. All individuals have a common probability belief P, under which $\tilde{X}$ is normally distributed with mean m_x and variance σ_x^2.

Before trading takes place, individual i receives a private signal $\tilde{Y}_i$,

$$\tilde{Y}_i = \tilde{X} + \tilde{\epsilon}_i, \tag{9.6.1}$$

where $\tilde{X}$ and $(\tilde{\epsilon}_i)_{i=1}^{I}$ are mutually independent and normally distributed and $E[\tilde{\epsilon}_i] = 0, \forall i$. The variance of $\tilde{\epsilon}_i$ is denoted by $\sigma_{\epsilon_i}^2$.

Implicit in the above setup is a state space Ω, on which all the random variables are defined. This state space has infinitely many elements, because the random variables are normally distributed. Each realization of $\tilde{Y}_i$, denoted simply by y_i, tells individual i that some states are possible and some are not. Individual i then updates his probability assessments about $\tilde{X}$ according to Bayes rule.

If the realization of his private signal is y_i, individual i's problem is

$$\max_{\alpha_i, \theta_i} E\left[-\exp\{-a_i \tilde{W}_i\} | \tilde{Y}_i = y_i\right] \tag{9.6.2}$$

$$\text{s.t. } \tilde{W}_i = (\bar{\theta}_i - \theta_i)S_x + \theta_i \tilde{X}.$$

where we have normalized the price of the riskless asset at time 0 to be 1, S_x is the price of the risky asset at time 0, and θ_i is the number of shares of the risky asset individual i chooses to hold. With the time–0 price of the riskless asset normalized to be 1, the rate of return on the riskless asset is zero. Note that, conditional on $\tilde{Y}_i = y_i$, $\tilde{X}$ is normally distributed with mean and variance as follows:

$$E[\tilde{X}|\tilde{Y}_i = y_i] = m_x + \beta_{xy_i}(y_i - m_x) \tag{9.6.3}$$

$$\text{Var}(\tilde{X}|\tilde{Y}_i = y_i) = \sigma_x^2 - \beta_{xy_i}\sigma_x^2, \tag{9.6.4}$$

where

$$\beta_{xy_i} \equiv \frac{\sigma_x^2}{\sigma_x^2 + \sigma_{\epsilon_i}^2}.$$

Note that the conditional mean of $\tilde{X}$ given $\tilde{Y}_i = y_i$ is equal to the unconditional mean of $\tilde{X}$, m_x, plus the "beta" of $\tilde{X}$ on $\tilde{Y}_i$, denoted by β_{xy_i}, times the deviation of y_i from m_x. Similarly, the conditional variance of $\tilde{X}$ given $\tilde{Y}_i = y_i$ is equal to the unconditional variance, σ_x^2, minus β_{xy_i} times σ_x^2. As we noted before, the conditional variance of (9.6.4) is independent of the realizations of $\tilde{Y}_i$. Arguments similar to those used in deriving (9.5.3) and (9.5.5) show that

$$\theta_i = \frac{E[\tilde{X}|\tilde{Y}_i = y_i] - S_x}{a_i \operatorname{Var}(\tilde{X}|\tilde{Y}_i = y_i)} \quad i = 1, 2, \ldots, I. \tag{9.6.5}$$

Putting

$$\tilde{R}_x \equiv \tilde{X}/S_x,$$

where $\tilde{R}_x$ is the return on the risky asset, and substituting this expression into (9.6.5) gives

$$\theta_i S_x = \frac{E[\tilde{R}_x|\tilde{Y}_i = y_i] - 1}{a_i \operatorname{Var}(\tilde{R}_x|\tilde{Y}_i = y_i)} \quad i = 1, 2, \ldots, I. \tag{9.6.6}$$

Relation (9.6.5) says that individual i will invest in the risky asset if and only if he expects, conditional on his signal, that the time–1 payoff of the risky asset will be strictly greater than its time–0 price. His demand for the risky asset is a decreasing function of its price. On the other hand, (9.6.6) implies that the dollar demand for the risky asset is strictly positive if and only if the *risk premium* is strictly positive. (Recall that the riskless interest rate is zero.) In addition, the more risk averse individual i is (or the larger a_i), the smaller the absolute values of θ_i and $\theta_i S_x$ are. These results are consistent with our analysis in Chapter 1. Note also that (9.6.5) and (9.6.6) are independent of individual i's endowment, $\bar{\theta}_i$, because negative exponential utility functions exhibit constant absolute risk aversion and there is no wealth effect.

9.7. Having computed individuals' demands for risky assets, we are now ready to construct a competitive equilibrium. As we have normalized the price of the riskless asset to be equal to one, a competitive equilibrium is composed of a price, S_x, for the risky asset at time 0 such that the market for the risky asset clears. By Walras law, once the market for the risky asset clears, the market for the riskless asset clears also. Our task, therefore, is to find S_x such that

$$\sum_{i=1}^{I} \theta_i = 1. \tag{9.7.1}$$

We can accomplish this by summing (9.6.5) across individuals and equating it to 1:

$$1 = \sum_{i=1}^{I} \frac{E[\tilde{X}|\tilde{Y}_i = y_i] - S_x}{a_i \operatorname{Var}(\tilde{X}|\tilde{Y}_i = y_i)}$$

$$= \sum_{i=1}^{I} \frac{E[\tilde{X}|\tilde{Y}_i = y_i]}{a_i \operatorname{Var}(\tilde{X}|\tilde{Y}_i = y_i)} - S_x \sum_{i=1}^{I} \frac{1}{a_i \operatorname{Var}(\tilde{X}|\tilde{Y}_i = y_i)}.$$

Solving for S_x gives

$$S_x = \frac{\sum_{i=1}^{I} \frac{E[\tilde{X}|\tilde{Y}_i = y_i]}{a_i \operatorname{Var}(\tilde{X}|\tilde{Y}_i = y_i)}}{\sum_{i=1}^{I} \frac{1}{a_i \operatorname{Var}(\tilde{X}|\tilde{Y}_i = y_i)}} - \left(\sum_{i=1}^{I} \frac{1}{a_i \operatorname{Var}(\tilde{X}|\tilde{Y}_i = y_i)} \right)^{-1}. \tag{9.7.2}$$

Relation (9.7.2) gives a competitive equilibrium price for the risky asset. This equilibrium price for the risky asset is equal to the *certainty equivalent* of its time–1 payoff. The certainty equivalent is a weighted average of individuals' expectations of $\tilde{X}$ given the signals they received minus a *risk adjustment factor*. The weight for individual i's conditional expectation of $\tilde{X}$ is

$$\frac{1}{a_i \operatorname{Var}(\tilde{X}|\tilde{Y}_i = y_i)} \left(\sum_{k=1}^{I} \frac{1}{a_k \operatorname{Var}(\tilde{X}|\tilde{y}_k = y_k)} \right)^{-1},$$

which is larger the smaller a_i and $\operatorname{Var}(\tilde{X}|\tilde{Y}_i = y_i)$ are, *ceteris paribus*. That is, the less risk averse individual i and the more precise the signal $\tilde{Y}_i$ (as captured by a smaller $\operatorname{Var}(\tilde{X}|\tilde{Y}_i = y_i)$) are, the more highly weighted individual i's estimate about $\tilde{X}$ is in the equilibrium price. Similarly, the risk adjustment factor will be smaller when individuals are less risk averse and their signals are more precise.

The competitive equilibrium constructed above makes a great deal of intuitive sense. The comparative statics discussed all seem to go the right direction. Unfortunately, this competitive equilibrium is not *stable* in the following sense. Note that the price of the risky asset in the competitive equilibrium is a linear function of individuals' signals. To see this, we simply substitute (9.6.4) into (9.7.2) and observe that $\text{Var}(\tilde{X}|\tilde{Y}_i = y_i)$ is independent of the realization of $\tilde{Y}_i$. In order to trade, individuals must know the equilibrium price of the risky asset, since their demands as characterized in (9.6.5) depend on that price. If they understand the relationship between the price and the signals $(\tilde{Y}_1, \ldots, \tilde{Y}_I)$, as would happen if, for example, the economy were repeated and individuals learned from history, they would realize that the risky asset price contained valuable information about the payoff of the risky asset. In such event, after observing the equilibrium price in the competitive equilibrium, individuals would acquire extra information and form their demands for the risky asset using their new posterior beliefs. It then follows that the competitive equilibrium price may fail to clear the market and the competitive equilibrium may break down.

Suppose instead that there is a price function

$$S_x(\tilde{Y}_1, \ldots, \tilde{Y}_I),$$

which gives prices for the risky asset for all possible realizations of the *joint signal*, $(\tilde{Y}_1, \ldots, \tilde{Y}_I)$, in that, for a given realization of the joint signal, $(y_1, \ldots, y_I)$, $S_x(y_1, \ldots, y_I)$ is the price for the risky asset. Moreover, the functional relationship between S_x and the joint signal is *known* to individuals in that for every realization $(y_1, \ldots, y_I)$ of $(\tilde{Y}_1, \ldots, \tilde{Y}_I)$, an individual i calculates his optimal demand for the risky asset using the posterior belief conditional on his own signal $\tilde{Y}_i = y_i$ and the price $S_x(\tilde{Y}_1, \ldots, \tilde{Y}_I) = S_x(y_1, \ldots, y_I)$ and the market clears. Then the price functional gives an equilibrium price for the risky asset for all possible realizations of the joint signal. This equilibrium is stable in the sense that it will not break down even after many repetitions of the economy, because individuals *know* the functional relation between the equilibrium price and the joint signal and have already taken it into consideration in calculating their optimal demands. This equilibrium is a *rational expectations equilibrium*. Individuals are said to have rational expectations if, in equilibrium, they understand the functional relation between the equilibrium price (of the risky asset) and the joint signal. In a rational expectations equilibrium, all individuals have rational expectations.

9.8. We will show that there exists a rational expectations equilibrium in the economy constructed in Section 9.6, when we add the assumptions that $\sigma_{\epsilon_i}^2 = \sigma_{\epsilon}^2$, $\forall i$. The proof is by construction: construct a price functional and show that it is indeed a rational expectations equilibrium price functional. Before proving this assertion, however, we discuss some results in probability theory that will be useful.

Let $\tilde{Z}$ be a random variable, let z denote its realization, and let $f_i(y_i, z|x)$ be the joint density of $\tilde{Y}_i$ and $\tilde{Z}$ conditional on $\tilde{X}$. The random variable $\tilde{Z}$ is a *sufficient statistic* for $f_i(y_i, z|x)$ if there exist functions $g_1(\cdot)$ and $g_2(\cdot)$ such that for all y_i and z,

$$f_i(y_i, z|x) = g_1(y_i, z)g_2(z, x). \qquad (9.8.1)$$

If $\tilde{Z}$ is a sufficient statistic for $f_i(y_i, z|x)$, the conditional density of $\tilde{X}$ given $\tilde{Y}_i$ and $\tilde{Z}$, denoted by $h(x|y_i, z)$, is independent of $\tilde{Y}_i$. To see this, we note that by Bayes rule,

$$h(x|y_i, z) = \frac{g(x)f_i(y_i, z|x)}{\int_{-\infty}^{+\infty} g(x)f_i(y_i, z|x)dx}, \qquad (9.8.2)$$

where $g(\cdot)$ is the density function for $\tilde{X}$. As $\tilde{Z}$ is a sufficient statistic for $f_i(y_i, z|x)$, we substitute (9.8.1) into (9.8.2) to get

$$
\begin{aligned}
h(x|y_i, z) &= \frac{g(x)g_1(y_i, z)g_2(z, x)}{\int_{-\infty}^{+\infty} g(x)g_1(y_i, z)g_2(z, x)dx} \\
&= \frac{g(x)g_2(z, x)}{\int_{-\infty}^{+\infty} g(x)g_2(z, x)dx}.
\end{aligned}
\qquad (9.8.3)
$$

The right–hand side of (9.8.3) is independent of y_i, which was to be proved.

Now we claim that

$$\bar{Y} \equiv \frac{\sum_{i=1}^{I} \tilde{Y}_i}{I}$$

is a sufficient statistic for $f_i(y_i, \bar{y}|x)$, the joint density of $\tilde{Y}_i$ and $\bar{Y}$ conditional on $\tilde{X}$, where $\bar{y}$ is a realization of $\bar{Y}$. Intuitively, this follows because, with the additional assumptions about the distributions of $\tilde{\epsilon}_i$, individuals are getting signals that are independent and identically distributed conditional on $\tilde{X}$. Thus the mean of the signals is more informative than any individual $\tilde{Y}_i$. More formally, we want to show that (9.8.1) holds when we take $\tilde{Z}$ to be $\bar{Y}$. Conditional on $\tilde{X} = x$, $\tilde{Y}_i$ is normally distributed with mean x and variance σ_ϵ^2, and $\bar{Y}$ is normally distributed with mean x and variance σ_ϵ^2/I. Conditional on $\tilde{X} = x$, the covariance of $\tilde{Y}_i$ and $\bar{Y}$ is σ_ϵ^2/I. Thus conditional on $\tilde{X} = x$, $(\tilde{Y}_i, \bar{Y})$ are bivariate normal with a mean vector (x, x) and a variance–covariance matrix

$$\begin{pmatrix} \sigma_\epsilon^2 & \sigma_\epsilon^2/I \\ \sigma_\epsilon^2/I & \sigma_\epsilon^2/I \end{pmatrix}.$$

Therefore,

$$f_i(y_i, \bar{y}|x) = (2\pi)^{-1} \begin{vmatrix} \sigma_\epsilon^2 & \sigma_\epsilon^2/I \\ \sigma_\epsilon^2/I & \sigma_\epsilon^2/I \end{vmatrix}^{-\frac{1}{2}}$$

$$\times \exp\left\{ -\frac{1}{2} \begin{pmatrix} y_i - x \\ \bar{y} - x \end{pmatrix}^{\mathsf{T}} \begin{pmatrix} \sigma_\epsilon^2 & \sigma_\epsilon^2/I \\ \sigma_\epsilon^2/I & \sigma_\epsilon^2/I \end{pmatrix}^{-1} \begin{pmatrix} y_i - x \\ \bar{y} - x \end{pmatrix} \right\}.$$

Define

$$g_1(y_i, \bar{y}) \equiv (2\pi)^{-1} \frac{I}{\sigma_\epsilon^2 \sqrt{I-1}} \exp\left\{ -\frac{1}{2} \frac{I}{\sigma_\epsilon^2(I-1)} (y_i^2 - 2\bar{y}y_i) \right\},$$

and

$$g_2(\bar{y}, x) \equiv \exp\left\{ -\frac{1}{2} \frac{I}{\sigma_\epsilon^2(I-1)} (2x\bar{y} - x^2 + I(\bar{y} - x)^2) \right\}.$$

Then $f_i(y_i, \bar{y}|x) = g_1(y_i, \bar{y})g_2(\bar{y}, x)$, and we have proved our assertion.

As $\bar{Y}$ is a sufficient statistic for $f_i(y_i, \bar{y}|x)$, the density of $\tilde{X}$ conditional on $\tilde{Y}_i = y_i$ and $\bar{Y} = \bar{y}$, $h(x|y_i, \bar{y})$, is independent of y_i. As a consequence,

$$
\begin{aligned}
E[\tilde{X}|\tilde{Y}_i = y_i, \bar{Y} = \bar{y}] &= E[\tilde{X}|\bar{Y} = \bar{y}] \\
&= m_x + \beta_{x\bar{y}}(\bar{y} - m_x), \\
\mathrm{Var}(\tilde{X}|\tilde{Y}_i = y_i, \bar{Y} = \bar{y}) &= \mathrm{Var}(\tilde{X}|\bar{Y} = \bar{y}) \\
&= \sigma_x^2 - \beta_{x\bar{y}}\sigma_x^2,
\end{aligned}
\tag{9.8.4}
$$

where

$$
\beta_{x\bar{y}} \equiv \frac{\sigma_x^2}{\sigma_x^2 + \sigma_\epsilon^2/I}
$$

is the "beta" of $\tilde{X}$ on $\bar{Y}$. The interpretation of (9.8.4) is similar to that for (9.6.3) and (9.6.4).

Using similar arguments, we can show that $\bar{Y}$ is a sufficient statistic for the joint density of $(\tilde{Y}_1, \ldots, \tilde{Y}_I, \bar{Y})$ conditional on $\tilde{X}$ and, thus,

$$
\begin{aligned}
E[\tilde{X}|\tilde{Y}_1 = y_1, \ldots, \tilde{Y}_I = y_I, \bar{Y} = \bar{y}] &= E[\tilde{X}|\bar{Y} = \bar{y}] \\
&= m_x + \beta_{x\bar{y}}(\bar{y} - m_x), \\
\mathrm{Var}(\tilde{X}|\tilde{Y}_1 = y_1, \ldots, \tilde{Y}_I = y_I, \bar{Y} = \bar{y}) &= \mathrm{Var}(\tilde{X}|\bar{Y} = \bar{y}) \\
&= \sigma_x^2 - \beta_{x\bar{y}}\sigma_x^2.
\end{aligned}
\tag{9.8.5}
$$

9.9. Now we are ready to construct a rational expectations equilibrium. First we note from (9.7.2) that if every individual received a signal equal to $\bar{Y}$, the competitive equilibrium price functional would be a linear function of $\bar{Y}$. This functional will be our candidate for a rational expectations equilibrium price functional. The reasoning is as follows: As individuals have rational expectations, once they see the *equilibrium price* announced by the auctioneer, they can invert the price to solve for the realization of $\bar{Y}$. Knowing $\bar{Y}$, which is a sufficient statistic for $f_i(y_i, \bar{y}|x)$, a rational individual's optimal demand for the risky asset will be independent of his own signal. In fact, individuals' optimal demands are equal to those in an *artificial economy* where all individuals received the signal $\bar{Y}$. Thus our price functional clears the market for the risky asset and is a rational expectations equilibrium price functional.

Formally, consider an *artificial economy* identical to the one currently being analyzed except that all individuals receive a signal equal to $\bar{Y}$. As there is no differential information among individuals in this artificial economy, we simply look for a competitive equilibrium. Given a realization $\bar{y}$ of $\bar{Y}$, the optimal demands for the risky asset are

$$\theta_i = \frac{E[\tilde{X}|\bar{Y} = \bar{y}] - S_x}{a_i \operatorname{Var}(\tilde{X}|\bar{Y} = \bar{y})}, \quad i = 1, 2, \ldots, I, \tag{9.9.1}$$

and the competitive equilibrium price for the risky asset is

$$
\begin{aligned}
S_x &= E[\tilde{X}|\bar{Y} = \bar{y}] - \operatorname{Var}(\tilde{X}|\bar{Y} = \bar{y}) \left(\sum_{i=1}^{I} \frac{1}{a_i} \right)^{-1} \\
&= m_x + \beta_{x\bar{y}}(\bar{y} - m_x) \\
&\quad - \left(\sigma_x^2 - \beta_{x\bar{y}}\sigma_x^2 \right) \left(\sum_{i=1}^{I} \frac{1}{a_i} \right)^{-1},
\end{aligned}
\tag{9.9.2}
$$

where we have used (9.7.2) and (9.8.4). Observe that S_x is a linear function of $\bar{y}$ with fixed coefficients in (9.9.2). We will use $S_x(\bar{y})$ to denote the value of this linear functional when $\bar{Y} = \bar{y}$. Note that there is a one–to–one correspondence between $\bar{y}$ and $S_x(\bar{y})$, and $S_x(\bar{Y})$ is therefore invertible.

The price functional of (9.9.2) is intuitively appealing. The price of the risky asset is higher the higher the realized average signal $\bar{y}$, *ceteris paribus*. For a given change of $\bar{y}$, the response of S_x is proportional to $\beta_{x\bar{y}}$, which lies in $(0, 1)$ by the definition given in (9.8.4). The proportional increase of S_x is higher the smaller σ_ϵ^2 is, or equivalently the more precise the signals are. Also, *ceteris paribus*, the more risk averse individuals are, the lower the price for the risky asset, since they require a higher risk premium to hold the risky asset. The comparative statics of S_x with respect to σ_ϵ^2 and σ_x^2 are left for the reader.

Note that the competitive price functional of (9.9.2) is also an equilibrium price in another artificial economy where individuals share their signals before trading, that is, where individuals observe the joint signal $(\tilde{Y}_1, \ldots, \tilde{Y}_I)$ before trading. This is so, because $\bar{Y}$ is also a sufficient statistic for the joint density of $(\tilde{Y}_1, \ldots, \tilde{Y}_I, \bar{Y})$ given $\tilde{X}$. The reader will be asked to prove this claim in Exercise 9.2.

Now we claim that the price functional of (9.9.2) is a rational expectations price functional. Given this price functional, individual i's rational expectations demand for the risky asset is

$$
\begin{aligned}
\theta_i &= \frac{E[\tilde{X}|\tilde{Y}_i = y_i, S_z(\bar{Y}) = S_z(\bar{y})] - S_z(\bar{y})}{a_i \mathrm{Var}(\tilde{X}|\tilde{Y}_i = y_i, S_z(\bar{Y}) = S_z(\bar{y}))} \\
&= \frac{E[\tilde{X}|\tilde{Y}_i = y_i, \bar{Y} = \bar{y}] - S_z(\bar{y})}{a_i \mathrm{Var}(\tilde{X}|\tilde{Y}_i = y_i, \bar{Y} = \bar{y})} \\
&= \frac{E[\tilde{X}|\bar{Y} = \bar{y}] - S_z(\bar{y})}{a_i \mathrm{Var}(\tilde{X}|\bar{Y} = \bar{y})},
\end{aligned}
\tag{9.9.3}
$$

where the first equality follows from the fact that $S_z(\bar{y})$ is an invertible function of $\bar{y}$, and the second equality follows from (9.8.4) and the fact that $\bar{Y}$ is a sufficient statistic for $f_i(y_i, \bar{y}|x)$. Note that the right–hand side of the third equality is identical to the right–hand side of (9.9.1) when we take S_z to be $S_z(\bar{y})$. Thus a rational individual's optimal demand when faced with the price functional $S_z(\bar{Y})$ is identical to that in the artificial economy. We know that the price functional clears the market in the artificial economy. Thus the price functional clears the market in the rational expectations economy and is a rational expectations equilibrium price functional.

9.10. The rational expectations equilibrium constructed in Section 9.9 has the following properties. First, the information conveyed by the equilibrium price is superior to any private signal in the sense that the price information is a sufficient statistic. Thus, given the equilibrium price, private information becomes redundant. Second, the rational expectations equilibrium is identical to a competitive equilibrium in an artificial economy where individuals share their private information. These two properties amount to saying that the rational expectations equilibrium price system *symmetrizes* the differences in information among individuals and thus is a *fully revealing* price system. A rational expectations equilibrium with a fully revealing price system is said to be a *fully revealing rational expectations equilibrium.*

A fully revealing rational expectations equilibrium seems economically attractive. The equilibrium price system aggregates diverse private information among individuals efficiently in that it reveals a sufficient statistic for the diverse information. Moreover, the equilibrium allocation cannot be improved on by a social planner who has access to the joint private signals.

A fully revealing rational expectations equilibrium, however, has the following problems. As the equilibrium price system conveys information that is superior to an individual's private signal, the optimal demand for the risky asset is independent of the individual's private signal! The optimal demand depends only upon the equilibrium price. If an individual's optimal demand is independent of his or her private signal, how can the equilibrium price system *aggregate* individuals' diverse private signals? In addition, an individual will not have an incentive to collect private information if it is costly to do so — a fully revealing equilibrium price system renders the information collection activity an unprofitable proposition. It then follows that if no individuals collect private information, certainly there is no diverse private information to aggregate. These are the paradoxes associated with a fully revealing price system.

The paradoxes can be resolved if the price system aggregates information only partially in the sense that the price information is *not* a sufficient statistic for an individual's private signal. In such event, the optimal demand of an individual for the risky asset will depend not only upon the price information but also upon his own private signal. This solves the first paradox. Since the optimal demands for the risky asset depend upon individuals' private signals, individuals have incentives to collect private information even at a cost. This solves the second paradox.

Now the question is under what scenario will a price system be *partially revealing*? Note that in the fully revealing rational expectations equilibrium considered earlier, there is only one source of uncertainty, namely the time-1 payoff of the risky asset $\tilde{X}$. Individuals receive private signals about $\tilde{X}$, and the equilibrium price system reveals a sufficient statistic about individuals' private signals. The price system is fully revealing, because it is a nontrivial linear function of the sufficient statistic and is thus invertible. When the price of the risky asset increases, individuals can infer that this occurs because the demand for the risky asset increases, which is in turn due to more optimistic private signals, on average.

Suppose instead that there is an additional source of uncertainty in the economy, for example, the aggregate supply of the risky asset. Then when the price of the risky asset increases, individuals may not be able to tell for sure whether it is because the private signals are more optimistic or because the aggregate supply is smaller. In such an event, the price system does not provide information that is superior to an individual's private signal and is not fully revealing. We will show in the next section that such an equilibrium exists. Note that the assumption of an uncertain aggregate supply is not the most natural. For example, in a stock market economy, the total supply of a common stock is the number of shares outstanding and is common knowledge. This somewhat contrived assumption, however, provides tractability to our analysis.

9.11. Consider again the economy constructed in Section 9.6. Assume that individuals have rational expectations and the same coefficient of absolute risk aversion. Assume in addition that individual i's endowment of shares of the risky asset is a draw of a normally distributed random variable $\tilde{V}_i$. The random variables $(\tilde{V}_1, \ldots, \tilde{V}_I)$ are independent and identically distributed with mean zero and variance σ_v^2. The zero mean assumption is made for convenience and can be relaxed easily. A realization of $\tilde{V}_i$ is denoted by v_i. It follows that the total supply of the risky asset is a realization of the random variable

$$\tilde{Z} \equiv \sum_{i=1}^{I} \tilde{V}_i,$$

which is normally distributed with mean zero and variance $I\sigma_v^2$, where we recall that I is the total number of individuals. A realization of $\tilde{Z}$ is denoted by z. We also assume that $\tilde{X}$, $\tilde{V}_i$, and the $\tilde{\epsilon}_i$'s are mutually independent and $\tilde{\epsilon}_i$ has mean zero and variance σ_ϵ^2, which is constant across individuals. Given that a realization of $(\tilde{V}_1, \ldots, \tilde{V}_I)$ is $(v_1, \ldots, v_I)$, the market clearing condition for the risky asset is

$$\sum_{i=1}^{I} \theta_i = \sum_{i=1}^{I} v_i.$$

We want to show that there exists a partially revealing rational expectations equilibrium. As in the fully revealing case, our proof will be by construction.

9.12. We first conjecture that the equilibrium price system is a linear function of the sufficient statistic $\bar{Y}$ and the aggregate supply $\tilde{Z}$:

$$S_x(\bar{Y}, \tilde{Z}) = \gamma + b_1 \bar{Y} - b_2 \tilde{Z}, \qquad (9.12.1)$$

where γ, $b_1 > 0$, and $b_2 > 0$ are some unknown constants. This price functional is an increasing function of $\bar{Y}$ and a decreasing function of the aggregate supply $\tilde{Z}$. Given this conjectured price functional, we can compute an individual's optimal demand conditional on a realization of the price functional, his private signal, and his endowment of shares of the risky asset. We then ask what the values of γ, b_1, and b_2 should be such that the optimal demands of individuals clear the market.

Given that the realizations of $\tilde{V}_i$, $\tilde{Y}_i$, and $\tilde{Z}$ are v_i, y_i, and z, respectively, and given the price functional of (9.12.1), individual i's optimal demand for the risky asset is

$$\theta_i = \frac{E[\tilde{X}|\tilde{V}_i = v_i, \tilde{Y}_i = y_i, S_x = S_x(\bar{y}, z)] - S_x(\bar{y}, z)}{a\mathrm{Var}(\tilde{X}|\tilde{V}_i = v_i, \tilde{Y}_i = y_i, S_x = S_x(\bar{y}, z))}. \qquad (9.12.2)$$

The derivation of (9.12.2) is identical to that for (9.6.5), except that now individual i forms expectations about $\tilde{X}$ conditional on his own private signal as well as on his endowment of shares of the risky asset and the realized price of the risky asset. As (9.12.1) is a linear function of normally distributed random variables, $S_x(\bar{Y}, \tilde{Z})$ is normally distributed with mean and variance:

$$(\gamma + b_1 m_x, \ b_1^2(\sigma_x^2 + \sigma_\epsilon^2/I) + I b_2^2 \sigma_v^2).$$

Therefore, $(\tilde{X}, \tilde{V}_i, \tilde{Y}_i, S_x(\tilde{Z}, \bar{Y}))$ are multivariate normally distributed with a mean vector

$$(m_x, 0, m_x, \gamma + b_1 m_x),$$

and a variance–covariance matrix

$$\begin{pmatrix} V_{11} & V_{12} \\ V_{21} & V_{22} \end{pmatrix}$$

$$\equiv \begin{pmatrix} \sigma_x^2 & 0 & \sigma_x^2 & b_1\sigma_x^2 \\ 0 & \sigma_v^2 & 0 & -b_2\sigma_v^2 \\ \sigma_x^2 & 0 & \sigma_x^2 + \sigma_\epsilon^2 & b_1(\sigma_x^2 + \sigma_\epsilon^2/I) \\ b_1\sigma_x^2 & -b_2\sigma_v^2 & b_1(\sigma_x^2 + \sigma_\epsilon^2/I) & b_1^2(\sigma_x^2 + \sigma_\epsilon^2/I) + Ib_2^2\sigma_v^2 \end{pmatrix},$$

where $V_{11} = \sigma_x^2$, V_{12} is a 1×3 vector, V_{21} is a 3×1 vector, and V_{22} is a 3×3 matrix.

The conditional expectation and conditional variance of relation (9.12.2) can be explicitly computed using multivariate normal distribution theory. They are

$$E[\tilde{X}|\tilde{V}_i = v_i, \tilde{Y}_i = y_i, S_x = S_x(\bar{y}, z)]$$

$$= m_x + V_{12}V_{22}^{-1} \begin{pmatrix} v_i \\ y_i - m_x \\ b_1(\bar{y} - m_x) - b_2 z \end{pmatrix}$$

$$= m_x + \Gamma^{-1} \{ (b_1 b_2 \sigma_x^2 \sigma_v^2 \sigma_\epsilon^2 (1/I - 1)) v_i$$
$$+ (b_2^2 \sigma_x^2 (\sigma_v^4 - \sigma_v^2 \sigma_\epsilon^2))(y_i - m_x)$$
$$+ b_1 \sigma_x^2 \sigma_v^2 \sigma_\epsilon^2 (1/I - 1)(b_1(\bar{y} - m_x) - b_2 z) \}$$

$$\equiv \varsigma_0 + \varsigma_1 v_i + \varsigma_2 y_i + \varsigma_3 \bar{y} + \varsigma_4 z,$$

and

$$\mathrm{Var}(\tilde{X}|\tilde{V}_i = v_i, \tilde{Y}_i = y_i, S_x = S_x(\bar{y}, z))$$

$$= V_{11} - V_{12}V_{22}^{-1}V_{21}$$

$$= \sigma_x^2 + \Gamma^{-1}\left(b_1^2 \sigma_x^4 \sigma_v^2 \sigma_\epsilon^2 \left(1 - \frac{1}{I}\right) + b_2^2 \sigma_x^4 \sigma_v^2 (\sigma_\epsilon^2 - \sigma_v^2) \right)$$

$$(9.12.3)$$

where

$$\Gamma \equiv b_1^2 \sigma_v^2 (\sigma_x^2 + \sigma_\epsilon^2/I)^2 + b_2^2 \sigma_v^2 (\sigma_x^2 + \sigma_\epsilon^2) - \sigma_v^2 (\sigma_x^2 + \sigma_\epsilon^2)(b_1^2(\sigma_x^2 + \sigma_\epsilon^2/I) + b_2^2 \sigma_x^2).$$

Note that $(\varsigma_0, \ldots, \varsigma_4)$ are nonlinear functions of b_1 and b_2 and are independent of individual indices and that the conditional variance is independent of the realizations of $\tilde{V}_i$, $\tilde{Y}_i$, S_x, and individual indices. To simplify our notation, we denote the conditional variance of (9.12.3) by H^{-1}, which we note is a nonlinear function of b_1 and b_2. H is the inverse of the conditional variance and is usually termed the *precision* of the information contained in $\tilde{V}_i$, $\tilde{Y}_i$, and S_x

9.13. The optimal demands for the risky asset of individuals derived in (9.12.2) and (9.12.3) are based on a conjectured price functional (9.12.1). For the conjectured price functional to be a rational expectations equilibrium price functional, it must be that the optimal demands clear the market for the risky asset. That is, we must have

$$\sum_{i=1}^{I} \frac{\varsigma_0 + \varsigma_1 v_i + \varsigma_2 y_i + \varsigma_3 \bar{y} + \varsigma_4 z - \gamma - b_1 \bar{y} - b_2 z}{a H^{-1}}$$

$$= \frac{(\varsigma_0 - \gamma)I + (\varsigma_2 + \varsigma_3 - b_1)I\bar{y} + (I\varsigma_4 + \varsigma_1 - Ib_2)z}{aH^{-1}} \qquad (9.13.1)$$

$$= z,$$

for every possible realization of $\tilde{V}_i$, $\tilde{Y}_i$, $\bar{Y}$, and $\tilde{Z}$. As $\tilde{Z}$ is independent of $\bar{Y}$, for (9.13.1) to hold for every possible realization of $\bar{Y}$ and $\tilde{Z}$, we must have

$$\varsigma_0 - \gamma = 0$$

$$\varsigma_2 + \varsigma_3 - b_1 = 0 \qquad (9.13.2)$$

$$I\varsigma_4 + \varsigma_1 - Ib_2 = aH^{-1}.$$

Recall that $(\varsigma_0, \ldots, \varsigma_4)$ and H^{-1} are all nonlinear functions of b_1 and b_2. Thus, (9.13.2) is a system of three nonlinear equations in as many unknowns (γ, b_1, b_2).

One can verify that a (unique) solution to (9.13.2) is

$$
\gamma = \frac{(\sigma_v^2 \sigma_\epsilon^2 + 1)m_x}{1 + I\sigma_x^2/\sigma_\epsilon^2 + \sigma_v^2(\sigma_\epsilon^2 + \sigma_x^2)},
$$

$$
b_1 = \frac{I\sigma_x^2/\sigma_\epsilon^2 + \sigma_v^2 \sigma_x^2}{1 + I\sigma_x^2/\sigma_\epsilon^2 + \sigma_v^2(\sigma_x^2 + \sigma_\epsilon^2)}, \qquad (9.13.3)
$$

$$
b_2 = \frac{I\sigma_x^2 + \sigma_x^2 \sigma_v^2 \sigma_\epsilon^2}{I(1 + I\sigma_x^2/\sigma_\epsilon^2 + \sigma_v^2(\sigma_x^2 + \sigma_\epsilon^2))}.
$$

It is then easily verified that the values of γ, b_1, and b_2 in (9.13.3) are not only necessary but also sufficient for a rational expectations equilibrium. That is, there exists a rational expectations equilibrium with the price functional

$$
S_x(\bar{Y}, \tilde{Z}) = \gamma + b_1 \bar{Y} - b_2 \tilde{Z},
$$

where γ, b_1, and b_2 are defined in (9.13.3).

Note that in this equilibrium, $b_1 > 0$ and $b_2 > 0$. Thus, the equilibrium price for the risky asset is an increasing function of $\bar{Y}$, the *sufficient statistic*, and a decreasing function of $\tilde{Z}$, the aggregate supply of the risky asset. Because the aggregate supply of the risky asset is also a random variable, there is no one–to–one relationship between the price of the risky asset and the sufficient statistic $\bar{Y}$. When the risky asset price increases, an individual is uncertain whether it is because on average everybody is getting a better signal or because the aggregate supply of the risky asset is smaller. Therefore, an individual's optimal demand for the risky asset depends on the information conveyed by the price of the risky asset, on his private signal, and on his own endowment of the risky asset. This resolves the paradox that if a price system is *fully revealing*, an individual's optimal demand is independent of his own private signal and the price system cannot, therefore, *aggregate* diverse private information among individuals. Moreover, as the price system aggregates diverse private information only partially, there exists an incentive to collect information even when it is costly to do so. This resolves the paradox associated with costly information discussed in Section 9.10.

9.14. From previous discussions, we learned that fully revealing rational expectations equilibria are not very interesting as they are not likely to arise – recall the paradoxes associated with fully revealing equilibria. We have constructed a partially revealing rational expectations equilibrium in Section 9.13 for a very special economy – one with negative exponential utility functions and normally distributed returns and private signals. Unfortunately, little is known about partially revealing rational expectations equilibria outside the special case discussed. The combined effects of negative exponential utility functions and multivariate normally distributed returns and private signals make a linear price functional a feasible solution to the equilibrium problem. This gives tractability to an inherently very difficult problem. On the other hand, the tractability is not without cost. The normally distributed return on the risky asset implies unlimited liability and negative consumption in equilibrium.

We also know very little about rational expectations equilibria in multiperiod economies. Even in the special case discussed above, the multiperiod extension is a formidable task. This extension, when successful, will give rise to a much richer model. Questions such as to what extent historical prices contain information about future prices and whether historical volumes of trade play any informational role can only be answered in models of a multiperiod economy.

9.15. We concentrated our discussion in earlier sections on securities markets equilibrium when individual traders possess diverse private information about the return on the risky asset. In the remainder of this chapter, we will consider situations where entrepreneurs possess inside information about projects for which they seek financing. Outside investors would benefit from knowing the true characteristics of the projects. However, the entrepreneurs cannot be expected to convey truthfully their inside information to the outside investors, as there may be substantial rewards for exaggerating positive qualities of their projects.

If the qualities of projects can be verified ex post, financing contracts between the entrepreneurs and the outside investors can be written with terms dependent upon the ex post verifiable qualities. On the other hand, if the qualities of projects cannot be verified ex post, the markets for financing may break down and projects with good qualities cannot be carried out resulting in inefficiency. To see this, we consider the financing of a family of projects whose quality is highly variable. While the entrepreneurs know the quality of their own projects, the outside investors do not. Therefore, the financing cost must reflect some *average quality*. For entrepreneurs with projects having above average quality, the financing cost may be too high to justify undertaking the projects. As a consequence, the high quality projects are withdrawn from the financing markets, and the average quality of projects seeking financing is lowered. This process may continue until the only projects seeking financing are of the lowest quality. This is the so–called the *lemon's problem* or the problem of *adverse selection*.

For projects of good quality to be financed, the private information possessed by entrepreneurs must be transferred to the outside investors when ex post verifiability of the quality of projects is lacking. This can be done by observable actions taken by the entrepreneurs. One such action, observable because of disclosure rules, is the willingness of the entrepreneurs to retain the ownership of the projects. The larger the proportion of a project retained by an entrepreneur, the less diversified his portfolio is. The cost of a nondiversified portfolio is smaller for entrepreneurs having good quality projects, because they will be compensated by, for example, higher expected returns on their projects. Outside investors can then infer the quality of the project from the proportion of a project retained by an entrepreneur. From the entrepreneurs' perspective, they use their actions to *signal* the outside investors about the qualities of their projects.

Outside investors can announce a *schedule* of financing cost depending on the proportion of the project retained by an entrepreneur. Through choosing financing from the schedule, an entrepreneur will reveal his or her private information about the project quality. This is called *screening* by the outside investors. Clearly, signalling and screening are two sides of a coin.

In the subsequent sections, we will develop a simple model of financial markets in which entrepreneurs seeking financing possess private information about the quality of their projects. A *signalling equilibrium* will be established. This equilibrium differs in important ways from models without asymmetric information.

9.16. Consider a family of investment projects indexed by "quality", $\mu \in [\underline{\mu}, \bar{\mu}]$. All investments require a capital outlay of K at time 0. An investment project with quality μ has a time-1 cash flow $\tilde{X} = \mu + \tilde{\epsilon}$, where μ is the expected future cash flow and $\tilde{\epsilon}$ is a normally distributed random variable with mean zero and variance σ_ϵ^2. Each investment project is accessible to an entrepreneur, who plans to hold α proportion of the equity, raising the remainder of the equity from outside investors, once he decides to undertake the project. A project will be 100% equity financed.

An entrepreneur has private information and knows the true value of μ. Outside investors do not know the true value of μ. They, however, are informed that μ has a strictly positive density function on $[\underline{\mu}, \bar{\mu}]$. The ex post realization of $\tilde{X}$, observable to both an entrepreneur and the outside investors, does not allow outside investors to tell the value of μ with certainty. However, outside investors will respond to a signal sent by an entrepreneur about the true value of μ, if they believe that it is in an entrepreneur's best interest to send such a signal. The signal we will examine here is the proportion α of the equity retained by an entrepreneur. Outside investors believe that there exists a functional relation between μ and α and make inferences about μ from the observed α. A *signalling equilibrium* is a situation where outside investors' beliefs about the functional relation between α and μ are indeed correct. A signalling equilibrium is said to be a *separating* equilibrium if the functional relation between α and μ is strictly monotone. In such an event, the true μ will be learned in equilibrium. We will only be interested in separating equilibria and will therefore use the term *signalling equilibria* to refer to separating equilibria.

Suppose that outside investors infer the value of μ according to the schedule $g(\alpha)$, in that when α is observed, they conclude that $\mu = g(\alpha)$. We assume that the value of equity is determined by the CAPM relation:

$$V(\alpha) = \frac{g(\alpha) - \lambda}{1 + r_f}, \qquad (9.16.1)$$

where

$$\lambda \equiv \frac{\text{Cov}(\tilde{X}, \tilde{r}_m)}{\sigma_m^2}(E[\tilde{r}_m] - r_f)$$

$$= \frac{\text{Cov}(\tilde{\epsilon}, \tilde{r}_m)}{\sigma_m^2}(E[\tilde{r}_m] - r_f), \qquad (9.16.2)$$

where $\tilde{r}_m$ denotes the normally distributed rate of return on the market portfolio, and σ_m^2 is the variance of $\tilde{r}_m$. We assume that

$$\frac{\mu - \lambda}{1 + r_f} - K < 0. \qquad (9.16.3)$$

That is, the lowest quality project has a strictly negative net present value.

In addition to investing in his own project, an entrepreneur can invest in the market portfolio and borrow and lend on personal account at the riskless rate r_f. Assume that he has a negative exponential utility function. We shall also make the *perfect competition* assumption that an entrepreneur's decision about undertaking the project has no effect on the return on the market portfolio. An entrepreneur's problem is to decide whether to undertake the project and, if he decides to do so, to choose the proportion to retain of his project, α, the dollar amount invested in the market portfolio, a, and the dollar amount invested in the riskless asset, b, to maximize his expected utility:

$$\max_{\alpha \in [0,1], a, b} E[-\exp\{-\tilde{W}\}]$$

$$\text{s.t. } \tilde{W} = \alpha(\mu + \tilde{\epsilon}) + a(1 + \tilde{r}_m) + b(1 + r_f) \qquad (9.16.4)$$

$$a + b + K = W_0 + (1 - \alpha)V(\alpha),$$

where W_0 is an entrepreneur's initial wealth. The left–hand side of the second constraint of (9.16.4) is the cash outlay for an entrepreneur at time 0, while the right–hand side is the cash available after selling a $(1 - \alpha)$ proportion of the project. The value an entrepreneur can get from selling part of the project, $(1 - \alpha)V(\alpha)$, depends on the proportion he is selling.

9.17. Substituting (9.16.1) and the second constraint of (9.16.4) into the first constraint of (9.16.4) to eliminate b gives

$$\tilde{W} = \alpha(\mu + \tilde{\epsilon} - g(\alpha) + \lambda) + a(\tilde{r}_m - r_f) + (W_0 - K)(1 + r_f) + g(\alpha) - \lambda. \tag{9.17.1}$$

Note that $\tilde{W}$ is normally distributed, because $\tilde{r}_m$ and $\tilde{\epsilon}$ are.

Using (9.17.1) and the arguments used in deriving (9.5.2), we know that (9.16.4) is equivalent to

$$\max_{\alpha, a} \alpha(\mu - g(\alpha) + \lambda) + a(E[\tilde{r}_m] - r_f) + (W_0 - K)(1 + r_f)$$

$$+ g(\alpha) - \lambda - \frac{1}{2}(\alpha^2 \sigma_\epsilon^2 + a^2 \sigma_m^2 + 2a\alpha \text{Cov}(\tilde{\epsilon}, \tilde{r}_m)). \tag{9.17.2}$$

Note that b, the dollar amount invested in the riskless asset does not appear in the maximization. It will be determined by the second constraint of (9.16.4) after a and α are determined. We will assume that there exists a solution $\alpha \in (0, 1)$ and proceed to characterize that solution.

The first order necessary conditions are

$$\mu - g(\alpha) + \lambda + (1 - \alpha)g'(\alpha) - \alpha\sigma_\epsilon^2 - a\text{Cov}(\tilde{\epsilon}, \tilde{r}_m) = 0, \tag{9.17.3}$$
$$E[\tilde{r}_m] - r_f - a\sigma_m^2 - \alpha\text{Cov}(\tilde{\epsilon}, \tilde{r}_m) = 0. \tag{9.17.4}$$

Substituting (9.16.2) and (9.17.4) into (9.17.3) for λ and a, respectively, gives

$$\mu - g(\alpha) + (1 - \alpha)g'(\alpha) - \alpha\gamma = 0, \tag{9.17.5}$$

where

$$\gamma \equiv \frac{\sigma_\epsilon^2 \sigma_m^2 - (\text{Cov}(\tilde{\epsilon}, \tilde{r}_m))^2}{\sigma_m^2}.$$

It is easily verified that $\gamma \geq 0$. We will assume that $\gamma > 0$. Relation (9.17.5) must be satisfied by α, given that outside investors infer μ using the functional $g(\alpha)$ when α is observed.

The second order necessary conditions are

$$-2g'(\alpha) + (1 - \alpha)g''(\alpha) - \sigma_\epsilon^2 \leq 0,$$
$$-\sigma_m^2 \leq 0, \tag{9.17.6}$$
$$\sigma_m^2 (2g'(\alpha) - (1 - \alpha)g''(\alpha) + \sigma_\epsilon^2) - (\text{Cov}(\tilde{\epsilon}, \tilde{r}_m))^2 \geq 0,$$

where g' and g'' denote the first and second derivatives of g, respectively.

Now we turn to analyze the problem of the outside investors.

9.18. As mentioned in Section 9.15, the outside investors' problem is to *screen* entrepreneurs. That is, they want to announce a *schedule* $g(\cdot)$ to determine the quality of projects seeking financing as a function of α, the proportion retained. The schedule should have the property that an entrepreneur, knowing the value μ, will optimally choose an $\alpha(\mu)$ such that

$$g(\alpha(\mu)) = \mu, \qquad (9.18.1)$$

when faced with the schedule $g(\cdot)$. In other words, given the schedule $g(\cdot)$, the optimal behavior of an entrepreneur is to tell the truth. Equivalently, entrepreneurs reveal their true types by *self-selection*. Relations (9.17.5) and (9.18.1) together characterize a *signalling equilibrium*.

Now we turn to closed form solutions of signalling equilibria. Substituting (9.18.1) into (9.17.5) gives

$$(1 - \alpha)g'(\alpha) = \alpha\gamma. \qquad (9.18.2)$$

There exists a family of solutions to (9.18.2) parameterized by an arbitrary constant C:

$$g(\alpha) = -\gamma(\ln(1 - \alpha) + \alpha) + C. \qquad (9.18.3)$$

Any member of (9.18.3) is a candidate for an equilibrium schedule and makes the program of (9.17.2) a strictly concave program, for which the second order conditions are automatically satisfied. Thus the first order conditions are also sufficient for a unique optimum in this case. Note that every member of (9.18.3) is strictly increasing and strictly convex in $(0, 1)$. As α approaches 1, $g(\alpha)$ asymptotically approaches infinity:

$$\lim_{\alpha \to 1} g(\alpha) = +\infty.$$

If a member of (9.18.3) is a signalling equilibrium, its relevant domain may be a subinterval of $[0, 1)$. To see this, we first note

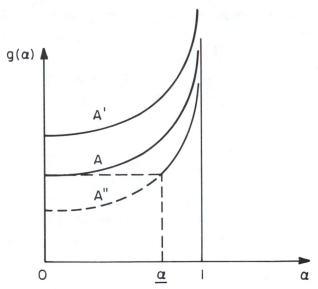

Figure 9.18.1: Solutions to (9.18.2)

that an entrepreneur with $\mu < \lambda + (1 + r_f)K$ will *not* undertake the project and seek outside financing, as, in equilibrium, the project has a strictly negative net present value. The project that just breaks even in equilibrium has a quality $\mu = \lambda + (1 + r_f)K$. Thus the relevant domain of an equilibrium schedule is

$$g^{-1}([\lambda + (1 + r_f)K, +\infty)), \tag{9.18.4}$$

the inverse image of the qualities of projects that have a positive net present value. Three members of (9.18.3) are depicted in Figure 9.18.1. According to (9.18.4), the relevant domains of A and A' are $[0, 1)$, while the relevant domain of A'' is $[\underline{\alpha}, 1)$, where $\underline{\alpha}$ is the solution to

$$-\gamma(\ln(1 - \alpha) + \alpha) + C'' = \lambda + (1 + r_f)K,$$

where C'' is the constant that corresponds to A''.

Not every member of (9.18.3), in its relevant domain, is an optimal solution to the outside investors' problem, however. Consider the schedule A' in Figure 9.18.1. The constant C' associated with this schedule is strictly greater than $\lambda + (1 + r_f)K$. According to this schedule, if an entrepreneur retains no equity, outside investors will conclude that

$$\mu = g(0) = C' > \lambda + (1+r)K.$$

Thus, an entrepreneur with $\mu < C'$ will find it profitable to undertake his project by investing K and choosing $\alpha = 0$ to sell the project for

$$V(0) = \frac{g(0) - \lambda}{1 + r_f}$$

$$> \frac{\lambda + (1+r_f)K - \lambda}{1 + r_f} = K.$$

By doing so, he makes a strictly positive profit of $V(0) - K$. Thus, all the entrepreneurs with a $\mu < C'$ will undertake the project and choose a signal level of $\alpha = 0$. This violates (9.18.1), and outside investors incur losses. (Recall that, by (9.16.3), there exists a strictly positive proportion of entrepreneurs having $\mu < \lambda + (1 - r_f)K$.)

In Exercise 9.4, the reader will be asked to show that the problem associated with schedule A' cannot be avoided by requiring a minimum level of strictly positive retained equity, since entrepreneurs with a μ smaller than but arbitrarily close to the minimum level will find it profitable to undertake the project and retain the minimum level. This violates (9.18.1). Thus we must have

$$C \leq \lambda + (1+r_f)K. \tag{9.18.5}$$

Next, consider the schedule A in Figure 9.18.1. The constant C that corresponds to A is equal to $\lambda + (1 + r_f)K$. Similar problems arise. An entrepreneur having $\mu < \lambda + (1+r_f)K$ can undertake the project and retain no equity. He just breaks even in this transaction and is indifferent as to whether or not to undertake the project. This again violates (9.18.1) at $\alpha = 0$. In Exercise 9.4, the reader is also asked to show that, if we require $\alpha > 0$, then entrepreneurs with $\mu < \lambda + (1+r_f)K$ will find it sub–optimal to undertake the project. Hence schedule A on the domain $(0,1)$ satisfies (9.18.1) and is a *signalling equilibrium.*

Next, we consider schedule A'' in Figure 9.18.1, which corresponds to a constant $C'' < \lambda + (1 + r_f)K$. The kind of problem associated with schedules A and A' does not arise. One can show that entrepreneurs with $\mu < \lambda + (1+r_f)K$ will find it unprofitable to undertake their projects and retain a strictly positive proportion of the equity. Thus A'' with a domain $[\underline{\alpha}, 1)$ is a signalling equilibrium schedule. The same arguments apply to any member of the family (9.18.3) with a constant strictly less than $\lambda + (1+r_f)K$ on its relevant domain. Hence there exists a continuum of signalling equilibria.

9.19. We identified a continuum of signalling equilibria in Section 9.18. In each equilibrium, an entrepreneur who chooses to undertake his project will get the desired financing by revealing the true quality of the project. However, all equilibria but one are inefficient in two senses.

First, we note that the proportion of equity retained can be viewed as an indication of the *signalling cost*. To see this, we note that, for a project having positive net present value, if there were no information asymmetry, the first order conditions of an entrepreneur's problem would be

$$\lambda - a\sigma_\epsilon^2 - a\mathrm{Cov}(\tilde{\epsilon}, \tilde{r}_m) = 0,$$
$$E[\tilde{r}_m] - r_f - a\sigma_m^2 - \alpha\mathrm{Cov}(\tilde{\epsilon}, \tilde{r}_m) = 0. \tag{9.19.1}$$

These imply that $\alpha = 0$. That is, without information asymmetry, the optimal solution involves no retained equity. In signalling equilibria where an entrepreneur chooses to retain a strictly positive proportion, his expected utility will be strictly lower than what would be attained without information asymmetry. Moreover, for a fixed μ, it is easily seen that the expected utility attained for a low α is higher than that which can be attained for a higher α. As a consequence, the proportion retained is a proxy for the cost paid for obtaining outside financing. For a fixed proportion, α, the signalling cost to an entrepreneur with a high μ is less than that to another with a low μ. This is the reason an entrepreneur with a high μ will optimally choose a high signal – he or she can better afford it! Among the continuum of signalling equilibria, the one that has the least signalling cost is schedule A in Figure 9.18.1. Compare schedules A and A'', for example. For a given level of μ, schedule A'' requires a strictly higher retained proportion. Thus A is the most efficient in the sense that the signalling costs in equilibrium are the lowest. In fact, schedule A is the only equilibrium which is competitive in that if schedule A were offered by some investors while some others were offering a different schedule, all entrepreneurs would do business with the investors offering schedule A.

Schedule A is the only equilibrium schedule under which all projects with a strictly positive net present value are undertaken. To see this, we note that an entrepreneur with a μ which yields a zero net present value is indifferent between undertaking his project and remaining at his status quo when facing schedule A. He will find it sub–optimal to undertake his project if he has to retain a strictly positive proportion. On the other hand, it can be shown that an entrepreneur with a μ that yields a strictly positive net present value finds it optimal to undertake his project when faced with schedule A. Thus all projects with a strictly positive net present value will be undertaken. On the other hand, when facing the schedule A'', an entrepreneur with a μ equal to $\lambda + (1 + r_f)K$ will find it sub–optimal to undertake his project, because he has to retain a proportion $\underline{\alpha}$. This is so, because he is just indifferent between accepting the project and remaining at his status quo when no proportion must be retained. When a strictly positive proportion must be retained, he will certainly find it sub–optimal to undertake his project. By a continuity argument, one can show that an entrepreneur with a μ strictly above but close to $\lambda + (1 + r_f)K$ will also find it sub–optimal to undertake his project. Thus, in equilibrium, some projects having a strictly positive net present value will not be undertaken. This is clearly inefficient relative to schedule A.

We have thus identified a unique efficient signalling equilibrium. Although efficient among all the signalling equilibria, it results in an expected utility loss for the entrepreneur compared to the case without information asymmetry.

9.20. In the previous discussions of this chapter, we only touched upon very limited aspects of informational issues related to financial markets. Readers interested in the general area of information economics as applied to financial markets will find Bhattacharya (1987) useful reading.

Among the subjects not discussed previously, the *moral hazard* problem is perhaps the most important. Moral hazard usually arises in a gaming situation where some players involved can take an unobservable action that affects the payoffs to be shared. A classical moral hazard problem arises in the context of insurance. The probability of, say, a fire can be influenced by the care exerted by the insured. There is no incentive for an individual who is fully insured to exert any care. Thus the insurance premium should vary for different levels of coverage. Arrow (1970) contains the original discussion of moral hazard issues in the context of health insurance.

In the entrepreneurs/outside investors example discussed in Sections 9.16 to 9.19, there is no moral hazard problem, as the quality of a project is outside an entrepreneur's control. It is, however, more reasonable to think that the quality of a project depends on some effort on the part of an entrepreneur. For example, we can think of μ as a function of an action taken by an entrepreneur. When the action taken by an entrepreneur is not observable and not ex post verifiable, the problem of moral hazard arises. The outside investors' problem is then not only to screen entrepreneurs who have exerted different levels of efforts but also to design a compensation scheme to provide the right incentives. Spence and Zeckhauser (1971), Holmstrom (1979), and Mirrlees (1976) are early discussions of general moral hazard/incentive problems, to which we refer interested readers. Recent discussions on this subject in the context of financial markets are Allen (1985) and Bhattacharya and Pfleiderer (1985).

Exercises

9.1. Consider a complete markets two–period economy, where trading occurs at time 0, and the consumption of a single consumption good occurs at time 1. Show that a necessary characteristic for an equilibrium price system when individuals learn from observing the system is that it symmetrize the differences in information among individuals.

9.2. Consider an economy identical to the artificial economy of Section 9.9 except that individuals observe the joint signal $(\tilde{Y}_1, \ldots, \tilde{Y}_I)$ before trading. Show that (9.9.2) also gives the competitive equilibrium price for the risky asset.

9.3. Consider an economy identical to the one constructed in Section 9.11 except that the coefficients of absolute risk aversion are not equal across individuals. Conjecture that the price functional for the risky asset is

$$S_x(\tilde{Y}_1, \ldots, \tilde{Y}_I, \tilde{Z}) = \gamma + \sum_{i=1}^{I} b_i \tilde{Y}_i + b_0 \tilde{Z}.$$

Show that if $(b_0, \ldots, b_I)$ is a solution to a system of nonlinear equation in as many unknowns, then there exists a rational expectations equilibrium with the conjectured price functional.

9.4. Show that the problem associated with schedule A' discussed in Section 9.18 cannot be avoided by requiring a minimum level of retained equity $\underline{\alpha} > 0$. Also show that the similar problem associated with schedule A in Figure 9.18.1 disappears when we require that $\alpha > 0$.

Remarks. The example of nonexistence in Section 9.5 is due to Kreps (1977). The competitive equilibrium of Sections 9.6 and 9.7 is taken from Lintner (1969). Discussions in Sections 9.8 to 9.10 are freely borrowed from Grossman (1976) and Grossman and Stiglitz (1980). The closed form solution of the noisy rational expectations equilibrium of Sections 9.11 to 9.13 is taken from Diamond and Verrecchia (1981). The signalling model of Sections 9.15 to 9.19 is due to Leland and Pyle (1977). In the same context as Exercise 9.3, Hellwig (1980) shows the existence of a noisy rational expectations equilibrium. He obtains a closed form solution when the number of individuals in the economy increases to infinity.

Our discussion in this chapter on some applications of information economics to financial markets is very limited in scope. Readers interested in rational expectations equilibrium should consult Jordon and Radner (1982) and the references therein. Admati (1987) has a more recent summary account of the literature including applied work. Pfleiderer (1984) studies comparative statics on volumes of trade in a rational expectations model. Kyle (1985) uses monopolistic competition to model speculation and information transmission through prices.

Signalling models began with Akerlof (1970) and Spence (1973). Riley (1975) and Rothschild and Stiglitz (1975) also made important contributions. For a more recent discussion on signalling equilibria, see Cho and Kreps (1987). Early applications of signalling models to financial economics include Bhattacharya (1976, 1980) and Ross (1977). Bhattacharya and Ritter (1983) is the first to consider models where a signal to financial markets is also observed by competitors in the product markets. Gertner, Gibbons, and Scharfstein (1987) also model this situation. Readers interested in this class of models as well as applications of other ideas in information economics to financial markets should consult Bhattacharya (1987) and the references therein.

References

Akerlof, G. 1970. The market for "lemons." *Quarterly Journal of Economics* **89**, 488–500.

Admati, A. 1985. A noisy rational expectations equilibrium for multi–asset securities markets. *Econometrica* **53**, 629–657.

Admati, A. 1987. Information in financial markets: The rational expectations approach. In *Frontiers of Financial Theory*. Edited by G. Constantinides and S. Bhattacharya. Rowman and Littlefield. Totowa, New Jersey.

Allen, F. 1985. Contracts to sell information. Mimeo. Wharton School, University of Pennsylvania.

Arrow, K. 1970. Essays in the Theory of Risk–Bearing. North–Holland. Amsterdam.

Bhattacharya, S. 1976. Imperfect information, dividend policy, and the "bird in the hand" fallacy. *Bell Journal of Economics* **10**:259–270.

Bhattacharya, S. 1980. Nondissipative signalling structures and dividend policy. *Quarterly Journal of Economics* 95:1–24.

Bhattacharya, S. 1987. Financial markets and incomplete information: A review of some recent developments. In *Frontiers of Financial Theory*. Edited by G. Constantinides and S. Bhattacharya. Rowman and Littlefield. Totowa, New Jersey.

Bhattacharya, S., and P. Pfleiderer. 1985. Delegated portfolio management. *Journal of Economic Theory* 36:1–25.

Bhattacharya, S., and J. Ritter. 1983. Innovation and communication: Signalling with partial disclosure, *Review of Economic Studies* 50:331–346.

Cho, I.-K., and D. Kreps. 1987. Signalling games and stable equilibria. *Quarterly Journal of Economics* 52:179–221.

Diamond, D., and R. Verrecchia. 1981. Information aggregation in a noisy rational expectations economy. *Journal of Financial Economics* 9, 221–235.

Gertner, R., R. Gibbons, and D. Scharfstein. 1987. Simultaneous signalling to the capital and product markets. Mimeo. Sloan School of Management, Massachusetts Institute of Technology. Cambridge, Massachusetts.

Grossman, S. 1976. On the efficiency of competitive stock markets when agents have diverse information. *Journal of Finance* 31, 573–585.

Grossman, S., and J. Stiglitz. 1980. On the impossibility of informationally efficient markets. *American Economic Review* 70, 393–408.

Hellwig, M. 1980. On the aggregation of information in competitive markets. *Journal of Economic Theory* 22, 477–498.

Holmstrom, B. 1979. Moral hazard and observability. *Bell Journal of Economics* 10:74–91.

Jordon, J., and R. Radner. 1982. Rational expectations in microeconomic models: An overview. *Journal of Economic Theory* 26, 201–223.

Kreps, D. 1977. A note on fulfilled expectations equilibria. *Journal of Economic Theory* 44, 32–43.

Kyle, A. 1985. Informed speculation with imperfect competition. Working Paper, Woodrow Wilson School, Princeton University.

Princeton, New Jersey.

Leland, H., and D. Pyle. 1977. Informational asymmetries, financial structure, and financial intermediation. *Journal of Finance* 32:371–387.

Lintner, J. 1969. The aggregation of investors' diverse judgement and preferences in purely competitive security markets. *Journal of Financial and Quantitative Analysis* 4:103–124.

Mirrlees, J. 1976. The optimal structure of incentives and authority within an organization. *Bell Journal of Economics* 7:105–131.

Pfleiderer, P. 1984. Private information, price variability and trading volume. Mimeo. Graduate School of Business, Stanford University. Stanford, California.

Riley, J. 1975. Competitive signalling. *Journal of Economic Theory* 10:174–186.

Ross, S. 1977. The determination of financial structure: The incentive-signalling approach. *Bell Journal of Economics* 8:23–40.

Rothschild, M., and J. Stiglitz. 1975. Equilibrium in competitive insurance markets: An essay on the economics of imperfect information. *Quarterly Journal of Economics* 90:812–824.

Spence, M. 1973. Job market signalling. *Quarterly Journal of Economics* 87, 355–379.

Spence, M., and R. Zeckhauser. 1971. Insurance, information, and individual action. *American Economic Review* 61:380–387.

CHAPTER 10
ECONOMETRIC ISSUES
IN TESTING THE
CAPITAL ASSET PRICING MODEL

10.1. In this chapter, econometric issues related to testing the Capital Asset Pricing Model (CAPM) will be discussed. Many test statistics will be given interpretations in the framework of Chapter 3. To provide a conceptual basis for interpreting these econometric issues, we shall first briefly discuss the testable implications of the CAPM. Throughout our discussion, we will assume that there exists a riskless lending opportunity.

10.2. In Chapter 3, we examined the mathematics of the portfolio frontier. There we derived the first order condition necessary and sufficient for a portfolio to be on the frontier and proved that any portfolio that is a linear combination of frontier portfolios is itself a frontier portfolio. In Chapter 4, we provided conditions on the distributions of asset returns necessary and sufficient for individuals' optimal portfolios to be frontier portfolios. In such an event, the market clearing condition implies that the market portfolio is a convex combination of individuals' optimal portfolios and is thus a frontier portfolio. The CAPM then follows immediately once the market portfolio is identified to be on the portfolio frontier. Thus, the CAPM is merely the combination of the first order conditions for a portfolio to be on the portfolio frontier and the market clearing condition.

10.3. Using time–series sample means, variances, and covariances we can construct a portfolio frontier, referred to as an *ex post* portfolio frontier. A portfolio on an *ex post* portfolio frontier is an *ex post frontier portfolio*. An *ex post* frontier portfolio could be constructed even if means, variances, and covariances were generated randomly. If the betas on individual assets are measured relative to an *ex post* frontier portfolio, it follows from the mathematics of the portfolio frontier that the average realized rates of returns on these assets would have an exact linear relation to these betas. This is a mathematical fact and has nothing to do with an equilibrium pricing relation. Thus, it is tautological to say that there exists a single "factor" that will "explain" rates of return. In addition, such a frontier portfolio may have large negative weights for many assets. Thus, without an underlying valuation theory, we cannot predict, *a priori*, that there is a positive association between average realized rates of return and betas measured relative to a prespecified market proxy portfolio that is well–diversified and has positive weights for all assets. This observation also relates to an important conceptual problem in testing the Arbitrage Pricing Theory that does not pre–identify the "factors" based on economic models of portfolio choice. For example, if factor analysis is used to determine the set of factors "explaining" ninety–five percent of the variation of the rates of returns on individual assets, a linear combination of these factors may closely approximate the rate of return on an *ex post* frontier portfolio. A test of the proposition that these factors are the sole determinants of risk premiums might fail to be rejected even if the underlying returns were generated randomly.

10.4. Financial theories provide internally consistent models of asset prices that have testable implications. A positive theory of the valuation of risky assets should not be judged by the realism of its assumptions. Indeed, incorrect assumptions are sometimes necessary to abstract from the complex and detailed circumstances and to build a model that focuses on more important aspects. For example, although we are well aware of the fact that many individuals have different probability beliefs, we abstract from this consideration by assuming homogeneous probability beliefs. This assumption and other equally implausible assumptions permit the derivation of the CAPM. A long and detailed list of realistic assumptions that are impossible to model is merely an institutional description and has in itself no predictive value. The correct test of a positive theory of asset pricing is the accuracy of its predictions concerning security returns and/or security prices. If the assumptions used to derive a theory abstract from the most critical considerations, then the theory's predictions would very likely prove inaccurate. The more general are the assumptions necessary to derive a given theory, the less precise its predictions will be. For example, allowing for the possibility that borrowing is either prohibited or is done at a rate strictly higher than the lending rate is more general than assuming unconstrained borrowing, or equivalently, unlimited borrowing and lending at the same rate. Recall from Section 4.14 that the CAPM based on unconstrained borrowing predicts a proportional relation between risk premiums (with respect to the riskless rate) and betas. The more general model that allows for constraints on borrowing merely predicts a linear relation between risk premiums and betas with a positive intercept.

10.5. Positive theories have strong predictions and weak predictions. A strong prediction is a prediction whose validity is implied by and implies the underlying theory. Thus, strong predictions are equivalent to necessary and sufficient conditions for the underlying theory. A strong prediction of the CAPM is two fund separation. Two fund separation may be refuted by the finding that an individual's optimal portfolio is not spanned by the optimal portfolios of two other individuals. While to the best of our knowledge no researcher takes such a prediction seriously, another strong prediction that the market portfolio is on the portfolio frontier has been subjected to extensive testing. Since meaningful positive theories are often based on unrealistic assumptions, their strong predictions are unlikely to be perfectly accurate. Indeed, failure to reject statistically a strong prediction of a positive theory is usually due to a lack of power of the statistical test. Strong predictions of positive theories, like two fund separation, are not often examined because their rejection is usually obvious *a priori*.

In contrast, a weak prediction is a prediction whose validity is "broadly" implied by but does not imply the underlying theory. An example of a weak prediction of the CAPM is that *ex post* betas measured relative to a broadly based market index are positively related to the average *ex post* realized returns. This weak prediction does not imply an exact linear relation between *ex ante* expected rates of return and betas. For example, *ex ante* expected returns may be related to betas and a second variable that is independent of the betas. Under stationarity conditions, *ex post* betas would then be related to *ex post* average returns. Empirically verified weak predictions have, however, yielded useful applications in financial economics.

10.6. In its most general form, the CAPM implies the following cross–sectional relation between *ex ante* risk premiums and betas, when there exists a riskless asset:

$$E[\tilde{r}_j] = E[\tilde{r}_{zc(m)}] + \beta_{jm}(E[\tilde{r}_m] - E[\tilde{r}_{zc(m)}]), \qquad (10.6.1)$$

where $\tilde{r}_j$ is the excess rate of return on security j, $\tilde{r}_m$ is the excess rate of return on the market portfolio of all assets, $\tilde{r}_{zc(m)}$ is the excess rate of return on the frontier portfolio having a zero covariance with respect to the market portfolio, β_{jm} is $\text{Cov}(\tilde{r}_j, \tilde{r}_m)/\text{Var}(\tilde{r}_m)$, the "beta" of security j (with respect to the market portfolio), and $E[\cdot]$ is the expectation operator. Here we caution the reader to note that, for notational simplicity, we have used $\tilde{r}_j$ to denote the "excess" rate of return on asset j with respect to the riskless lending rate in contrast to the notation used in earlier chapters, and likewise for $\tilde{r}_m$

and $\tilde{r}_{zc(m)}$. In empirical work, one often uses the treasury bill rate as the short term riskless lending rate.

10.7. When there are unlimited borrowing and lending opportunities at a constant riskless interest rate, the traditional version of the CAPM predicts that the expected rate of return on $zc(m)$ is equal to the riskless rate, or, equivalently, that risk premiums on assets are proportional to their market betas. In this case, (10.6.1) holds with

$$E[\tilde{r}_{zc(m)}] = 0 \quad \text{and} \quad E[\tilde{r}_m] > 0. \tag{10.7.1}$$

The constrained borrowing version of the CAPM makes the less precise prediction that the risk premium on $zc(m)$ is positive and that the difference between the risk premium on the market portfolio and the risk premium on $zc(m)$ is strictly positive. In this case, (10.6.1) holds with

$$E[\tilde{r}_{zc(m)}] \geq 0 \quad \text{and} \quad E[\tilde{r}_m] - E[\tilde{r}_{zc(m)}] > 0. \tag{10.7.2}$$

Thus, the predictions of the constrained borrowing version of the CAPM are somewhat less precise than those of the traditional version of the model. It should, therefore, come as no surprise that the empirical tests are more consistent with the constrained borrowing version of the model.

10.8. There are, in general, three major conceptual problems associated with the testing of the CAPM. First, the CAPM implies relationships concerning *ex ante* risk premiums and betas, which are not directly observable. Second, empirical tests use time–series data to calculate mean excess rates of return and betas; however, it is unlikely, that risk premiums and betas on individual assets are stationary over time. When time–series data are used to calculate betas and mean rates of return on assets, it is implicitly assumed that the CAPM holds period by period, since the CAPM is a two period model. Third, many assets are not marketable and tests of the CAPM are invariably based on proxies for the market portfolio that exclude major classes of assets such as human capital (the capitalized value of wage and salary income), private businesses, and private real estate. Different approaches for dealing with these problems have been taken in the literature.

10.9. Concerning the first conceptual problem, the unobservability of *ex ante* expected returns and betas, the assumption of rational expectations is implicitly made. Under *rational expectations*, the realized rates of return on assets in a given time period are drawings from the *ex ante* probability distributions of returns on those assets. Here we remind the reader that the definition of *rational expectations* can be found in Section 7.7.

10.10. As for the second problem, the nonstationarity of risk premiums and betas on individual assets, two complementary approaches have evolved. The first approach is to form portfolios that are constructed to have stationary betas and to assume that the risk premiums on these constructed portfolios, on the market portfolio, and on $zc(m)$ are stationary over time. Note that constant risk premiums are consistent with equal percentage point changes in the riskless interest rate and in the expected rates of return on risky assets. The second approach is to interpret the tests in terms of the distributions of asset returns conditional on a coarser information set and assume that these distribution are time–stationary. Even when risk premiums and betas conditional on information sets available to investors over time are nonstationary, they can be stationary conditional on a coarser information set. We will discuss this second approach in detail below.

As mentioned in Section 10.8, empirical testing of the CAPM implicitly assumes that the CAPM holds period by period. In particular, we assume that, at each time $t-1$, an individual i maximizes expected utility of time t random wealth conditional on the information that he has at time $t-1$. The first order condition for his time t random wealth, $\tilde{W}_t^i$, to be optimal is

$$E[u_{it}'(\tilde{W}_t^i)(\tilde{r}_{jt} - \tilde{r}_{zc(m)t})|\mathcal{F}_{t-1}] = 0, \quad \forall j, \qquad (10.10.1)$$

where $u_{it}(\cdot)$ denotes individual i's utility function for time t wealth, $\tilde{r}_{jt}$ denotes the rate of return on asset j from time $t-1$ to time t,

$\tilde{r}_{zc(m)t}$ denotes the rate of return on the zero covariance portfolio with respect to the market portfolio from time $t-1$ to time t, and $\mathcal{F}_{t-1}$ denotes the information possessed by individuals at time $t-1$. Taking expectations on both sides of (10.10.1) conditional on the aggregate wealth at time $t-1$ gives

$$E[u'_{it}(\tilde{W}^i_t)(\tilde{r}_{jt} - \tilde{r}_{zc(m)t})|\tilde{M}_{t-1}] = 0, \quad \forall j, \tag{10.10.2}$$

where $\tilde{M}_{t-1}$ denotes the time $t-1$ aggregate wealth. Assume that distributions of $\tilde{W}^i_t$, $\tilde{r}_{jt}$, and $\tilde{r}_{zc(m)t}$ are multivariate normal conditional on $\tilde{M}_{t-1}$. Using the definition of covariance, the Stein's Lemma, and the line of argument used in deriving (4.15.3), and assuming that $\tilde{M}_t$ and $\tilde{r}_{zc(m)t}$ are uncorrelated conditional on M_{t-1} we can rewrite (10.10.2) as

$$\vartheta^{i-1}_t(E[\tilde{r}_{jt}|\tilde{M}_{t-1}] - E[\tilde{r}_{zc(m)t}|\tilde{M}_{t-1}]) = \text{Cov}(\tilde{W}^i_t, \tilde{r}_{jt} - \tilde{r}_{zc(m)t}|\tilde{M}_{t-1}), \tag{10.10.3}$$

where

$$\vartheta^i_t \equiv \frac{-E[u''_{it}(\tilde{W}^i_t)|\tilde{M}_{t-1}]}{E[u'_{it}(\tilde{W}^i_t)|\tilde{M}_{t-1}]}$$

is the i-th individual's *global absolute risk aversion* for the time t utility function on wealth conditional on time $t-1$ total wealth. Summing (10.10.3) across i and using the market clearing condition

$$\sum_{i=1}^{I} \tilde{W}^i_t = \tilde{M}_t$$

gives

$$E[\tilde{r}_{jt}|\tilde{M}_{t-1}] - E[\tilde{r}_{zc(m)t}|\tilde{M}_{t-1}]$$

$$= \left(\sum_{i=1}^{I} \frac{1}{\vartheta^i_t}\right)^{-1} \text{Cov}(\tilde{r}_{jt}, \tilde{M}_t|\tilde{M}_{t-1})$$

$$= \left(\sum_{i=1}^{I} \frac{1}{\vartheta^i_t}\right)^{-1} \tilde{M}_{t-1} \text{Cov}(\tilde{r}_{jt}, \tilde{r}_{mt}|\tilde{M}_{t-1}), \quad \forall j \tag{10.10.4}$$

where

$$\tilde{r}_{mt} \equiv \frac{\tilde{M}_t}{\tilde{M}_{t-1}} - 1$$

is the rate of return on the market portfolio from time $t-1$ to t. Relation (10.10.4) certainly holds when we take asset j to be the market portfolio and thus

$$E[\tilde{r}_{mt}|\tilde{M}_{t-1}] - E[\tilde{r}_{zc(m)t}|\tilde{M}_{t-1}]$$

$$= \left(\sum_{i=1}^{I} \frac{1}{\theta_t^i}\right)^{-1} \tilde{M}_{t-1}\text{Var}(\tilde{r}_{mt}|\tilde{M}_{t-1}), \quad \forall j. \tag{10.10.5}$$

Substituting (10.10.5) into (10.10.4) gives

$$E[\tilde{r}_{jt}|\tilde{M}_{t-1}] - E[\tilde{r}_{zc(m)t}|\tilde{M}_{t-1}]$$
$$= \beta_{jmt}(\tilde{M}_{t-1})(E[\tilde{r}_{mt}|\tilde{M}_{t-1}] - E[\tilde{r}_{zc(m)t}|\tilde{M}_{t-1}]), \quad \forall j, \tag{10.10.6}$$

where

$$\beta_{jmt}(\tilde{M}_{t-1}) \equiv \frac{\text{Cov}(\tilde{r}_{jt}, \tilde{r}_{mt}|\tilde{M}_{t-1})}{\text{Var}(\tilde{r}_{mt}|\tilde{M}_{t-1})},$$

is the time t beta of assets j conditional on $\tilde{M}_{t-1}$. Note that in (10.10.6) the expected returns and betas are measured with respect to the distribution of asset returns conditional on $\tilde{M}_{t-1}$. When the distributions of asset returns conditional on aggregate wealth are independent of aggregate wealth, (10.10.6) becomes

$$E[\tilde{r}_{jt+1}] - E[\tilde{r}_{zc(m)t+1}] = \beta_{jmt}(E[\tilde{r}_{mt+1}] - E[\tilde{r}_{zc(m)t+1}]), \quad \forall j, \tag{10.10.7}$$

where

$$\beta_{jmt} \equiv \frac{\text{Cov}(\tilde{r}_{jt+1}, \tilde{r}_{mt})}{\text{Var}(\tilde{r}_{mt})}$$

is the unconditional beta for asset j. Note that (10.10.7) is specified under the unconditional distribution and is thus termed the *unconditional CAPM*. If the unconditional distributions of asset returns are stationary over time, β_{jmt} of (10.10.7) is a constant independent of time. It then follows that even though risk premiums and betas conditional on the information set available to investors may be non-stationary, a time–series of returns on assets may be used to test the unconditional CAPM.

Also note that (10.10.2) does not imply (10.10.1). This is because a zero conditional expectation conditional on an information partition does not imply that the expectation conditional on a finer information partition will be identically zero. Along the lines of argument used in deriving (10.10.6), (10.10.1) together with multivariate normality of the rates of return on assets conditional on $\mathcal{F}_{t-1}$ implies that

$$
\begin{aligned}
&E[\tilde{r}_{jt}|\mathcal{F}_{t-1}] - E[\tilde{r}_{zc(m)t}|\mathcal{F}_{t-1}] \\
&= \beta^c_{jmt}(E[\tilde{r}_{mt}|\mathcal{F}_{t-1}] - E[\tilde{r}_{zc(m)t}|\mathcal{F}_{t-1}]), \quad \forall j,
\end{aligned}
\tag{10.10.8}
$$

where the random variable

$$
\beta^c_{jmt} \equiv \frac{\mathrm{Cov}(\tilde{r}_{jt}, \tilde{r}_{mt}|\mathcal{F}_{t-1})}{\mathrm{Var}(\tilde{r}_{mt}|\mathcal{F}_{t-1})}
$$

is the conditional beta of asset j at time t. Relation (10.10.8) will be termed the conditional CAPM. The validity of the unconditional CAPM does not imply the validity of the conditional CAPM. Thus, the market portfolio being on the portfolio frontier based on the unconditional distributions of asset returns should be viewed as a weak prediction of the conditional form of the CAPM but a strong prediction of the unconditional form of the CAPM. Most existing tests of the CAPM and our discussion which follows focus on the unconditional form of the model.

10.11. Concerning the third conceptual problem, the unobservability of the true market portfolio, three related approaches have been taken. The first approach ignores the problem by implicitly assuming that the disturbance terms from regressing the asset returns on the return on the market proxy portfolio are uncorrelated with the true market portfolio and that the proxy portfolio has a unit beta. If the market proxy is a portfolio constructed from the individual assets or portfolios contained in the test sample, this assumption is equivalent to assuming that the market proxy is the minimum variance unit beta portfolio of the set of all feasible portfolios constructed from the assets in the test sample. This implicit assumption will be discussed in more detail in Section 10.12.

The second approach merely interprets the test as a test of whether the market proxy is on the portfolio frontier. The third approach is to view the test as a test of a single factor APT with a prespecified factor. This approach is empirically indistinguishable from the second approach.

10.12. Now we will demonstrate explicitly the implicit assumption made when the unobservability of the true market portfolio is ignored. Suppose that the market proxy, $\hat{m}$, has unit beta and that the disturbance terms in the regressions

$$\tilde{r}_j = \alpha_j + \beta_{j\hat{m}}\tilde{r}_{\hat{m}} + \tilde{e}_j, \quad j = 1, 2, \ldots, N \qquad (10.12.1)$$

are uncorrelated with the true market, where

$$\beta_{j\hat{m}} \equiv \frac{\mathrm{Cov}(\tilde{r}_j, \tilde{r}_{\hat{m}})}{\mathrm{Var}(\tilde{r}_{\hat{m}})} \qquad (10.12.2)$$

is the "beta" of asset j with respect to the market proxy. By definition, the true beta of asset j is

$$\beta_{jm} = \frac{\mathrm{Cov}(\tilde{r}_j, \tilde{r}_m)}{\mathrm{Var}(\tilde{r}_m)}. \qquad (10.12.3)$$

Substituting (10.12.1) into (10.12.3) gives

$$\beta_{jm} = \beta_{j\hat{m}}\frac{\mathrm{Cov}(\tilde{r}_{\hat{m}}, \tilde{r}_m)}{\mathrm{Var}(\tilde{r}_m)}, \qquad (10.12.4)$$

where we have used the hypothesis that $\tilde{e}_j$ is uncorrelated with $\tilde{r}_m$. Since the market proxy has unit beta, we know that

$$\frac{\mathrm{Cov}(\tilde{r}_{\hat{m}}, \tilde{r}_m)}{\mathrm{Var}(\tilde{r}_m)} = 1.$$

Substituting this into (10.12.4) gives

$$\beta_{jm} = \beta_{j\hat{m}}, \qquad (10.12.5)$$

that is, the beta with respect to the market proxy is equal to that with respect to the true market portfolio. Thus, even though the true market portfolio is not observable, the true betas can be estimated if the market proxy has unit beta and the disturbance terms of (10.12.1) are uncorrelated with the true market portfolio.

Next we show that if the proxy, $\hat{m}$, is constructed from the individual assets or portfolios contained in the test sample and is the unit beta minimum variance portfolio among all the portfolios constructed from the test sample, the betas measured with respect to $\hat{m}$ are equal to the true betas. Consider a set of N risky assets which is a proper subset of the set of all assets. Let $\mathbf{V}$ be the unconditional variance–covariance matrix of their rates of return, $\mathbf{w}$ be the $N \times 1$ vector of the weights of a portfolio, $\mathcal{B}_m$ be a $N \times 1$ vector of betas measured relative to the true market portfolio, and $\mathcal{B}_{\hat{m}}$ be a $N \times 1$ vector of betas measured relative to the rate of return on the minimum variance unit beta portfolio.

Let $\mathbf{w}_{\hat{m}}$ be the portfolio weights on risky assets for the minimum variance unit beta portfolio. Since covariances are additive, the beta of $\hat{m}$ is a weighted average of betas of individual assets, that is, $\mathcal{B}_{\hat{m}} = \mathbf{w}_{\hat{m}}\mathcal{B}_m$. Then $\mathbf{w}_{\hat{m}}$ is a solution to the following problem,

$$\min_{\{\mathbf{w}\}} \frac{1}{2}\mathbf{w}^\top\mathbf{V}\mathbf{w}$$
$$\text{s.t. } \mathbf{w}^\top\mathcal{B}_m = 1. \tag{10.12.6}$$

The weights on risky assets in (10.12.6) are not constrained to sum to unity because the portfolio weights can be later rescaled with a riskless asset without changing the beta or the variance.

Assuming that $\mathbf{V}$ is nonsingular, $\mathbf{w}_{\hat{m}}$ is the unique solution to (10.12.6) and satisfies the following first order conditions:

$$\mathbf{w}_{\hat{m}} = \lambda\mathbf{V}^{-1}\mathcal{B}_m \tag{10.12.7}$$

and

$$\mathbf{w}_{\hat{m}}^\top\mathcal{B}_m = 1, \tag{10.12.8}$$

where λ is the Lagrangian multiplier for the constraint of (10.12.6). Relations (10.12.7) and (10.12.8) imply that

$$\lambda = \frac{1}{\mathcal{B}_m^\top\mathbf{V}^{-1}\mathcal{B}_m}. \tag{10.12.9}$$

Next note that, by definition, the $N \times 1$ vector of betas with respect to the minimum variance unit beta portfolio, denoted by $\mathcal{B}_{\hat{m}}$, is

$$\mathcal{B}_{\hat{m}} = \frac{\mathbf{V}\mathbf{w}_{\hat{m}}}{\mathbf{w}_{\hat{m}}^{\top}\mathbf{V}\mathbf{w}_{\hat{m}}}$$

$$= \frac{\lambda \mathcal{B}_m}{\lambda^2 \mathcal{B}_m^{\top}\mathbf{V}^{-1}\mathcal{B}_m} = \mathcal{B}_m \, , \qquad (10.12.10)$$

where the second equality follows from (10.12.7), and the third equality follows from (10.12.9).

Relation (10.12.10) demonstrates that the betas of all assets in this proper subset of assets with respect to the minimum variance unit beta portfolio (constructed from the same subset of assets) are identical to their betas with respect to the true market portfolio. Thus, even if the market portfolio is not observable, the betas can still be estimated when an appropriate market proxy is used. In Exercise 10.1 we ask the reader to solve (10.12.6) by replacing the constraint with $\mathbf{w}^{\top}\mathcal{B}_m = \rho$ for some constant $\rho \neq 0$. The solution is a portfolio with a beta equal to ρ that has a minimum variance. Denoting this solution still by $\hat{m}$, the reader is also asked to show that $\mathcal{B}_{\hat{m}} = \mathcal{B}_m/\rho$.

10.13. Most tests of the CAPM have used a time–series of monthly rates of return on common stocks listed on the New York Stock Exchange (NYSE). The CAPM suggests three related empirical models. The first is a cross–sectional regression model involving average monthly excess rates of return, $\bar{r}_j$ (average realized rate of return in excess of the short term lending rate), and betas with respect to the NYSE index, denoted by $\beta_{j\hat{m}}$. This model is

$$\begin{aligned} \bar{r}_j &= a + b\beta_{j\hat{m}} + \tilde{u}_j, \qquad j = 1, 2, \ldots N, \\ \tilde{u}_j &= \bar{r}_j - E[\tilde{r}_j], \\ a &= E[\tilde{r}_{zc(\hat{m})}], \\ b &= E[\tilde{r}_{\hat{m}}] - E[\tilde{r}_{zc(\hat{m})}]. \end{aligned} \qquad (10.13.1)$$

The second is a series of monthly cross–sectional regressions of the realized excess rates of return on the betas. That is, for all

$t = 0, 1, \ldots, T,$

$$\tilde{r}_{jt} = a_t + b_t \beta_{j\hat{m}} + \tilde{u}_{jt} \qquad j = 1, 2, \ldots N,$$
$$\tilde{u}_{jt} = \tilde{r}_{jt} - E[\tilde{r}_j | \tilde{r}_{zc(\hat{m})t}, \tilde{r}_{mt}],$$
$$a_t = \tilde{r}_{zc(\hat{m})t}, \tag{10.13.2}$$
$$b_t = \tilde{r}_{\hat{m}t} - \tilde{r}_{zc(\hat{m})t},$$

where we have used $\tilde{r}_{jt}$, $\tilde{r}_{\hat{m}t}$, and $\tilde{r}_{zc(\hat{m})t}$ to denote the random excess rates of return at time t on security j, the NYSE index, $\hat{m}$, and the minimum variance zero covariance portfolio with respect to the NYSE index, respectively.

The third is a series of time–series regressions for each asset or portfolio in the sample: $\forall j = 1, 2, \ldots, N$,

$$\tilde{r}_{jt} = \alpha_j + \beta_{j\hat{m}} \tilde{r}_{\hat{m}t} + \tilde{e}_{jt} \quad t = 1, 2, \ldots T,$$
$$\alpha_j = E[\tilde{r}_{zc(\hat{m})}](1 - \beta_{j\hat{m}}), \tag{10.13.3}$$
$$\tilde{e}_{jt} = \tilde{r}_{jt} - E[\tilde{r}_{jt} | \tilde{r}_{\hat{m}t}].$$

In this model, the expected excess rate of return on $zc(m)$ and the betas are assumed to be constant over time.

Note that the $\beta_{j\hat{m}}$'s are treated as a fixed independent variable in the cross–sectional regression models given in (10.13.1) and (10.13.2), while they are parameters to be estimated in the time–series regression model given in (10.13.3). Note also that in the above model specifications, we have used a *tilde* on top of r_{jt}, $r_{\hat{m}t}$, and u_{jt} to signify the fact that they are random variables. When the same symbols appear without a *tilde*, they represent realizations of random variables or the observations in a sample. We will refer to the $\tilde{u}_j$, $\tilde{u}_{jt}$, and $\tilde{e}_{jt}$ of (10.13.1), (10.13.2), and (10.13.3), respectively, as disturbance terms. In later sections, when they appear without a *tilde*, the same symbols represent "residuals" from a fitted linear model.

10.14. An example of the type of test of (10.13.1) is Blume and Friend (1973). The focus of their study was on a weak prediction of the traditional CAPM. Specifically, they tested the predictions that $a = 0$ and $b > 0$. Thus, they were testing whether $E[\tilde{r}_{zc(\hat{m})}] = 0$ and

$E[\tilde{r}_{\hat{m}}] - E[\tilde{r}_{zc(\hat{m})}] > 0$. They found that both a and b were strictly positive and this finding was statistically significant.

An example of a test of (10.13.2) is Fama and MacBeth (1973). The primary focus of their study was the same weak form predictions. They tested the predictions that

$$\sum_{t=1}^{T} a_t/T = 0 \quad \text{and} \quad \sum_{t=1}^{T} b_t/T > 0$$

when return distributions are stationary over time. Thus, like Blume and Friend they were essentially testing whether $E[\tilde{r}_{zc(\hat{m})}] = 0$ and $E[\tilde{r}_m] - E[\tilde{r}_{zc(\hat{m})}] > 0$. They found that the means of both $\hat{a}_t$ and $\hat{b}_t$ were significantly strictly positive, where $\hat{a}_t$ and $\hat{b}_t$ denote estimates of a_t and b_t, respectively.

An example of the third type of test is Black, Jensen and Scholes (1972), who tested the weak prediction that

$$\sum_{j=1}^{N} \frac{\alpha_j}{N(1 - \beta_{j\hat{m}})} = 0.$$

Equivalently, they were testing whether $E[\tilde{r}_{zc(\hat{m})}] = 0$, which they rejected.

Another example of the third type of test is Gibbons (1982), who tested whether

$$\alpha_j = (1 - \beta_{j\hat{m}})E[\tilde{r}_{zc(\hat{m})}], \quad \forall j.$$

The Gibbons' test was a test of whether or not the market proxy portfolio was on the portfolio frontier of the assets included in his sample.

The tests discussed above are closely related. Before discussing them in detail, we will first develop a general framework for analyzing the methods used by these authors.

10.15. In addition to the conceptual problems associated with testing the CAPM, there are three major econometric problems. These problems will be briefly discussed in this and the next two sections and their detailed solutions will be developed in later sections.

The first major econometric problem is that the disturbance terms of (10.13.1) and (10.13.2) are heteroscedastic and correlated across assets, because variances of rates of return differ across assets and asset returns are correlated. Therefore, ordinary least squares (OLS) estimators of a and b and a_t and b_t are inefficient (have higher variances) relative to generalized least square (GLS) estimators. This indicates that tests based on OLS estimators would be less powerful than tests based on GLS estimators. The lower power means that there is a higher probability of failing to reject the null hypotheses that $E[\tilde{r}_{zc(\hat{m})}] = 0$ and $E[\tilde{r}_m] - E[\tilde{r}_{zc(m)}] > 0$ when the alternative hypotheses that $E[\tilde{r}_{zc(m)}] > 0$ and $E[\tilde{r}_m] - E[\tilde{r}_{zc(m)}] \leq 0$ are true. Therefore, empirical findings that reject the null hypotheses cannot be attributed to a lack of power in the testing procedures. Moreover, estimates of the variances of the regression coefficients are biased if standard formula for the OLS estimators are used. Thus, values of the t–statistic given by "canned" OLS regression packages are biased. Note, however, that if the $\beta_{j\hat{m}}$'s are observed without error, the OLS estimators of a and b and a_t and b_t are unbiased.

Possible solutions to the first problem are to use GLS estimators or to use OLS estimators and to calculate the correct variances of the coefficients. The former approach was taken by Litzenberger and Ramaswamy (1978) based on a restricted variance covariance matrix. The latter approach was adopted by Fama and MacBeth (1972), Black, Jensen and Scholes (1972), and Kraus and Litzenberger (1976). These solutions, however, require estimation of the variance–covariance matrix. We will discuss these estimation procedures in considerable detail in later sections.

10.16. The second major econometric problem is that we do not observe the true betas but rather their estimates which contain measurement errors. Under this condition, OLS and GLS estimators of a and b and a_t and b_t are biased and inconsistent. There are three possible solutions to this problem. First, use grouped data to reduce the variances of the measurement errors in betas. Second, use an instrumental variables approach. Third, use an adjusted GLS approach that takes account of the variances of the measurement errors in betas. The first approach was used by Blume and Friend (1973), Fama and Macbeth (1972), Black, Jensen and Scholes (1972), Black and Scholes (1974), and Kraus and Litzenberger (1976) among others. The second approach was used by Rosenberg and Marathe (1979). The third approach was adopted by Litzenberger and Ramaswamy (1979). This problem and alternative solutions will be discussed in considerable detail later in this chapter.

10.17. The third major econometric problem is that the CAPM implies a non–linear constraint on the return generating process as expressed in relation (10.13.3). In testing whether or not a market proxy portfolio is on the portfolio frontier, estimation of betas, variances and covariances should take account of this constraint. However, the constraint itself depends upon the parameters that are to be estimated. This problem can be solved by using a maximum likelihood estimation that takes these interactions into account. This approach was developed by Gibbons (1982) and later extended by Stambaugh (1982), Jobson and Korkie (1982), Kandel (1984), Shanken (1985), and MacKinlay (1987).

10.18. In order to focus on the problems of heteroscedasticity and correlation of the disturbance terms, assume until further notice that the betas are fixed known independent variables observable without error. Also assume that our test sample consists of N assets having linearly independent realized monthly rates of return. When the variance–covariance matrix is estimated using realized monthly rates of return, we require that the number of observations in the sample exceed the number of assets. Under these conditions, the variance–covariance matrix is non–singular. Furthermore, as variances are strictly positive even when portfolio weights do not sum to unity, the variance–covariance matrix is positive definite. We will consider a pooled cross-sectional time–series regression of realized monthly excess rates of return on betas and other independent variables. The other independent variables that have been examined in the literature include residual risk (see Fama and Macbeth (1973)), dividend yield (see Black and Scholes (1972), Litzenberger and Ramaswamy (1979, 1982), and Miller and Scholes (1982)), log of firm size (see Banz (1981), Reinganum (1983) and Schwert (1983)), and systematic skewness (see Kraus and Litzenberger (1978) and Friend and Westerfield (1980)).

10.19. To consider tests of extended forms of the CAPM that involve more than one independent variable, the econometric model is expressed as:

$$\tilde{\mathbf{r}} = \mathbf{X}\mathbf{b} + \tilde{\mathbf{u}},$$
$$E[\tilde{\mathbf{u}}] = \mathbf{0}, \tag{10.19.1}$$

where $\tilde{\mathbf{r}}$ is a $TN \times 1$ vector of monthly random excess rates of return, $\tilde{r}_{jt}$, T is the number of months, N is the number of assets, $\mathbf{b}$ is a $k \times 1$ vector of coefficients, $\mathbf{X}$ is a $TN \times k$ matrix of independent variables, $\tilde{\mathbf{u}}$ is a $TN \times 1$ vector of disturbance terms, and $\mathbf{0}$ is a $T \times N$ vector of zeros. The first column of $\mathbf{X}$ is a column of $1's$, the second column contains the $\beta_{j\hat{m}t}$'s, and the k-th column contains the (k-1)–th independent variable. Note that the betas are allowed to differ each month and that we have used $\beta_{j\hat{m}t}$ to denote the beta of asset j with respect to the market proxy in month t. This is consistent with many studies that use different estimates of betas for each monthly cross–sectional regression. However, betas being constant is consistent with a stationary multivariate distribution of asset returns, and this case will be considered in detail later.

The variance–covariance matrix of the disturbance terms is

$$\mathbf{V} \equiv E[\tilde{\mathbf{u}}\tilde{\mathbf{u}}^\top]$$

$$= \begin{pmatrix} E[\tilde{u}_{11}\tilde{u}_{11}] & E[\tilde{u}_{11}\tilde{u}_{21}] & \cdots & E[\tilde{u}_{11}\tilde{u}_{NT}] \\ E[\tilde{u}_{21}\tilde{u}_{11}] & E[\tilde{u}_{21}\tilde{u}_{21}] & \cdots & E[\tilde{u}_{21}\tilde{u}_{NT}] \\ \vdots & \vdots & \ddots & \vdots \\ E[\tilde{u}_{N1}\tilde{u}_{11}] & E[\tilde{u}_{N1}\tilde{u}_{21}] & \cdots & E[\tilde{u}_{N1}\tilde{u}_{NT}] \\ E[\tilde{u}_{12}\tilde{u}_{11}] & E[\tilde{u}_{12}\tilde{u}_{21}] & \cdots & E[\tilde{u}_{12}\tilde{u}_{NT}] \\ \vdots & \vdots & \ddots & \vdots \\ E[\tilde{u}_{NT}\tilde{u}_{11}] & E[\tilde{u}_{NT}\tilde{u}_{21}] & \cdots & E[\tilde{u}_{NT}\tilde{u}_{NT}] \end{pmatrix}.$$

If $\mathbf{V}$ is known, the GLS estimator of $\mathbf{b}$ is

$$\hat{\mathbf{b}}_{(GLS)} = (\mathbf{X}^\top\mathbf{V}^{-1}\mathbf{X})^{-1}\mathbf{X}^\top\mathbf{V}^{-1}\mathbf{r}. \tag{10.19.2}$$

The variance–covariance matrix of the estimator $\hat{\mathbf{b}}_{(GLS)}$ is

$$\text{Var}(\hat{\mathbf{b}}_{(GLS)}) = (\mathbf{X}^\top \mathbf{V}^{-1} \mathbf{X})^{-1}. \qquad (10.19.3)$$

The OLS estimator of $\mathbf{b}$ is

$$\hat{\mathbf{b}}_{(OLS)} = (\mathbf{X}^\top \mathbf{X})^{-1} \mathbf{X}^\top \mathbf{r}. \qquad (10.19.4)$$

The variance–covariance matrix of $\hat{\mathbf{b}}_{(OLS)}$ is

$$\text{Var}(\hat{\mathbf{b}}_{(OLS)}) = (\mathbf{X}^\top \mathbf{X})^{-1} \mathbf{X}^\top \mathbf{V} \mathbf{X} (\mathbf{X}^\top \mathbf{X})^{-1}. \qquad (10.19.5)$$

The GLS estimator of (10.19.2) reduces to the OLS estimator of (10.19.5) when the OLS assumption on the disturbance terms that

$$\mathbf{V} = \sigma_u^2 \mathbf{I}_{TN} \qquad (10.19.6)$$

for some $\sigma_u^2 > 0$ is satisfied, where $\mathbf{I}_{TN}$ is the $TN \times TN$ identity matrix. It can be verified that if (10.19.6) is not true, then the diagonal elements of $\text{Var}(\hat{\mathbf{b}}_{(OLS)})$ is greater than the corresponding diagonal elements of $\text{Var}(\hat{\mathbf{b}}_{(GLS)})$, and thus OLS estimators are not efficient compared to GLS estimators.

   For expositional purposes, the analysis in most of this chapter will be done under the assumption that there are two independent variables so that $\mathbf{b}$ is a 3×1 vector and $\mathbf{X}$ is a $TN \times 3$ matrix whose second and third column are vectors of the two independent variables. The second independent variable will henceforth be referred to as the dividend yield, for convenience, and the dividend yield for security j at time t will be denoted by d_{jt}. In this case, we can write

$$\tilde{\mathbf{r}} = \begin{pmatrix} \tilde{r}_{11} \\ \tilde{r}_{21} \\ \vdots \\ \tilde{r}_{NT} \end{pmatrix}, \mathbf{b} = \begin{pmatrix} b_0 \\ b_1 \\ b_2 \end{pmatrix}, \mathbf{X} = \begin{pmatrix} 1 & \beta_{1\hat{m}1} & d_{11} \\ 1 & \beta_{2\hat{m}1} & d_{21} \\ \vdots & \vdots & \vdots \\ 1 & \beta_{N\hat{m}T} & d_{NT} \end{pmatrix}, \tilde{\mathbf{u}} = \begin{pmatrix} \tilde{u}_{11} \\ \tilde{u}_{21} \\ \vdots \\ \tilde{u}_{NT} \end{pmatrix}.$$

Our discussion will not be changed if the second independent variable is residual risk, the log of firm size, or systematic skewness.

   Note that in practice the true variance–covariance matrix is unknown and its elements are estimated using realized excess rates of return. In small samples, GLS estimators based on an estimated variance–covariance matrix are not necessarily more efficient than OLS estimators. However, as the number of months in the sample increases $(T \to \infty)$, the estimates of the variances and covariances based on time–series data approach the true variances and covariances. Thus, GLS estimators based on time–series estimates of variances and covariances are said to be *asymptotically efficient*. Note that asymptotic efficiency is achieved as the number of time periods approaches infinity, not as the number of assets approaches infinity. As the number of months in the sample increases to infinity, the sample distribution of asset returns approaches the true underlying distribution.

10.20. We will assume that excess rates of return are serially uncorrelated, which is consistent with most empirical work. Therefore, $\mathbf{V}$ is a block diagonal matrix, and its inverse, $\mathbf{V}^{-1}$, may be expressed as

$$\mathbf{V}^{-1} = \begin{pmatrix} \mathbf{V}_1^{-1} & \cdots & 0 & \cdots & 0 \\ \vdots & \ddots & \vdots & \ddots & \vdots \\ 0 & \cdots & \mathbf{V}_t^{-1} & \cdots & 0 \\ \vdots & \ddots & \vdots & \ddots & \vdots \\ 0 & \cdots & 0 & \cdots & \mathbf{V}_T^{-1} \end{pmatrix},$$

where $\mathbf{V}_t^{-1}$ denotes the inverse of the period t variance–covariance matrix of asset returns. The element in the j–th row and k–th column of $\mathbf{V}_t$ is the covariance of the excess rates of return on the j–th and k–th asset at time t. Because $\mathbf{V}$ is block diagonal, separate GLS regressions may be run cross–sectionally using data in each period, and the pooled time–series cross–sectional GLS estimates that are based on a combined sample of monthly observations for all months and on model (10.19.1) are weighted averages of the individual period estimates. The weights are proportional to the variances of the individual period estimates.

Formally, consider the period t sub–model of the two independent variable version of (10.19.1):

$$\tilde{\mathbf{r}}_t = \mathbf{X}_t \mathbf{b}_t + \tilde{\mathbf{u}}_t, \tag{10.20.1}$$

where

$$\tilde{\mathbf{r}}_t = \begin{pmatrix} \tilde{r}_{1t} \\ \tilde{r}_{2t} \\ \vdots \\ \tilde{r}_{Nt} \end{pmatrix}, \mathbf{b}_t = \begin{pmatrix} b_{0t} \\ b_{1t} \\ b_{2t} \end{pmatrix}, \mathbf{X}_t = \begin{pmatrix} 1 & \beta_{1\hat{m}t} & d_{1t} \\ 1 & \beta_{2\hat{m}t} & d_{2t} \\ \vdots & \vdots & \vdots \\ 1 & \beta_{N\hat{m}t} & d_{Nt} \end{pmatrix}, \tilde{\mathbf{u}}_t = \begin{pmatrix} \tilde{u}_{1t} \\ \tilde{u}_{2t} \\ \vdots \\ \tilde{u}_{Nt} \end{pmatrix}$$

The GLS estimator of $\mathbf{b}_t$, denoted by $\mathbf{b}_{t(GLS)}$, is

$$\hat{\mathbf{b}}_{t(GLS)} \equiv (\mathbf{X}_t^\top \mathbf{V}_t^{-1} \mathbf{X}_t)^{-1} \mathbf{X}_t^\top \mathbf{V}_t^{-1} \mathbf{r}_t. \qquad (10.20.2)$$

The variance–covariance matrix of the estimator is

$$\mathrm{Var}(\hat{\mathbf{b}}_{t(GLS)}) = (\mathbf{X}_t^\top \mathbf{V}_t^{-1} \mathbf{X}_t)^{-1}. \qquad (10.20.3)$$

Note that, similar to the discussion in Section 10.19, when $\mathbf{V}_t = \sigma_{u_t}^2 \mathbf{I}_N$ for some $\sigma_{u_t}^2 > 0$, where $\mathbf{I}_N$ is the $N \times N$ identity matrix, the GLS estimator of (10.20.2) reduces to an OLS estimator. Note also that when $\mathbf{V}_t$ is stationary over time, its elements can be estimated by the time–series variances and covariances of the excess rates of return on assets.

Denoting by $\hat{b}_{kt(GLS)}$ the k–th element of $\hat{\mathbf{b}}_{t(GLS)}$ and by $\hat{b}_{k(GLS)}$ the k–th element of $\hat{\mathbf{b}}_{(GLS)}$, it is easily verified that

$$\hat{b}_{k(GLS)} = \sum_{t=1}^{T} w_t \hat{b}_{kt(GLS)}, \qquad (10.20.4)$$

where

$$w_t = \cfrac{1}{\cfrac{\mathrm{Var}(\hat{b}_{kt(GLS)})}{\sum_{t=1}^{T} (1/\mathrm{Var}(\hat{b}_{kt(GLS)}))}}. \qquad (10.20.5)$$

The variance of $\hat{b}_{k(GLS)}$, denoted by $\mathrm{Var}(\hat{b}_{k(GLS)})$, can be verified to be

$$\mathrm{Var}(\hat{b}_{k(GLS)}) = \sum_{t=1}^{T} w_t^2 \mathrm{Var}(\hat{b}_{kt(GLS)}).$$

Note that the w_t's of (10.20.5) are the positive weights on the $\hat{b}_{kt(GLS)}$'s that minimize the variance of the linear combination of the

$\hat{b}_{kt(GLS)}$'s on the right–hand side of (10.20.4). Note also that when $\text{Var}(\hat{b}_{kt(GLS)})$ is a constant over time, $w_t = 1/T$ and the estimates of the pooled model of (10.19.1) are simple averages of the separate monthly estimates. That is,

$$\hat{b}_{k(GLS)} = \sum_{t=1}^{T} \frac{\hat{b}_{kt(GLS)}}{T}. \qquad (10.20.6)$$

Moreover, we have in this case,

$$\text{Var}(\hat{b}_{k(GLS)}) = \frac{\text{Var}(\hat{b}_{kt(GLS)})}{T}. \qquad (10.20.7)$$

Note from (10.20.3) that $\text{Var}(\hat{\mathbf{b}}_t)$ is a constant over time if $\mathbf{X}_t$ and $\mathbf{V}_t$ are time stationary. Indeed, this will be the case in point in Exercises 10.6.2–10.6.4.

Blume and Friend (1973) applied OLS to the cross–sectional relation between time–series average excess rates of return and betas of (10.13.1) but relied on a "canned" OLS program to generate the variances. Thus, they obtained estimates of a and b which would be unbiased in the absence of measurement error but obtained biased t–statistics. In contrast, Fama and Macbeth (1973) applied OLS to monthly excess rates of return and betas by using (10.13.2) for each month. They then calculated the time–series means of the regression coefficients and their time–series variances. Except for small monthly differences in betas, the average of the estimates of a_t's and b_t's would be identical to the estimates of a and b of Blume and Friend (1973). However, the estimators of the variances of the OLS estimators of b in Fama and Macbeth (1973) take account of the full variance–covariance matrix. Although emphasizing a time–series based interpretation, Black, Jensen and Scholes (1972) also obtained OLS estimates of a_t's and calculated their time–series mean and variance. They found that a was strictly positive and statistically significant. In Exercise 10.2, the reader is asked to verify that the Black, Jensen and Scholes estimator of the intercept term a is identical to that given in (10.20.6) and that their estimator of its variance is identical to that given in (10.20.7).

10.21. The relationship between portfolio theory and the linear regression model is helpful in interpreting tests of the CAPM. We will see that the GLS procedure is identical to a portfolio problem. This follows as any linear estimator is a linear combination of the observations of the dependent variable. Since the dependent variable is the excess rate of return, a GLS estimator of a regression coefficient is the excess rate of return on a portfolio (whose weights sum to either zero or unity depending on the parameters estimated). It is well known that GLS estimators are BLUE (for Best Linear Unbiased Estimators). The "best" means that a GLS estimator has the minimum variance among all the linear unbiased estimators. Thus, each coefficient in (10.20.1) is estimated as the linear combination of the securities excess rates of return that has minimum variance subject to the unbiasedness condition. The unbiasedness condition is that the expected value of the estimator be equal to the true value of the coefficient of interest.

The estimator for b_{kt} is identical to the rate of return on a portfolio obtained by solving the following portfolio problem in month t:

$$\min_{\{w_{jt}; j=1,2,\ldots,N\}} \sum_{j=1}^{N} \sum_{l=1}^{N} w_{jt} w_{lt} \sigma_{jlt}$$

$$\text{s.t. } E\left[\sum_{j=1}^{N} w_{jt} \tilde{r}_{jt}\right] = b_{kt}, \tag{10.21.1}$$

where w_{jt} denotes the portfolio weight on asset j at time t and σ_{jlt} denotes the covariance at time t of excess rates of return on securities j and l.

Using the two independent variables model of Section 10.19 and the definition of a linear estimator, the unbiasedness constraints for the coefficients of the two independent variables are implemented as follows: First, we note that

$$\sum_{j=1}^{N} w_{jt} \tilde{r}_{jt} = b_{0t} \sum_{j=1}^{N} w_{jt} + b_{1t} \sum_{j=1}^{N} w_{jt} \beta_{j\hat{m}t}$$

$$+ b_{2t} \sum_{j=1}^{N} w_{jt} d_{jt} + \sum_{j=1}^{N} w_{jt} \tilde{u}_{jt}. \tag{10.21.2}$$

The unbiasedness constraint on the coefficient for betas is

$$E[\sum_{j=1}^{N} w_{jt}\tilde{r}_{jt}] = b_{1t},$$

or, equivalently,

$$b_{0t}\sum_{j=1}^{N} w_{jt} + b_{1t}\sum_{j=1}^{N} w_{jt}\beta_{j\hat{m}t} + b_{2t}\sum_{j=1}^{N} w_{jt}d_{jt} = b_{1t}, \qquad (10.21.3)$$

where we have used the fact that the disturbance terms have zero expectations. For (10.21.3) to hold for arbitrary betas and dividend yields, it is necessary and sufficient that

$$\sum_{j=1}^{N} w_{jt} = 0, \quad \sum_{j=1}^{N} w_{jt}\beta_{j\hat{m}t} = 1, \quad \text{and} \quad \sum_{j=1}^{N} w_{jt}d_{jt} = 0. \quad (10.21.4)$$

Therefore, (10.21.1) is equivalent to minimizing the same objective function as in (10.21.1) subject to the constraints of (10.21.4). Note that $\sum_{j=1}^{N} w_{jt} = 0$ implies that the "portfolio" is a self–financing portfolio; $\sum_{j=1}^{N} w_{jt}\beta_{j\hat{m}t} = 1$ implies that the "portfolio" has unit beta with respect to the proxy; and $\sum_{j=1}^{N} w_{jt}d_{jt} = 0$ implies that this "portfolio" has a zero dividend yield. Of all feasible self–financing portfolios meeting these conditions, the portfolio with the smallest variance would be the one that meets the efficiency property of a GLS estimator. The corresponding unbiasedness conditions for the coefficient on the dividend yield are

$$\sum_{j=1}^{N} w_{jt} = 0, \quad \sum_{j=1}^{N} w_{jt}\beta_{j\hat{m}t} = 0, \quad \text{and} \quad \sum_{j=1}^{N} w_{jt}d_{jt} = 1. \quad (10.21.5)$$

The corresponding unbiasedness conditions for b_{0t} are

$$\sum_{j=1}^{N} w_{jt} = 1, \quad \sum_{j=1}^{N} w_{jt}\beta_{j\hat{m}t} = 0, \quad \text{and} \quad \sum_{j} w_{jt}d_{jt} = 0. \quad (10.21.6)$$

In words, the GLS estimate of b_{2t} is the excess rate of return on a
self–financing portfolio that has zero beta and unit dividend yield
and that of b_{0t} is the excess rate of return on a "normal" portfolio
that has zero beta and zero dividend yield. The standard deviations
of the rates of return on these portfolios are, of course, the standard
deviations of the estimated coefficients.

To understand the intuition behind the analogy between the
GLS procedure and a portfolio problem recall that the GLS estimators are the best linear unbiased estimators. Since we have no prior
knowledge of the betas and the dividend yields, unbiasedness can
only be assured by the constraints of (10.21.4)–(10.21.6). The best
linear unbiased estimator is the excess rate of return on the minimum
variance portfolio that meets those constraints.

10.22. In the GLS procedure discussed above, it was assumed
that V_t is known. In practice, the variance–covariance matrix of
asset returns is not known and must be estimated. To simplify this
estimation, it can be assumed that the variance–covariance matrix
has a certain special structure and the GLS estimation is then said to
be based on a restricted variance–covariance matrix. In this section,
we discuss a special structure of the variances and covariances of
asset returns – the *single index model*.

We will assume, throughout this section, that betas, variances,
and covariances are stationary over time so we will drop their time
subscripts. Assume also that excess rates of return on assets satisfy

$$\tilde{r}_{jt} = \alpha_j + \beta_{j\hat{m}}\tilde{r}_{\hat{m}t} + \tilde{e}_{jt}, \quad \forall t = 1, 2, \ldots, T,$$

$$\mathrm{Cov}(\tilde{e}_{jt}, \tilde{e}_{kt}) = \begin{cases} 0, & \text{for } j \neq k, \\ \sigma_{e_j}^2 & \text{for } j = k. \end{cases} \tag{10.22.1}$$

Note that $\sigma_{e_j}^2$ is independent of t. Under the assumption of the
single index model, the covariances among individual asset returns
are explained by their common covariances with the market index:

$$\sigma_{jk} = \begin{cases} \beta_{j\hat{m}}\beta_{k\hat{m}}\sigma_{\hat{m}}^2 & \text{if } j \neq k; \\ \beta_{j\hat{m}}^2\sigma_{\hat{m}}^2 + \sigma_{e_j}^2 & \text{if } j = k; \end{cases} \tag{10.22.2}$$

where $\sigma_{\hat{m}}^2$ is the time stationary variance of the rate of return on the market proxy. From (10.22.2), we can see that the variance–covariance matrix is completely specified by knowledge of the $\beta_{j\hat{m}}$'s, $\sigma_{\hat{m}}^2$, and the $\sigma_{e_j}^2$'s.

The single index model is an overly simplified model of the return generating process. If $\tilde{r}_{\hat{m}t}$ is a linear combination of the $\tilde{r}_{jt}$'s, this linear combination will not have a disturbance term. That is, a linear combination of the $\tilde{e}_{jt}$'s will be identically equal to zero. This means that covariances of asset returns cannot all be zero and contradicts (10.20.1). However, this assumption greatly reduces the amount of information required in the estimation process. An alternative procedure is to use a multiple index model incorporating industry specific indices in addition to the market index.

The variance of a linear estimator in the context of the single index model may be expressed as

$$\text{Var}(\sum_{j=1}^{N} w_{jt}\tilde{r}_{jt}) = \sum_{j=1}^{N} w_{jt}^2(\beta_{j\hat{m}}^2\sigma_{\hat{m}}^2 + \sigma_{e_j}^2) + \sum_{j=1}^{N}\sum_{k\neq j} w_{jt}w_{kt}(\beta_{j\hat{m}}\beta_{k\hat{m}}\sigma_{\hat{m}}^2)$$

$$= (\sum_{j=1}^{N} w_{jt}\beta_{j\hat{m}})^2\sigma_{\hat{m}}^2 + \sum_{j=1}^{N} w_{jt}^2\sigma_{e_j}^2.$$

Thus, the problem of minimizing the variance of an estimator reduces to the minimization of $\sum_{j=1}^{N} w_{jt}^2\sigma_{e_j}^2$, because the unbiasedness condition necessitates that $\sum_{j=1} w_{jt}\beta_{j\hat{m}} = 1$ or 0 depending on the coefficient being estimated. Note that when the assumption of a single index model is not made, an additional term involving the covariance of the disturbance terms,

$$\sum_{j=1}^{N}\sum_{k\neq j} w_{jt}w_{kt}\sigma_{e_je_k},$$

must be added, where $\sigma_{e_je_k}$ denotes the time stationary covariance of $\tilde{e}_{jt}$ and $\tilde{e}_{kt}$. When the assumption that $\sigma_{e_j}^2 = \sigma_e^2$, a constant, is made, a GLS estimator reduces to an OLS estimator. This is the case considered by Black and Scholes (1972), where the independent variables are betas and dividend yields.

10.23. We have discussed the estimation procedure for the model (10.20.1) for general $\mathbf{V}_t$. When $\mathbf{V}_t$ is a diagonal matrix, GLS estimators for the model (10.20.1) may be obtained by making a simple heteroscedasticity correction and using OLS. This is accomplished by deflating the excess rate of return, beta, and dividend yield of an asset by the standard deviation of its disturbance term, $\sigma_{u_{jt}}$. Note that this involves an OLS regression with the constant term suppressed. This procedure is a *weighted least squares regression* (WLS), where the weights are the standard deviations of the disturbance term of each asset. When $\sigma_{u_{jt}}$ is constant across assets, this estimator is, of course, identical to the OLS estimator with the undeflated variable and a constant term. The WLS estimators are

$$\hat{\mathbf{b}}_{t(WLS)} = (\mathbf{X}_t^{*\top}\mathbf{X}_t^*)^{-1}\mathbf{X}_t^{*\top}\mathbf{r}_t^*, \qquad (10.23.1)$$

where

$$\mathbf{r}_t^* = \begin{pmatrix} r_{1t}/\sigma_{u_{1t}} \\ \vdots \\ r_{Nt}/\sigma_{u_{Nt}} \end{pmatrix} \quad \text{and} \quad \mathbf{X}_t^* = \begin{pmatrix} \frac{1}{\sigma_{u_{1t}}} & \frac{\beta_{1\dot{m}t}}{\sigma_{u_{1t}}} & \frac{d_{1t}}{\sigma_{u_{1t}}} \\ \vdots & \vdots & \vdots \\ \frac{1}{\sigma_{u_{Nt}}} & \frac{\beta_{N\dot{m}t}}{\sigma_{u_{Nt}}} & \frac{d_{Nt}}{\sigma_{u_{Nt}}} \end{pmatrix}.$$

Note that in this case

$$\mathbf{u}_t^* = \begin{pmatrix} u_{1t}/\sigma_{u_{1t}} \\ \vdots \\ u_{Nt}/\sigma_{u_{Nt}} \end{pmatrix}$$

and

$$E(\mathbf{u}_t^*\mathbf{u}_t^{*\top}) = \mathbf{I}_N,$$

where as usual $\mathbf{I}_N$ denotes the $N \times N$ identity matrix.

Note also that by the definition of $\mathbf{X}_t^*$ and $\mathbf{r}_t^*$ and the assumption that $\mathbf{V}_t$ is diagonal, we have

$$(\mathbf{X}_t^\top\mathbf{V}_t^{-1}\mathbf{X}_t)^{-1}\mathbf{X}_t^\top\mathbf{V}_t^{-1}\mathbf{r}_t = (\mathbf{X}_t^{*\top}\mathbf{X}_t^*)^{-1}\mathbf{X}_t^{*\top}\mathbf{r}_t^*. \qquad (10.23.2)$$

Recall the left–hand side of (10.23.2) is the GLS estimator of $\mathbf{b}_t$ given in (10.20.2), and the left–hand side is the WLS estimator of $\mathbf{b}_t$ given in (10.23.1). Thus, the WLS estimator are identical to the GLS estimator when the variance–covariance matrix is restricted to be diagonal.

10.24. The previous analysis treated the betas as a fixed independent variable observable without error. In actuality, only estimates of the true betas are available. Even if the estimates of betas are unbiased, the resulting OLS or GLS estimators of the coefficients would be biased. Moreover, the OLS or GLS estimators are inconsistent. These problems will be discussed in the following sections.

10.25. Consider the case of a single independent variable. Assume that the cross–sectional model we desire to estimate for month t is

$$\tilde{r}_{jt} = a_t + b_t \beta_{j\hat{m}t} + \tilde{u}_{jt}, \qquad j = 1, 2, \ldots, N. \tag{10.25.1}$$

However, instead of using the unobservable true beta, $\beta_{j\hat{m}t}$, we use an unbiased estimate, $\hat{\beta}_{j\hat{m}t}$. To simplify the discussion, assume that an equally weighted index of the N assets used in the test is used as the market proxy and that (10.25.1) satisfies the OLS assumption that $E[\tilde{u}_t \tilde{u}_t^T] = \sigma_u^2 I_N$ throughout our discussion about the measurement errors.

The equally weighted average of the excess rates of return on these N assets would obviously equal the excess rate of return on the market index, that is, $\sum_{j=1}^{N} r_{jt}/N = r_{\hat{m}t}$. Furthermore, because covariances are additive, the equally weighted average of the betas (both true and estimated) of the N assets used in the test is equal to unity, that is, $\sum_{j=1}^{N} \beta_{j\hat{m}t}/N = 1$. The case of a value weighted market index would not change the conclusions substantively.

The OLS estimate of b_t is

$$\hat{b}_{t(OLS)} = \frac{\sum_{j=1}^{N}(r_{jt} - r_{\hat{m}t})(\hat{\beta}_{j\hat{m}t} - 1)}{\sum_{j=1}^{N}(\hat{\beta}_{j\hat{m}t} - 1)^2}. \tag{10.25.2}$$

The estimated beta, $\hat{\beta}_{j\hat{m}t}$, may be expressed as the true beta, $\beta_{j\hat{m}t}$, plus a measurement error, $\tilde{v}_{jt}$,

$$\hat{\beta}_{j\hat{m}t} = \beta_{j\hat{m}t} + \tilde{v}_{jt}. \tag{10.25.3}$$

Since $\hat{\beta}_{j\hat{m}t}$ is unbiased,

$$E[\tilde{v}_{jt}] = 0, \quad j = 1, 2, \ldots, N. \tag{10.25.4}$$

Before we proceed, substitute the right hand side of (10.25.3) for $\hat{\beta}_{jm}$ in (10.25.2) to get

$$\hat{b}_{t(OLS)} = \frac{\sum_{j=1}^{N} \frac{(r_{jt}-r_{\hat{m}t})(\beta_{j\hat{m}t}-1)}{N} + \sum_{j=1}^{N} \frac{(r_{jt}-r_{\hat{m}t})v_{jt}}{N}}{\sum_{j=1}^{N} \frac{(\beta_{j\hat{m}t}-1)^2}{N} + \sum_{j=1}^{N} \frac{v_{jt}^2}{N} + \sum_{j=1}^{N} \frac{2(\beta_{j\hat{m}t}-1)v_{jt}}{N}}.$$

$$(10.25.5)$$

Our purpose now is to show that even under a set of plausible assumptions about the measurement errors, $\hat{b}_{t(OLS)}$ is inconsistent. We will take probability limit of (10.25.5) when the number of assets included in the sample goes to infinity. Note that as the number of assets in the sample increases, the equally weighted index and the corresponding asset betas will change. We will not, however, denote this dependence for notational simplicity.

We will make the following plausible assumptions about $\tilde{v}_{jt}$:

$$E[\tilde{v}_{jt}\tilde{v}_{kt}] \begin{cases} = 0 & \text{if } j \neq k, \\ \leq \bar{\sigma}_{vt}^2 < \infty & \text{if } j = k, \end{cases} \qquad (10.25.6)$$

$$\text{Cov}(\tilde{v}_{jt}, \tilde{u}_{kt}) = 0 \quad \forall j, k. \qquad (10.25.7)$$

$$\text{Var}(\tilde{v}_{jt}^2) \leq \bar{\sigma}_{vt}^4, \ j = 1, 2, \ldots \qquad (10.25.8)$$

Note that $\bar{\sigma}_{vt}^2$ and $\bar{\sigma}_{vt}^4$ are upper bounds of $\text{Var}(\tilde{v}_{jt})$ and $\text{Var}(\tilde{v}_{jt}^2)$ across assets, respectively. Relations (10.25.6) and (10.25.7) basically say that measurement errors are cross sectionally uncorrelated and are uncorrelated with the disturbance terms. We will further assume that

$$\lim_{N \to \infty} \frac{\sum_{j=1}^{N} \beta_{j\hat{m}t}^2}{N^2} = 0. \qquad (10.25.9)$$

That is, the sum of the squares of true betas increases more slowly than the square of the sample size as the sample size goes to infinity. Note that a sufficient condition for (10.25.9) is that the true betas are uniformly bounded as the the number of assets in the sample goes to infinity.

In Exercise 10.3, we ask the reader to demonstrate that relations (10.25.4) and (10.25.6)–(10.25.9) imply

$$\plim_{N \to \infty} \frac{\sum_{j=1}^{N} (\tilde{r}_{jt} - \tilde{r}_{\hat{m}t})\tilde{v}_{jt}}{N} = 0, \qquad (10.25.10)$$

$$\plim_{N\to\infty} \frac{\sum_{j=1}^{N} \beta_{j\hat{m}t}\tilde{v}_{jt}}{N} = 0, \qquad (10.25.11)$$

$$\plim_{N\to\infty} \frac{\sum_{j=1}^{N} \tilde{v}_{jt}}{N} = 0, \qquad (10.25.12)$$

and

$$\plim_{N\to\infty} \frac{\sum_{j=1}^{N} \tilde{v}_{jt}^2}{N} = \lim_{N\to\infty} \frac{\sum_{j=1}^{N} \text{Var}(\tilde{v}_{jt})}{N}, \qquad (10.25.13)$$

respectively. Now define

$$\overline{\text{Var}}(\beta_t) \equiv \lim_{N\to\infty} \frac{\sum_{j=1}^{N}(\beta_{j\hat{m}t} - 1)^2}{N}, \qquad (10.25.14)$$

the asymptotic sample variation of the true betas. We assume that $\overline{\text{Var}}(\beta_t) \neq 0$. Taking the probability limit of (10.25.5) by using (10.25.10)–(10.25.13) gives

$$\plim_{N\to\infty} \hat{b}_{t(OLS)} = \frac{b_t}{1 + \frac{\overline{\text{Var}}(\tilde{v}_t)}{\overline{\text{Var}}(\beta_t)}}, \qquad (10.25.15)$$

where

$$\overline{\text{Var}}(\tilde{v}_t) \equiv \lim_{N\to\infty} \frac{\sum_{j=1}^{N} \text{Var}(\tilde{v}_{jt})}{N}. \qquad (10.25.16)$$

Thus, $\hat{b}_{t(OLS)}$ is not a consistent estimator of b_t. From (10.25.15), we see that the magnitude of inconsistency can be improved either when $\overline{\text{Var}}(\tilde{v}_t)$ is small or $\overline{\text{Var}}(\beta_t)$ is large.

The OLS estimator of a_t is

$$\hat{a}_{t(OLS)} \equiv r_{\hat{m}t} - \hat{b}_{t(OLS)}.$$

Moreover, since $\hat{b}_{t(OLS)}$ is not consistent, $\hat{a}_{t(OLS)}$ is not either.

10.26. There are at least three approaches to the problem of measurement errors in the betas. The first approach groups assets into portfolios. Under the assumption that the measurement errors are uncorrelated across assets, the variance of the measurement errors for the portfolio betas would approach zero as the number of

assets in each portfolio increases. The second approach is an instrumental variables approach, in which an instrumental variable that
is highly correlated with the true beta but uncorrelated with the
measurement errors is used to obtain consistent estimators of a_t and
b_t. The third approach estimates the variances of the measurement
errors and subtracts the average variance of the measurement error from the cross–sectional sample variation of the estimated betas.
These approaches will be developed in Sections 10.27 to 10.32.

10.27. The most frequently used approach to the problem of
measurement errors in variables is grouping assets into portfolios. If
the measurement errors associated with the betas satisfy (10.25.5)
and are uncorrelated with the criterion used to group the assets into
portfolios, the variance of the measurement errors associated with
the portfolio betas approaches zero as the number of assets in the
portfolios increases. It then follows from (10.25.15) that $\hat{b}_{t(OLS)}$ will
be consistent. To see this, note that the variance of the measurement
error of the beta for portfolio g consisting of L assets is

$$\text{Var}(\tilde{v}_{gt}) = \sum_{j=1}^{L} \frac{\text{Var}(\tilde{v}_{jt})}{L^2} \leq \frac{\bar{\sigma}_{vt}^2}{L}.$$

Then

$$\lim_{L \to \infty} \text{Var}(\tilde{v}_{gt}) \leq \bar{\sigma}_{vt}^2 \lim_{L \to \infty} \frac{1}{L} = 0.$$

However, when measurement errors associated with beta estimates are correlated, grouping would only asymptotically reduce the
variance of the measurement error of the group beta and cannot
eliminate it even in the limit. Empirically, the estimates of betas for
large portfolios of assets have non–trivial variances. This indicates
that grouping cannot make OLS estimators of (10.25.1) consistent
estimators. It can only reduce the magnitude of inconsistency of
OLS estimators.

10.28. The grouping procedure discussed in Section 10.27 reduces the magnitude of inconsistency resulting from measurement
errors. It, however, causes a loss of efficiency of the estimators. To

see this, assume that the N assets are divided into G mutually exclusive groups with L assets in each group. Let g be an index denoting the group to which an asset belongs. The group excess rate of return, $\tilde{r}_{gt}$, is a simple average of those of the individual assets contained in the group,

$$\tilde{r}_{gt} = \sum_{j=1}^{L} \frac{\tilde{r}_{gjt}}{L}.$$

Since covariances are additive, the beta of a group is also equal to the average of betas of the individual assets contained in the group,

$$\beta_{g\hat{m}t} = \sum_{j=1}^{L} \frac{\beta_{gj\hat{m}t}}{L},$$

and similarly for the estimate of a group beta,

$$\hat{\beta}_{g\hat{m}t} = \sum_{j=1}^{L} \frac{\hat{\beta}_{gj\hat{m}t}}{L}.$$

The OLS estimator of b_t based on individual (ungrouped) data and estimates of betas is

$$\hat{b}_{t(OLS)} \equiv \frac{\sum_{g=1}^{G} \sum_{j=1}^{L} (\tilde{r}_{gjt} - \tilde{r}_{\hat{m}t})(\hat{\beta}_{gj\hat{m}t} - 1)}{\sum_{g=1}^{G} \sum_{j=1}^{L} (\hat{\beta}_{gj\hat{m}t} - 1)^2}, \qquad (10.28.1)$$

and the variance of $\hat{b}_{t(OLS)}$ (under the OLS assumption of homoscedasticity and uncorrelated disturbance terms) is

$$\text{Var}(\hat{b}_{t(OLS)}) \equiv \frac{\sigma_{u_t}^2}{\sum_{g=1}^{G} \sum_{j=1}^{L} (\hat{\beta}_{gj\hat{m}t} - 1)^2}, \qquad (10.28.2)$$

where $\sigma_{u_t}^2$ is the variance of $\tilde{u}_{jt}$ for all j. Note that the variance of the estimator is inversely proportional to the total cross–sectional variation in the estimated betas.

Now consider the OLS estimator of b_t based on the group returns and estimated group betas,

$$\hat{b}_{t(OLS)}^{G} \equiv \frac{\sum_{g=1}^{G} (r_{gt} - r_{\hat{m}t})(\hat{\beta}_{g\hat{m}t} - 1)}{\sum_{g=1}^{G} (\hat{\beta}_{g\hat{m}t} - 1)^2}, \qquad (10.28.3)$$

where $\hat{\beta}_{g\hat{m}t}$ is an estimate of $\beta_{g\hat{m}t}$. Note that under the assumption of uncorrelated disturbance terms for individual assets, the variance of the disturbance term of $\tilde{r}_{gt}$ is inversely proportional to the number of assets in each group. Therefore, the variance of the OLS estimator of b_t based on the group returns and estimated group betas is

$$\text{Var}(\hat{b}_{t(OLS)}^G) \equiv \frac{\sigma_{\tilde{u}t}^2/L}{\sum_{g=1}^{G}(\hat{\beta}_{g\hat{m}t} - 1)^2}. \tag{10.28.4}$$

Thus, the relative efficiency of the OLS estimators based on grouped and ungrouped observations is equal to the ratio of the between group variation in estimated betas to the total variation in estimated betas:

$$\frac{\text{Var}(\hat{b}_{t(OLS)})}{\text{Var}(\hat{b}_{t(OLS)}^G)} = \frac{L\sum_{g=1}^{G}(\hat{\beta}_{g\hat{m}t} - 1)^2}{\sum_{g=1}^{G}\sum_{j=1}^{L}(\hat{\beta}_{gj\hat{m}t} - 1)^2}. \tag{10.28.5}$$

This ratio is less than unity, because the total variation in estimated betas is equal to the sum of the between group variation and the within group variation in the estimated betas:

$$\sum_{g=1}^{G}\sum_{j=1}^{L}(\hat{\beta}_{gj\hat{m}t} - 1)^2$$

$$= L\sum_{g=1}^{G}(\hat{\beta}_{gmt} - 1)^2 + \sum_{g=1}^{G}\sum_{j=1}^{L}(\hat{\beta}_{gj\hat{m}t} - \hat{\beta}_{g\hat{m}t})^2, \tag{10.28.6}$$

where the first term on the right–hand side is the between group variation and the second term is the within group variation. It follows that grouping always results in a loss of efficiency.

Assuming a given group size, the loss of efficiency is minimized by using a criterion for placing the assets into groups that maximizes the between group variation. Note that random assignment of the assets into groups may minimize the between group variation and result in the greatest loss of efficiency. Forming groups by ranking assets using the independent variable, the true beta, would minimize the within group variation and thereby maximize the between group variation and minimize the loss of efficiency. For example, rank assets according to betas and divide them into ten groups. The first group is composed of assets having betas among the top 10%, the tenth group is composed of assets having betas among the lowest 10%, etc. However, the true betas are unobservable and the estimates of betas contain measurement errors. Rankings of assets based on estimated betas will be correlated with measurement errors, and the variance of the measurement errors will not go to zero as the number of assets in each group approaches infinity. For instance, consider the extreme case where the true betas were equal, then the rankings based on estimated betas would be perfectly correlated with the measurement errors.

The ideal way to rank assets is to use a criterion that is highly correlated with the true betas but uncorrelated with the measurement errors. The use of a criterion that is highly correlated with the true betas will result in substantial between group variation in the true betas. The use of a criterion that is uncorrelated with the measurement errors in estimated betas will result in the within group measurement errors being uncorrelated across assets and the variance of the measurement error of the group beta approaching zero when the number of assets in the group approaches infinity. Non–contemporaneous estimates of betas calculated using time–series of individual asset returns that do not overlap with the time–series of returns used to calculate the estimated group betas are an ideal instrument for ranking assets into groups. Measurement errors in betas calculated over non–overlapping periods should be uncorrelated, because asset returns are serially uncorrelated. Empirically, estimated betas calculated from non–overlapping periods have a statistically significant correlation, which is consistent with a stationary distribution of asset returns. The grouping procedures used by Blume and Friend (1973), Fama and Macbeth (1973), and Black and Jensen and Scholes (1973) were based on non–contemporaneous beta estimates. This procedure is consistent with the assumption of stationary unconditional betas. The loss of efficiency through grouping based on historical betas is quite small.

10.29. The errors in variables problem when there are two or more independent variables but only one of them is subject to measurement error is quite similar to the single independent variable case. However, previous statements concerning the cross–sectional sample variation in the independent variable relate instead to the cross–sectional sample variation in a given independent variable that is orthogonal to (uncorrelated with) the cross–sectional sample variation in the other independent variables. That is, the regression coefficient on a given independent variable in an OLS multiple regression is equal to the regression coefficient in a simple OLS regression on the same independent variable orthogonalized using the other independent variables. Consider the case of two independent variables, estimated betas and dividend yields. Only the estimated betas are subject to measurement error. The orthogonalization of the estimated betas and the dividend yields can be accomplished by running the following cross–sectional OLS regressions of estimated betas on dividend yields and of dividend yields on estimated betas, respectively,

$$\hat{\beta}_{j\hat{m}t} = \hat{\gamma}_{0t} + \hat{\gamma}_{1t}d_{jt} + e_{\hat{\beta}_{j\hat{m}t}}, \qquad (10.29.1)$$

and

$$d_{jt} = \hat{\alpha}_{0t} + \hat{\alpha}_{1t}\hat{\beta}_{j\hat{m}t} + e_{d_{jt}}, \qquad (10.29.2)$$

where $\hat{\gamma}_{0t}$, $\hat{\gamma}_{1t}$, $\hat{\alpha}_{0t}$, and $\hat{\alpha}_{1t}$ are OLS regression coefficients and where $e_{\hat{\beta}_{j\hat{m}t}}$ and $e_{d_{jt}}$ are residuals. The residuals, $e_{\hat{\beta}_{j\hat{m}t}}$'s and $e_{d_{jt}}$'s, are the orthogonalized betas and the orthogonalized dividend yields, respectively.

Then the multiple OLS regression coefficients in the following cross–sectional regression

$$\tilde{r}_{jt} = b_{0t} + b_{1t}\hat{\beta}_{j\hat{m}t} + b_{2t}d_{jt} + \tilde{u}_{jt}, \quad j = 1, 2, \ldots, N,$$

may be expressed as

$$\hat{b}_{1t(OLS)} = \frac{\sum_{j=1}^{N} e_{\hat{\beta}_{j\hat{m}t}}(r_{jt} - r_{\hat{m}t})}{\sum_{j=1}^{N} e_{\hat{\beta}_{j\hat{m}t}}^2},$$

$$\hat{b}_{2t(OLS)} = \frac{\sum_{j=1}^{N} e_{d_{jt}}(r_j - r_{\hat{m}t})}{\sum_{j=1}^{N} e_{d_{jt}}^2},$$

and

$$\hat{b}_{0t(OLS)} = r_{\hat{m}t} - \hat{b}_{1t(OLS)} - \hat{b}_{2t(OLS)}d_{\hat{m}t},$$

where $d_{\hat{m}t}$ is the time t dividend yield for the market proxy and where we have used the fact that

$$\sum_{j=1}^{N} e_{\hat{\beta}_{j\hat{m}t}} = 0 \quad \text{and} \quad \sum_{j=1}^{N} e_{d_{jt}} = 0,$$

that is, the sum of the residuals is equal to zero. This observation and (10.28.2) imply that the efficiency of an estimator of a given coefficient is inversely proportional to that part of the sample variation in that independent variable which is not explained by the other independent variables. Grouping by only one independent variable and doing a multiple regression may maximize the loss of efficiency of the estimator of the coefficient on the other independent variable. The most appropriate grouping criterion would be to maximize the between group orthogonal variation in the independent variable of interest. For example, if the dividend yield is the variable of interest, maximizing the between group variation in dividend yield that is uncorrelated with the cross–sectional variation in betas would be appropriate.

One possible procedure is to group the assets by betas into L groups and to rank the assets in each beta group into L dividend yield sub-groups. The resulting $L \times L$ groups should have substantial orthogonal variation in dividend yields. Black and Scholes (1974) ranked assets into quintiles based on the dividend yields and then into subquintiles based on the betas, thereby achieving substantial orthogonal variation in betas and some orthogonal variation in the dividend yields. They found the coefficient on the betas to be strictly positive and statistically significant, but the coefficient on the dividend yields to be insignificantly different from zero. An alternative approach is to form separate groups based on each independent variable and combine all the groups. When there are only two independent variables, this procedure should also result in significant orthogonal variation in each of the independent variables. This approach was used by Kraus and Litzenberger (1978), who found that the coefficients on both beta and coskewness were significant even though the betas and the coskewnesses of the groups were highly correlated.

10.30. An instrumental variable approach to the problem of errors in variables is closely related to the previously discussed grouping approach. An ideal instrumental variable would be uncorrelated with both the measurement errors in betas and the disturbance terms but have a high correlation with the true betas. To simplify our exposition, in this section and Sections 10.31 and 10.32, we will consider the single independent variable model of (10.25.1):

$$\tilde{r}_{jt} = a_t + b_t \beta_{j\hat{m}t} + \tilde{u}_{jt}, \qquad j = 1, 2, \ldots, N.$$

Let $\tilde{z}_{jt}$, $j = 1, 2, \ldots, N$, denote an instrumental variable with the properties that

$$\operatorname*{plim}_{N\to\infty} \sum_{j=1}^{N} \frac{\tilde{u}_{jt}(\tilde{z}_{jt} - \tilde{z}_{mt})}{N} = 0, \qquad (10.30.1)$$

$$\operatorname*{plim}_{N\to\infty} \sum_{j=1}^{N} \frac{\tilde{v}_{jt}(\tilde{z}_{jt} - \tilde{z}_{mt})}{N} = 0, \qquad (10.30.2)$$

and

$$\operatorname*{plim}_{N\to\infty} \sum_{j=1}^{N} \frac{\beta_{j\hat{m}t}(\tilde{z}_{jt} - \tilde{z}_{mt})}{N} = \text{a nonzero constant}, \quad (10.30.3)$$

where $\tilde{z}_{mt}$ denotes the cross–sectional mean of the instrumental variable $\tilde{z}_{jt}$. Note that, as usual, we did not denote the dependence of the betas and the cross–sectional mean of the $\tilde{z}_{mt}$'s on the the number of assets in a sample. Sufficient conditions for (10.30.1) and (10.30.2) include the uncorrelatedness of $\tilde{z}_{jt}$ and $\tilde{u}_{kt}$ and $\tilde{z}_{jt}$ and $\tilde{v}_{kt}$, for all j, k. The instrumental variable estimator of b_t is

$$\begin{aligned}
\hat{b}_{t(INST)} &= \frac{\sum_{j=1}^{N} r_{jt}(z_{jt} - z_{mt})/N}{\sum_{j=1}^{N} \hat{\beta}_{j\hat{m}t}(z_{jt} - z_{mt})/N} \\
&= \frac{b_t \sum_{j=1}^{N} \beta_{j\hat{m}t}(z_{jt} - z_{mt})/N + \sum_{j=1}^{N} u_{jt}(z_{jt} - z_{mt})/N}{\sum_{j=1}^{N} \beta_{j\hat{m}t}(z_{jt} - z_{mt})/N + \sum_{j=1}^{N} v_{jt}(z_{jt} - z_{mt})/N}.
\end{aligned} \qquad (10.30.4)$$

Taking the probability limit of $\hat{b}_{t(INST)}$ and using (10.30.1)–(10.30.3) gives

$$\operatorname*{plim}_{N\to\infty} \hat{b}_{t(INST)} = b_t.$$

Thus the instrumental variable estimator is consistent.

The previously discussed estimates based on grouped data may be interpreted as instrumental variable estimators. When the group membership is constant over the periods in which the betas are estimated, the estimators based on grouped data are identical to the instrumental variable estimators based on the ungrouped data with the group rank of each asset being used as the instrument (See Johnston (1984), pp. 430–432).

10.31. Two stage least squares (TSLS) is a special case of the instrumental variables approach. In the first stage, the independent variable that has measurement errors is regressed on a number of variables including the other independent variables and at least one other exogenous variable. In the single independent variable model of (10.25.1), we regress, cross–sectionally, the estimated betas on a number of variables not included in the model to be estimated. The first stage model is

$$\hat{\beta}_{j\hat{m}t} = \alpha_{0t} + \sum_{k=1}^{K} \alpha_{kt} y_{kjt} + \tilde{u}'_{jt}, \; j = 1, 2, \ldots, N. \qquad (10.31.1)$$

The variables y_{kjt}'s are usually termed as *descriptors* and can be accounting variables, for example. Let the fitted values of (10.31.1) be denoted by $\bar{\beta}_{j\hat{m}t}$'s. That is,

$$\bar{\beta}_{j\hat{m}t} = \hat{\beta}_{j\hat{m}t} - u'_{jt} \quad j = 1, 2, \ldots, N, \qquad (10.31.2)$$

where we remind the reader that u'_{jt}'s are without a *tilde* and thus denote the residuals from (10.31.1). By the fact that u'_{jt}'s are residuals, we also know that

$$\sum_{j=1}^{N} \frac{u'_{jt} \bar{\beta}_{j\hat{m}t}}{N} = 0, \qquad (10.31.3)$$

that is, the u'_{jt}'s are cross–sectionally uncorrelated with $\bar{\beta}_{j\hat{m}t}$, and

$$\sum_{j=1}^{N} \frac{u'_{jt}}{N} = 0. \qquad (10.31.4)$$

Relations (10.31.2) and (10.31.3) imply that

$$\sum_{j=1}^{N} \frac{\hat{\beta}_{j\hat{m}t}\bar{\beta}_{j\hat{m}t}}{N} = \sum_{j=1}^{N} \frac{\bar{\beta}_{j\hat{m}t}^2}{N}. \tag{10.31.5}$$

Moreover, (10.31.4) and the fact that the market proxy is an equally weighted index imply

$$\sum_{j=1}^{N} \frac{\bar{\beta}_{j\hat{m}t}}{N} = \sum_{j=1}^{N} \frac{\hat{\beta}_{j\hat{m}t}}{N} = 1. \tag{10.31.6}$$

Now we consider the second stage regression. In this stage, we use the following model

$$\tilde{r}_{jt} = \gamma_{0t} + \gamma_{1t}\bar{\beta}_{j\hat{m}t} + \tilde{u}_{jt}, \quad j = 1, 2, \ldots, N. \tag{10.31.7}$$

The OLS estimator of the γ_{1t} of (10.31.7) is the two stage least squares estimator of b_t of (10.25.1), denoted by $\hat{b}_{t(TSLS)}$. We know

$$\hat{b}_{t(TSLS)} = \frac{\sum_{j=1}^{N} r_{jt}(\bar{\beta}_{j\hat{m}t} - 1)/N}{\sum_{j=1}^{N} (\bar{\beta}_{j\hat{m}t} - 1)^2/N}, \tag{10.31.8}$$

where we have used (10.31.6). We claim that $\hat{b}_{t(TSLS)}$ is equivalent to $\hat{b}_{t(INST)}$ of (10.30.4) when the instrumental variable is $\bar{\beta}_{j\hat{m}t}$. To see this, we first substitute (10.25.1) and (10.31.5) into the right–hand side of (10.31.8) to get

$$\begin{aligned}
\hat{b}_{t(TSLS)} &= \frac{b_t \sum_{j=1}^{N} \beta_{j\hat{m}t}(\bar{\beta}_{j\hat{m}t} - 1)/N + \sum_{j=1}^{N} u_{jt}(\bar{\beta}_{j\hat{m}t} - 1)/N}{\sum_{j=1}^{N} \hat{\beta}_{j\hat{m}t}(\bar{\beta}_{j\hat{m}t} - 1)/N} \\
&= \frac{b_t \sum_{j=1}^{N} \beta_{j\hat{m}t}(\bar{\beta}_{j\hat{m}t} - 1)/N + \sum_{j=1}^{N} u_{jt}(\bar{\beta}_{j\hat{m}t} - 1)/N}{\sum_{j=1}^{N} \beta_{j\hat{m}t}(\bar{\beta}_{j\hat{m}t} - 1)/N + \sum_{j=1}^{N} v_{jt}(\bar{\beta}_{j\hat{m}t} - 1)/N}.
\end{aligned} \tag{10.31.9}$$

Note that the right–hand side of the second equality of (10.31.9) is identical to the right–hand side of (10.30.4) when we substitute $\bar{\beta}_{j\hat{m}t}$ for z_{jt}, and we have proved our claim.

We used OLS in the above TSLS regression for ease of exposition. A two stage generalized least squares approach was used by Rosenberg and Marathe (1978) to estimate the two independent variables model of (10.20.1). The dividend yields and a number of accounting variables were included in the first stage regression. The inclusion of the dividend yields was to ensure that the residuals from the first stage were uncorrelated cross–sectionally with the dividend yields. The coefficients of the fitted betas and dividend yields in the second stage were found to be strictly positive and statistically significant.

10.32. The third approach to the problem of errors in measurement in beta estimates is to take account of the impact of the measurement errors on the sample variation in estimated betas. We assume that the measurement errors satisfy (10.25.6)–(10.25.8) and the $\beta_{j\hat{m}t}$'s satisfy (10.25.9). Define an *adjusted* OLS estimator for b_t of (10.25.1) as follows:

$$\hat{b}_{t(A-OLS)} \equiv \frac{\sum_{j=1}^{N} (r_{jt} - r_{\hat{m}t})(\hat{\beta}_{j\hat{m}t} - 1)}{\sum_{j=1}^{N} (\hat{\beta}_{j\hat{m}t} - 1)^2 - \sum_{j=1}^{N} \text{Var}(\tilde{v}_{jt})}. \qquad (10.32.1)$$

Relations (10.25.10)–(10.25.13) then imply that

$$\plim_{N \to \infty} \hat{b}_{t(A-OLS)} = b_t,$$

and the adjusted OLS estimator of (10.32.1) is consistent. The adjusted OLS estimator of a_t is naturally

$$\hat{a}_{t(A-OLS)} \equiv r_{\hat{m}t} - \hat{b}_{t(A-OLS)}.$$

Since $\hat{b}_{t(A-OLS)}$ is consistent, $\hat{a}_{t(A-OLS)}$ is consistent.

Alternatively viewed in the context of 10.21, $\hat{a}_{t(A-OLS)}$ is the excess rate of return on an asymptotic portfolio whose beta with respect to $\hat{m}$ is equal to zero, and $\hat{b}_{t(A-OLS)}$ is the excess rate of return on a self–financing asymptotic portfolio whose beta with respect to $\hat{m}$ is equal to unity.

There are very few instances in economics where the econometrician has knowledge of the variances of measurement errors in an independent variable. However, betas are generally estimated based on a time–series OLS regression of the rate of return on an asset on the rate of return on the market proxy. Then a cross–sectional model of (10.25.1) is estimated. We know that

$$\text{Var}(\hat{\beta}_{j\hat{m}t}) = \text{Var}(\beta_{j\hat{m}t} + \tilde{v}_{jt}) = \text{Var}(\tilde{v}_{jt}). \qquad (10.32.2)$$

Thus the estimate of the variance of an OLS estimator of $\beta_{j\hat{m}t}$ is an estimate of the variance of measurement error $\tilde{v}_{jt}$. The estimate of the variance of a time–series estimate of a beta is easily calculated. Consider the time–series regression over, say, the sixty months prior to month t that satisfies the assumption of a stationary beta and the OLS assumption on the disturbance term:

$$\tilde{r}_{j\tau} = \alpha_j + \beta_{j\hat{m}t}\tilde{r}_{\hat{m}\tau} + \tilde{e}_{j\tau}. \quad \tau = t - 60, t - 59, \ldots, t - 1. \quad (10.32.3)$$

The variance of the OLS estimator of beta is

$$\text{Var}(\hat{\beta}_{j\hat{m}t}) = \sigma_{e_j}^2 / (\sum_{\tau=t-60}^{t-1} (r_{\hat{m}\tau} - \bar{r}_{\hat{m}t})^2), \qquad (10.32.4)$$

where $\sigma_{e_j}^2$ is the variance of the disturbance term and $\bar{r}_{\hat{m}t}$ is the time–series mean of the $r_{\hat{m}\tau}$'s. Then

$$\hat{b}_{t(A-OLS)} \equiv \frac{\sum_{j=1}^{N}(r_{jt} - r_{\hat{m}t})(\hat{\beta}_{j\hat{m}t} - 1)}{\sum_{j=1}^{N}(\hat{\beta}_{j\hat{m}t} - 1)^2 - \sum_{j=1}^{N}\text{Var}(\hat{\beta}_{j\hat{m}t})}$$

is a consistent estimator of b_t of (10.25.1) and similarly

$$\hat{a}_{t(A-OLS)} \equiv r_{mt} - \hat{b}_{t(A-OLS)},$$

is a consistent estimator for a_t of (10.25.1). When $\sigma_{e_j}^2$ of (10.32.4) is unknown, we replace it by an estimate

$$\frac{\sum_{\tau=t-60}^{t-1} e_{j\tau}^2}{58}, \qquad (10.32.5)$$

where we note that there is no *tilde* on top of the $e_{j\tau}$'s of (10.32.5) and they represent the "residuals" from the time–series regression model of (10.32.3). It is well–known that (10.32.5) is a consistent estimator of $\sigma_{e_j}^2$ and thus

$$\frac{\sum_{\tau=t-60}^{t-1} e_{j\tau}^2}{58} \Big/ \Big(\sum_{\tau=t-60}^{t-1} (r_{\hat{m}\tau} - \bar{r}_{\hat{m}t})^2 \Big)$$

is a consistent estimator for $\text{Var}(\hat{\beta}_{j\hat{m}})$ and for $\text{Var}(\tilde{v}_{jt})$.

10.33. In Section 10.32, we discussed the adjustment that can be made to $\hat{b}_{t(OLS)}$ to make it a consistent estimator of b_t when the disturbance terms of (10.25.1) satisfies the OLS conditions. In this section, we will show that the same principle applies to the GLS estimator in the case where $\mathbf{V}_t$ is a diagonal matrix.

Recall from Section 10.23 that when $\mathbf{V}_t$ is diagonal, GLS estimators can be obtained from an OLS estimator applied to the dependent and independent variables, including the unit vector for the intercept, deflated by $\sigma_{u_{jt}}$. This estimator was termed a WLS estimator in Section 10.23. This estimator is, however, inconsistent in the presence of measurement errors. Moreover, $\sigma_{u_{jt}}^2$ is unknown. A consistent estimator of $\sigma_{u_{jt}}^2$ is (10.32.5) when the residuals of the time–series model of (10.32.3) are used. We denote this estimator by $\hat{\sigma}_{u_{jt}}^2$. Thus a consistent estimator of $\text{Var}(\tilde{v}_{jt})$ is

$$\hat{\text{Var}}(\tilde{v}_{jt}) \equiv \hat{\sigma}_{u_{jt}}^2 \Big/ \Big(\sum_{\tau=t-60}^{t-1} (r_{\hat{m}\tau} - \bar{r}_{\hat{m}t})^2 \Big). \tag{10.33.1}$$

Note that $\hat{\text{Var}}(\tilde{v}_{jt})$ is proportional to $\hat{\sigma}_{u_{jt}}^2$. Thus we can deflate the dependent and independent variables by $\sqrt{\hat{\text{Var}}(\tilde{v}_{jt})}$ in a WLS estimator instead of by $\sqrt{\hat{\sigma}_{u_{jt}}^2}$. In this case, the WLS estimator is

$$\hat{\mathbf{b}}_{t(WLS)} = (\mathbf{X}_t^{*\top} \mathbf{X}_t^*)^{-1} \mathbf{X}_t^{*\top} \mathbf{r}_t^*, \tag{10.33.2}$$

where

$$\mathbf{r}_t^* = \begin{pmatrix} r_{1t}/\sqrt{\hat{\text{Var}}(\tilde{v}_{1t})} \\ \vdots \\ r_{Nt}/\sqrt{\hat{\text{Var}}(\tilde{v}_{Nt})} \end{pmatrix} \quad \text{and} \quad \mathbf{X}_t^* = \begin{pmatrix} \dfrac{1}{\sqrt{\hat{\text{Var}}(\tilde{v}_{1t})}} & \dfrac{\hat{\beta}_{1\hat{m}t}}{\sqrt{\hat{\text{Var}}(\tilde{v}_{1t})}} \\ \vdots & \vdots \\ \dfrac{1}{\sqrt{\hat{\text{Var}}(\tilde{v}_{Nt})}} & \dfrac{\hat{\beta}_{N\hat{m}t}}{\sqrt{\hat{\text{Var}}(\tilde{v}_{Nt})}} \end{pmatrix}.$$

This estimator is inconsistent, however, because of the presence of the measurement errors.

Note that a consistent estimate of the variance of the measurement error $\tilde{v}_{jt}$ deflated by $\sqrt{\widehat{\text{Var}}(\tilde{v}_{jt})}$ is equal to one. In Exercise 10.4, the reader is asked to show that consistent WLS estimators of the coefficients of (10.25.1) can be obtained by subtracting N from the sample variation in the deflated betas, that is,

$$\hat{\mathbf{b}}_{t(A-WLS)} \equiv \left(\mathbf{X}_t^{*\top} \mathbf{X}_t^* - \begin{pmatrix} 0 & 0 \\ 0 & N \end{pmatrix} \right)^{-1} \mathbf{X}_t^{*\top} \mathbf{r}_t^*, \qquad (10.33.3)$$

is a consistent estimator of coefficients of (10.25.1) under some regularity conditions. This was the approach used by Litzenberger and Ramaswamy (1978) in the more general model of (10.20.1) with two independent variables, the betas and the dividend yields. They found that the coefficients both on betas and dividend yields were strictly positive and significant.

10.34. The previous discussion of econometric problems in testing the CAPM focused on the cross–sectional tests of the weak prediction of the CAPM that *ex ante* expected rates of return have a positive correlation with betas. Note that the estimates of betas, variances, and covariances were not constrained by the *ex ante* relation between expected returns and betas implied by the CAPM. The estimates of variances and covariances that are based solely on *ex post* realized rates of return will be termed *unconstrained estimates of variances and covariances*. The relationship between *ex ante* expected rates of return and betas that is implied by the market proxy being on the portfolio frontier may be used to estimate betas, variances, and covariances. Consider the time–series model of (10.13.3):

$$\tilde{r}_{jt} = \alpha_j + \beta_{j\hat{m}}\tilde{r}_{\hat{m}t} + \tilde{e}_{jt} \quad t = 1, 2, \ldots, T, \, j = 1, 2, \ldots, N. \quad (10.34.1)$$

The market proxy throughout the discussion to follow will be a portfolio constructed from assets in the test sample. Under the null hypothesis that $\hat{m}$ is on the *ex ante* portfolio frontier, it follows from the mathematics of the portfolio frontier that

$$\alpha_j = a(1 - \beta_{j\hat{m}}) \quad \forall j = 1, 2, \ldots, N, \qquad (10.34.2)$$

where a is the expected excess rate of return on the minimum variance zero covariance portfolio with respect to the market proxy. Relation (10.34.2) is a non–linear constraint on the parameters to be estimated. The alternative hypothesis here is that the the market proxy is not on the *ex ante* portfolio frontier. We assume that the disturbance terms of (10.34.1) are multivariate normally distributed and will use a maximum likelihood method in estimation.

Under the null hypothesis that the market proxy is on the *ex ante* portfolio frontier, the non–linear constraint of (10.34.2) has to be taken into account in estimating the coefficients of (10.34.1).

10.35. To understand the impact on estimating betas, variances, and covariances of the non–linear constraint of (10.34.2), we first consider the relatively simpler case of the traditional version of the model. Under this version the risk premium on a zero beta portfolio is zero. Thus $a = 0$ in (10.34.2), and conditioning on this constraint implies a proportional relationship between excess rates of return and betas. Note that in this case, the non–linear constraint reduces to the linear constraint that $\alpha_j = 0$, $\forall j$. Assuming that the disturbance terms of (10.34.1) are serially uncorrelated in that

$$E[\tilde{u}_{jt}\tilde{u}_{ks}] = 0 \quad \forall j, k \text{ if } t \neq s$$

and have a time–stationary distribution, betas, variances, and covariances can be estimated with the linear constraint by using the following procedure: First, obtain an estimate of beta for each of the N assets by an OLS regression of the asset's monthly excess rates of return on the market proxy's monthly excess rates of return, with the intercept terms suppressed. Formally, the model is

$$\tilde{r}_{jt} = \beta^c_{j\hat{m}}\tilde{r}_{\hat{m}t} + \tilde{e}^c_{jt}, \quad t = 1, 2, \ldots, T, \; j = 1, 2, \ldots, N. \quad (10.35.1)$$

Let $\hat{\beta}^c_{j\hat{m}}$ denote the beta estimate for asset j, where the superscript c signifies the fact that this estimate is based on the constraint that the intercept terms are zero. Next, the time–stationary cross–sectional variance–covariance matrix of the disturbance terms of (10.35.1) is estimated as

$$\hat{V}^c_e \equiv (\sum_{t=1}^{T} e^c_t e^{c\top}_t)/T, \quad (10.35.2)$$

where

$$\mathbf{e}_t^c = \begin{pmatrix} e_{1t}^c \\ \vdots \\ e_{Nt}^c \end{pmatrix}$$

is the N–vector of time t residuals for the N assets in the sample.

Note also that the OLS estimates of betas are identical to the estimates obtained by using the seemingly unrelated regression (SUR) technique which takes account of the estimated variance–covariance matrix, since the pooled time–series and cross–sectional model of (10.34.1) has the same independent variable for every asset equation, namely the excess rates of return on the market proxy portfolio.

The unconstrained estimates of betas, variances, and covariances can also be obtained by a procedure similar to that discussed above except that the intercept terms are not constrained to be zero. Let the unconstrained estimates of betas and the variance–covariance matrix of the residuals be denoted by $\hat{\beta}_{j\hat{m}}$ and $\hat{\mathbf{V}}_e$, respectively.

10.36. We discussed the constrained and unconstrained estimation of $\beta_{j\hat{m}}$ and the variance–covariance matrix in Section 10.35. We will now consider the test statistic of the null hypothesis that $\hat{m}$ is on the *ex ante* portfolio frontier. The log of the likelihood function of r_{jt}'s using unconstrained estimates of betas, variances, and covariances is

$$\ln L = -(\frac{NT}{2}) \ln 2\pi - \frac{T}{2} \ln |\hat{\mathbf{V}}_e| - \frac{1}{2} \sum_{t=1}^{T} \mathbf{e}_t^\top \hat{\mathbf{V}}_e^{-1} \mathbf{e}_t, \qquad (10.36.1)$$

where $|\hat{\mathbf{V}}_e|$ denotes the determinant of $\hat{\mathbf{V}}_e$ and $\mathbf{e}_t$ is the N vector of residuals at time t from the unconstrained time–series model of (10.34.1) for the N assets. The log of the likelihood function using the constrained estimates of betas, variances, and covariances is

$$\ln L^c = -(\frac{NT}{2}) \ln 2\pi - \frac{T}{2} \ln |\hat{\mathbf{V}}_e^c| - \frac{1}{2} \sum_{t=1}^{T} \mathbf{e}_t^{c\top} \hat{\mathbf{V}}_e^{c-1} \mathbf{e}_t^c, \qquad (10.36.2)$$

where $|\hat{\mathbf{V}}_e^c|$ denotes the determinant of $\hat{\mathbf{V}}_e^c$. The reader can verify

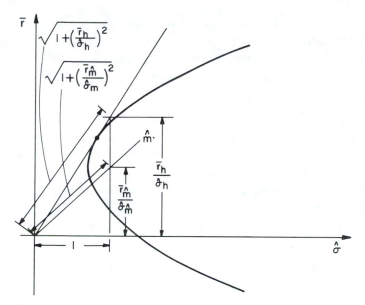

Figure 10.36.1: A graphical demonstration of the test statistic of (10.36.4) and (10.36.5)

that

$$\frac{1}{2}\sum_{t=1}^{T} \mathbf{e}_t^{c\top}\hat{\mathbf{V}}_e^{c-1}\mathbf{e}_t^c = \frac{1}{2}\sum_{t=1}^{T} \mathbf{e}_t^{\top}\hat{\mathbf{V}}_e^{-1}\mathbf{e}_t = \frac{NT}{2}. \qquad (10.36.3)$$

Note that since $\hat{\beta}_{j\hat{m}}^c$, $\hat{\beta}_{j\hat{m}}$, $\hat{\mathbf{V}}_e^c$, and $\hat{\mathbf{V}}_e$ are maximum likelihood estimates, they maximize their respective likelihood functions. Since L^c is the maximand with an additional constraint, $\ln L^c - \ln L \le 0$. A test statistic for the null hypothesis that the market proxy is on the *ex ante* portfolio frontier is

$$-2(\ln L^c - \ln L) = T(\ln|\hat{\mathbf{V}}_e^c| - \ln|\hat{\mathbf{V}}_e|), \qquad (10.36.4)$$

where we have used (10.36.3). When the market proxy is on the *ex ante* portfolio frontier, we will likely find that L^c is close to L, the test statistic is close to zero, and we will fail to reject the null hypothesis. Gibbons (1982) showed that this test statistic is asymptotically distributed according to χ_{N-1}^2 when $T \to \infty$.

The test statistic of (10.36.4) was shown by Gibbons, Ross, and Shanken (1986) to have an intuitively appealing economic interpretation. First, using the unconstrained estimates of variances and covariances and the time–series means of the rates of return on assets, one can construct an *ex post* portfolio frontier. Call this an unconstrained portfolio frontier. This frontier is a half line since there is a riskless asset. This frontier is shown in Figure 10.36.1. Note that unlike the figures in Chapter 3, the vertical axis of Figure 10.36.1 is the time–series mean of the excess rate of return and the horizontal axis is the standard deviation of asset (portfolio) excess rates of return using unconstrained estimates. The riskless asset is at the origin.

Let h denote the portfolio having the highest reward to variability ratio (mean excess rate of return to standard deviation) using the unconstrained estimates. Any portfolio on the unconstrained portfolio frontier can be h. The tangent portfolio of Figure 10.36.1 is such a portfolio. Let $(\hat{\sigma}_h, \bar{r}_h)$ be the coordinate of the tangent portfolio in Figure 10.36.1. It can be shown that

$$\frac{|\hat{\mathbf{V}}_e^c|}{|\hat{\mathbf{V}}_e|} = \left(\frac{1 + \left(\frac{\bar{r}_h}{\hat{\sigma}_h} \right)^2}{1 + \left(\frac{\bar{r}_{\hat{m}}}{\hat{\sigma}_{\hat{m}}} \right)^2} \right). \qquad (10.36.5)$$

Hence (10.36.4) can be rewritten as

$$-2 \ln \left(\ln L^c - \ln L \right) = T \ln \left(\frac{1 + \left(\frac{\bar{r}_h}{\hat{\sigma}_h} \right)^2}{1 + \left(\frac{\bar{r}_{\hat{m}}}{\hat{\sigma}_{\hat{m}}} \right)^2} \right), \qquad (10.36.6)$$

where $\bar{r}_{\hat{m}}$ and $\hat{\sigma}_{\hat{m}}$ denote the time–series mean and standard deviation of the market proxy. Since the market proxy is a portfolio constructed by the assets in the test sample, $(\sigma_{\hat{m}}, \bar{r}_{\hat{m}})$ must be below the tangent line in Figure 10.36.1. From (10.36.6), we see that the test may be interpreted as a test of whether there is a statistically significant difference between the reward to variability ratio for the market proxy and the highest reward to variability ratio using the unconstrained estimates. If the market proxy were on the *ex ante* portfolio frontier, it would likely be close to the constrained frontier, the test statistic would thus likely be close to zero, and we would fail to reject the null hypothesis that the market proxy is on the *ex ante* portfolio frontier.

The derivation of (10.36.5) is rather lengthy. We will not present it here but refer interested readers to Gibbons, Ross and Shanken (1986).

10.37. Now consider the case of the constrained borrowing version of the CAPM. In this case, the non–linear constraint of (10.34.2) can not be reduced to a linear constraint. The constrained maximum likelihood estimates of betas, variances, and covariances are based on the following model:

$$\tilde{r}_{jt} - a = \beta_{j\hat{m}}^c (\tilde{r}_{\hat{m}t} - a) + \tilde{e}_{jt}^c, \quad t = 1, 2, \ldots, T. \tag{10.37.1}$$

Unlike the case of the traditional CAPM, where $a = 0$, the a needs to be estimated. To illustrate the interactions involved in estimating a, $\beta_{\hat{m}}^c$, and the variance–covariance matrix, Gibbons (1982) has presented the following algorithm:

1. Use OLS to estimate α_j and $\beta_{j\hat{m}}$ of the time–series model of (10.34.1) for every j without the constraint. Note that since the same independent variable is used in the N time–series regressions, the OLS estimators are identical to the seemingly unrelated regression estimators.

2. Use the residuals from the N time–series regression equations in step 1 to compute the unconstrained estimate of the variance–covariance matrix of N assets, denoted by $\hat{V}_e$, as in (10.35.2) and calculate the unconstrained estimates of the expected excess rates of return, the $\bar{r}_j$'s. Note that $\bar{r}_j$ is simply the time–series sample mean of r_{jt}.

3. Use $\hat{V}_e$ and the $\bar{r}_j$'s to obtain the GLS estimate of a. That is, solve for the portfolio weights that minimize the portfolio variance subject to the constraint that the portfolio has a zero covariance with respect to the market proxy. The solution to this problem is derived in Section 3.15. The GLS estimate of a is then computed by applying these portfolio weights to the $\bar{r}_j$'s.

4. Use the GLS estimate of a obtained in step 3 to re–estimate

the $\beta_{j\hat{m}}$'s using (10.37.1) and OLS. The residuals from this constrained regression are then used to estimate the variance covariance matrix as in (10.35.2). We can also compute the constrained estimates of the expected excess rates of returns on assets by

$$\bar{r}_j^c \equiv \hat{a} + \hat{\beta}_{j\hat{m}}^c(\bar{r}_{\hat{m}} - \hat{a}), \quad j = 1, 2, \ldots, N,$$

where the $\hat{\beta}_{j\hat{m}}^c$ are the OLS estimates of betas obtained in this step, and $\hat{a}$ denotes the GLS estimate of a in step 3.

5. Use the expected excess rates of returns and the variance covariance matrix estimated in step 4 to obtain a new GLS estimator of a as in step 3. Then carry out step 4. Continue iterating this process until a satisfactory level of convergence is achieved.

10.38. While the algorithm presented in Section 10.37 is useful to illustrate the impact of the non–linear constraint of (10.34.2), the estimate of a may be obtained directly as follows: First, maximize the likelihood function to choose the maximum likelihood estimators for the $N \times N$ variance–covariance matrix of the N assets in the sample and the betas conditional on a given estimate a' of a. Denote these estimators by $\hat{\mathbf{V}}_e(a')$ and $\hat{\beta}_{j\hat{m}}(a')$. Next, substitute $\hat{\mathbf{V}}_e(a')$ and $\hat{\beta}_{j\hat{m}}(a')$ into the original likelihood function to produce the *concentrated likelihood function* as a function of only a'. Finally, maximize the concentrated likelihood function with respect to a' to produce a maximum likelihood estimator of a. Kandel (1984) showed that the maximum likelihood estimator of a is a solution to the following quadratic equation in x:

$$Fx^2 + Gx + H = 0, \qquad (10.38.1)$$

where
$$F = -1,$$

$$G = \frac{-\hat{C}\hat{\sigma}_{\hat{m}}^2 - \hat{C}\bar{r}_{\hat{m}}^2 + 1 + \hat{B}}{\hat{A} - \hat{C}\bar{r}_{\hat{m}}},$$

$$H = \frac{\hat{A}\hat{\sigma}_{\hat{m}}^2 + \hat{A}\bar{r}_{\hat{m}}^2 - \bar{r}_{\hat{m}} - \hat{B}\bar{r}_{\hat{m}}}{\hat{A} - \hat{C}\bar{r}_{\hat{m}}},$$

$$\hat{A} = \bar{r}^\top \hat{V}^{-1} 1_N,$$
$$\hat{B} = \bar{r}^\top \hat{V}^{-1} \bar{r},$$
$$\hat{C} = 1_N^\top \hat{V}^{-1} 1_N,$$

$\bar{r}$ denotes the N–vector of $\bar{r}_j$'s, the time–series means of the excess rates of return on assets, $\hat{V}$ denotes the unconstrained variance–covariance matrix of the excess rates of return on assets as defined in Exercise 10.6.3, 1_N denotes the N–vector of 1's, and $\hat{\sigma}_{\hat{m}}^2$ denotes the time–series variance of the excess rates of return on the market proxy. Note that $\hat{A}$, $\hat{B}$, and $\hat{C}$ are simply the unconstrained estimates of the A, B, and C defined in Section 3.9. There are two solutions to (10.38.1), denoted by x_1 and x_2. Assume without loss of generality that $x_1 < x_2$. Denoting by $\hat{a}_{(MLE)}$ the maximum likelihood estimate of a, Kandel (1984) showed that

1. if $\bar{r}_{\hat{m}} > \hat{A}/\hat{C}$, then $x_1 < (\hat{A}/\hat{C}) < \bar{r}_{\hat{m}} < x_2$ and $\hat{a}_{(MLE)} = x_1$;

2. if $\bar{r}_{\hat{m}} < \hat{A}/\hat{C}$, then $x_1 < \bar{r}_{\hat{m}} < (\hat{A}/\hat{C}) < x_2$ and $\hat{a}_{(MLE)} = x_2$.

10.39. In fact, $\hat{a}_{(MLE)}$ is a GLS estimator based on the constrained estimates of the expected excess rates of return on assets and of the variance–covariance matrix of the excess rates of return on assets. To see this, note that we can use $\hat{a}_{(MLE)}$ to estimate the constrained betas as in Step 4 in the algorithm presented in Section 10.38. The constrained estimates of expected excess rates of return and covariances are

$$\bar{r}_j^c \equiv \hat{a}_{(MLE)} + \hat{\beta}_{j\hat{m}}^c (\bar{r}_m - \hat{a}_{(MLE)}),$$
$$\hat{\sigma}_{jk}^c \equiv \sum_{t=1}^{T} (r_{jt} - \bar{r}_j^c)(r_{kt} - \bar{r}_k^c)/T. \tag{10.39.1}$$

The constrained estimates in (10.39.1) can then be used to construct the *constrained portfolio frontier*. Alternatively viewed, $\hat{a}_{(MLE)}$ is the estimated expected excess rate of return on $zc(\hat{m})$ using the constrained estimates in (10.39.1). It is a GLS estimate because it is based on a full variance–covariance matrix and has a minimum variance among all estimates whose expected value is equal to $E[\bar{r}_{zc(\hat{m})}]$.

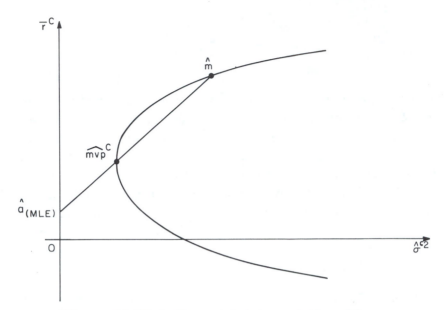

Figure 10.39.1: Geometric interpretation of $\hat{a}_{(MLE)}$ based on constrained estimates of means, variances, and covariances of excess rates of return

Note that $\hat{m}$ will be on the constrained portfolio frontier. Thus, it follows from Section 3.15 that the geometric position of $\hat{a}_{(MLE)}$ can be determined by drawing, in mean–variance space, a straight line from the market proxy, $\hat{m}$, through the the minimum variance portfolio on the constrained portfolio frontier, denoted by $\widehat{mvp}^c$. The intersection of that line with the estimated expected excess rate of return axis is $\hat{a}_{(MLE)}$. The geometric position of $\hat{a}_{(MLE)}$ is demonstrated in Figure 10.39.1.

Next we will demonstrate the geometric representation of the GLS estimator of a based on the unconstrained estimates of the variance–covariance matrix and the expected excess rates of return as discussed in Step 3 of the algorithm of Section 10.37. We will denote this GLS estimate of a by $\hat{a}_{(GLS)}$. The portfolio frontier of risky assets in Figure 10.39.2 is the frontier based on the unconstrained estimates as defined in Exercise 10.6.3. Consider the portfolio frontier formed by the market proxy and the minimum variance portfolio based on the unconstrained estimates. As we discussed

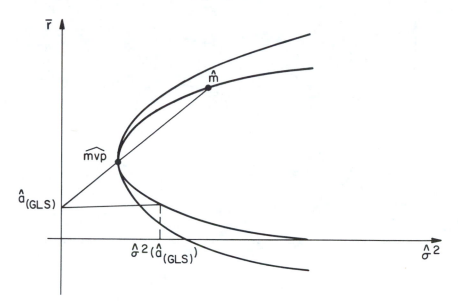

Figure 10.39.2: Geometric interpretation of $\hat{a}_{(GLS)}$ based on unconstrained estimates of means, variances, and covariances of excess rates of return

in Section 3.15, this frontier lies inside of and touches the unconstrained portfolio frontier of all risky assets at the single point $\widehat{mvp}$, the global minimum variance portfolio on the unconstrained frontier. Recall also from Section 3.15 that the minimum variance zero covariance portfolio with respect to the market proxy, based on the unconstrained estimates, will be on the parabola generated by $\hat{m}$ and $\widehat{mvp}$. The coordinate of this portfolio along the estimated expected excess rate of return axis is $\hat{a}_{(GLS)}$. The geometric position of $\hat{a}_{(GLS)}$ can be identified by drawing a line from $\hat{m}$ through $\widehat{mvp}$. This is demonstrated in Figure 10.39.2.

Note that if $\hat{m}$ were on the unconstrained portfolio frontier, the constraint of (10.34.2) would not be binding, and the constrained and unconstrained portfolio frontiers would be identical. Suppose that this is not true and $\bar{r}_{\hat{m}} > \bar{r}_{\widehat{mvp}}$, where $\bar{r}_{\widehat{mvp}}$ denotes the unconstrained estimate of the excess rate of return on $\widehat{mvp}$. Then one can show that the constrained portfolio frontier lies inside the unconstrained portfolio frontier and is tangent to it at a single point. Moreover, the constrained estimate of the excess rate of return on $\widehat{mvp}^c$ is strictly

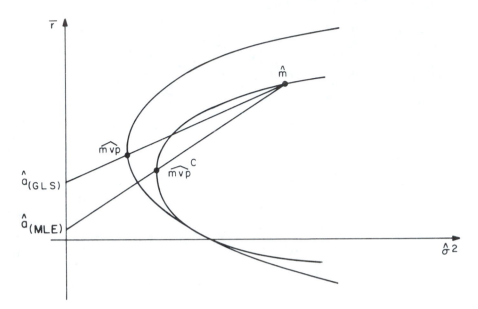

Figure 10.39.3: Geometric comparison of $\hat{a}_{(MLE)}$ and $\hat{a}_{(GLS)}$

lower than the unconstrained estimate of that on $\widehat{mvp}$. We will not prove these statements here but refer the reader to Kandel (1984) for details.

Figure 10.39.3 graphs the constrained and unconstrained portfolio frontier together. Note that the constrained and unconstrained estimates of the expected excess rate of return and variance on $\hat{m}$ agree. They are simply the time–series mean and variance of $r_{\hat{m}t}$. Thus, the position of $\hat{m}$ in the variance–mean space is invariant with respect to whether the constrained or unconstrained frontier is graphed. It then follows from the relative position of $\widehat{mvp}^c$ and $\widehat{mvp}$ that $\hat{a}_{(GLS)} > \hat{a}_{(MLE)}$.

10.40. Kandel (1984) showed that the test statistic of the likelihood ratio test of the null hypothesis that the market proxy is on the *ex ante* portfolio frontier can be written as

$$T \ln \left(\frac{\overline{r}_{\widehat{mvp}} - \hat{a}_{(MLE)}}{\hat{\sigma}^2_{\widehat{mvp}}} \Bigg/ \frac{\overline{r}^c_{\widehat{mvp}^c} - \hat{a}_{(MLE)}}{\hat{\sigma}^{c2}_{\widehat{mvp}^c}} \right), \qquad (10.40.1)$$

where $\bar{r}^c_{mvp^c}$ and $\bar{r}_{mvp}$ are the constrained and unconstrained estimates of the expected excess rate of return on the minimum vari-
ance portfolio, respectively, and $\hat{\sigma}^{c2}_{mvp^c}$ and $\hat{\sigma}^2_{mvp}$ are the constrained
and unconstrained estimates of the variance of the minimum vari-
ance portfolio, respectively. Under the null hypothesis, this statistic
is asymptotically distributed as χ^2_{N-2}.

The test statistic of (10.40.1) has a very intuitive interpretation. If the market proxy is on the *ex ante* portfolio frontier, then
the constrained and unconstrained portfolio frontiers would be likely
to be close. Contrast the slope of the line connecting $\hat{a}_{(MLE)}$ and
$\widehat{mvp}^c$ with the slope of the line connecting $\hat{a}_{(MLE)}$ and $\widehat{mvp}$. If the
two frontiers were close, the slopes of these two lines would be close.
In this case, the test statistic would be close to zero and we would
fail to reject the null hypothesis that the market proxy is on the *ex
ante* portfolio frontier. If the slopes were significantly different, or,
equivalently, the constrained and the unconstrained portfolio frontier frontiers were significantly different, the test statistic would be
significantly different from zero and the null hypothesis would be rejected. The geometry of the test statistic of (10.40.1) is demonstrated
in Figure 10.40.1.

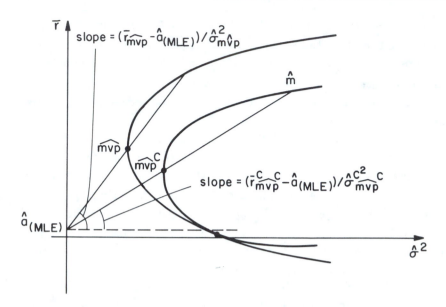

Figure 10.40.1: Geometric interpretation of the likelihood ratio test statistic

Exercises

10.1. Show that the betas of assets in a proper subset of all assets with respect to a portfolio, constructed from the same proper subset of assets, that has a given "true" beta with respect to the market portfolio and a minimum variance, are equal to the true betas times a scalar.

10.2. Read Black, Jensen, and Scholes (1972) and show that their estimator of the intercept term a discussed in Section 10.20 is identical to that given in (10.20.2) and that their estimator of its variance is identical to that given in (10.20.3).

10.3. Show that (10.25.4) and (10.25.6)–(10.25.9) imply (10.25.10)–(10.25.13).

10.4. Give sufficient conditions, in the context of Section 10.33, for

$$\hat{b}^A_{t(WLS)} \equiv \left(\mathbf{X}^{*\top}_t \mathbf{X}^*_t - \begin{pmatrix} 0 & 0 \\ 0 & N \end{pmatrix} \right)^{-1} \mathbf{X}^{*\top}_t \mathbf{r}^*_t$$

to give consistent estimators of coefficients of (10.25.1).

10.5. Assume that the single index model of (10.22.1) is a valid description of the return generating process. Derive the portfolio weights for the minimum variance zero covariance portfolio with respect to the market proxy in the context of Section 10.22. Show that the excess rate of return on this portfolio is identical to the WLS estimator of the intercept term of (10.23.1).

10.6. This exercise uses a data set consisting of monthly excess rates of return on the ten beta decile portfolios. These data may be derived from the data file maintained by the Chicago Center for Security Prices (CRSP) to which a large number of universities subscribe. For individuals at universities subscribing to CRSP but where beta decile portfolios are not readily available, the authors will provide the data if they are sent a $5\frac{1}{2}$ inch floppy disk with a stamped self–addressed disk envelope. Note that the ten beta decile portfolios are constructed by grouping individual assets into ten groups according to estimated betas as discussed in Section 10.28. The market proxy portfolio in the following exercises can be taken to be the equally weighted portfolio of the ten beta decile portfolios.

10.6.1. Use the monthly excess returns on the ten beta decile portfolios from January 1931 through December 1983 to compute the estimates of the betas of the ten beta decile portfolios and their standard errors by using the time–series model (10.13.2). Do an OLS regression using the cross–sectional model of (10.13.1) and calculate the standard errors of the OLS estimators of a and b based on the sample variance–covariance matrix of the mean excess rates of return. Note that the sample covariance of the excess rates of return on assets j and l is

$$\bar{\sigma}_{jl}^2 \equiv \frac{\sum_{t=1}^{T}(r_{jt} - \bar{r}_j)(r_{lt} - \bar{r}_l)}{T(T-1)}.$$

Compare these standard errors with the standard errors based on the OLS assumption that

$$E[\tilde{u}_j \tilde{u}_l] = \begin{cases} \sigma_u^2 & \text{if } j = l; \\ 0 & \text{if } j \neq l. \end{cases}$$

10.6.2. Do an OLS regression of the monthly excess rates of return on the ten decile portfolios on the betas estimates for each month from 1931 through 1983 using the model of (10.13.2). Calculate the time–series means and standard deviations of $\hat{a}_{t(OLS)}$ and $\hat{b}_{t(OLS)}$. Compare these means and standard deviations with those calculated in Exercise 10.6.1.

10.6.3. Do a GLS regression of the monthly excess rates of return on the ten decile portfolios on the betas estimates for each month from 1931 through 1983 using the model of (10.13.2) and the sample variance–covariance matrix. Note that the sample covariance of excess rates of return on asset j and l is

$$\hat{\sigma}_{jl}^2 \equiv \frac{\sum_{t=1}^{T}(r_{jt} - \bar{r}_j)(r_{lt} - \bar{r}_l)}{(T - 1)}.$$

Calculate the time–series means and standard deviations of $\hat{a}_{t(GLS)}$ and $\hat{b}_{t(GLS)}$. Compare these standard deviations with those of the OLS estimators in Exercise 10.6.2.

10.6.4. Do a WLS regression of the monthly excess rates of return on the ten decile portfolios on the betas estimates for each month from 1931 through 1983 using the model of (10.13.2) and the sample variance–covariance matrix. As in Exercise 10.6.3, the sample covariance of excess rates of return on asset j and l is

$$\hat{\sigma}_{jl}^2 \equiv \frac{\sum_{t=1}^{T}(r_{jt} - \bar{r}_j)(r_{lt} - \bar{r}_l)}{(T - 1)}.$$

Calculate the time–series means and standard deviations of $\hat{a}_{t(WLS)}$ and $\hat{b}_{t(WLS)}$. Compare these standard deviations with those of the OLS estimators in Exercise 10.6.2 and those of the GLS estimators in Exercise 10.6.3.

10.6.5. Use a maximum likelihood method to test whether the equally weighted market proxy is on the *ex ante* portfolio frontier generated by the ten beta decile portfolios using monthly data from 1931 to 1983.

10.6.6. Use monthly returns for the ten beta decile portfolios from 1931–1983 to estimate the parameters of the unconstrained *ex post* portfolio frontier and plot this portfolio frontier in mean–variance space. Demonstrate on the graph the position of $\hat{a}_{(GLS)}$ relative to the plotted *ex post* portfolio frontier.

10.6.7. Constrain the equally weighted market proxy to be on the *ex ante* portfolio frontier to estimate the parameters of the constrained frontier. Plot the unconstrained and constrained frontier on the same graph. Show the tangency of the two frontiers and the relationship between the GLS and MLE estimators of a on the graph.

Remarks. For a general discussion of linear estimators see Johnston (1984, pp. 28–29 and pp.31–32). The discussion of the role of assumptions in the development of a positive theory of the valuation of risky assets in Section 10.4 is inspired by Friedman (1956). The discussion in Sections 10.3 and 10.5 is stimulated by the critique of CAPM tests contained in Roll (1977). The discussion of the unconditional form of the CAPM in Section 10.10 and the discussion of the minimum variance unit beta portfolio in Section 10.12 are adapted from Breeden, Gibbons and Litzenberger (1986). The derivation of linear estimators as portfolio returns discussed in Section 10.21 first appeared in Black and Scholes (1974). The discussion of weighted least square estimators and generalized least square estimators in Section 10.23 and the discussion of the third approach to errors in variables in Section 10.33 are adapted from Litzenberger and Ramaswamy (1979). The discussion of an iterative maximum likelihood approach in Section 10.36 is adapted from Gibbons (1982). Gibbons used seemingly unrelated regression in step 4 of the algorithm presented in Section 10.37, rather than OLS as described above. The estimates from the two procedures coincide. The discussion of the geometric interpretation of the likelihood ratio test and the GLS and MLE estimators of a in Section 10.39 and Section 10.40 is based on Kandel (1984).

This chapter focused on the econometric procedures used in testing the CAPM rather than the actual test results. The intent of this chapter is to provide a discussion of econometric issues that will enrich the reader's understanding of the empirical literature on testing the CAPM. It is not intended as a substitute for reading the original articles. Our discussion is not exhaustive, however. For a discussion of the power and small sample bias of tests based on asymptotic distributions in the context of Sections 10.36–10.39 see MacKinlay (1987), Amsler and Schmidt (1985), and Jobson and Korkie (1982). For the development of tests that do not implicitly assume that the market proxy is the minimum variance unit beta portfolio, see Shanken (1987) and Kandel and Stambaugh (1987).

This chapter emphasizes tests involving only a single independent variable, the beta. While other independent variables are briefly discussed, the econometric problem related to the measurement of these independent variables is not discussed. For a dialogue concerning econometric issues associated with the testing of an after–tax CAPM that includes a dividend yield term see Litzenberger and Ramaswamy (1979, 1982) and Miller and Scholes (1982).

We did not discuss tests of other asset pricing models. For pioneering work on testing of the APT, see Roll and Ross (1980). For a test of the Consumption–Oriented CAPM, see Breeden, Gibbons and Litzenberger (1986). For an important paper using the method of moments for testing non–linear pricing models, see Hansen and Singleton (1982). See Gibbons and Ferson (1985) for a test of the conditional form of the CAPM. Readers interested in the problems associated with seasonality in the relation between risk and return should consult Tinic and West (1984).

References

Amsler, C., and P. Schmidt. 1985. A Monte Carlo investigation of the accuracy of multivariate CAPM tests. *Journal of Financial Economics* **14**:359–376.

Banz, R. 1981. The relationship between return and market value of common stocks. *Journal of Financial Economics* **9**:3–18.

Black, F. 1972. Capital market equilibrium with restricted borrowing. *Journal of Business* **45**:444–454.

Black, F., M. Jensen, and M. Scholes, 1972. The Capital Asset Pricing Model: Some empirical tests. In *Studies in the Theory of Capital Markets*, Edited by M. Jensen. Praeger, New York.

Black, F., and M. Scholes. 1974. The effects of dividend yield and dividend policy on common stock, prices and returns. *Journal of Financial Economics* 1:1–22.

Blume, M., and I. Friend. 1973. A new look at the Capital Asset Pricing Model. *Journal of Finance* 28:19–33.

Breeden, D. 1979. An intertemporal asset pricing model with stochastic consumption and investment opportunities. *Journal of Financial Economics* 7:265–296.

Breeden, D., M. Gibbons, and R. Litzenberger. 1986, Tests of the consumption oriented Capital Asset Pricing Model. Mimeo. Stanford University.

Fama, E., and J. MacBeth. 1973. Risk, return and equilibrium: Empirical tests. *Journal of Political Economy* 81:607–636.

Friedman, M. 1956. The methodology of positive economics. In *Essays in Positive Economics*. University of Chicago Press. Chicago.

Friend, I., and R. Westerfield. 1980, Co–skewness and Capital Asset Pricing. *Journal of Finance* 35:897–913.

Gibbons, M. 1982. Multivariate tests of financial models: A new approach. *Journal of Financial Economics* 10:3–27.

Gibbons, M., and W. Ferson. 1985. Testing asset pricing models with changing expectations and an unobservable market portfolio. *Journal of Financial Economics* 14:217–236.

Gibbons, M., S. Ross, and J. Shanken. 1986. A test of the efficiency of a given portfolio. Research Paper #853. Graduate School of Business, Stanford University.

Hansen, L., and K. Singleton. 1982. Generalized instrumental variables estimation of non–linear rational expectations models. *Econometrica* 50:1269–1286.

Jobson, J., and R. Korkie. 1982. Potential performance and tests of portfolio efficiency. *Journal of Financial Economics* 10:433–466.

Johnston, J. 1984. *Econometric Methods*. McGraw–Hill. New York.

Kandel, S. 1984. The likelihood ratio test statistic of mean–variance efficiency without a riskless asset. *Journal of Financial Economics* 13:575–592.

Kandel, S., and R. Stambaugh. 1987. On correlations and the sensitivity of inferences about mean–variance efficiency. *Journal of Financial Economics* **18**:61–90.

Kraus, A., and R. Litzenberger. 1976, Skewness preference and the valuation of risk assets. *Journal of Finance* **31**:1085–1100.

Lintner, J. 1965. The valuation of risk assets and the selection of risky investment in stock portfolios and capital budgets. *Review of Economics and Statistics* **47**:13–37.

Litzenberger, R., and K. Ramaswamy. 1979. The effect of personal taxes and dividends on capital asset prices. *Journal of Financial Economics* **7**:163–195.

Litzenberger, R., and K. Ramaswamy. 1982. The effects of dividends on common stock prices: Tax effects or information effects? *Journal of Finance* **37**:429–443.

MacKinlay, A. 1987. On multivariate tests of the CAPM. *Journal of Financial Economics* **18**:341–371.

Merton, R. 1973. An intertemporal capital asset pricing model. *Econometrica* **41**:867–887.

Miller, M., and M. Scholes. 1982. Dividends and taxes: Some empirical evidence. *Journal of Political Economy* **90**:1118–1141.

Reinganum, M. 1983. Misspecification of capital asset pricing: Empirical anomalies based on earnings yields and market values. *Journal of Financial Economics* **9**:19–46.

Roll, R. 1977. A critique of the asset pricing theory's tests – Part 1: On past and potential testability of the theory. *Journal of Financial Economics* **4**:129–176.

Roll, R., and S. A. Ross. 1980. An empirical investigation of the arbitrage pricing hypothesis. *Journal of Finance* **35**:1073–1104.

Rosenberg, B., and V. Marathe. 1979. Tests of capital asset pricing hypothesis. *Research in Finance* **1**:115–223.

Ross, S. 1976. The arbitrage theory of capital asset pricing. *Journal of Economic Theory* **13**:341–360.

Schwert, G. 1983. Size and stock returns and other empirical regularities. *Journal of Financial Economics* **12**:3–12.

Shanken, J. 1985. Multivariate tests of the zero–beta CAPM. *Journal of Financial Economics* **14**:32–348.

Shanken, J. 1987. Proxies and asset pricing relations: Living with the Roll critique. *Journal of Financial Economics* **18**:91–110.

Sharpe, W. 1964. Capital asset prices: A theory of market equilibrium under conditions of risk. *Journal of Finance* **19**, 425–442.

Tinic, S., and R. West. 1984. Risk and return: January vs. the rest of the Year. *Journal of Financial Economics* **13**:561–574.

INDEX